P9-AZX-505

Handbook for SCIENTIFIC PHOTOGRAPHY

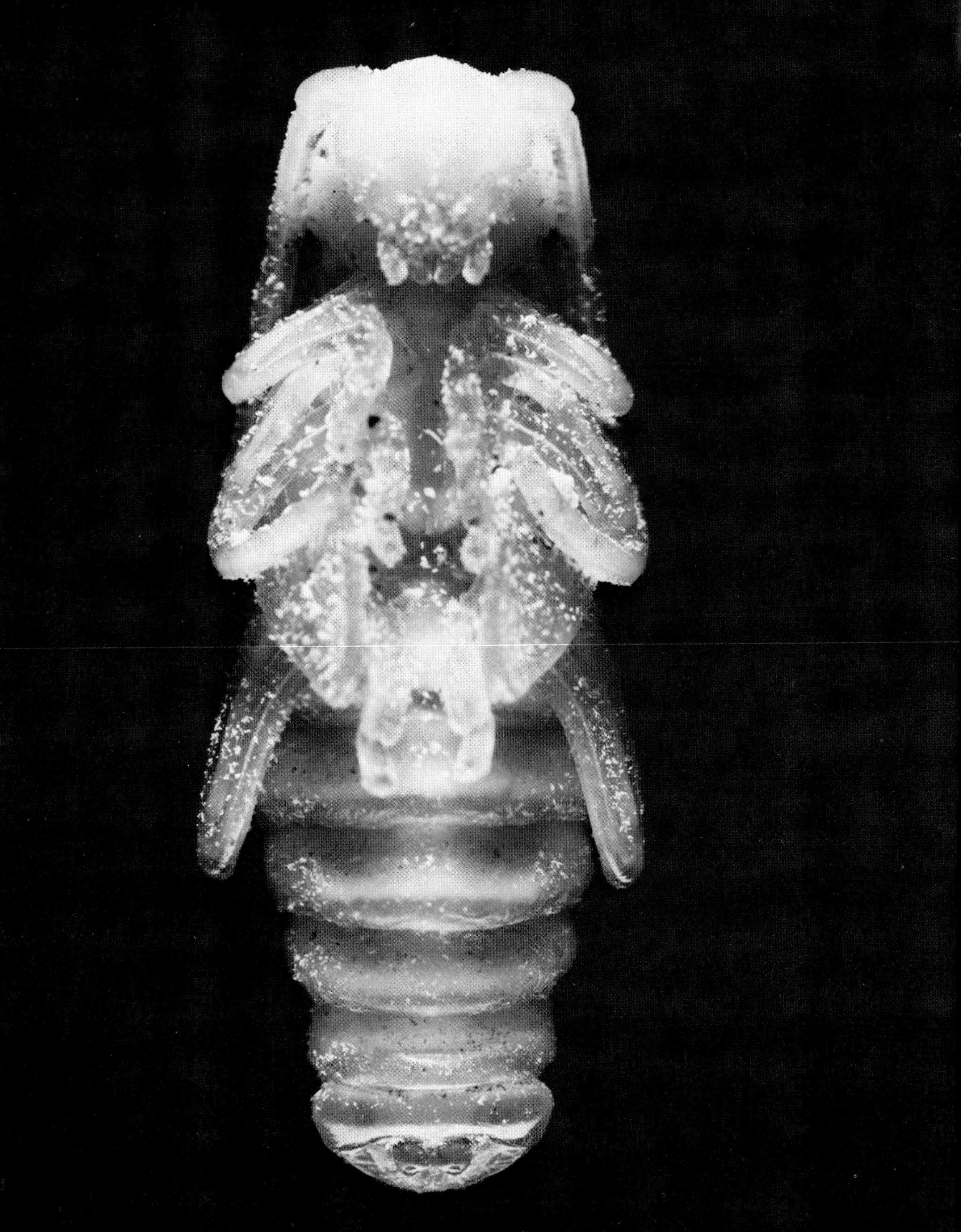

Handbook for SCIENTIFIC PHOTOGRAPHY

Alfred A. Blaker, RBP

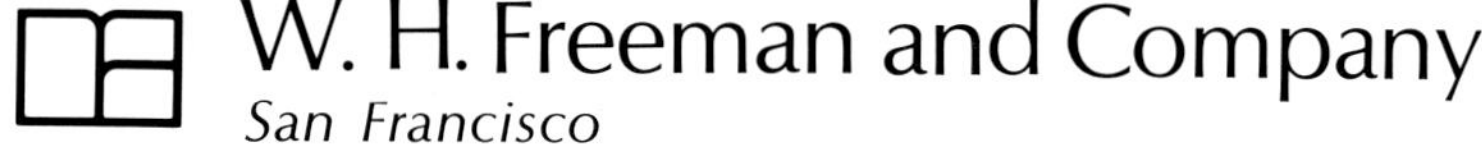

Frontispiece: Translucent pupa ($\times$9.2). See the caption for Plate 36C (page 226) for details.

Library of Congress Cataloging in Publication Data

Blaker, Alfred A 1928–
Handbook for scientific photography.

"A greatly expanded revision of [the author's] Photography for scientific publication . . . published in 1965."

Bibliography: p.
Includes index.
1. Photography—Scientific applications.
2. Scientific illustration. I. Title.
TR692.5 1977 778.3 77-24661
ISBN 0-7167-0285-1

Printed in the United States of America

9 8 7 6 5 4 3 2 1

The contemplation of things as they are
Without error or confusion
Without substitution or imposture
Is in itself a nobler thing
Than a whole harvest of invention.

—Francis Bacon

Preface

This handbook is based upon *Photography for Scientific Publication* (W. H. Freeman and Company, 1965), but the material presented has been so greatly revised, expanded, and reorganized that the book has been retitled. Virtually everything that was in the earlier version has been retained in some form, but much entirely new text and many new text figures and photographs have been added. The result is a new book rather than a simple revision.

Handbook for Scientific Photography is intended to be a compact source of useful and practical information about photography in the laboratory, or for laboratory-related purposes, for people who need to illustrate scientific articles or books. Many researchers, lacking access to a suitable photographic service laboratory or being unable to pay for professional assistance, must learn to do their own photography. The available literature on the subject, however, often leaves them without the particular knowledge they most need, and most photographic instruction gives no more than very general aid. Consequently, the quality of scientific photographs in journals and books is often inferior to that of the text they accompany. Because the clarity of a scholarly publication depends in part upon the clarity of its illustrations, and because the likelihood of acceptance of one's thesis will be enhanced by its clarity, it is obvious that one should strive to produce the best possible photographs for such purposes.

The main concern of this book is black-and-white still photography of subjects encountered in scientific research. There is supplementary material on color photography but, since color reproduction is costly and hence relatively uncommon in scientific publication, this material is not extensive. There is a substantial emphasis on the photography—using commonly available equipment—of subjects whose small size requires the application of closeup and photomacrographic techniques, in magnifications up to about ×80. There is also a chapter on photography through the microscope, subdivided according to simple and more complex methods, in which general techniques are discussed rather than specific equipment. Although most of the text deals with the photography of subjects that are motionless or nearly so at the moment of exposure, one section describes a particularly useful and versatile method of photographing small, lively subjects. Throughout the book the approach is pragmatic, being in terms of what one *needs to know* to accomplish the stated ends, rather than in terms of theory or ideal circumstances.

The coverage of basic photography is skeletal, on the assumption that most readers will have some general knowledge of the field. If you need a greater depth or breadth of knowledge of the basics, or if your laboratory work also entails frequent field studies requiring photography, you should see my other recent book, *Field Photography: Beginning and Advanced Techniques* (W. H. Freeman and Company, 1976), which concentrates on field and field-related photography and includes much more detailed coverage of basic photographic techniques.

No attempt is made here to describe specialized techniques already well covered elsewhere, except as is necessary to provide a summary knowledge for better understanding of a given problem. This exclusion applies particularly to techniques requiring special equipment, such as the photography of spectra, oscilloscope traces, or aerodynamic flow fields. Such highly specialized techniques are discussed thoroughly in separate books, technical articles, or the literature accompanying the equipment in question.

The reader should keep in mind that knowledge of photographic techniques can be readily transferred from one type of subject to another, if they share some common characteristics. Thus, even if your immediate concerns seem to require reference to only a single small portion of this handbook, an initial reading of the whole text will be of material help in solving your specific problem. Simply referring to the index for notations on a particular subject will give no true idea of the usefulness of the book. Remember that, although the subject matter of a given illustrative plate may be foreign to your field of study, the characteristics being shown and the principles comprehended in the photography may well apply to your own subject matter. Thus, for instance, the relatively widespread appearance of insect materials in the plates is due both to the easy availability of suitable specimens and—more importantly—to the inherently great structural variety of such materials. The characteristics displayed in many of these photographs may be readily seen in other, vastly different types of subject matter. The very unpredictability of a researcher's needs may make a seemingly unrelated piece of information just what is needed to solve some new problem.

No claims are made to complete knowledge or to originality of technique. The methods described here are those that have been found most useful by me, my associates, and my predecessors. I hope that they will prove useful to many others.

All the photographs in this book—except as noted below—were made by me; the blame for any deficiencies can thus be clearly assigned. Most of them were made as part of my daily work at the Scientific Photographic Laboratory of the University of California, Berkeley, where I was employed for many years. Some were made expressly to illustrate matters discussed in the text; a few others were existing examples of my personal photographic interests. The last two plates in the book are photographs made in 1885 and 1906, respectively, and were reprinted by me from negatives in the posession of the Museum of Vertebrate Zoology at the University of California, Berkeley.

A handbook such as this is necessarily a synthesis. The author of such a book must read, observe, be taught—and then adapt widely and freely. In a very real sense this book is the sum of the experience of a great many people, not all of whom can be identified. But some direct help can be clearly recognized, and those who gave it can be given the deserved credit.

Without the five years of excellent on-the-job training at the Scientific Photographic Laboratory under Victor G. Duran, I could not have undertaken this work. Much credit must also be given to Dr. E. S. Evans, Dr. Max Alfert, and Dr. Robert D. Raabe, who were members of the Laboratory's guiding faculty committee, for encouraging the experimentation necessary to develop and refine many of the techniques described in this handbook.

Nor could the great variety of specifically illustrative photographs have been collected without the cooperation of many of the people who have had work done at the Laboratory and who have allowed me to use the resulting pictures here. Those who have given such permissions, or who provided subject matter for photographic experimentation, are credited in the plate captions. Dr. David Wake, Director of the Museum of Vertebrate Zoology, was very helpful in allowing access to the museum's negative files and in granting permission for the publication of pictures found there.

Grateful thanks are due Zev Pressman of the Stanford Research Institute, Dr. Edward S. Ross of the California Academy of Sciences, and Dr. Richard D. Zakia of the Rochester Institute of Technology for reading the manuscript and offering much helpful criticism. Many of their suggestions have been incorporated into the text. Much of the book still reflects the valuable advice and criticism given by Dr. Ralph Emerson of the University of California, Berkeley, when I was writing the original edition.

Any author would be helpless without the assistance of a great many people in the office of his publisher. Most cannot be credited by name because of the group nature of a publishing effort, but I must single out two people for special consideration—Fred Raab, whose editing of the manuscript has been a magnificent effort, and Jack Nye, whose performance as designer is obvious from cover to cover. My association with the personnel of W. H. Freeman and Company, over more than thirteen years, has been uniformly satisfying to me.

Last, but certainly not least, I would like to thank my wife, Sally, and my children (all six of them) for their patience during a period of unusual neglect, with special thanks to John, Frances, Barbara, and Elizabeth for their service as "galley slaves."

ALFRED A. BLAKER

Walnut Creek, California
July, 1977

Contents

Formulas and Tables

FORMULAS

TABLES

Illustrations

FIGURES

BLACK-AND-WHITE PLATES

COLOR PLATES
(*following page 104*)

Handbook for SCIENTIFIC PHOTOGRAPHY

PART I

A Review of Essentials

In any work of this sort it is necessary to assume that the reader already has a working knowledge of the fundamentals of photography. However, it is appropriate to provide a brief review of the essentials. And, paradoxically, in such a review it is safest to assume nothing, since there is no way of telling which elements are weak or missing in the knowledge of any individual reader.

CHAPTER 1

Basic Photography

This chapter will cover only the most fundamental aspects of photographic method: the achievement of correct film exposure and the processing of films and papers to obtain finished pictures.

The initial act of photography consists of one operation that is relatively intuitive and two that are rather mechanical. The first one is the whole combined operation of choosing, isolating, and lighting the subject; the other two are the determination of correct exposure and the operation of the camera itself. These operations are followed by the development of the exposed film, the making of the photographic print, and any further operations required to prepare final materials for use in the classroom or in a publication.

Since operating the camera is generally a simple matter of manual dexterity, with the special features of any given make and model being explained in the camera instruction booklet, this topic will receive little attention here. Camera operations requiring special knowledge, such as closeup and photomacrographic techniques, will be described in later chapters.

Choosing, isolating, and lighting the subject, and the methods used to prepare final materials for classroom or publication use, are major topics that will make up the bulk of this handbook. But first let us review the basics.

BLACK-AND-WHITE FILMS

Although there are many special films for special purposes, it is fair to state, in general, that black-

and-white films are divided into three groups: panchromatic, orthochromatic, and non-color-sensitive.

Panchromatic Films

Panchromatic films, which record the relative brightnesses of the various colors in a scene roughly as the eye does, are the most commonly used films in scientific photography, as discussed in this book. The approximate correspondence of panchromatic films to the sensitivity of the eye is exceptionally useful. One can use filters to differentiate a wide range of colors from one another (in varying shades of grey, of course). One can also roughly determine the effect of a filter simply by looking through it and observing the resulting changes in relative brightness in various subject areas.

Orthochromatic Films

Orthochromatic films (or simply "ortho" films) are sensitive to yellow, green, blue, and violet, but not to the reds. These films are useful where their sensitivity range accords with the colors of the subject matter or with the photographer's notion of what he wishes to record. Orthochromatic effects can usually be simulated by using suitable filters with panchromatic films, but only at a great cost in film speed (see section on film speed, below). Ortho films are very commonly used in copying. They are rarely found in roll form, but are readily available in sheet form.

Non-Color-Sensitive Films

Non-color-sensitive films record only in the blue-violet region of the spectrum. These films are no longer used in general photography, but are usually reserved for making transparencies or for other similarly limited uses.

Specialized discussions of matters covered above are given in the following sections, and more detailed information can be had by reference to information sources listed in the Bibliography.

THE BASIS OF CORRECT EXPOSURE

The determination of correct film exposure depends upon the interaction of three factors and upon finding the proper balance among them. These factors are:

1. Film speed;
2. Diaphragm opening; and
3. Exposure time (shutter speed).

In most circumstances the correct exposure can readily be determined within acceptable limits by using a light meter according to the instructions provided with it. But *intelligent* use of the camera and meter requires a little more knowledge.

Film Speed

The film speed, as listed by the manufacturer, is a constant that is based upon the response of the film to the action of light under specified "normal" conditions. (In the United States these conditions are established by the American National Standards Institute, which was formerly the American Standards Association.) The characteristics of films are described in more detail later in this chapter. In general, slow films are fine-grained and show relatively brilliant overall tonal gradation (high contrast), whereas fast films have larger grain structure and show less contrast. By "slow" or "fast" films we mean films requiring relatively longer or shorter exposures, respectively, under given conditions. For most purposes in laboratory scientific photography a slow film is preferred for reasons of photographic quality, particularly if a small-format film, requiring subsequent enlargement of the images, is being used.

Film speed is designated differently in different parts of the world, but here we will use only the American Standards Association ratings, usually called ASA. A comparison of this scale with its foreign equivalents is shown in Table 1. A film rated at ASA 25 or 50 is considered slow; one rated at ASA 500 or 1600 is fast. Greater extremes of film speed exist in both directions. Films with intermediate ratings are simply called medium-speed films.

Functions of Diaphragm and Shutter

Examination of any adjustable camera will show that the amount of light reaching the film can be varied by opening or closing the iris diaphragm at the lens, or by changing the shutter speed. Current practice is to graduate the diaphragm scale as shown in Table 2 and to designate the shutter speeds according to one of the two systems shown there. The individual diaphragm graduations are generally called *f*-numbers or *f*-stops, and the difference between any two adjacent graduations on *either* scale (diaphragm *or* shutter) is a difference of one "stop."

By using a light meter that has been set for the speed of the film being used, one can measure the light available in a given situation and read from the meter scale a variety of diaphragm-opening/shutter-speed combinations, any of which will provide correct exposure of

TABLE 1
Equivalent American and foreign film-speed scales.

ASA & BSI (US & UK)	BSI (log) (UK)	GOST (USSR)	DIN (EUROPE)	SCHEINER (EUROPE)
3	16°	6	6	17°
4	17°	8	7	18°
5	18°	10	8	19°
6	19°	12	9	20°
8	20°	16	10	21°
10	21°	20	11	22°
12	22°	25	12	23°
16	23°	32	13	24°
20	24°	40	14	25°
25	25°	50	15	26°
32	26°	65	16	27°
40	27°	80	17	28°
50	28°	100	18	29°
65	29°	125	19	30°
80	30°	160	20	31°
100	31°	200	21	32°
125	32°	230	22	33°
160	33°	320	23	34°
200	34°	400	24	35°
250	35°	500	25	36°
320	36°	650	26	37°
400	37°	800	27	38°
500	38°	1000	28	39°
650	39°	1250	29	40°
800	40°	1600	30	41°
1000	41°	2000	31	42°
1200	42°	2400	32	43°
1600	43°	3200	33	44°

TABLE 2
Common diaphragm and shutter settings.

DIAPHRAGM OPENING (f-NUMBER)	SHUTTER SPEED (SECONDS) SYSTEM 1	SHUTTER SPEED (SECONDS) SYSTEM 2
1.4	1	1
2	1/2	1/2
2.8	1/5	1/4
4	1/10	1/8
5.6	1/25	1/15
8	1/50	1/30
11	1/100	1/60
16	1/200	1/125
22	1/400	1/250
32	1/800	1/500
45		1/1000
64		1/2000
90		

In each column the top figure represents the most light transmitted, and each succeeding figure represents roughly half the light transmission of the preceding one.

the film. Then, however, one must choose the combination that will *best* fulfill the needs of the task at hand.

Adjustment of the exposure time is, of course, the means by which any motion of either the camera or the subject is "stopped": fast shutter speeds stop motion better than slow speeds. Thus the shutter serves the double function of varying the amount of light reaching the film and controlling the degree to which motion is stopped.

The diaphragm also serves a double function. It varies the amount of light reaching the film and, in addition, controls the *depth of field,* which is defined as that amount of fore-and-aft depth in the scene being photographed that is seen as acceptably "in focus" on the ground glass of the camera or in the resulting picture. A wide opening of the diaphragm (such as $f/2$) provides only shallow depth of field, whereas a small opening (such as $f/64$) gives much greater depth of field. Obviously a lens focused at a distance of 4 feet gives an image that is truly in focus only at that distance. If the diaphragm is opened to $f/2$ or wider this becomes quite evident, with only a very narrow band of space acceptably in focus. But if the diaphragm is "stopped down" to $f/22$ the depth of the scene rendered acceptably sharp in the image will be much greater (from about 3 feet to about 5 feet, if the focus is at about 4 feet). Depth of field will be discussed at greater length in Chapter 6.

Selection of Camera Settings

With the foregoing clearly in mind one can arrive at a reasonable choice of shutter speed and diaphragm opening (f-stop). It depends upon the relative importance of the speed of the motion to be stopped and the depth of field desired. Three-dimensional motionless subjects allow depth to determine the choice. A subject that is in a single plane of focus allows speed to determine the choice. All other situations require a compromise in one direction or the other. The situation as a whole therefore rules, subject to the needs and desires of the photographer. When speed and depth must both be considered, it will help to use a faster film if the intensity of the light illuminating the scene cannot be increased. The negative, however, will have larger grain and less overall contrast. Whether this is important depends upon the subject matter and the use to be made of the negative.

The Reciprocity Law

Determining correct exposures requires a clear understanding of the *law of reciprocity.* This law can be stated as follows: For a film of any given speed, a long exposure with a small diaphragm opening is equivalent to a short exposure with a large diaphragm opening, provided that each such combination transmits the same total amount of light to the film. This simple relation is diagramed in Figure 1. What it means in practice is that, if you wish to increase the speed (decrease the exposure time) by one stop *and keep the same exposure,* you must open the diaphragm one stop to compensate; and vice versa. The same applies for two stops, etc.

The reciprocity law applies *except* when the exposure time is either very long or very short—for practical purposes, shorter than 1/1000 second or longer than about 1 second with black-and-white films, or shorter than 1/1000 second or longer than about 1/5 second with most color films. In either case the exposure is said to suffer from *reciprocity failure,* and in both cases the correction required is the same: relatively *more* exposure is needed than the initial calculation indicated. If your work requires such short or long exposures, you may have to test the film to determine how much additional exposure is needed. Film manufacturers do provide some information on correcting for reciprocity failure, but it is often not specific.

To correct for reciprocity failure in long exposures with black-and-white films, a useful rule of thumb is to increase the exposure (either by increasing the time or by opening the lens diaphragm) by one-half stop to one stop at the 1-second level, by one to two stops at 10 seconds, or by two to three stops at about 100 seconds. With color films it is best to avoid the problem entirely, since the effects of reciprocity failure are not equal in the different emulsion layers and thus a color shift is introduced. The simplest way to avoid long-exposure reciprocity failure is to use flash lighting at unusually short distances, to provide enough light intensity to allow the exposure time to be shortened. Flashbulbs or electronic flash units can be used, but the latter are usually less powerful and less flexible. The effective light output of electronic flash units cannot be changed by changing the shutter speed because the duration of the flash is too short—usually about 1/1000 second or less. Flashbulbs, on the other hand, have a relatively long curve of light output—about 1/50 second—which is normally controlled by chopping it to

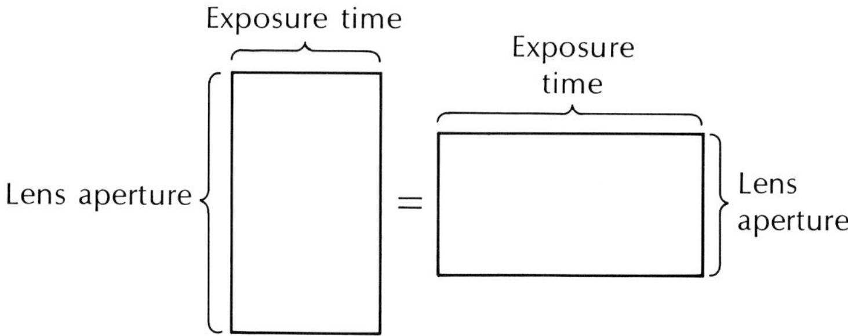

FIGURE 1
The reciprocity law states that equal exposure results whether the lens aperture is large and the exposure time is short, or the aperture is small and the time is long—provided that the total amounts of light transmitted to the film are equal.

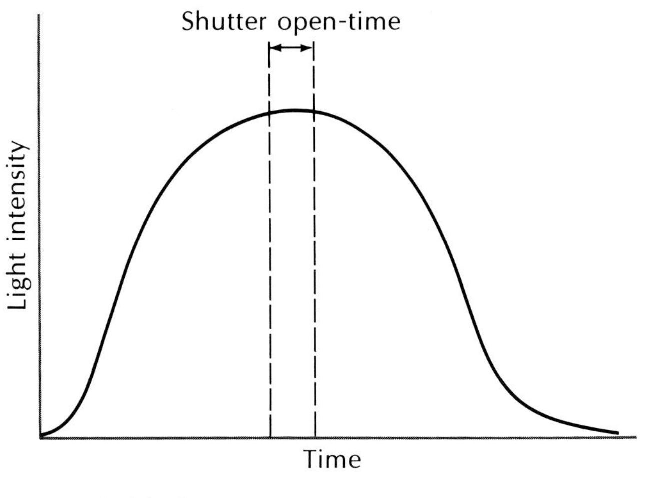

A Flashbulb

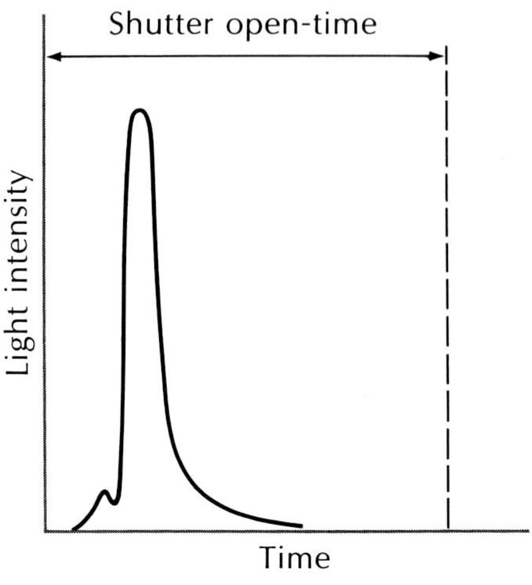

B Electronic flash

FIGURE 2
Flash duration vs. shutter speed. The curves are approximate, and the coordinates do not show actual comparative light intensities or flash durations (these factors vary with type and make).

A Flashbulb exposure is controlled by the shutter open-time.
B Electronic flash exposure is controlled by the flash duration; the shutter is used only to trigger the flash and limit the capture of ambient light.

any desired shorter length with the camera shutter (see Figure 2 for illustration of this point). Maximum light capture is achieved by using a shutter speed of $1/_{30}$ second or longer. Thus, when the shutter is open, as for a time exposure, a flashbulb can be used to maximum effect to shorten the exposure time; in effect, the latter becomes the duration of the bulb emission—about $1/_{50}$ second with most bulbs. (Flash photography using this method is further described in Chapter 6.)

Short-exposure reciprocity failure was encountered by few photographers until recently. But the introduction of automatic-feedback electronic flash units, which provide exposure correction over decreasing flash-to-subject distances by progressively shortening the duration of the flash, has brought the problem (at least theoretically) even to amateur photographers. At very short distances these units may have flash durations as short as $1/_{50,000}$ second. Such ultra-high speeds are sometimes needed to freeze very rapid subject movements; you may then have to test the exposure results and correct for reciprocity failure by opening the lens diaphragm as needed. Otherwise, just avoid the problem by not bringing the flash unit too close to the subject. (Or, override the feedback feature by setting the unit for manual operation, and then calculate the exposure as with a standard flash unit; in manual operation most such units have a flash duration of about $1/_{1000}$ second, where there is no problem.)

The Inverse-Square Law

A second law affecting photographic exposure in certain circumstances is called the *inverse-square law.* This can be stated as follows: The intensity of light from a point source (or from any relatively small source) falls off with the square of the distance. Thus, if you double the distance from a small light source to the subject, as in flash photography, or from a lens to the projected image, as inside the camera in photomacrography (see Chapter 6), the light energy is spread over four times the original area, so the light intensity falls to one-fourth the original level (see Figure 3). If the distance is tripled, the light intensity falls to one-ninth; and so on. And, of course, it also works in reverse: if you halve the distance, the light intensity quadruples, and so on.

EXPOSURE DETERMINATION

The determination of photographic exposure is most commonly done using a photoelectric exposure meter to measure the light. In flash photography it is done by simple arithmetical calculation or by the use of a dial calculator built into the flash unit.

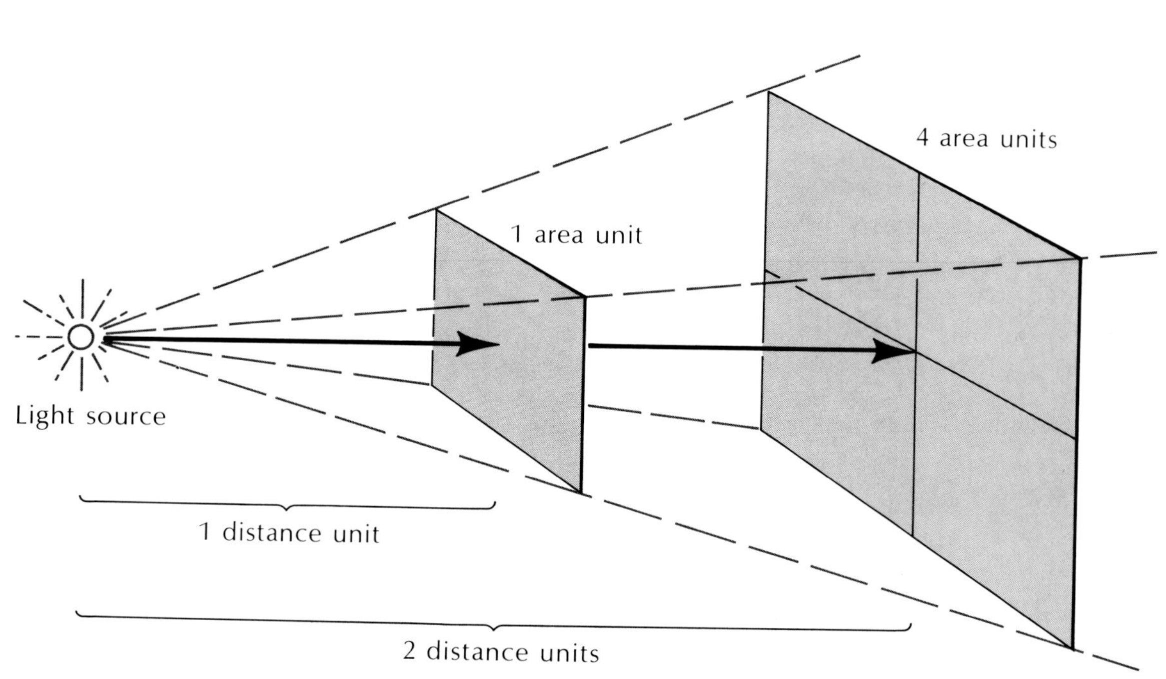

FIGURE 3
The inverse-square law states that, as the light source-to-subject (or lens-to-film) distance increases, the light energy is spread over an ever increasing area and the light intensity falls off with the square of the distance.

Light Metering

Photoelectric light meters operate by means of a light-sensing cell connected to a sensitive galvanometer. There are several types of sensing cells, with significant differences in circuitry, but the basic method of use is the same. The light meter is keyed to the sensitivity of the film being used by setting a film-speed marker on the meter. The meter reading, however obtained, is then transferred to a circular dial calculator to get a series of shutter-speed/diaphragm-opening combinations, from which the photographer chooses the one that represents the best compromise between motion-stopping ability and depth of field.

Light meters that are built into cameras operate in a manner similar to that of separate, handheld meters, but in addition are usually mechanically coupled to the diaphragm-setting and/or shutter-speed-setting dials of the camera.

As with the camera itself, details of the operation of any particular light meter are best obtained from the instruction booklet supplied with it upon purchase.

Flash Calculations

Flash photography, in which exposure is by the light produced by a pulsed source, can be accomplished with either of two types of light source: (1) flashbulbs (including such specialized forms as flashcubes, light bars, etc.), which are one-shot, disposable glass envelopes containing any of several forms of finely divided metal that is ignited by an electric current through a rather simple triggering circuit; and (2) electronic flash (often miscalled "strobelight"—actual stroboscopic light is a controlled series of light pulses from an electronic flash), in which a gas—usually xenon or a mixture of xenon with other rare gases—enclosed in a glass tube is caused to glow brightly for an instant as the result of excitation by a pulsed electric discharge. An electronic flash tube can be fired an indefinite number of times.

Flashbulbs are individually cheap and produce a great deal of light for their size and weight. Electronic flash is much cheaper in the long run, and provides a much shorter flash, with the potential for impressive motion-stopping ability; but great light output is obtainable only with large, heavy units, because of the bulky capacitors needed for energy storage. Both types of flash sources are highly useful, and are by no means mutually exclusive in their applications. And a flash unit or bulb need not be especially large to be very useful in quite varied situations.

To determine correct photographic exposure with most flash sources one must employ a simple arithmetical formula, shown here as Formula 1. It states that to obtain the correct *f*-number one divides the guide number by the flash-to-subject distance in feet. The key to this formula is the *guide number* (*GN*), which is a numerical statement of the light output of the source and is related to the speed of the film to be used. This formula is a way of expressing the inverse-square law, as it applies to light emitted by a small source.

Disposable flashbulbs emit a rather long burst

FORMULA 1
Standard flash-exposure formula.

$$f\text{-number} = \frac{\text{guide number}}{\text{flash-to-subject distance (feet)}}$$

$$f = \frac{GN}{D}$$

of light, usually about $1/50$ second but varying according to the type of bulb. At best, this is too slow for much motion stopping, so the shutter is synchronized with the flash, and the timing of the shutter is used to chop the flash into segments of any desired shorter length. A guide number must therefore be provided for each likely shutter-speed/film-speed combination. Guide-number charts for exposure computation are usually printed on the flashbulb package. Formula 1 is then used to obtain the correct film exposure for the given circumstances.

Since the effective exposure time with an electronic flash is the duration of that flash—usually from $1/1000$ to $1/3000$ second—only one guide number per film speed is assigned to such a unit. The shutter speed is largely irrelevant, being longer than the flash, and serves primarily to limit the effect of ambient light on the film. Any limitations on shutter speeds, as in cameras having focal-plane shutters, are mechanical in nature.

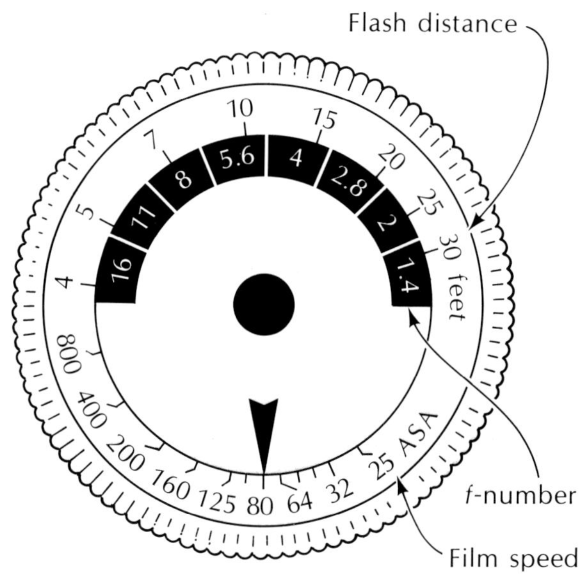

FIGURE 4
Flash-unit dial calculator, typical of those on small electronic flash units. Turning the outer ring to align the indicator with the film speed gives a series of correct flash-distance and *f*-number pairs. Multiplying any pair yields the guide number for that film speed (here the guide number is about 55).

The use of electronic flash in general photography is simplified by the dial-type exposure calculator now provided on nearly all such units (see Figure 4). You simply turn a setting ring to the applicable film speed, and the dial displays a series of flash-to-subject-distance/*f*-number settings. You use the *f*-number specified for the particular distance being used; or, conversely, you use the distance specified for the *f*-number you wish to use. If you need to *know* the guide number for your film, just multiply one of the intermediate distances by the opposed *f*-number. For example, if *f*/5.6 falls directly opposite 10 feet, the guide number for that film speed is 56.

The recently introduced automatic-feedback electronic flash units are even simpler to use. Having set the unit for the proper film speed, you just set the aperture, focus, and shoot. As the flash begins, a built-in sensing cell detects the flash light reflected from the subject and automatically adjusts the duration of the flash to give a correct exposure at the aperture setting being used. As with any flash exposure, this works for any reasonably nearby subject, at one or more specified aperture settings. You should realize, of course, that these devices cannot think, and so may give an inaccurate exposure if the area read by the sensor is not representative of the actual subject area of primary interest. However, all such units known to me have a "manual" setting, which bypasses the feedback circuit and allows operation of the device as a standard electronic flash unit. Then the normal guide-number method for determining correct exposure is used.

I should mention that correct flash exposures can be measured, rather than calculated, with a special device called a flash meter. However, the use of flash meters is presently so limited that I have assumed the calculation of exposure as normal procedure. See your dealer for information if you wish to use a meter.

BLACK-AND-WHITE FILM DEVELOPMENT

Laboratory scientific photography can entail the use of roll films, sheet films, or both. The processing is similar for both, but the details of handling vary. It is useful but not absolutely necessary to have had some formal instruction in film processing.

Roll Films

Most professionals and many amateurs agree that the most practical and durable equipment for developing small quantities of roll films is the stainless steel tank with wire reels, though some new designs of plastic tanks that have been introduced recently are also good. I personally prefer to stay with steel. Such tanks are cylindrical and have a widemouthed, lighttight, slip-on top that can be capped for inversion agitation. Tanks for processing anything from a single 35-mm roll up to four or more 35-mm or 120-size rolls of film simultaneously are available.

Loading the wire reels in the dark is not difficult if you practice it a few times in a lighted room with a waste roll of film. Some people prefer to use one of the special devices that are made to facilitate the loading. Detailed instructions for loading and use are supplied with the tanks upon purchase.

Films are loaded in total darkness (except for those few kinds of tanks designed for so-called daylight loading), using either a darkroom or a loading bag. The latter is a lighttight bag with a zippered closing and a pair of elastic-ended "sleeves" that allow you to insert your hands to do the loading by feel. The processing can be done in full room light, since the chemicals can be poured in and out through the lighttight opening in the tank.

The steps in film processing are as follows:

1. Developing. Developers are solutions of certain organic compounds. Check the instruction sheet supplied with the film for the type of developer to use, as well as the appropriate dilutions, temperatures, and times.
2. Rinsing with water or using "short-stop." The latter is dilute acetic acid, and is used with some films to instantaneously stop the action of any developer remaining in or on the film emulsion after the tank is emptied of developer; with most films a simple water rinse is sufficient.
3. Fixing. The image in the developed negative is rendered permanent and the remaining undeveloped light-sensitive compounds are removed from the emulsion in this step. The acid fixer—sometimes called "hypo"—is a solution primarily of sodium thiosulfate.
4. Washing. Residual fixer is removed, either by immersing the film (still on its reel) in a running water wash or by filling the tank with water, letting it stand several minutes, emptying it, and repeating this cycle five or six times.
5. Post-wash rinsing. Water-spotting of the negatives is prevented by a final immersion

in a dilute solution of a detergent (wetting agent), such as Kodak's Photo-Flo.

6. Drying. This is most easily accomplished by simply hanging the film to air-dry in a dust-free place, with a weight clipped to the bottom, if necessary, to prevent it from curling. The drying is speeded up by squeegeeing the excess moisture from the film with a *clean* photographic-grade plastic sponge when hanging the film up. Warm-air drying devices are unnecessary.

Sheet Films

Sheet films are single pieces of film meant to be exposed one at a time in manually operated press or view cameras (these are described in Chapter 2). There are certain advantages in using sheet films. If you use an appropriate film size it is possible to avoid the need for photo-enlarging (and thus the need for even having an enlarger), thus simplifying and speeding up the printing. It is also possible to make sequential exposures with entirely different types of film; this is a useful procedure in some circumstances, particularly in the photography of patients in hospitals. Perhaps most important is that, since the image will not be significantly enlarged (if at all) in printing, one can obtain high-quality prints with much less difficulty and less need for precision work than when roll films are used. Although I do a great deal of my field photography with 35 mm cameras, I prefer to use large sheet films—usually 5 × 7 or 8 × 10 inches—for most of my laboratory work, for the foregoing reasons.

I assume that most readers of this book will be doing relatively small volumes of photographic work, not requiring large-scale, factory-type processing equipment and facilities. With that in mind, I recommend that sheet films be processed in flat trays rather than in tanks. It is simple, convenient, and economical in the use of chemicals. With a little practice you can safely develop as many as twelve 4 × 5-inch, eight 5 × 7-inch, or four to six 8 × 10-inch films simultaneously in an ordinary 8 × 10-inch tray.

The processing procedure is basically the same for sheet films as for roll films and need not be repeated here, although separate trays are used for the developer, water rinse (shortstop is seldom needed with sheet films), and fixer. Panchromatic films must be processed in total darkness completely through the fixation stage, but washing can be done in room light. Orthochromatic and non-color-sensitive films can be developed under a red safelight.

Time and Temperature

In processing either roll or sheet films, among the most important considerations are time and temperature. Both are specified for various processing conditions in the film manufacturer's information sheets. Development time is important because it establishes the negative's basic range of contrasts, and both underdevelopment and overdevelopment can be detrimental to the image quality. Temperature is a very important factor. You must know what it is in order to establish the correct development time.

Most critical are temperature variations. Although many seem to think that temperature control is less important in black-and-white work than in color work, this is false. The tolerable limits of variation are the same for both: plus or minus about one-half degree Fahrenheit. Failure to keep the temperature within close limits during all liquid processing steps, from initial development right through the post-wash rinse, introduces the risk of *reticulation*. This is a prunelike wrinkling of the film emulsion caused by alternate swelling and shrinking. Gross temperature variations can cause the effect to increase to the point where the emulsion frills or breaks up at the edges of the film base, and even threatens to slough right off. Lesser effects may be so slight as to resemble, to the naked eye, an increase in film grain size. But examining the film under magnification will reveal the true nature of the effect. The problem can be avoided simply by keeping control of the temperature, which requires care and attention but is not difficult.

Agitation

Agitation is the movement of film relative to processing solutions that is necessary to prevent stagnation of the solutions. The consequences of stagnation are reduced chemical activity due to local exhaustion of the chemicals, and the risk of uneven development or incomplete fixation.

Roll films developed in tanks are best agitated by gently inverting the tank several times in succession at 30-second intervals throughout development. Developer by-products are inert and are heavier than water. If the tank is not inverted, the film is likely to develop unevenly while it stands on edge in a solution that is settling out.

Sheet films should be individually lifted from the tray, drained from alternate corners, and then carefully re-immersed in a manner that prevents the corner of one film from scratching the surface of another. This procedure should be done constantly throughout development, taking each film in turn. I slide out the bottom film of a group and then put it back on the top. The risk of scratching is reduced if the films are kept emulsion-side down in the tray. Agitation need not be as constant during fixation, but should still be done frequently. Keep in mind that overly vigorous agitation may result in streaking of the negative and an unwanted increase in contrast.

Negative Quality

A good negative is the first aim in all black-and-white photography, because a print—although subject to some manipulation—can only show what is already in the negative. Quality greatly enhances both the appearance and the scientific value of any illustration. It is the result of constant attention to detail. But if the basic requirements are held clearly in mind one can achieve quality without being fanatic about technical virtuosity, particularly since the individual worker's needs and usages are usually relatively limited.

Top-quality scientific photography, while varying widely in subject matter and in the conditions in which it is shown, has certain common features. These are sharpness, separation, and clarity.

Sharpness is the recording of the maximum amount of fine subject detail. *Separation* is the distinctness with which the boundaries of the important subject matter can be discerned, either against the background or within the subject itself, with no apparent blending of tones across edges in any important area. Good visual separation is most often the result of careful lighting, although color filtering can be important, too. *Clarity* is the presentation of the relevant subject matter without extraneous intrusions or ambiguity. This includes the positioning of the subject of main importance within the picture area, and introduces the somewhat touchy matter of composition.

People who see photography primarily as an

art form often criticize scientific photographs as stodgy or "textbooky," without thinking of the special needs of science. In scientific photography, if the main subject is small relative to the area of the picture, it should usually be in the center of the picture. If it is not in the center, the subsidiary portions of the picture should be arranged, if possible, to lead the eye to it. Composition should be simple and straightforward. Because of what we may call "the human principle of misunderstanding wherever possible" (a variant of Murphy's Law), complex or subtle compositions should be avoided unless the nature of the subject matter requires it. With the aid of a brief caption, the point illustrated should be obvious. A picture that looks poor from an artistic point of view may be excellent as a scientific illustration. Conventional standards of artistry may be irrelevant in a particular instance. However, keep in mind that there is no special scientific virtue in a dull picture. The more attractive a picture, other factors being equal, the better it will carry its message.

Technically, a good negative has a sharp, clear image, has sufficient density to contain all of the tones of the subject without being so dense as to reduce highlight contrast or require unusually long printing time, is not excessively grainy, and has a range of tonal gradations (internal contrasts) consistent with the ability of the various grades of printing papers to reproduce them (films can encompass a considerably greater range of tones than printing papers).

The sharpness of the image depends upon using good lenses, focusing correctly, stopping any motion of camera or subject, and attaining a depth of field sufficient to contain the subject. Obtaining adequate density in the negative is primarily a matter of correct exposure. Density increases with the log of exposure time; thus, the greater the exposure, the denser the negative, up to the point of total exposure of all available light-sensitive material.

Grain in some degree is an integral part of the negative. It is not, however, part of the subject. Excessive graininess must be avoided wherever it might make the picture ambiguous by spuriously resembling subject texture. In the negative, visible grain is due to the random grouping, or clumping, of the silver grains—themselves microscopic in size—which form the image in the developed film emulsion. Excessive grain can be due to any of several causes. Faster films are generally grainier than slow ones. Overexposure and overdevelopment can result in enlarged grain, while the high-contrast printing required to make good prints from underexposed negatives also increases the contrast, and hence the visibility, of whatever grain is present. Unusually high processing temperatures and overly vigorous developers also tend to increase grain size. Finally, projection printing enlarges the grain structure just as it does the rest of the image, so overenlargement will result in overly visible grain.

Negative contrast is controlled in several ways. First, it is controlled in selecting the film to be used; fast films tend to be lower in overall contrast than slower ones. The major area of control is in the lighting of the subject. Then there are variations of contrast according to the degree of exposure. Any undue overexposure or underexposure will greatly lower the overall contrast in any black-and-white film. It will also tend to distort the range of tonal values: overexposure will lower the highlight and other light-area contrasts, and underexposure will dull and greatly diminish the visibility of shadow and other dark-area detail. Both overall negative contrast and internal contrasts within colored subjects can be changed, in many instances, by means of color filters.

Generally speaking, the best negative is one

that has had the minimum amount of exposure that will provide *complete* tonal coverage of the subject. Less conventionally and more practically, and especially in scientific photography, a good negative can be defined as one that prints well, according to the aims of the photographer.

BLACK-AND-WHITE PRINTING

If you wish to exercise any control over the visual impression presented by your black-and-white illustrations, you must do the printing yourself. I suggest that you use the processing chemicals and procedures recommended by the printing-paper manufacturers, as described in their literature. Prints are developed in trays, like sheet films, but using a different developer. As many as about six prints can be developed at one time, agitating by leafing them through in the manner described for sheet films. The use of a short-stop bath after development will extend the useful life of the fixer.

The most recent innovation in printing papers is resin-coated (RC) paper. This plastic-based material does not absorb chemicals, so washing times are very short and print permanence is very good. If you need glossy prints, which are usually required for publication, simple air drying will result in a good gloss, on glossy-type materials. There is no need to apply the prints to such glossing surfaces as ferrotype tins or chromed mechanical dryers, as would be required with normal printing papers. Just lay the prints out face up on a clean surface, or hang them by a corner from a wire with clothespins. Drying is rapid, and is speeded up if you lightly blot the surface of each print as you remove it from the wash. RC papers are also available in non-gloss surfaces, and these are dried the same way.

RC black-and-white printing papers have been the subject of some adverse criticism in the photographic press, but I lay most of this to prejudice arising from the common human failing of being unwilling to accept change. After considerable use and critical evaluation, I see no qualitative difference between RC prints and prints of the same negatives made on conventional papers. Meanwhile, I have found the advantages well worthwhile. These include substantial savings of water and time in print washing, ease and rapidity of drying and glossing, and unusual resistance to curling after drying. (Single-weight conventional prints will roll up into tight, springy cylinders if left unweighted in a dry place, but RC prints retain indefinitely only the slight curve that comes in initial drying.)

Variables in Printing

Obtaining good prints is simplified by the fact that there are only two basic variables in printing: paper contrast and exposure time.

Papers of different contrasts are needed because not all negatives contain exactly the same range of light-to-dark contrasts. Thus, one must choose the appropriate grades of paper if all prints are to be consistent in overall appearance.

There are two kinds of black-and-white printing papers: variable-contrast and graded-contrast. The former are used in conjunction with colored filters over the light source; with appropriate filters a single packet of paper can yield a good range of contrasts. A somewhat wider range of contrasts is offered by graded papers, but you must have a separate packet of paper for each desired contrast level. Graded papers start at 0 (very low contrast) and go up to 6 (very high contrast). Variable-contrast papers provide the approximate equivalent of 0 to about $3\frac{1}{2}$ on this scale. This is enough for a great many uses, but not for all. I prefer to use graded papers even though I have to stock a larger number of packages. In fact, almost anyone who does much printing will use enough paper to make it economically practical to carry the larger stock. The decision of which type of paper to use is not clear-cut, however. Most beginners find it best to start with the variable papers, and a surprising number of experienced photographers use nothing else.

Varying the printing exposure time varies the overall lightness or darkness of the print. Beyond the simple matter of lightness or darkness, there are several factors that, singly or in combination, determine the correct exposure time. One of these is the density of the negative. Another is the speed of the paper. Contact papers, which are printed by placing negative and paper in actual contact with each other, are slower than projection papers. The latter, which are intended for making enlargements, must be faster in order to cope with the effect of the inverse-square law: as the image magnification is increased with the enlarger, the light intensity at the paper decreases rapidly. So the degree of enlargement itself is another factor affecting the exposure time. The aperture setting of the enlarger lens is, of course, also a factor. And then there is paper contrast. A few makes of papers feature equal speed through the various grades, but it is generally true that the higher the contrast of the paper—or, with variable-contrast papers, the higher the contrast produced by filtering—the longer the exposure time.

Understanding all this, it is enough to say that, if the print appears to be too light overall, you must make another, using more time. If it is too dark, shorten the exposure time. (See Plate 1.)

Control Methods in Printing

For simple darkroom setups, such as mine, the basic method of determining both the correct grade of paper for contrast and the correct printing exposure time is to make some form of test strip. The common way of testing is to place a piece of printing paper below the enlarger lens after the image has been focused and then use a card to block the light from all but a narrow strip across the end of the paper during the first exposure. The time of this exposure is made shorter than is estimated to be correct. Then further exposures of equal duration are made, each time moving the card to widen the area of the printing paper that is exposed to the light. Upon development the print will appear as a series of stripes of ever-increasing overall darkness. To be useful in determining the correct exposure, such a test strip must have at least one stripe definitely too dark and one definitely too light, so that the correct exposure falls somewhere in between—though not necessarily exactly on one of the intermediate times. The method is illustrated in Figure 5.

The best stripe should give a good idea of whether the contrast is correct. If it is, in most cases the full range of tones in the negative will just barely be encompassed by the full tonal range of the paper. If the best stripe looks murky or muddy, a paper of higher contrast is needed, so a new test strip should be made. A new test is also needed if the contrast effect is one of "chalk and charcoal," with no detail showing in either the highlight or shadow areas, but in this case a paper of lower contrast must be chosen. You can visualize the relation between negative and paper by thinking of the combined pair as a continuum. If the negative contrast range takes up less than half the length of this continuum, by having low contrast, the paper must

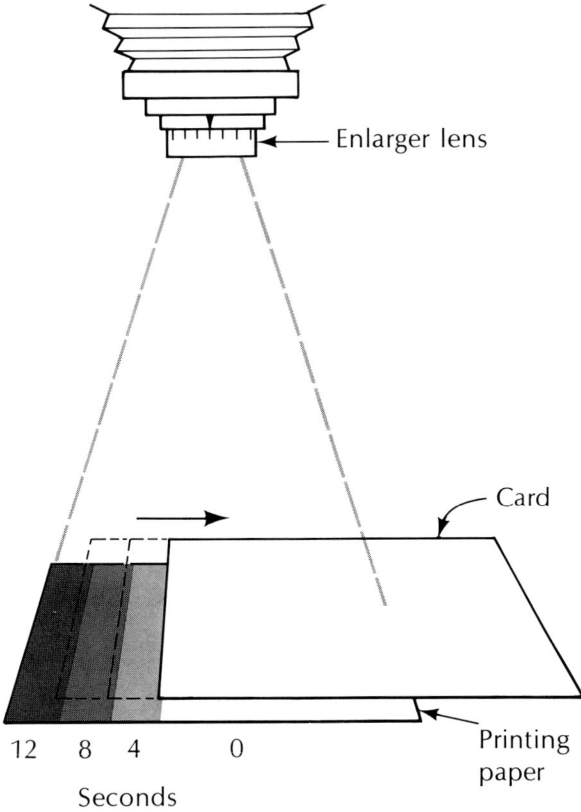

FIGURE 5
Test printing by progressive intermittent exposure, using a 4-second interval. The stripes appear only after the paper is processed.

make up the rest, by having high contrast; and vice versa.

When you have a test-strip section that looks right in both overall darkness and internal contrast, make a print of the whole picture, using the correct exposure time on the appropriate grade of paper. This allows you to gauge the overall effect. With the exceptions noted in the next paragraph, this will be a good print *if* the area of the image that was tested was representative of the negative as a whole.

It is common for some parts of the film to receive either more or less light than the overall picture area, through error or circumstances beyond the photographer's control. In the field, skylight is normally stronger than light reflected from the earth, and trees do throw shadows. In the laboratory, care in lighting the subject should prevent this sort of problem. Still, errors do occur, and besides, it is not always possible to make a single exposure that will be optimal for the entire image. I refer to the solution of this problem as *differential printing,* though this concept is commonly thought of as two separate procedures called dodging and burning in. *Dodging* consists of interrupting the light between the lens and a small area of the printing paper so as to give less exposure to that area, whereas *burning in* is the opposite—interrupting the light to the entire paper *except* for a small area, so as to give *more* exposure to that area. These procedures are illustrated in Figure 6.

PLATE 1 ▶

Basic Photography: Printing Levels and Contrasts.

Mineral specimen (×1.8). Lighting is with one direct flood lamp from the upper right, with minor reflective fill opposite. The background is a white card directly below the subject, receiving the same amount of light as the subject.

A Too low in contrast, with printing time adjusted to show good highlights. The general effect is muddy.
B Correct contrast and printing level. Highlight areas (the small, light inclusions) just show slight detail; the shadows do the same.
C Too high in contrast, with printing time adjusted to show good shadow detail. The highlights are washed out.
D Too high in contrast, with printing time adjusted to show good highlights. The shadow areas go dead black.

Note that neither part C nor D is a good overall print, although each shows some areas well.

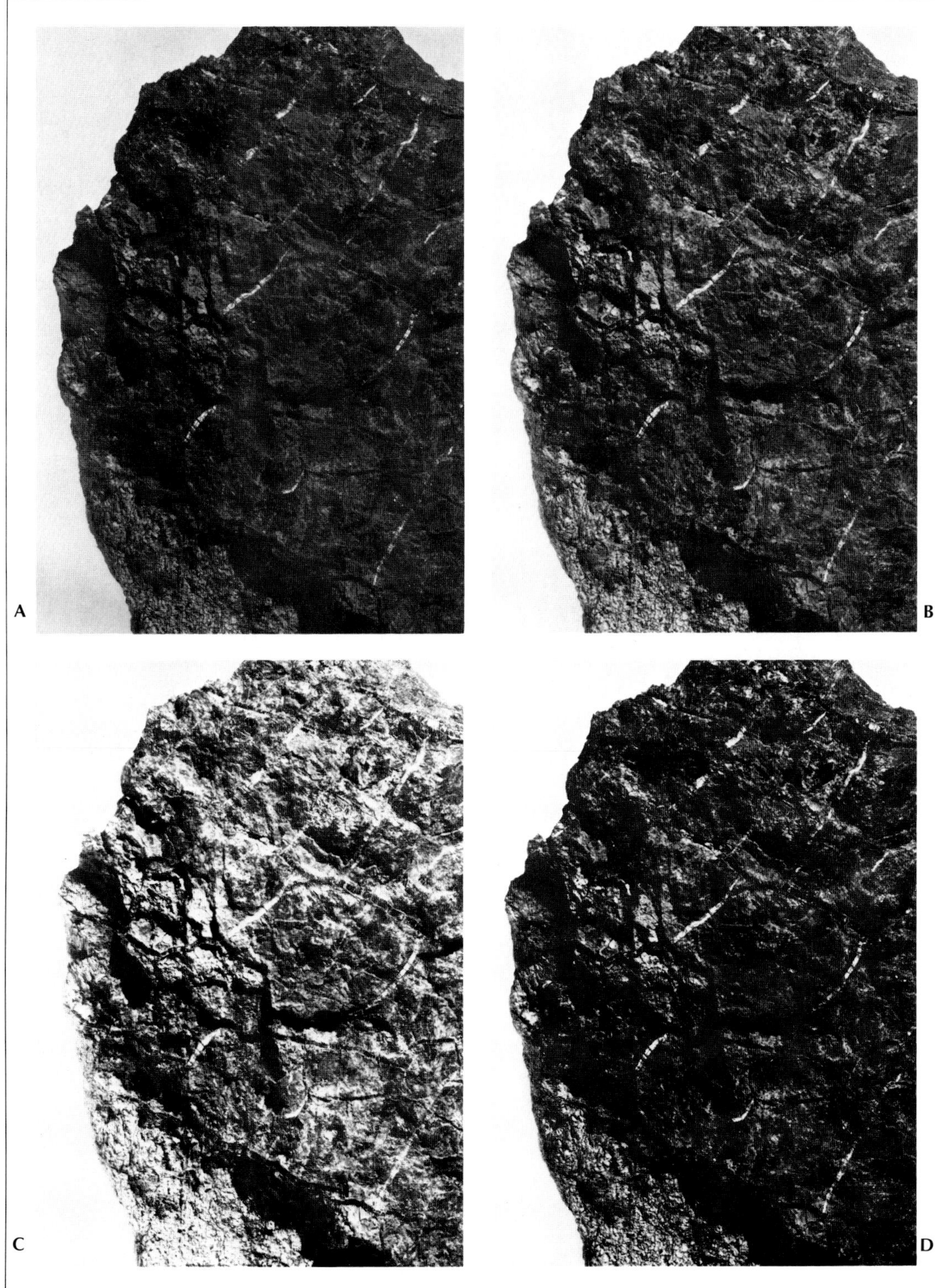
A
B
C
D

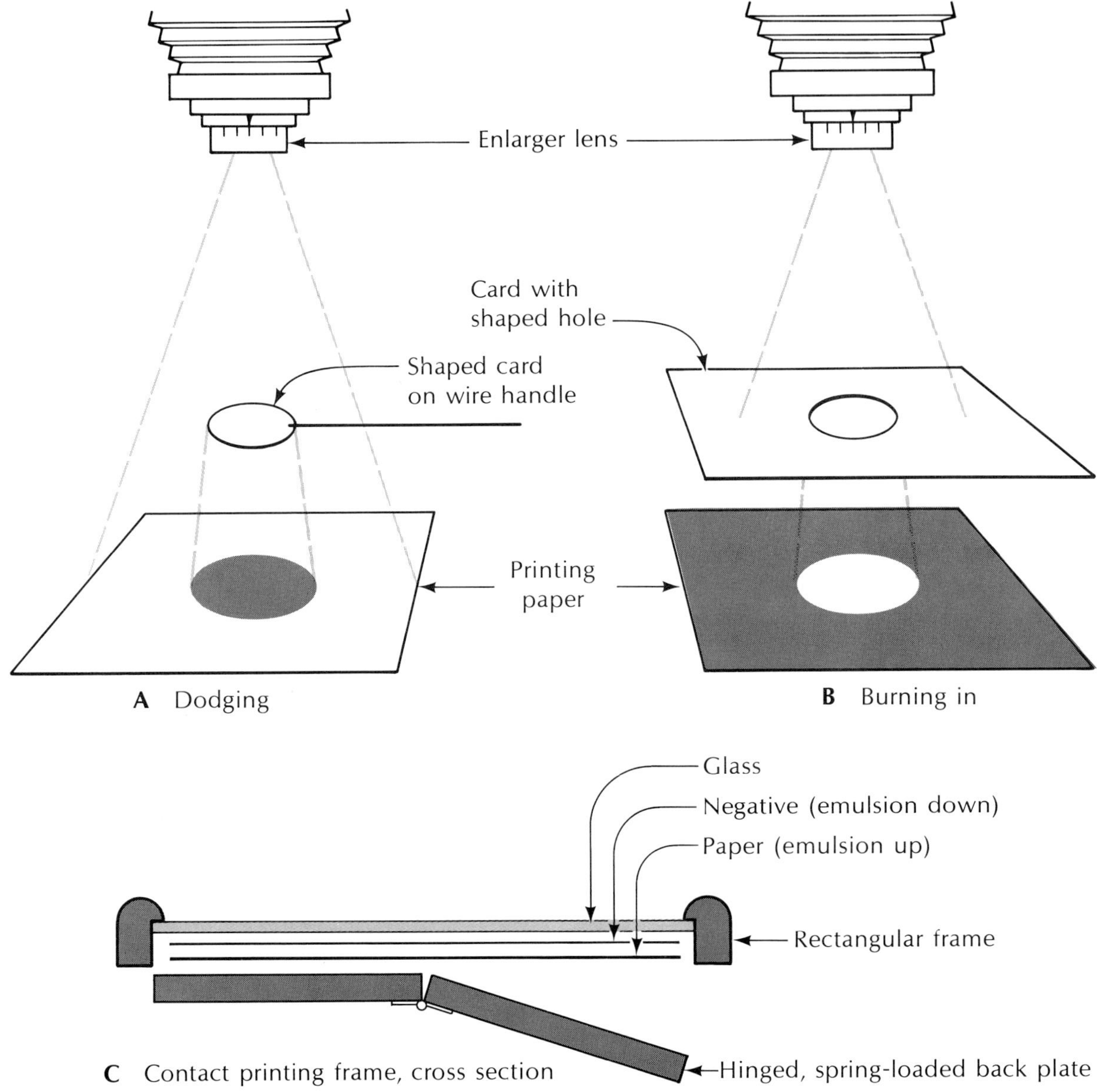

FIGURE 6
Differential printing. Uneven exposure in the negative can be corrected in printing by dodging or burning in. Keeping some distance between the card and the printing paper and constantly moving the card during exposure will "feather" the edge of the affected area. When correctly done, differential exposure is not detectable in the final print. This technique can also be used in contact printing, where the negative and the enlarging paper (contact printing paper is too slow for use with an enlarger as a light source) are sandwiched in a glass-fronted frame and placed on the enlarger baseboard.

In differential printing I prefer to use a simple additive system, in which I first establish a basic exposure time for the least dense area of the negative image. The whole print is given this basic exposure, and then other areas of the image are given additional exposure, progressively longer according to need, until the whole print looks correct when processed. You must test for or accurately estimate the amount of additional time needed for each area.

The only difficulty in learning to do good differential printing lies in teaching yourself to analyze the needs in a logical manner. A little effort should solve the problem. And, as with film processing, it is useful to take instruction from a good teacher.

Brilliance is a term often used to describe fine prints. In a brilliant print there is a richness of detail visible in each of the major tonal areas—there is relatively high contrast within the light areas, the middle tones, and the dark areas, as differentiated from simple overall good contrast. As a quality, it results from successful handling of all aspects of the photography: good lighting, correct color filtering, correct exposure of the film, and careful printing.

In printing there is a special problem that arises to produce a lack of brilliance when the negative has been slightly underexposed. The effect is that, although the highlights and middle tones have good internal tonal separation, the shadows or dark tones are abnormally low in contrast.

When a slightly underexposed negative is printed on a normal grade of paper, the lack of dark-area contrast results in a peculiarly unbalanced appearance; it somewhat resembles a muddy, low-contrast print, such as that shown in Plate 1A. Because the deficiency occurs only in the dark areas, however, simply reprinting to a higher overall contrast is no remedy. Doing so will correct the dark-area contrasts, but will also result in excessively high contrasts in the other tonal areas.

The best method that I have found for solving this problem is to print on a paper that would be one grade too high in contrast if developed normally, and then to process it in a *divided developer.* Such a developer consists of two separate solutions. In the first there is only the developing agent; in the second there are the accelerator and other chemical constituents. The exposed paper is soaked in the first solution (with no need for agitation) for 30–45 seconds, drained above the tray for 5 seconds to remove excess developer from the print surface, and then placed in the second solution for an additional 30–45 seconds with minimum agitation (only that amount needed to spread the solution evenly over the surface of the paper).

Nothing visible occurs in the first bath, since a developing agent by itself works very slowly. The paper remains white until it is put into the second bath, whereupon the image appears almost immediately. Development is complete when the developing agent retained in the paper's emulsion after draining is chemically exhausted. Longer immersion in the second solution is pointless. Printing exposure time is critical, because deliberate underdevelopment or overdevelopment is impractical. See Plate 2 for an example of divided development.

There is no commercially prepared divided developer known to me that works as well as a formula published by Paul Farber in 1962 and 1972 (the former in *U.S. Camera* magazine, the latter in P. D. Dignan's book—see the Bibliography).* Although it must be mixed from

*Both sources are copyrighted, so are not reproduced here. The chemicals can be bought at well-equipped camera stores, or by mail from Dignan at the address given in the Bibliography.

scratch, this formula uses only a few chemicals, all in rather small quantities and all relatively inexpensive and easily obtained. The shelf life is excellent, the first solution lasting indefinitely and the second for 4 to 6 months.

Points of Technique

Paper should never be underdeveloped; the result will be uneven development and/or a generally muddy look with poor reproduction of light areas and no true blacks. Contact paper should be developed not less than 45 seconds and preferably for a full minute. Projection papers require at least 1½ minutes and preferably 2 full minutes. I personally use the longer of these times. Both types of paper can be developed for up to twice the recommended times in normal developers if the safelights are used as specified by the manufacturer, and doing so may improve the print quality if the exposure was slightly short. Too much development, however, introduces the risk of fogging—a greying of light and middle tones through the development of unexposed light-sensitive substances in the emulsion.

During development, the print should be agitated frequently. Simply rocking the tray to move the solution is often insufficient, because standing waves may be created that look good but do not actually move the developer much (the waves move, but the liquid in them remains in essentially the same place). As noted earlier, the print should also be agitated during fixing. Beginners often forget this, with the result that fixation is incomplete. Staining of the print then occurs, either immediately upon exposure to light, or later.

Print Quality

For scientific purposes, the best print is one that reveals the maximum amount of significant information about the subject while presenting an attractive appearance. The latter function, of course, must be subordinate to the former, for if a picture does not show all that is desired, it hardly matters how superficially fine it may appear.

In normal photographic practice, a good print is said to have a just discernible detailing visible in its lightest areas, a wide range of intermediate tones, and good shadow or dark-tone detail, with the darkest tones just approaching total blackness. Such a print makes a good visual impression; that is, it looks "right." In some prints, areas of total black may be included for visual emphasis or for silhouetting.

PLATE 2 ▶

Basic Photography: Contrast Correction through Divided Development.

Cocoons of *Rhyacionia zozana,* the Ponderosa Pine-Tip Moth, on a pine branch (×1). The contrast of the negative fell between contrast grades of printing paper, with a major lack of dark-tone contrast due to marginal underexposure. Divided development was employed to correct the fault. (Originally photographed for R. E. Stevens.)

A Printing on normal-contrast #2 paper, with normal development, gives low overall image contrast.
B A print on #3 paper, still with normal development, is an improvement but is too brilliant in the highlights and deficient in dark-area contrast.
C A print on #3 paper, with divided development instead of normal development, gives greatly improved overall contrast.

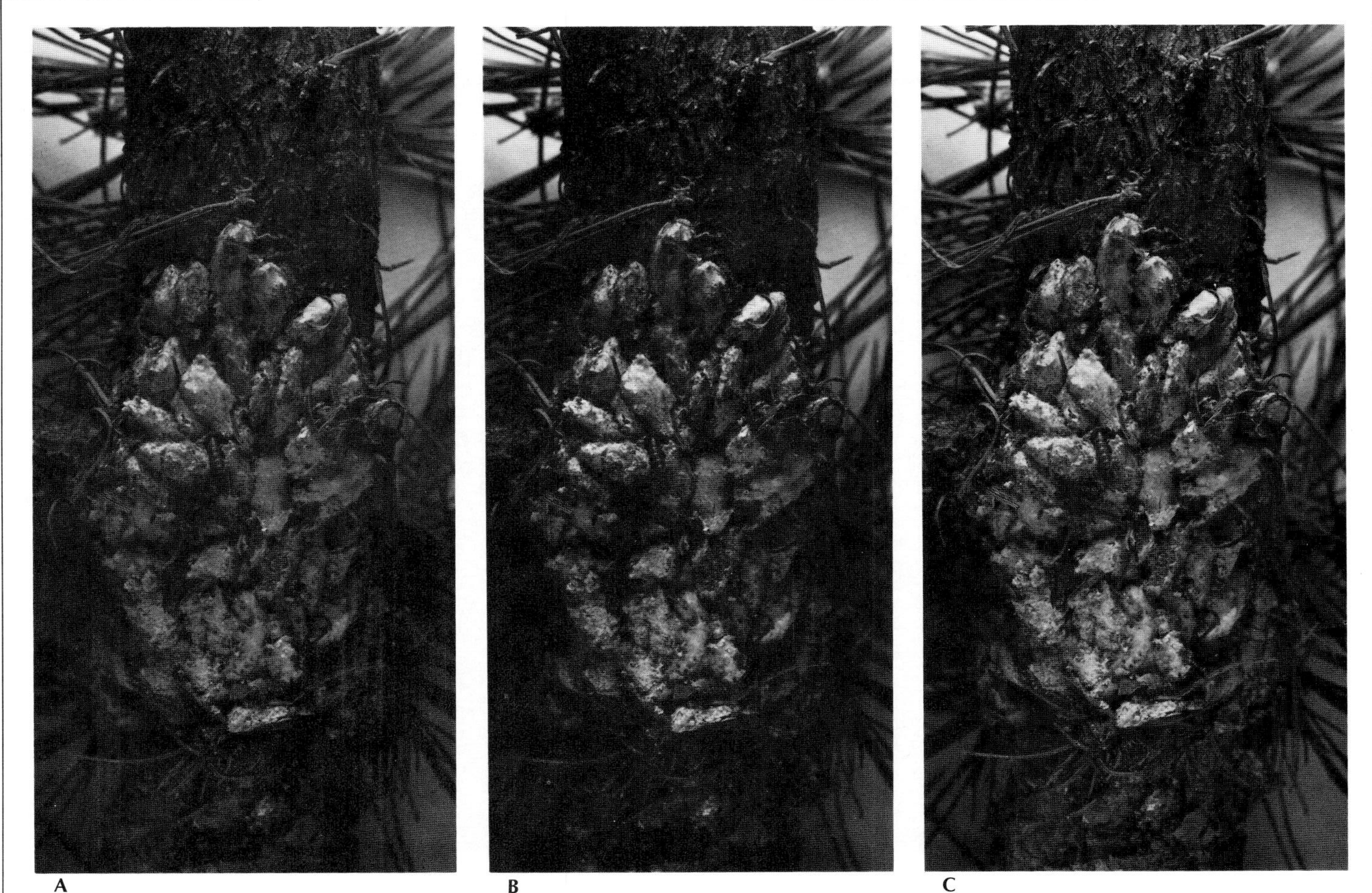
A B C

These criteria also apply generally in scientific photography. Sometimes, however, it may be necessary to avoid loss of detail in the very light and very dark areas, and here one may have to print to a slightly lower than normal contrast. This will produce light grey highlights and dark grey dark areas, for a slightly muddy-looking but more informative picture. This practice should be necessary only rarely, and should not be overdone. And pure white or pure black should be reserved for use as backgrounds.

In terms of purely photographic quality, the surface of a finished print should be as glossy as the intended use will allow. For publication, the normal practice is to use glossy papers, either fully glossed or just air-dried to a semi-gloss (air-dried RC glossy papers come to a full gloss naturally). Printers prefer the glossy surface because any texturing tends to break up the image in reproduction.

All non-gloss (matte, semi-matte, linen, etc.) surfaces reflect light diffusely, by definition, and the result is a reduced overall print quality, especially a loss of contrast in the more subtle dark tones. You can demonstrate this effect very well by making a good print on a semi-matte paper and then spraying one-half of it with a clear gloss enamel.

Matte surfaces should be reserved for wall display, and then preferably for very large prints only. Large photographs may require a non-gloss surface to avoid undue viewing difficulties when there are sizable surface reflections. Glossy prints up to 16 × 20 inches or more can be wall-mounted without reflection problems, however, if the floor is relatively dark in tone, if the prints are suspended so as to lean slightly forward, and if all light sources in the room are at or above the level of the prints.

COLOR FILM PROCESSING

Although almost anyone can learn to do an adequate job of processing either transparency or negative color films, I do not feel that it is either necessary or economically worthwhile for most photographers to do so. In earlier years I did a lot of color processing—enough to convince me that it takes a pretty large operation to be worth the doing. For small operations, then, I recommend that color films be sent to a reputable commercial laboratory. Folklore to the contrary notwithstanding, good color laboratories routinely maintain quality standards that are superior to all but the very best of private setups. They do make errors upon occasion, as do all human enterprises (and once in a while I have been the victim of some little beauties), but in truth their lapses are remarkably few. If you do choose to do your own work, see your dealer and the literature published by film manufacturers for details.

CHAPTER 2
Choice of Equipment

CAMERAS

In amateur photography the choice of the camera to be used depends primarily on the preferences and prejudices of the buyer—whether he values easy mobility most of all, or perhaps the ability to record infinite detail. Generally the casual photographer chooses the small, light camera for its ease of handling and its inconspicuousness. These reasons are usually excellent, and in skilled hands many such cameras are capable of producing fine photographs. There remain, however, a few hardy souls willing to use (and even backpack into the countryside) large view cameras of up to 8 × 10 inches in film size, and some even larger. Again, the reasons for doing so are usually excellent, and if ably used these cameras can yield pictures of superb photographic quality.

In scientific photography, as in any other branch of professional photography, the choice of camera must also depend to some extent upon your preference, but you should also look carefully at the requirements of the particular subject matter and the capabilities of the particular equipment before deciding. Although most of the photographic techniques to be discussed later can be carried out with nearly any type of camera—depending, of course, on the availability of accessories in some cases—it will be worthwhile to discuss the various types available in some detail. We will begin with a brief discussion of one of the most important components of all cameras: the shutter.

Shutters

One fundamental difference among cameras is the type of shutter used. There are two basic types: the leaf shutter and the curtain shutter. Between-the-lens shutters are of the leaf type, in which a number of metal leaves open and close concentrically. This concentric operation tends to expose the film unevenly, with the center receiving more light than the edges, unless the shutter is located at the point of tightest convergence in the bundle of light rays passing into the camera—hence its usual placement between the main lens components.

The curtain design is used in focal-plane shutters, which are located, as the name implies, just in front of the film (near the plane of focus). Most have a curtain of rubberized cloth or flexible metal, of rather complex construction, with an adjustable slit forming its opening. The curtain moves the slit along the long dimension of the film (in a very few makes, the slit moves across the short dimension). The main control over exposure time is variation in the width of the slit. At slow speeds—usually up to 1/30 or 1/60 second—the slit is the full width of the film, and the shutter just stays open for the requisite time. Faster speeds are obtained by using a narrower slit that is passed across the film in a wiping motion. The effective exposure time is the period in which a given point on the film is exposed to the light during this passage. A few cameras have leaf-type focal-plane shutters, most of which operate in a concentric rectangular pattern.

Leaf shutters located between the lens components expose the whole film virtually simultaneously at any shutter speed. Thus, flash synchronization at any speed is just a matter of closing an electrical contact to fire a flashbulb or electronic flash unit at the right time. With curtain shutters, flash synchronization is a little more complex. Flashbulbs can be synchronized (or "synched") at any shutter speed, provided the peak light output lasts at least as long as the total slit-movement time. Electronic flash is another matter, because of its brief duration. It can only be synched so as to expose the whole film when the width of the shutter slit equals the width of the film, as at the slower shutter speeds. With the shutter set at its fastest full-slit speed (usually 1/30 or 1/60 second, as noted above), it serves mainly to limit the capture of ambient light, and the film-exposure time is essentially the duration of the electronic flash (usually 1/1000 second). Since the two types of flash sources have different delay times for ignition, either type of shutter must be set for the type of flash to be used.

High shutter speeds tend to be less accurate in leaf shutters, and the stress limits of materials in motion have traditionally restricted the fastest speed to about 1/1000 second (with a probable error of about 20% bringing it to a real time as slow as 1/800 second). However, recent technical advances have produced leaf shutters as fast as 1/2000 second, with improved timing accuracy. It is mechanically simpler to attain accurate high shutter speeds with the curtain design, for focal-plane shutters.

The type of shutter mounted in a camera depends upon other design considerations in the instrument. Most small rangefinder cameras have between-the-lens leaf shutters because they are compact, durable, and quiet. Leaf shutters are also used in twin lens reflex cameras and in most view cameras. Nearly all single lens reflex cameras have focal-plane shutters, usually of the curtain type. It is mechanically simpler to provide for through-the-lens viewing if the shutter is near the film plane rather than in the lens mount. Press cameras have been made with either type of shutter, and the most famous make—the recently discontinued Speed Graphic—had both.

Small Cameras

For supreme mobility, for ease and speed of handling, for ability to follow motion, and for economy in film costs, by far the best choice is the high-quality small camera of 35 mm or 2¼-inch format. Quality in the design and manufacture of both lens and body is essential for fine work, because considerable enlargement is generally necessary for publication-sized prints, and any defects in the photograph will quickly become visible. Fortunately, there are many good models to choose from, and some are superb.

In the 35 mm format there are two types of cameras: the rangefinder camera and the single lens reflex, or SLR (see Figure 7). With the rangefinder camera, one views through an optical viewfinder, which incorporates a rangefinder coupled with the focusing mount of the lens. Such cameras are quite fast-handling, and the best of them are very good indeed. They are excellent for such uses as recording human activity, where the photographer must be inconspicuous and easy mobility is essential. One disadvantage is that they must be brought to the eye for focusing. Another is that framing of the image is never entirely accurate, because of what is known as *parallax.* The viewfinder does not see exactly the same view as the lens, because it is located off the optical axis of the camera; to avoid accidental exclusion of part of the subject, the viewfinder is designed to include a little less area than the film will record. Rangefinder cameras are generally poor for closeup or high-magnification work because without special equipment they cannot be focused closer than 2 to 3 feet. Attachments are often provided for these purposes but they are usually inconvenient to use, and many are expensive.

Single lens reflex cameras come in a variety of sizes, from the large cut-film formats on down, but the vast majority are either the 35 mm size or, in smaller numbers, the 2¼-inch-wide formats using 120-size roll film. These small sizes of cameras are generally similar in design and operation, except that most 35 mm cameras usually have a pentaprism to aid eye-level viewing, whereas in many of the 2¼-inch cameras, waist-level viewing is standard, with prisms as accessories. SLR cameras larger than the 2¼-inch sizes tend to be rather cumbersome.

With single lens reflex cameras, viewing is accomplished through the taking lens by way of an internal mirror, which flips out of the lens-film axis at the moment of exposure (see Figure 8). Nearly all features of the rangefinder camera are present, but the viewing system makes framing more accurate (in a few cameras, absolutely so), and makes telephoto, closeup, and high-magnification work convenient, easy, and speedy. These cameras are especially well suited for closeup photography of live, moving organisms. Models with waist-level viewfinders are good for inconspicuous photography of people, and in situations where right-angle viewing is a help (photographing subjects at ground level, etc.). A disadvantage is that the focal-plane shutters used in most SLR cameras are quite noisy compared to leaf shutters, and the audible "flop" of the internal mirror adds to the problem. But most SLR's accept a great

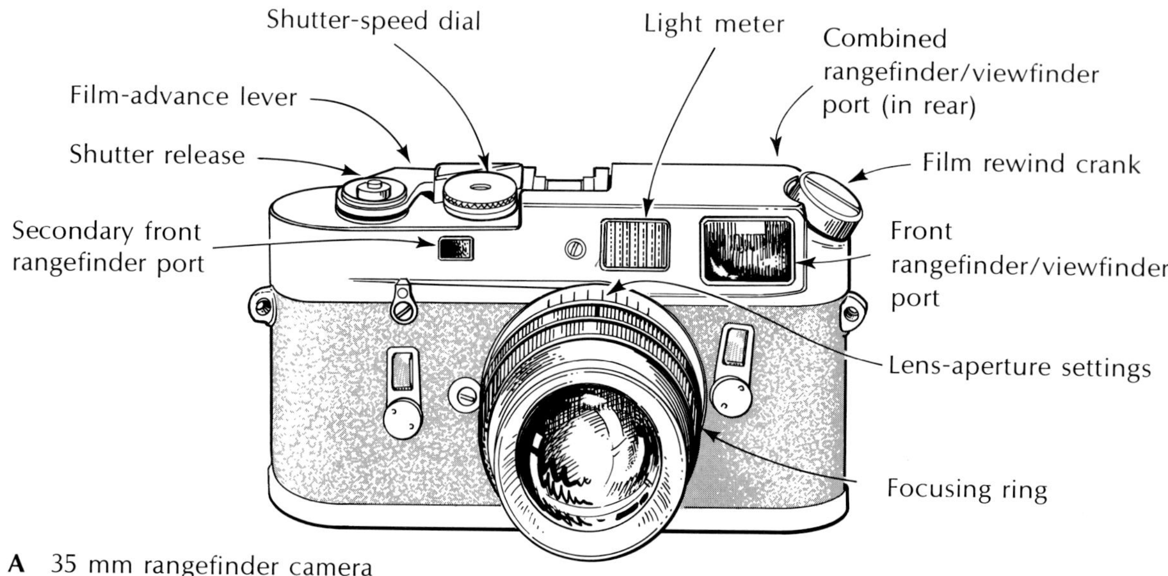

A 35 mm rangefinder camera

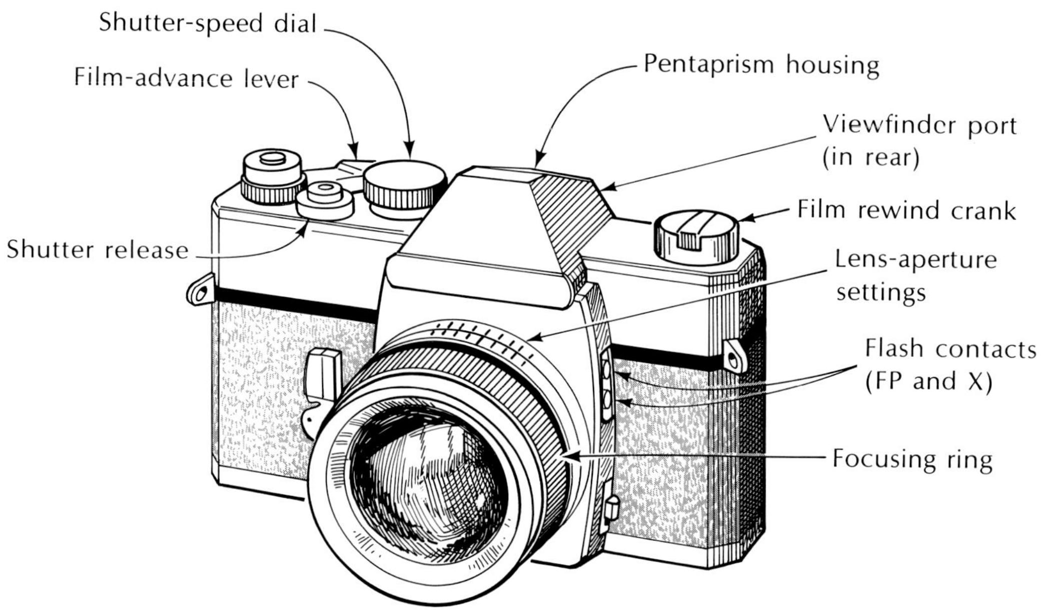

B 35 mm single lens reflex camera

FIGURE 7
Typical rangefinder and single lens reflex (SLR) cameras.

variety of lenses and accessories (the so-called systems approach), and hence offer much versatility.

A type of camera that has been popular among journalists and documentary photographers for many years is the twin lens reflex, an instrument that is, in effect, two cameras, one mounted on top of the other (see Figure 9). The top lens is combined with a mirror to provide viewing, from the top, of a good-sized (usually 2¼-inch-square) ground-glass image, and the bottom lens does the actual picture taking. The two lenses are of similar types and are coupled so that they focus together. The better cameras have automatic parallax correction, to compensate partially for the difference in viewing position of the two lenses. Being inconspicuous and quiet, these cameras are excellent for ethnological recording and other photography of people, but are less useful for other scientific work. They are particularly poor for closeup and high-magnification work. Accessories are limited, and interchangeability of lenses is either nonexistent or very limited.

All of these small cameras allow great economy in film costs, particularly with color film. This is partially offset by a general tendency of photographers to take advantage of the economy feature by making many exposures of the same subject, to "make sure." Forethought and good training can help to obviate such waste, but this economy feature is overrated anyway. In photography the cost of film is negligible compared to equipment and labor costs, ex-

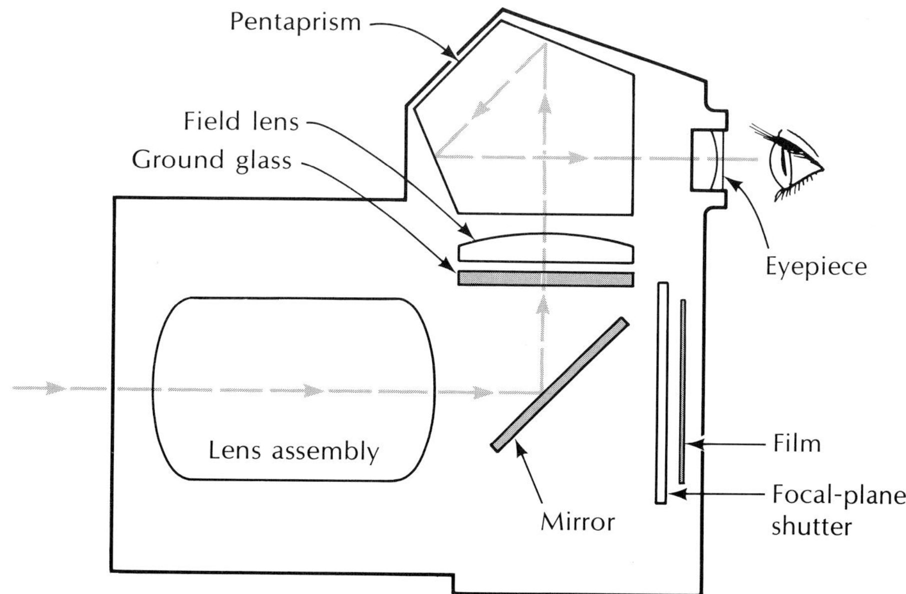

FIGURE 8
The light path in a typical single lens reflex camera. When the shutter release is pressed, the mirror swings up parallel to the ground glass, the focal-plane shutter opens, and the light passes straight through to the film.

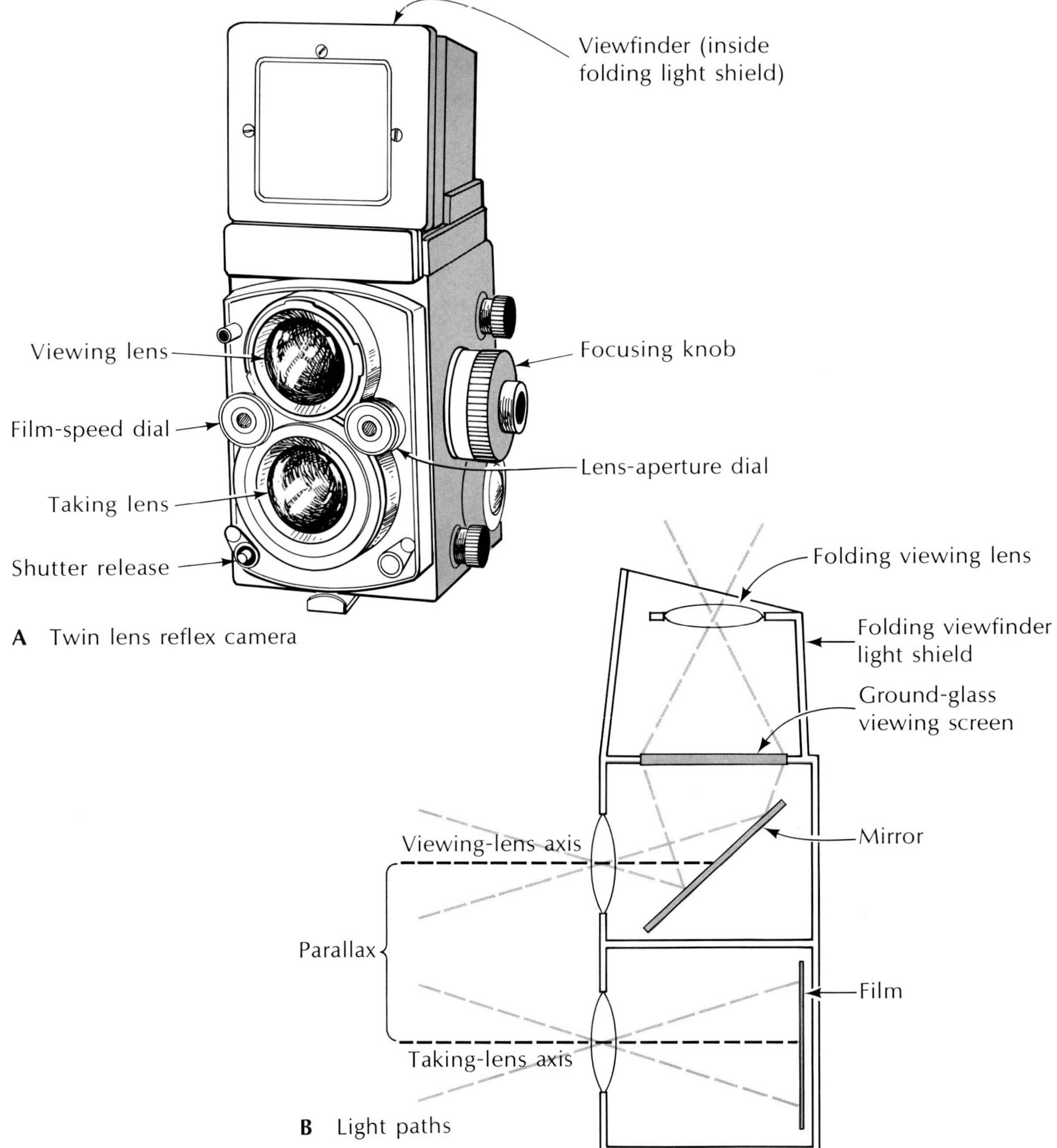

FIGURE 9
Typical twin lens reflex camera, with diagram of the light paths.

A Twin lens reflex camera.
B The internal light paths. The shutter is located between the elements of the taking lens.

cept when enormous numbers of pictures are needed, as is sometimes true in highly specialized scientific photography.

A disadvantage of small film sizes in general is the necessity to enlarge in printing. Enlarging is often expensive in terms of both time and auxiliary equipment, and introduces a good chance of loss of quality, particularly since only the best—and most expensive—enlarger lenses are of sufficient quality for professional results. The necessity to enlarge also requires that relatively slow films be used, if excessive grain is to be avoided.

Generally speaking, any subject can be photographed adequately with any of the basic types of cameras. However, the convenience of small cameras has been somewhat overemphasized in recent years. It seems to be forgotten that you have to work a great deal harder to obtain quality equal, or even comparable, to that which can be had routinely with larger film sizes. If you do need the mobility and versatility of a small single lens reflex camera, however, by all means use it. I do. But keep in mind the need to be extra careful, and consider the desirability of using high-resolution films and development (see Chapter 7) to enhance the quality.

Large Cameras

The ultimate in picture quality can be obtained when the negative is large enough to allow an unrestricted choice of films, whatever manipulation of the negatives may be desirable and permissible, and contact printing. Contact printing (in which the negative is in actual contact with the printing paper) requires less time than projection printing, and there is, of course, no need to have an enlarger or to suffer a loss of quality through its limitations or misuse. In the actual picture taking, the composition, setup, and lighting are often simplified by the photographer's ability to see the subject clearly on a large ground-glass viewing screen.

In large-format photography there are two main types of cameras: the press camera and the view camera (see Figure 10). (Single lens reflex designs are now available in some larger sizes, some of them as standard reflex cameras and some in a hybrid form possessing some view-camera characteristics.) Though smaller press and view cameras are available, the description here will be limited to those using films of 4 × 5 inches or larger.

The typical press camera consists essentially of a box body with a front plate that folds down to become a support and track mechanism for the lens. The shutter may be mounted with the lens, or there may be a focal-plane shutter in the camera body. The lens is coupled to an optical rangefinder. The back of the body carries a ground-glass viewing screen and an arrangement for inserting various types of film holders. For versatility, mobility, and speed and ease of handling, the 4 × 5 press camera is best among the larger cameras. Operating the camera in the manner of the 35 mm rangefinder camera is practical and common, and the negative is large enough to allow contact printing in most scientific uses. Furthermore, since these cameras have a long extension bellows and some view-camera movements (see below), they can often be used as view cameras and can provide good results in closeup and high-magnification photography. They are an excellent choice where one camera must serve for a wide variety of uses. The weight of the camera body is greater than those of small cameras, but, since relatively few accessories are needed, the overall weight that the photographer must carry is similar. Lens interchangeability is great, and usually convenient. Where film economy is important, small roll-

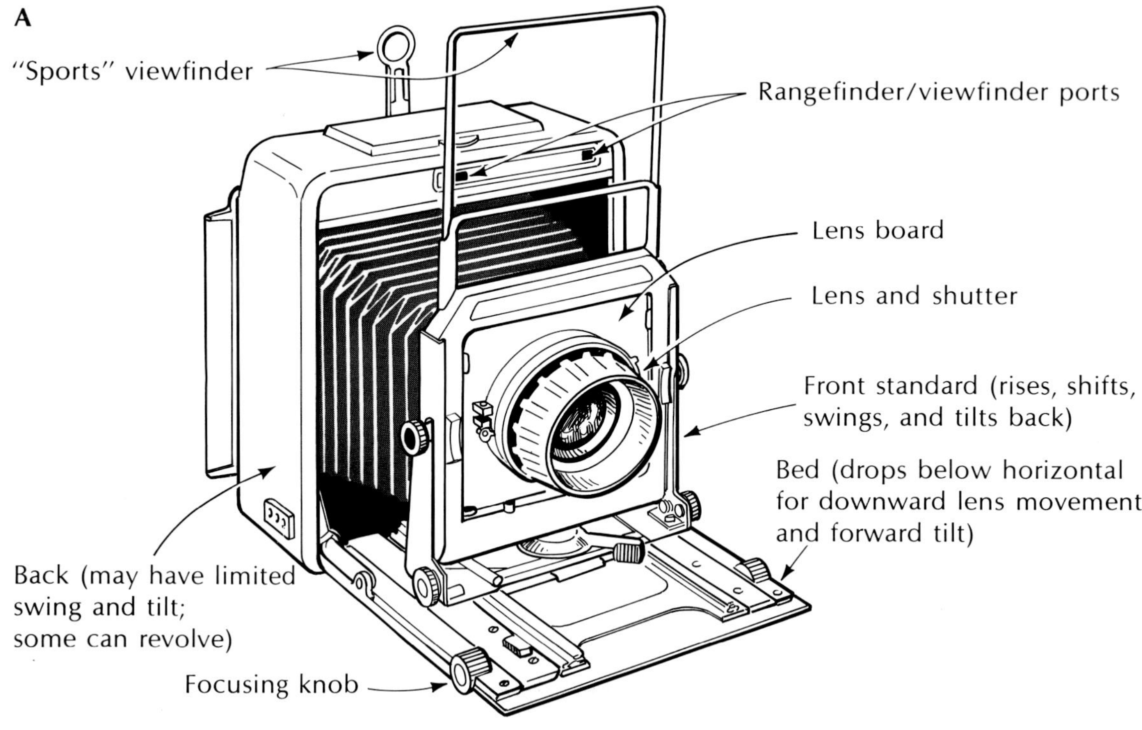

FIGURE 10
Typical press and view cameras.

A Press camera. There may be a focal-plane shutter in the rear body of a press camera, as well as a shutter in the lens mount.

film adapters are readily available and convenient to use.

If mobility is not a factor but extreme adjustability and the highest possible print quality are necessary, the best choice is a view camera. These cameras are also well adapted for work at high magnification. A view camera consists essentially of a film-holding back and a lens- and shutter-carrying front, each constructed so as to be three-dimensionally adjustable within moderate ranges; this assembly is mounted on a support base, usually a single rail or a folding flat bed with tracks. The front and back are, of course, connected by the bellows. View cameras are readily available in sizes using 4 × 5-inch, 5 × 7-inch, and 8 × 10-inch film. Both smaller and larger sizes can be had, but this range best covers the needs to be discussed here. In Europe and elsewhere, metric film sizes that are roughly equivalent are used, i.e., 9 × 12 cm, 13 × 18 cm, and 18 × 24 cm.

The one great advantage of the view camera, other than sheer size, is that you can move the front and back of the camera three-dimension-

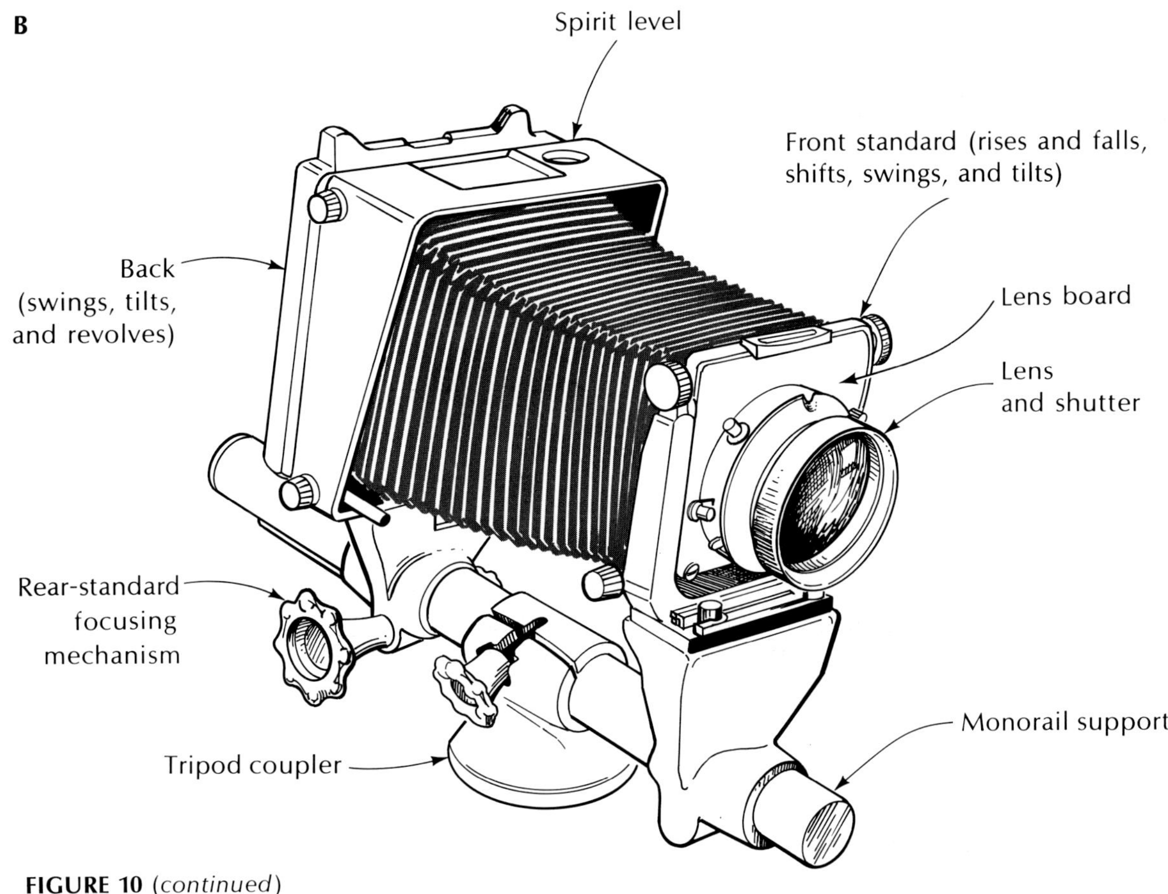

FIGURE 10 (*continued*)
B View camera.

ally with respect to each other and to the subject. This allows correction and adjustment of perspective, and makes it possible to increase greatly the apparent depth of field by bringing the principal plane of focus of the lens into coincidence with the principal plane of the subject, as seen in the ground-glass image. For architectural photography, for laboratory photography of apparatus, etc., this capacity for adjustment is very useful; this is especially true if large film sizes are used, since depth of field decreases as image magnification increases.

Each view-camera movement has a name. The lens board and camera back of a "full" view camera (as opposed to one not capable of a full range of movements) can: *rise and fall* (move vertically), *shift* (move sideways in either direction), *swing* (rotate about a vertical axis), and *tilt* (rotate about a horizontal axis). Collectively, these movements are just called swings and tilts; they can be made individually or in combinations, as compound movements. Front movements control the apparent depth of field; back movements adjust the perspective. To use swings and tilts effectively you must keep the separate functions clearly in mind, or confusion will result.

You must always start with the lens aperture wide open and with all components centered, i.e., with the front and back in the conventional camera orientation. If more than one view is to be photographed in one session, center the components between successive setups, even if the movements used were slight.

The basic camera angle is chosen first: level for most architectural photography and wherever else vertical subject lines are to appear parallel in the image, and tilted up or down for an angular view. The back is then adjusted if there is a need to control the apparent perspective. If one side of the image is to be made larger, that side of the ground glass is swung and/or tilted *away* from the subject.

Any swing or tilt of the back will put the image plane partially out of coincidence with the ground glass, and thus portions of the image will appear out of focus. The next step, therefore, is to swing and/or tilt the front of the camera to bring these two planes back into agreement. Theoretically, the plane of the lens board should intersect the angle formed by the film plane and the principal subject plane, i.e., the three planes should meet at a common location in space. In practice, the adjustment is made without measurement, while watching the ground-glass image. If a compound movement is being made, it is simplest to match up the swing and the tilt separately.

Any such front or back movements will also move the image across the ground glass to some extent, so horizontal or vertical shifts will be needed to restore the composition. Shifts can also be used to move the image even when no other movements are needed; for example, in the photography of tall buildings (or groups of trees, etc.) the camera is leveled to keep vertical lines parallel, and then the lens is shifted upward to move the top of the building into view on the ground glass. If the whole camera were simply tilted upward, vertical lines would converge. Your eye and brain can discount this effect when you look at the subject, but it will be unpleasantly obvious in a picture.

Finally, the lens diaphragm is closed down as needed to give complete depth of field; you are then ready to calculate exposure and make the picture. Don't forget to close the shutter before inserting the film holder (I get caught every now and then).

There will be no attempt here to survey comprehensively the movements and uses of view cameras, because relatively few scientists use them. Those needing additional information are referred to the Bibliography (see especially the book by Stroebel, 1976).

Some disadvantages of view cameras are that handheld use is usually impractical and their operation in general is relatively slow. The cost of sheet films is relatively high per exposure, but this is at least partially offset by the lesser need or inclination to make multiple exposures to "be sure." And even 8 × 10-inch films are cheap enough, even in color, that the cost is more than recompensed by the high quality of the result. For general laboratory work, view cameras offer such great qualitative advantages that, wherever space and other circumstances allow and easy mobility is not imperative, their use is highly recommended.

CAMERA SUPPORTS

For the best control of composition and for eliminating camera movement with *any* camera, a tripod or other firm camera support is necessary, wherever practicable. But not just any tripod will do. Tripods for large cameras must be quite sturdy simply to carry the weight, and even small cameras need a tripod that is strong and sturdy enough to resist vibration and other stresses. Many of the very small, light tripods suggested for use with 35 mm cameras are so unstable and vibration-prone as to be worse than useless. *Camera movement during exposure is probably the single greatest cause of unsharpness in pictures.* Even with quite high shutter speeds and careful attention to camera-holding technique, there is often a distinctly visible difference between pictures made with handheld and tripod-held cameras. Because poorly designed tripods are likely to be least dependable just when they are most needed, and because sharpness is one of the most important characteristics of scientific photographs, a tripod should be chosen with great care.

For large studio view cameras one can obtain very good camera stands that can be moved about on casters and that provide great flexibility in the choice of camera position, angle, and height. For tabletop use of small cameras there are a number of devices that allow great versatility of operation. There are also medium-sized mechanisms that incorporate the camera and stand into a single unit. Typical of these are the MP-series cameras produced by Polaroid. Certain enlargers are similarly convertible to camera use. For example, I have a 5 × 7-inch Beseler enlarger that is easily converted to a 5 × 7-inch camera. The normal vertical mounting can be changed to a horizontal position if needed, and in both positions there is a simple sideways movement that facilitates composition of the ground-glass image. In addition, the whole camera moves up and down by means of an electric motor, a great labor saver when many pictures are being made at varying image magnifications.

PART II

General Techniques

CHAPTER 3

Backgrounds

It may at first seem odd to discuss backgrounds before discussing the photographic subject itself, but in reality it is a most logical thing to do. For scientific illustration, the background serves an immediate and important function: isolating the subject and focusing the viewer's attention upon it. The background should be uncluttered, impossible to confuse with the subject, and well suited to the techniques of both photographic and publication printing.

Owing to their peripheral nature, backgrounds are too often not considered when planning a picture. The result is often a poorly differentiated subject, scarcely visible as a separate and important entity. Both the importance of the background's function and the logical planning of a picture setup demand early consideration of background problems.

Backgrounds are much more limited in kind, nature, and purpose than are subjects. In black-and-white photography there are only four kinds: white, black, grey, and natural. The last of these is a background that exists as part of the subject matter and is unalterable by the nature of the situation. Backgrounds for color work will be discussed in Chapter 11.

PLAIN WHITE BACKGROUNDS

Where practical, plain white backgrounds are generally to be preferred over others because they serve particularly well to isolate the subject and they reproduce best in printing. A background that prints photographically as pure white will, unless given special treatment by the pressman, reproduce as a very light grey, which is very satisfactory for publication. (See Plate 25 for comparative examples.) No matter how a white background is achieved, it will print photographically as pure white only if it receives about 100% more light than the subject, unless that subject is unusually dark.

Every negative has a *characteristic curve* representing its range of tones (often called the *D* log *E* curve, because density increases with the log of exposure; it is also called the H and D curve, because the effect was first explored by Hurter and Driffield, in the nineteenth century). Internal contrast in the negative is indicated by the slope of the curve: the steeper the slope, the higher the contrast. The two ends, where the darkest and the lightest tones are recorded, are lower in contrast than the middle, or *straight-line,* portion. The least dense portion of the negative, where shadows and dark tones are recorded, is represented by the *toe* of the curve; the densest portion, where the light areas or highlights are recorded, is represented by the *shoulder.* See Figure 11.

By controlling the lighting contrast when photographing a subject, it is possible to contain all of the tones of that subject within a portion of the characteristic curve of the negative; and by controlling the exposure, the subject tones can be limited to the toe and straight-line portions. Then, if the white background is given about 100% (1 stop) more light than the lightest part of the subject, a gap in the tonal scale of the negative is produced, in effect. This will guarantee visual separation of the subject from the background in the print.

Separating the subject from the background by differential exposure in this manner has a side effect that is very useful. The highlight areas of a negative are normally less contrasty than the middle tones. By working as I have described, we place the lightest tones of the subject within the relatively more contrasty straight-line portion of the curve; thus there will be a greater degree of contrast in those light areas. In most scientific photography this is a worthwhile effect (the primary exception being in photomicrography, where the important information is most commonly in the middle and dark tones; this is discussed in Chapter 9).

For large subjects photographed outdoors, and where a natural background is undesirable for some reason, the easiest way to achieve a white background is to use the sky, particularly if it is overcast. The background will then be at least very light, and if conditions are right it will print as pure white. The additional light necessary to provide a pure white in the print can be obtained either by turning the subject so that the brightest part of the sky is behind it (on an overcast day or if one is working in a shaded area) or by using a light blue filter to reproduce the blue sky as white (see Chapter 5 for details). Such filtering can also have the effect of removing unwanted scattered small clouds.

In laboratory work with moderately large subjects, the white background—whether paper, cloth, or other material—can be placed vertically behind the subject at a little distance. Then either the lighting is so arranged as to provide the necessary extra background light, or a double exposure can be made with little or no light on the subject during the second exposure. To avoid confusing shadows, light sources should be placed off the optical axis and enough distance kept between subject and background to allow the shadows to pass off to one side. A top view of a typical setup is shown in Figure 12.

In scientific photography the great majority of subjects are quite small and are most easily photographed under a vertically mounted cam-

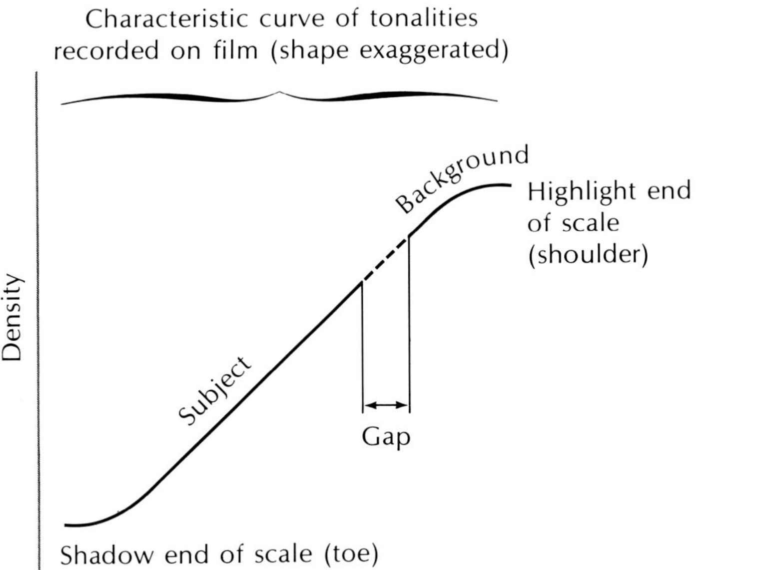

FIGURE 11
Tonal-scale break with a white background. In a negative, the density increases approximately with the log of exposure, with slightly lesser increases at very low and very high densities. This can be plotted on a graph to produce a characteristic curve for each choice of film and developer. The slope of the plotted line indicates contrast: the steeper the slope, the higher the contrast. The toe of the curve represents what will be the darker tones or shadows in the print, the straight-line portion the middle tones, and the shoulder the light tones or highlights. The gap shown here represents unused recording potential when the background is exposed about one stop more than the lightest part of the subject. In the negative these tones will be less dense than those of the background; thus it will be possible to print them so that they do not blend into it.

era. The most convenient method of producing a white background here is to suspend a sheet of glass some distance above the surface to be used as the background, lay the subject on it, and photograph it. This method works well even at moderately high magnifications, as in photomacrography.

It will be found useful to construct one or more glass-topped tables in sizes suited to your subject matter. These can be anywhere from an inch or two high to perhaps 2 feet high, with glass plates of from 1 × 3 inches to about 20 × 24 inches or more. Two useful designs are illustrated in Figure 13.

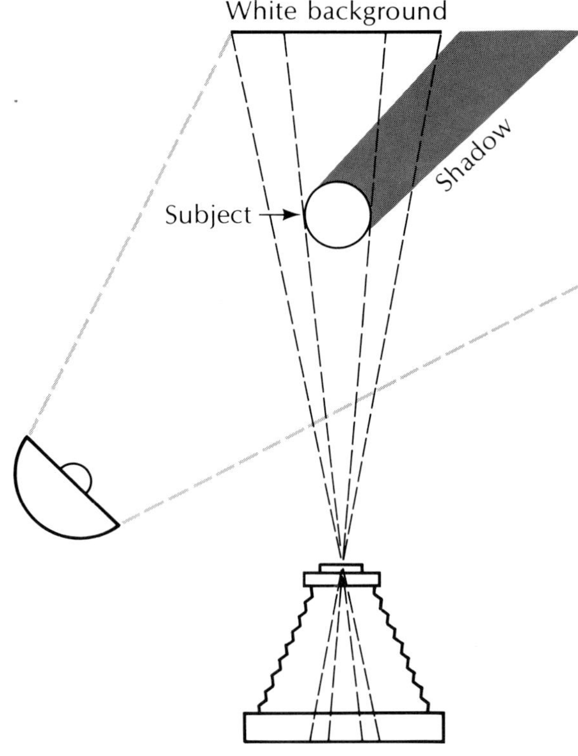

FIGURE 12
Basic horizontal camera setup, seen from above. Placing the main light to one side throws the subject shadow out of the picture area when there is space between the subject and the background. Basic vertical camera setups are illustrated in Figures 17 and 19.

Another method of getting a white background is useful when the lighting is axial or near-axial (that is, incident on the subject from the direction of the camera lens) and the subject is not larger than a few inches across. In this case, use a sheet of heavy-duty household aluminum foil for the background, and lay the subject directly upon it. Such foil is mirror-bright on one side and slightly matte on the other. If it is shiny-side up, it will reflect an image of the light source into the camera. But if it is matte-side up, the result is a fine, soft glow surrounding the subject (see Figure 14 for a typical setup). There will probably be a slight penumbra visible around the subject but, unless the subject is unusually light or bright, even this will be white in the print. In any case it will not be so dark as to disturb the eye or confuse the edge of the subject. This setup is particularly useful in photographing coins and medallions.

Wherever a white background is used, it should cover an area not much larger than the subject. If it is too large, there will be two difficulties. First, the background will reflect so much extra light to the lens that there will be internal flare in the camera, which has the effect of drastically lowering the overall contrast of the picture. (This will also be true if the background is overlit and delivers too much light to the camera—that is, much over 100% more than to the subject.) Second, with any but two-dimensional subjects, a background that is too large causes disturbing edge reflections on the subject.

One can obtain white backgrounds by using internally lighted boxes topped with a sheet of opal (translucent) glass. Such items are commercially available, but they are relatively inflexible in use and most of them are quite expensive. Some types of photo-enlargers have what is called a cold-light head, which is simply a box containing a cold cathode tube, twisted and coiled so as to make up a basically rectangular pattern. This box is covered with a sheet of opal glass to produce an even light output. My 5 × 7-inch Beseler enlarger has one that is easily removed. You can invert such a lamphouse under your camera and use it as a light box for photography where a white background is wanted. The difficulty in using light boxes is that they must be taken into account when determining exposures, to avoid overexposure and flare. But by switching them on and off at appropriate times during time exposures, you can control the relative exposures of subject and background easily.

BLACK BACKGROUNDS

Black backgrounds are somewhat less useful because they are difficult to reproduce well in any but high-quality printing. Poorer-quality printing, which is unfortunately common in many of the less well-financed journals, results in greyness and in breaks that produce quantities of white spots instead of a uniform black area. If the press is inked heavily enough to print the background as a uniformly deep black, there is the risk of overprinting the subject area of the picture, so that it appears too dark and loses shadow detail. For sheer drama of presentation, however, black backgrounds are unbeatable in either color or black-and-white photography. They are also very effective wherever the subject is either white or very light in color.

The single best material for black backgrounds is a good grade of deep-nap velvet or velveteen—quite expensive but worth the cost. The need is for a material that reflects virtually no light at all, to assure separation from the subject matter. No other material approaches deep-nap velvet in quality; even shallow-nap velvets are poor, and napless black cloth or paper is very poor.

A second method of achieving a deep black background is to place the subject on a glass-topped box with a black lining, but this often gives reflections of the camera and/or the subject on the glass surface. Some variation of this method may be necessary if the subject is wet or must be immersed in water. If the overall background is really black, if the edge separations are clear, and if the negative is large

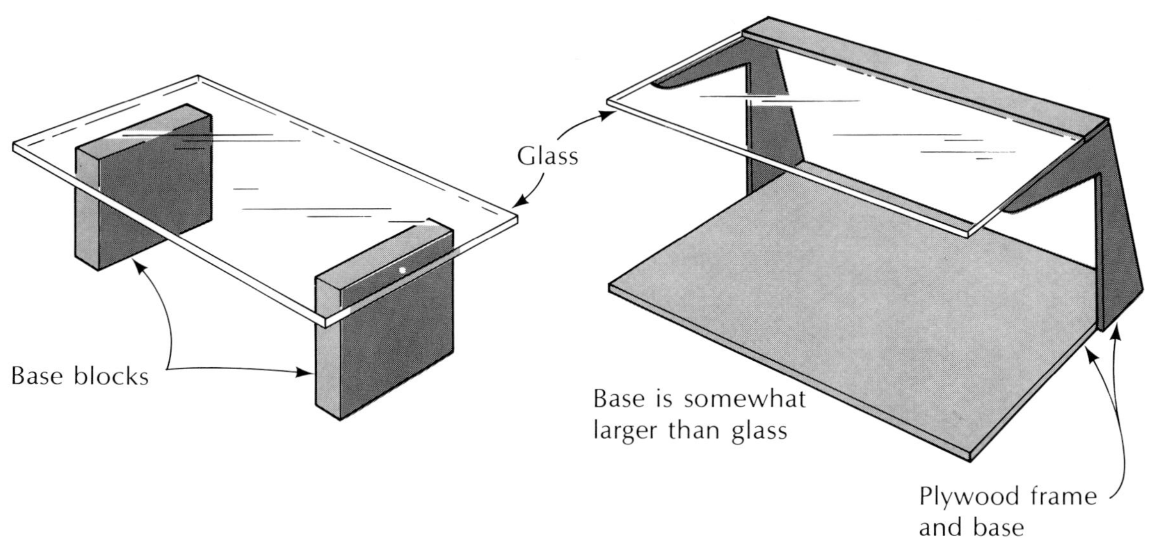

FIGURE 13
Glass-topped table designs for use with vertically mounted cameras.

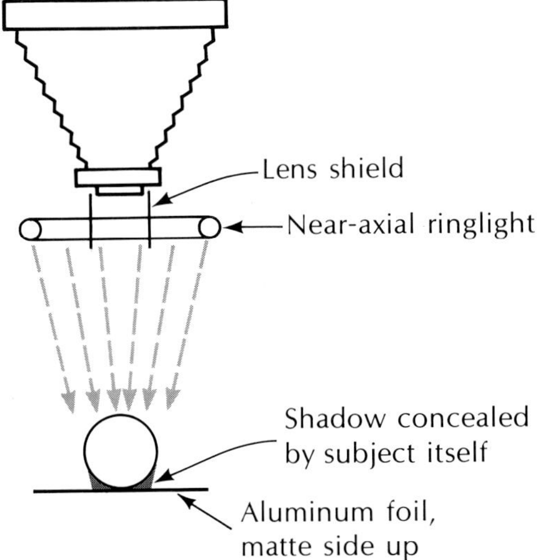

FIGURE 14
Using aluminum foil to obtain a white background with near-axial lighting. A matte-surface foil (heavy-duty foil has one matte side) reflects near-axial light so brightly that it appears white compared to most subjects.

enough (4 × 5 inches or over), the offending reflection images can be physically scraped off the negative without impairing the final print quality. After all, it doesn't matter how the negative looks in the areas that will print black anyway. Correctly printed, there will be no shades of grey in the print. And it is the print that counts.

If velvet is used, the subject is simply placed directly upon it. Shadows cast by the subject are completely absorbed by the background. No separation between the subject and the background is needed.

Other than problems of journal-printing quality, the only big trouble with black backgrounds is in lighting the subject so as to assure that shadowed areas will not merge into the blackness of the background. This will be discussed in detail in Chapter 4, but a good rule to follow is to see that the subject's shadows are only just discernible to the eye. If lighted properly, the shadowed areas will then appear natural in the print and will still differentiate at the edges.

PLAIN GREY BACKGROUNDS

Plain grey backgrounds are generally to be avoided. In journal reproduction a white background, unless specially treated, prints as a light

---

PLATE 3 ▶

Basic Photography: Isolating the Subject.

There are several methods by which a subject, or selected details within it, can be made to show better in a photograph.

A A mineral specimen of stepped structure that has a raised crystalline edge extending across a region of the same material (×1.8). In this picture it is not possible to differentiate that edge.
B The crystalline edge is revealed here by casting a shadow on the region behind it. The background in both pictures is black velvet.
C Color changes due to disease on bean leaves (×0.9), shown to best advantage through the use of a Wratten 25 medium red filter. The effect is to darken the healthy green areas relative to the affected yellow and yellow-green areas, and thus to increase the visual contrast. In the original print, the background below the supporting glass table was rendered pure white by controlled overexposure. (Originally photographed for C. E. Yarwood.)
D Soil nematode (×35), standing on end and waving about in search of prey. It is visually isolated from the background by differential focus. The unlit natural background printed as black. (Originally photographed for G. Poinar.)

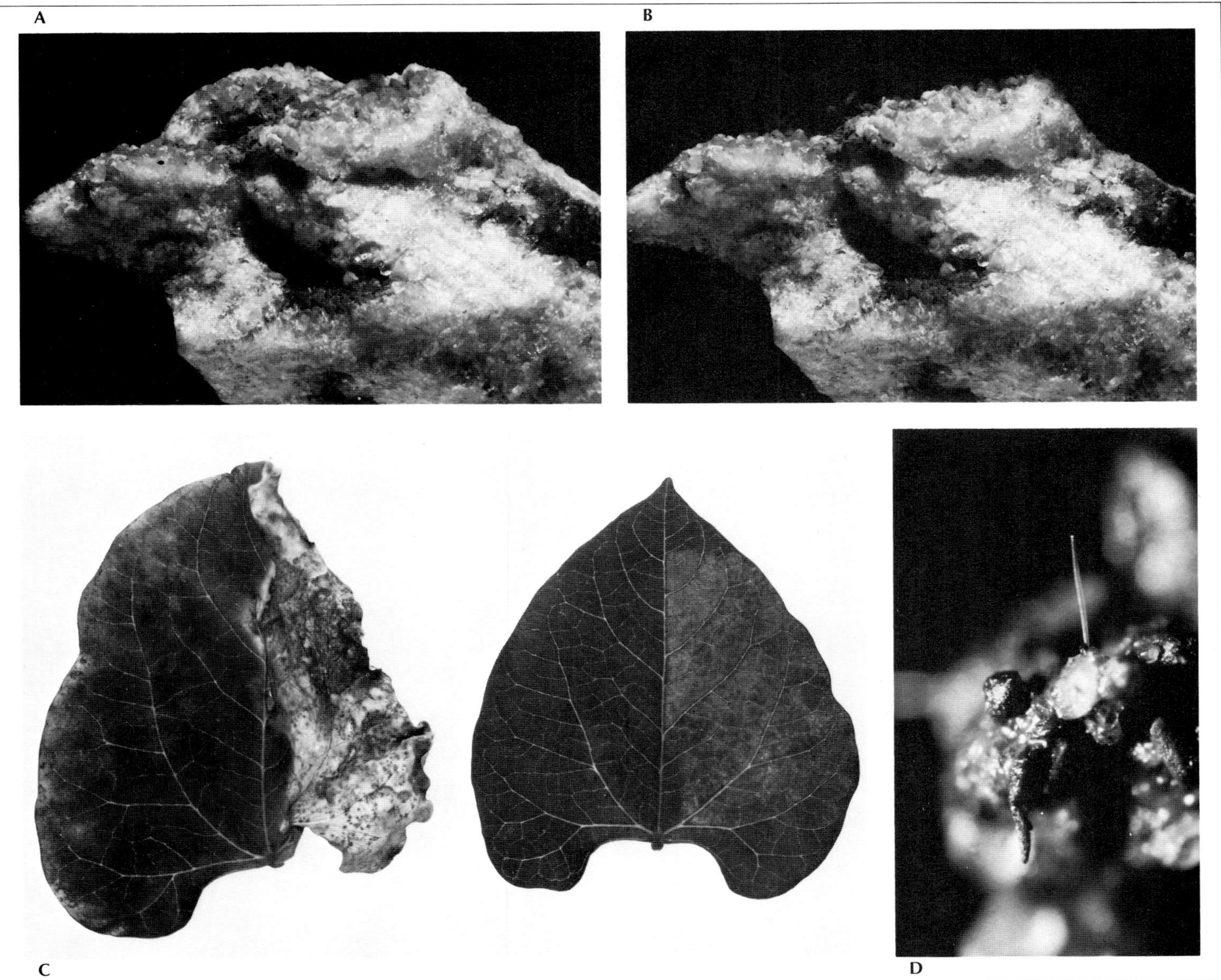
A
B
C
D

grey. (See Plate 25 for comparative examples.) Grey backgrounds, then, will reproduce as darker greys, and the result is usually unpleasantly muddy in appearance, with the subject itself difficult to differentiate. The commonest reason for using a plain grey background is to show best a subject having both white and black areas in it, such as a white root with some branches blackened by disease. Unfortunately, there will generally be transitional areas where the subject tone merges with the grey of the background. This can sometimes erroneously appear as a break in the subject; hence grey should be avoided here, too. With most such subjects the best rendering is against a white background, with the white subject areas printing as a light grey.

NATURAL BACKGROUNDS

Natural backgrounds, as noted earlier, are those that are part of the subject matter itself or that are for some reason an unalterable condition of the picture. It could also be that a natural background is simply the most desirable one for scientific accuracy, the preference of the worker, or other reasons. Differentiation between the naturally occurring background and the main subject can then be achieved by several means, and you should pay careful attention to its achievement.

For relatively small subjects, an excellent—and often virtually unavoidable—way to do it is to take advantage of the inherently shallow depth of field when image magnification is relatively great. You can readily have the main subject sharply in focus while all or nearly all of the rest of the picture is out of focus. The viewer's eye is naturally drawn to the in-focus portion, and so to the intended main subject.

A second method of differentiating between subject and background is through color. If one is dark and the other light, there is no problem. If they are different in color but similar in brightness—that is, if they are of colors that will be reproduced by panchromatic films as similar shades of grey—you can use color filters to cause an apparent light-and-dark difference in the final picture.

Where the colors of the subject and background are similar and there is too little spatial separation to allow differentiation by focus, you can use light to make the difference. You can either use a grazing direct light (to show the shape and texture of the subject) or cause a shadow to fall behind or under the subject and thereby show it as light against a darker background.

Nearly any problem of differentiation between subject and background can be solved by one of these methods, or by using them in combination. In difficult situations only informed experimentation will yield the solution. See Plate 3 for examples of ways of isolating subjects.

CHAPTER 4

Lighting Three-Dimensional Subjects

As the word photography implies, the most important single feature of the craft is the application of light to the subject. Unless the subject is suitably lit, the purpose of the photograph—exposure of the salient and significant features of that subject to the viewer—will not be accomplished. Lighting must be applied according to a knowledge of what it will do in terms of film and printing-paper response and how it will look in the final picture.

GENERAL CONSIDERATIONS

First to be decided is the kind of background, as already stated. Then the subject must be correctly oriented to the light, or the light to the subject. It is important that the light in the picture should appear to come roughly from the top. Whether from directly above or from top left or top right is relatively unimportant (except where convention decrees), but it must be *generally* from the top. If it comes from what will be the picture bottom, the appearance of relief will be deceptive. Hills will appear to be valleys, and vice versa. This can be confirmed by looking at pictures containing relief lighting effects while turning them at various angles. In some fields of science, conventions have arisen that decree that all pictures must appear to be lit from the upper left, or upper right. The photography of fossils, for instance, has suffered from this kind of rigidity. It is much more ap-

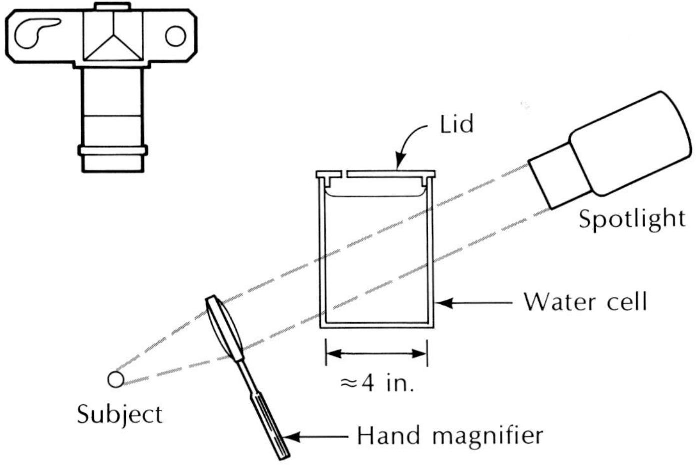

FIGURE 15
Lighting of small objects, cooled with a water cell. There should be a lid on the cell to retard evaporation, but it must be vented to allow steam to escape in case of overheating. The cell should be about 4 inches thick and should hold 1 or 2 quarts of water (distilled or boiled, to retard growth of algae).

propriate to light from whatever angle best reveals the detail of the subject. If you feel that the direction of light should be indicated to the viewer, use an arrow on the print to show it.

Steps must often be taken to protect the subject matter, especially small plant and animal materials, from the heat of the lights. This can be accomplished by introducing a water cell between lamp and subject. This is a transparent, water-filled container, which absorbs the infrared radiation while transmitting the visible light. It is especially necessary if a high light intensity is required (as in high-magnification work), or if a light-concentrating lens is used. A typical setup containing such a lens and a water cell is shown in Figure 15. A simple hand magnifier with its handle clamped to a common lab stand will serve admirably to increase the light intensity, but will literally shrivel up an insect or leaf if a water cell 3–4 inches thick is not interposed to absorb the heat.

One can also protect the subject by using a heat-absorbing glass filter. Corning makes a variety of these. However, nearly all glass heat absorbers have a color tint—usually greenish—that makes them rather unsuitable for use with color films. A further drawback is that they have definite limits of heat-absorbing capacity: if they become overheated they will crack. A water cell has no color tinge, and has a greater capacity for heat absorption. As it warms up you will eventually notice the formation of the small bubbles that precede boiling. At that point you should stop and cool things off. For safety purposes, any lid placed on a water cell, as for the prevention of water loss with time, should be pierced to allow the easy escape of steam when the water gets hot.

For a thorough understanding of lighting technique it is necessary to keep several principles clearly in mind. One is known as the *law of specular reflection:* the angle at which a ray of light is reflected from a surface (the angle of reflection) is equal to the angle at which it hits that surface (the angle of incidence). See Figure 16. Keeping this simple principle in mind will solve many of your lighting problems.

A second principle to remember is this: in black-and-white photography, apparent lighting contrasts are vastly increased by putting them on film and then on paper. What appears to the eye to be a just discernible shadow becomes, in the final print, a very distinct shadow indeed. This is because the range of illumination that the eye can perceive is vastly greater than that of the film, and the film's range is greater than that of the printing paper. Because of this, a shadow that is *distinctly* visible to the eye may lose detail in what will become deep shade in the final print. And what is deep shade to the eye will be opaque black shadow in the print. Acquiring a subtle eye for the detection of light and shade will be a great aid in research photography. Practice is essential. A simple way of seeing light and shade much as the print will record it is to squint your eyes and look through your lashes. You will find that *detail* disappears; the subject is seen as a mass or group of masses, and the *areas* of light and shadow are more readily seen. If you feel that you need an aid to viewing, try the Wratten 90 viewing filter, which is sold by Kodak. This is a sort of murky yellow filter. When you view a scene through it the effect of colors is greatly muted, and that of light and shadow becomes somewhat easier to discern. It is more effective than the blue filter used by some moviemakers (which is itself a holdover from the use of orthochromatic films).

A third point to keep in mind is that light on most three-dimensional subjects should appear to come from one direction only, to avoid ambiguity in relief and a confusing multiplicity of shadows. Thus, any supplementary lighting should generally be slightly weaker than the

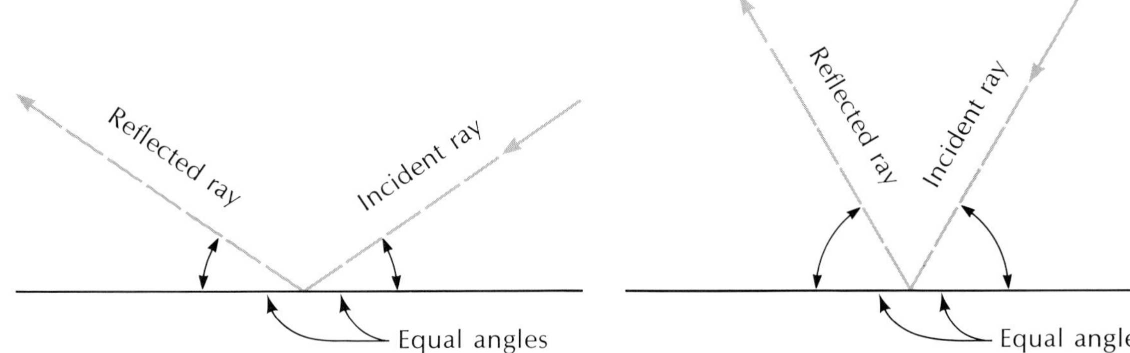

FIGURE 16
The reflection of light from a smooth surface. Each ray is reflected at an angle equal to its angle of incidence.

main light, and probably also more diffuse. This leads, of course, to a general preference for simplicity in lighting setups, which has the obvious advantages of being quick and easy and of requiring less investment in both equipment and the space required for its use. Exceptions will be pointed out later.

The exact type of lighting to be used on a particular job depends upon the nature of the subject and what is to be shown of it. Lighting for scientific subject matter is for the purpose of revealing maximum significant detail—of giving maximum significant information. The individual worker must decide what is significant in each case before proceeding.

Generally speaking, there are two aspects of the subject—shape and color—one of which it will be desirable to emphasize. In black-and-white photography, one big pitfall is the danger of confusing the differences between the two by poor lighting. If one is not careful, a light color may appear as a highlight or a dark color as a shadow, or vice versa. Lighting *must* reveal which is which.

Shape is shown either by casting shadows or by using a lighting that will direct light to the camera lens differentially according to the angles at which the various portions of the subject surface are inclined to that lens. Color tones are shown best in black-and-white by so reducing the light/shade contrasts that relief is scarcely noticeable in the final print; the various shades of grey in the picture are thus all accounted for by color differences in the subject. In color photography the problem is, of course, nearly negligible: colors are clearly colors. See Plate 4 for an example of color vs. shape in black-and-white photography.

For most purposes it is preferable to use the continuous light provided by natural light or by such artificial sources as floods and spotlights. One can then observe exactly the fall of the light under all circumstances. But the use of flash, either ordinary flashbulbs or electronic flash, can be very useful for stopping motion or for other special purposes. Where flash is used, you must be especially careful in determining the angle of lighting, since it cannot usually be directly observed prior to the exposure. In most cases you can ascertain the correct positions of your flash units by experimenting with continuous light sources. This can be as complex as working out a full-scale multiple lighting arrangement, or as simple as shining a flashlight around while observing through the camera to see when a suitable lighting angle is attained. Either way, of course, a last-minute substitution of flash units for lamps is made. Where time and movement considerations do not allow this method, the estimation of lighting effects will be aided by simply remembering that light travels in straight lines. If you hold a light source

---

PLATE 4 ▶

Basic Lighting Methods: Color vs. Shape.

A fossil leaf (×1.8), photographed two ways. The original plate was labeled as for journal publication, prior to printing here.

A In this picture very low lighting contrast de-emphasized surface sculpturing. A Wratten 45 deep blue-green filter rendered the color contrasts more visible. This effect was further enhanced by high-contrast development of the film (in Kodak D-11 developer) and extremely high-contrast printing (on Agfa Brovira #6 paper). Note the revelation of a leaf-miner trace at left center.
B The same fossil, given grazing direct lighting with minimal reflective fill, photographed so as to emphasize surface sculpturing. A Wratten 80B pale blue filter de-emphasized the color staining somewhat.

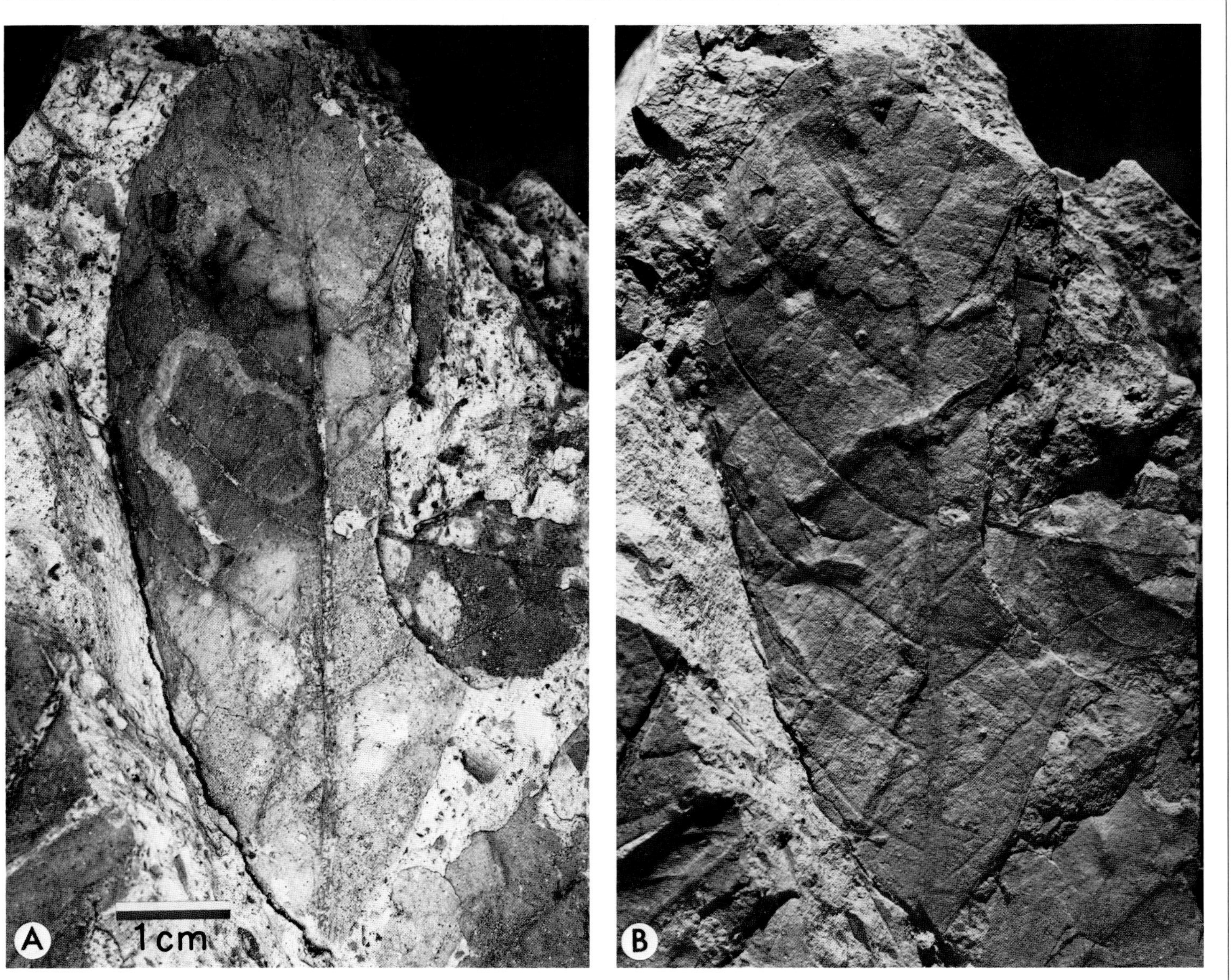
A
1 cm
B

in a given position, the shadows will fall directly opposite. And if you hold the flash unit in front of your face and sight along its axis, everything you can see will be lit, while everything you cannot see will be in shadow. The only other real worry then is specular reflections, which are covered by the law of reflection.

TECHNIQUES

For our purposes there are only a few really different lighting setups. We will take these up in the order of their usual importance.

Reflector-Diffuser Lighting

This type of lighting consists of one lamp inclined downward onto the subject, with a tissue-paper diffuser on the lamp side of the subject and a white-card reflector on the other side (see Figure 17). With this setup one can vary the lighting contrasts of the subject almost indefinitely by moving either the reflector or the diffuser back and forth to suit. The range is from equal light from both sides to a bright highlight opposed to a deep shadow. The effect can readily be observed during these adjustments by looking from the camera position. Where the subject matter is irregularly shaped, it may be desirable to use small subsidiary reflectors to add light to certain areas not well enough illuminated otherwise. This may be necessary when using black backgrounds, in order to keep the subject shadows light enough to separate from the background in printing.

This setup is the most generally useful one. The diffuser keeps the light relatively free of harshness, and the reflector fills in the shadow side to any degree desired. Figure 17 shows that, whereas the subject is completely "shaded" by the diffuser, the reflector is at least partly directly lit. This allows fuller flexibility and control than is possible if the reflector is completely shaded also.

Note, too, that Figure 17 shows a white background that is completely unshaded by the diffuser. Direct background light in this setup provides the extra 100% of light to allow it to print pure white in the final picture, with all but the lightest-colored subjects. (Extremely light subjects may need a certain amount of extra background lighting to assure complete separation in printing.) The basic setup is, of course, also readily usable with any other type of background.

When you are using a black background, and an irregularly shaped subject requires that you use one or more subsidiary reflectors close to portions of that subject, you may find it necessary to have them so close as to intrude on the picture area. In that case, just use a knife to scrape their images off the negative, as described in Chapter 3. Or, just cut away the offending portions of the negative with scissors. As long as the background is to be black anyway, these treatments will leave no visible trace on the print. (They are, of course, most practical with large films, but they can be done even on films as small as 35 mm, if you are exceedingly careful.)

Reflector-diffuser lighting serves for a very wide variety of subject matter, and should be tried first when in doubt. It can be used at high magnification as well as for subjects as large as a watermelon, provided that the reflectors and diffusers are sized in proportion to the size of the subject. It is a particularly good method to use when low lighting contrasts are needed in order to emphasize color over shape, al-

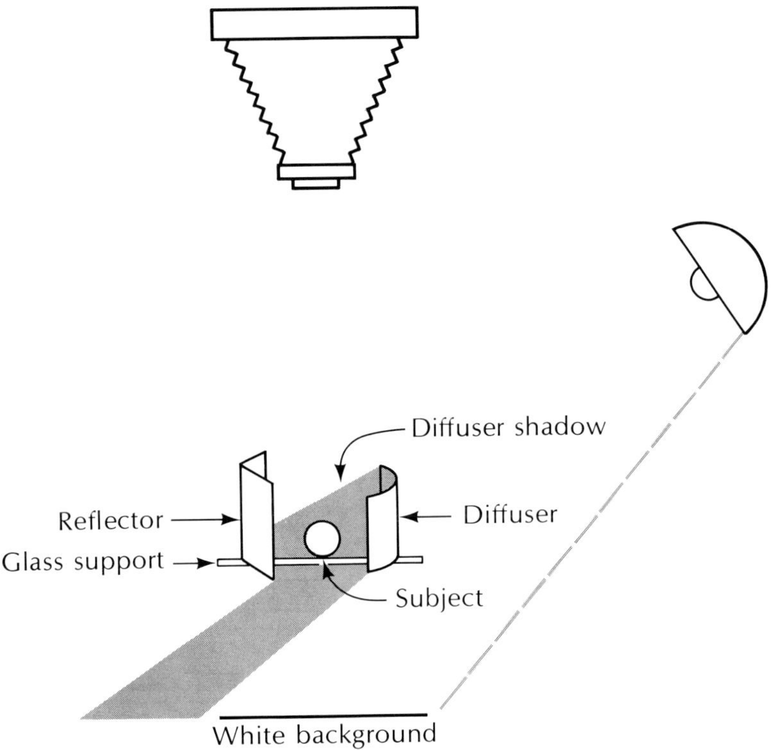

FIGURE 17
Reflector-diffuser lighting. The diffuser, usually made of white tracing tissue taped to a wire frame, casts a diffuse shadow across the subject. Little or no shadow falls on the reflector, which reflects light diffusely to the unlighted side of the subject. The overall effect is of directional but soft lighting. Contrast is controlled by the relative positions of the diffuser, subject, reflector, and lamp. With the diffuser close to the subject and the reflector further away, contrast is relatively high. With the diffuser further away and the reflector moved in, the contrast decreases. Moving the lamp closer increases the contrast, other factors remaining the same. Though shown here with a white background, a black one can also be used. (See Plate 5A.)

though shape can also be shown well simply by moving the reflector back to increase the lighting contrast. For examples of the use of reflector-diffuser lighting, see Plate 5A, as well as Plates 27B, 28A,C,D, 34A,C,D, 36B,D, 38, 43, 44A,C, and 47A,C, and Color Plate VIIIA.

Where the only important feature of the subject is color, but where the shape is very irregular or the surface heavily textured, a variation of this method—the *light tent*—is useful. Light tenting is also useful with small, bright metal objects, where harsh surface reflections must be subdued. In this method a truncated cone of white tissue paper extends from the lens to, or below, the subject, and is commonly lit from two or three sides to provide a uniform light intensity all around. (See Figure 18.) A complete lack of shadows and an absolutely even distribution of light result in subject differentiation by color alone; shape (except, of course, for outline) is visually nullified. With small subject matter this effect can be achieved by using ordinary reflector-diffuser lighting, if both the reflector and the diffuser are relatively large, close to the subject, and wrapped well around it.

Direct Lighting

The second most versatile setup is plain old direct lighting. In practice, this resembles the reflector-diffuser method just discussed, except that there is no diffuser (see Figure 19). If shadow detail is to be retained at all, a reflector is generally necessary on the shadowed side. In this case it is unlikely that completely uniform lighting is obtainable unless the reflector is a mirror (a useful technique itself upon occasion—see later sections in this chapter), but good contrast control can still be obtained. Since the usual reflector material is a matte white card, the usual fill-in light returned to the subject is soft and diffuse; thus the directionality of the light is clearly maintained even when its intensity is nearly uniform. Again, small subsidiary reflectors may be needed for best results with irregular subjects. This setup is excellent for showing surface textures, as well as for showing low- and medium-height relief. The lower the relief to be shown, the lower the angle at which the lamp must be placed.

To get a pure white background with this setup requires either a separate or brighter (or closer) lamp on the background. Alternatively, the subject can be shaded during part of the exposure by a circle of standing black cards. Black backgrounds require no special treatment. For examples of direct lighting, see Plate 5, parts B and C, as well as Plates 27A,C, 28B, 33, 36A,C, 39, 45, 46, and 47B.

Axial and Near-Axial Lighting

A specialized application of direct lighting is found in axial and near-axial lighting. To say that light is axial means that it comes, or appears to come, from the direction of the camera itself —that is, along the lens axis. To obtain this effect, a half-silvered mirror or a plain optical flat is

PLATE 5 ▶

Basic Lighting Methods: Reflector-Diffuser and Direct.

A Plant galls (×1.8), lit to medium contrast by reflector-diffuser lighting, to show the three-dimensional shapes. A Wratten 47 deep blue filter was used to increase visual color contrasts. (Originally photographed for P. A. Ark.)
B Mined Live-oak leaf (×0.9), lit directly by a single flood lamp from the direction of the leaf tip, at a grazing angle to emphasize surface relief. A Wratten 58 deep green filter was used to increase visual color contrasts.
C Insect eggs (×7.1) on a leaf, photographed by direct lighting at about a 30° downward angle to emphasize the spherical shape and somewhat translucent quality. (Originally photographed for W. W. Middlekauff.)

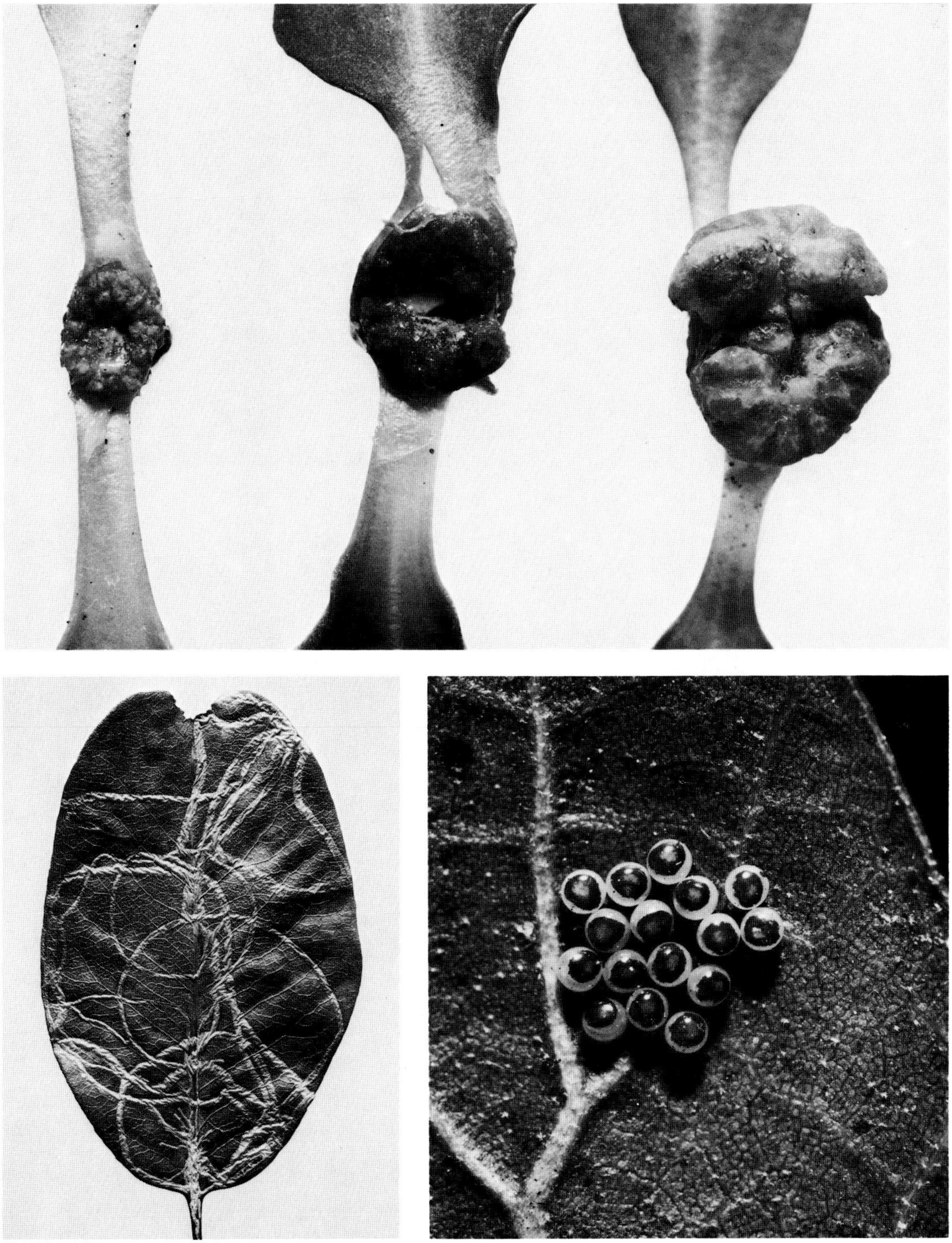

A

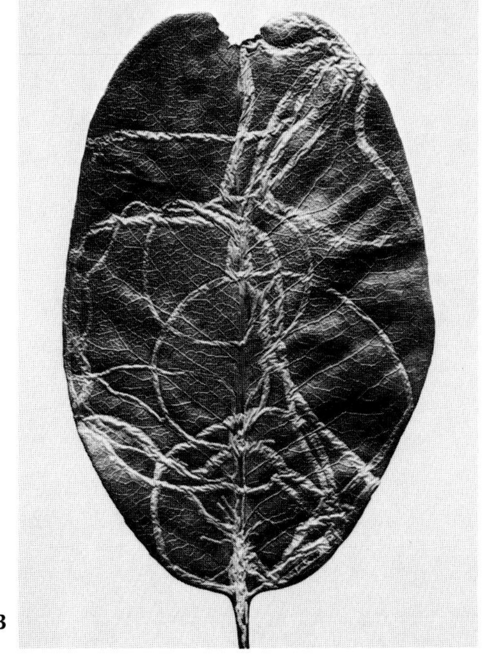

B

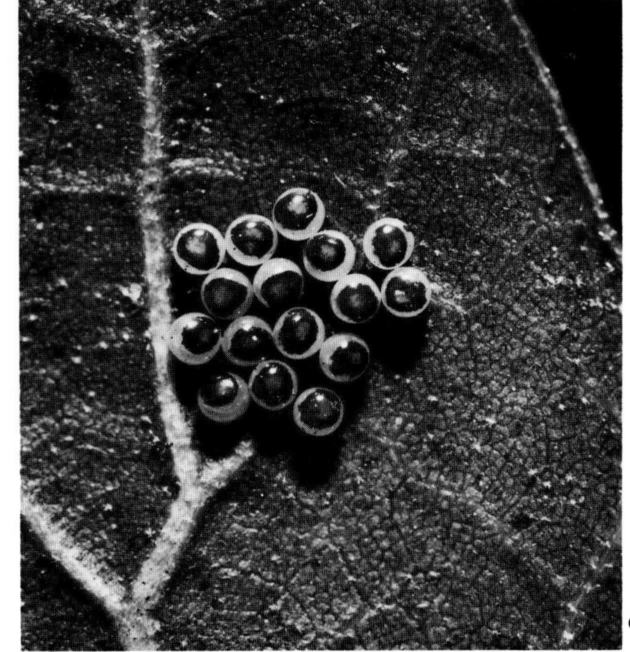

C

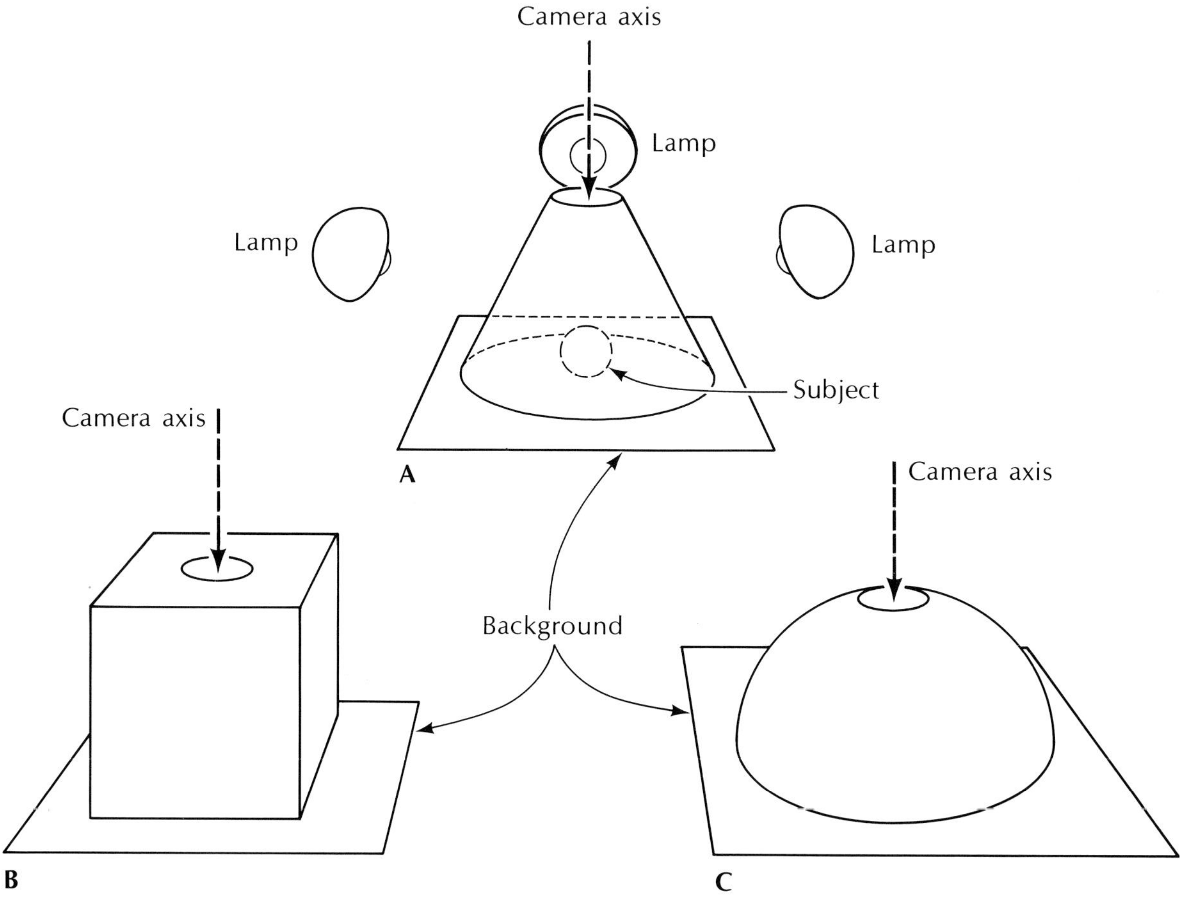

FIGURE 18
Light tenting in various forms. The effect is of nondirectional soft lighting.

A Truncated tissue-paper cone.
B Tissue-paper cube, using a wire frame.
C Hemisphere (half a Ping-Pong ball, a frosted plastic dome, a lighting-fixture globe, etc.).

used as a beam-splitter, and is mounted at a 45° angle in the center of a box that is open at one end. This box serves to cut out light or reflections from sources other than the intended one, as well as to absorb the light that passes through the beam-splitter (Figure 20). The box has one hole in the top, over the beam-splitter, and another in the bottom, under it. The box must be entirely lined with black velvet to cut out all stray reflections. The beam-splitter causes at least a 75% light loss, because in each of the two impingements of the light beam upon the mirror, less than 50% passes through; the rest is reflected or absorbed (see the light path in Figure 20).

Axial lighting is used for two purposes: (1) to light deep cavities from the outside and (2) to show very low relief. The latter is possible because surfaces that are inclined at an angle to the lens axis will reflect less light to the lens than will a surface at a right angle to the lens axis (and at a right angle to the light, in axial lighting). The effect will be harsh, and will thus exaggerate very low reliefs, thereby tending to show them better (Figure 21). This is simply a consequence of the law of reflection. For examples of axial lighting, see Plate 6, parts A and B, and also Plate 34B.

Beam-splitters must be optically flat or severe distortion of the image will result. Some linear distortion is probably present in all but the very best of these mirrors, because the light beam is offset by refraction (Figure 22), and any imperfections are thereby exaggerated. Thinner glass gives less distortion by giving less offset. In work at high magnification with this method, use the thinnest available microscope-slide cover glass as a mirror.

As noted above, axial lighting can be used to light very deep cavities, as well as objects within them, where no other method can accomplish it. It is also particularly good where one must show relief so low as to be virtually undetectable. For other purposes the light provided may be too harsh.

Where it is necessary to avoid the loss of light inherent in the beam-splitter, the effect of one can be closely simulated by using an interrupted two-piece mirror (see Figure 23). Here two mirrors are placed precisely parallel to each other but far enough apart to allow the lens to peer through. The angle of placement is 45° to both the lens axis and the lamp axis, as with a beam-splitter, and the near edges of the two must be aligned on the lamp axis. If this placement is exactly correct the effect will be that of a normal beam-splitter in terms of the light reaching the subject, but little or no light will be lost. Remember, however, that a setup this exact is quite difficult to make.

Near-axial lighting is, of course, lighting from a source close to but not on the optical axis. It can be achieved by using a light placed close to the camera lens (Figure 24A), a mirror placed close to the camera lens to reflect a beam of light correctly (Figure 24B), or a ringlight (either a fluorescent ring or an electronic-flash ringlight) surrounding the lens (Figure 24C). In this

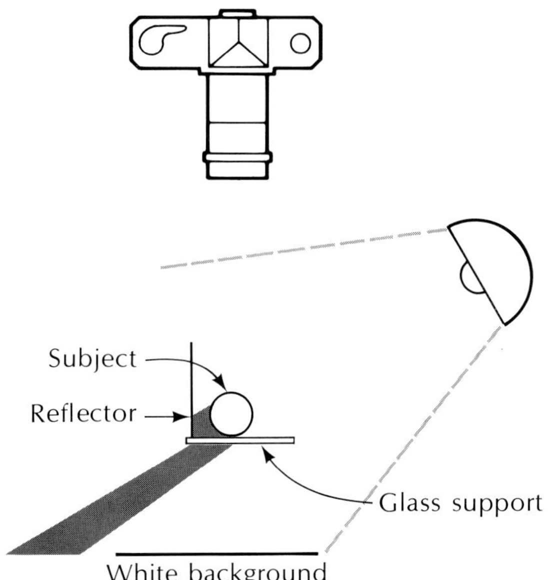

FIGURE 19
Direct lighting. The effect is of strongly directional lighting. Diffuse light reflected from a white card opposite the lamp gives some contrast control and illuminates the shadow details. (See Plate 5, parts B and C.)

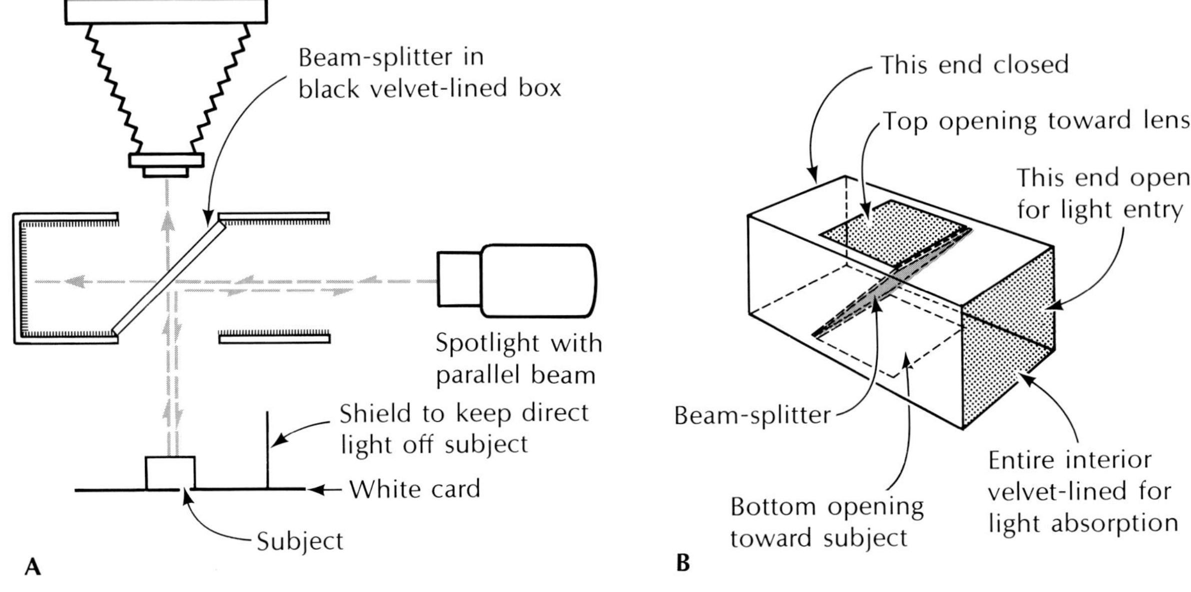

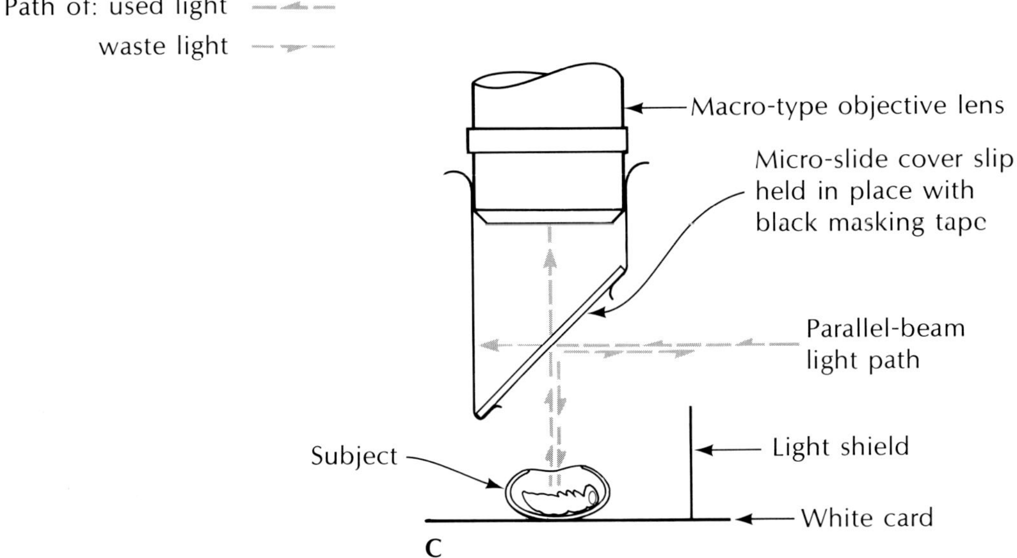

FIGURE 20
Axial lighting by means of a beam-splitter. This provides direct frontal lighting, along the lens axis. It makes possible the photographic penetration of deep cavities and enhances the contrast of low subject relief. (See Plate 6, parts A and B, and Plate 34B.)

A Diagram of the setup.
B Design for a beam-splitter housing.
C An improvised beam-splitter for very small subjects.

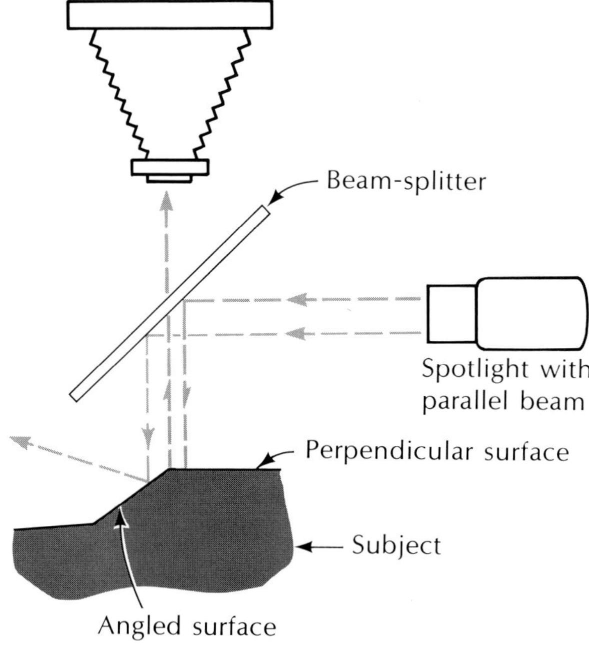

FIGURE 21
Reflections with axial lighting. A surface perpendicular to an axial beam reflects light back to the lens, and appears bright. Surfaces at other angles reflect relatively less light toward the lens, and appear dark.

last example the lens must be shielded from the direct light.

Near-axial lighting is useful for illuminating moderately deep cavities or, with ringlights, for showing very low relief with less harshness than with beam-splitter axial lighting and for giving an even, soft, shadowless, nondirectional light (see Plate 32B). For this last purpose, only the ringlight is suitable, not the first two near-axial methods mentioned above. Where practical, these lighting methods are to be preferred over true axial lighting, since one can avoid optical aberrations and the problem of light loss more easily than with the interrupted-mirror method. Fluorescent ringlights are not recommended for color work (see Chapter 11 for details).

For small subjects the effect of a ringlight can be well simulated by using a special mirror with a rectangular hole in it, mounted at a 45° angle just below the lens and illuminated by a spotlight off to one side (Figure 24D). A convenient way to make such a setup is to use as a mirror a small rectangle of heavy-duty household aluminum foil with a hole cut in it. When the foil

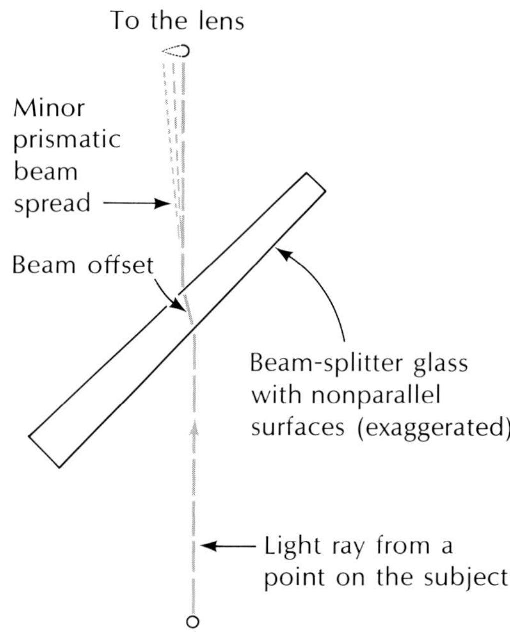

FIGURE 22
Refraction effect with beam-splitters. A beam-splitter with nonparallel surfaces acts like a thin prism. The refracted ray tends to spread, so that points on the subject will record on the film as short lines, thus distorting the image. The thinner the beam-splitter, the less the distortion.

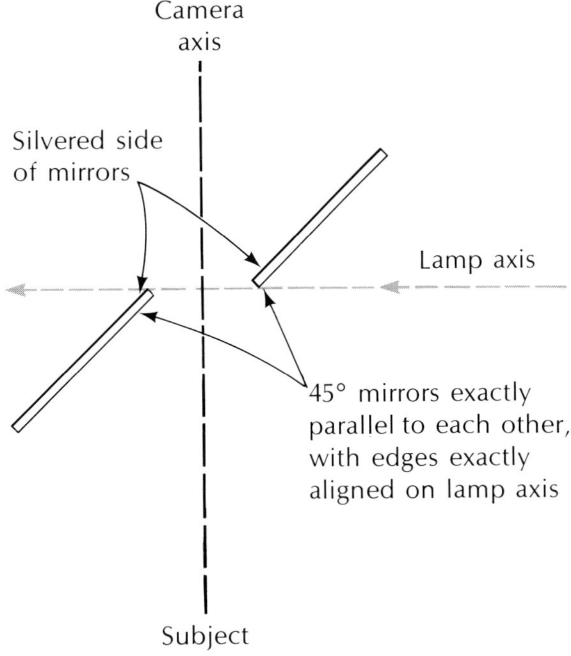

FIGURE 23
Axial lighting by means of an interrupted two-piece mirror. The mirrors lose less light than a true beam-splitter and do not introduce distortion, but are difficult to align. Any alignment failure will give near-axial rather than axial lighting.

rectangle is mounted, the lens views through the hole and the light is reflected down, ring-fashion, upon the subject. The matte side of the foil should face the subject in order to distribute the light evenly. (The shiny side tends to produce "hot spots" of light.) This lighting method is particularly useful where a small subject sits directly on a natural background and where no hint of shadow can be allowed, so as not to obscure edges or other important details.

For any of the methods of near-axial lighting, the background can be either black or white, as desired. With either the ringlight or the pierced mirror, a sheet of aluminum foil can be used to produce a white background (see Figure 14 and its accompanying text). With the near-axial lighting schemes of Figure 24, parts A and B, the directed light beam falls so as to make a white background difficult to use, but it can be done by placing the subject on a glass plate above a white card and illuminating that card separately with another lamp. Where a large fluorescent ringlight is used to provide soft, nondirectional light for a moderately large subject, the best method is probably just to place the subject directly on a white card. The background will be very nearly white in the final print, with just a tinge of off-white if the subject is light-colored. There will probably not be any

---

PLATE 6 ▶

Basic Lighting Methods: Axial and Transmitted.

A Adult beetle resting after emerging from the pupal stage (×1.8). This dark subject lying at the bottom of a rather deep cavity could not be lit effectively by any means other than axial lighting from a beam-splitter. (Originally photographed for A. Raske.)
B The face of the breechblock of a .380 automatic pistol (×4.7). The original photography was done at ×2, with further enlargement in printing. The breech was closed, and all light was provided by axial lighting from a beam-splitter, directly down the gun barrel. The machining marks are clearly visible, and one can even discern detail on the end of the firing pin.
C *Drosophila* with nematodes (×27), photographed by transmitted light. The insect was floating in a dish of liquid. Use of a Wratten 15 deep yellow filter (placed in the illumination beam rather than at the camera lens) helped to provide visual contrast. (Originally photographed for G. Poinar.)

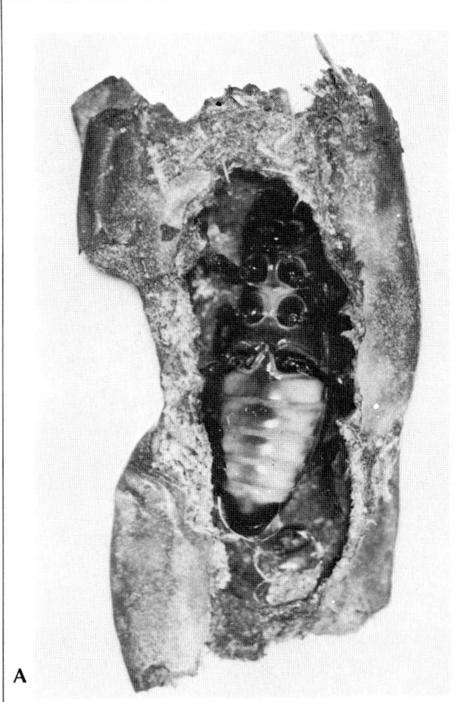

A

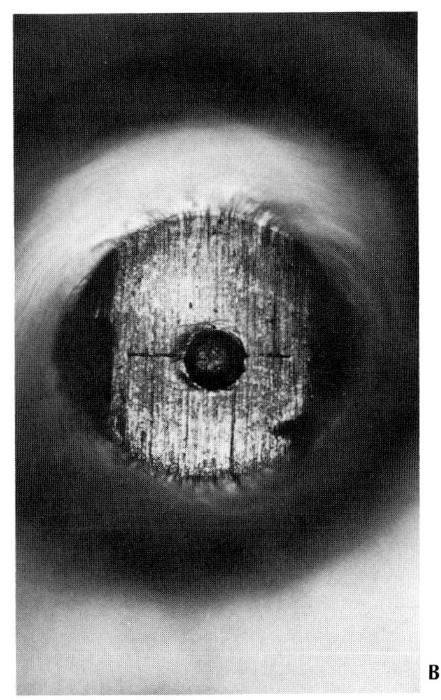

B

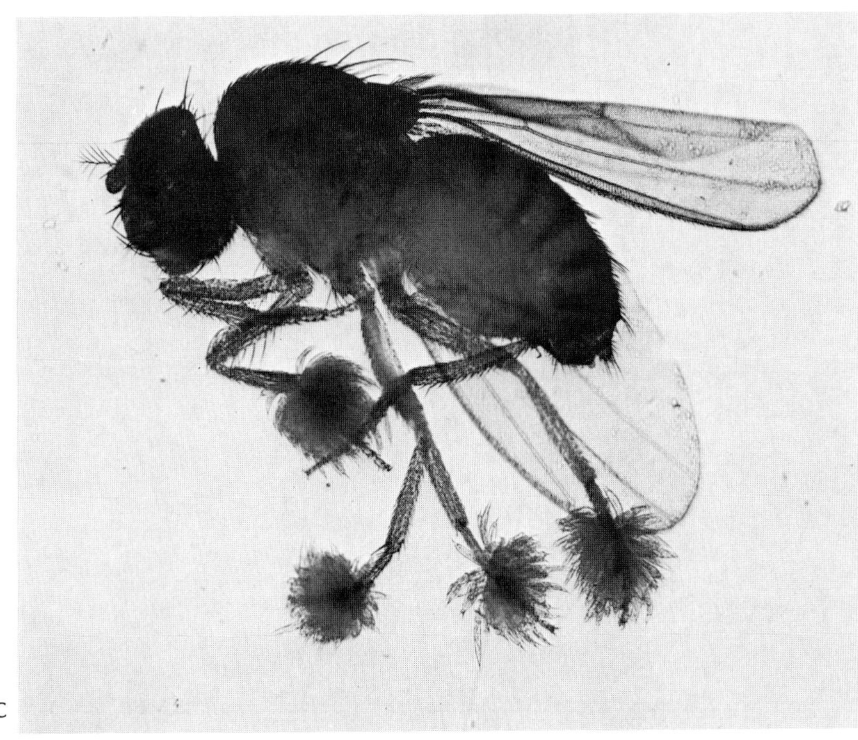

C

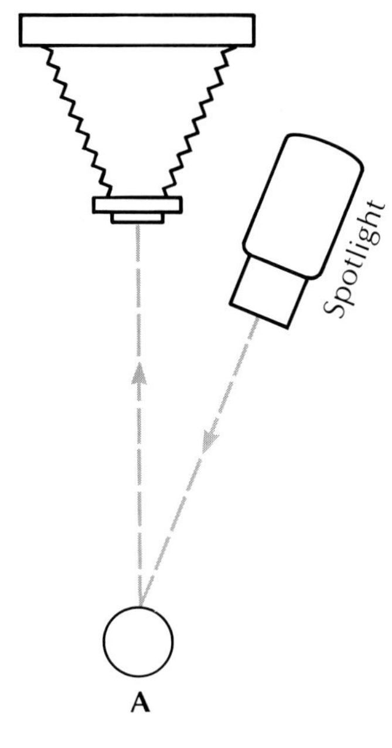
Spotlight
A

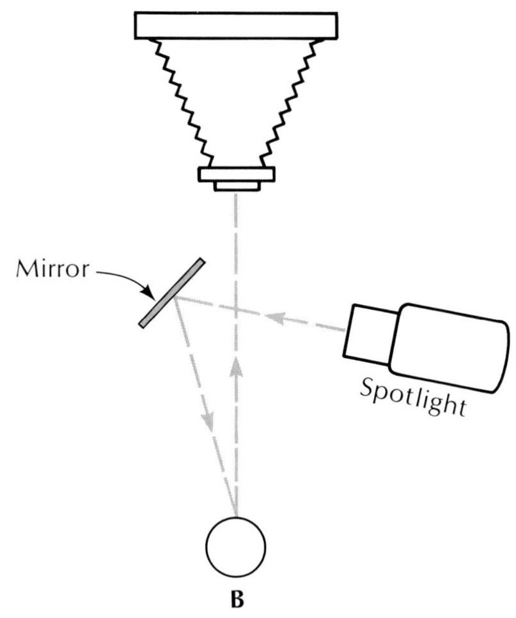
Mirror
Spotlight
B

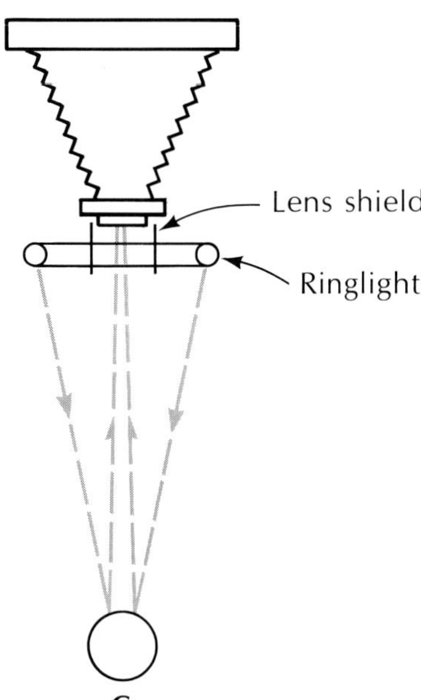
Lens shield
Ringlight
C

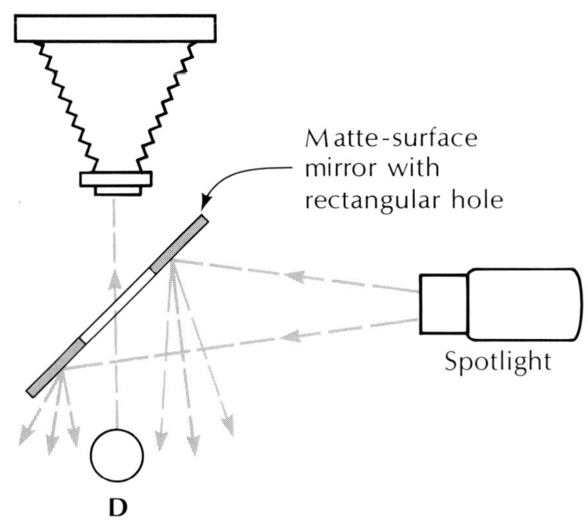
Matte-surface
mirror with
rectangular hole
Spotlight
D

shadowing here, and at worst it will be no more than a very pale penumbra. (This shadowing can be minimized by constructing and using a multiple lamp. Fluorescent rings come in three sizes, which can be mounted concentrically for this purpose. You can buy such a multiple lamp through photographic supply houses, but you will save a good deal of money by putting it together yourself. There is also available a cold-cathode version of it that is approximately balanced for use with color films; however, it is quite expensive.) Black backgrounds offer no difficulties when using ringlights, and the subject is simply laid on a piece of velvet, as usual.

Transmitted Light

As used in scientific photography, transmitted light is either an optically aligned beam or diffuse light. The commonest use of transmitted light is in photomicrography of mounted slides, where the aligned beam is the normal usage. This will be covered in Chapter 9.

For photographing any translucent or transparent subject of moderate size, such as geological thin sections, thin leaves, or tissue sections, or for making copies of color transparencies, a convenient way of producing diffuse transmitted light is to light a matte white card that has been placed a little distance behind the subject, which itself receives no direct light at all. With a vertical camera the setup is the same as for reflector-diffuser lighting with a white background, except that the subject is surrounded by a standing ring of black cards to keep all top light off it. Plate 6C is an example of the use of transmitted light on a special kind of three-dimensional subject.

Dark-Field Lighting

A special application of transmitted light is found in dark-field lighting. Here the idea is to light the subject from below or behind by light beams that enter the lens only if they are refracted or scattered by the subject. In microscopy this effect is contrived by introducing a center stop into the back of the condenser, thereby producing a hollow cone of light that is refracted by the subject into the microscope (see Chapter 9 for details). With larger subjects we can produce a similar effect by placing a ringlight below or behind the subject (see Figure 25). If a shield keeps the direct light of the ring from the lens, and if the distance between the ring and the subject is correctly set for maximum

◂ **FIGURE 24**

Near-axial lighting methods.

A Lamp axis close to lens axis.
B Mirror redirects the lamp axis close to the lens axis.
C Ringlight surrounds the lens to give all-around near-axial lighting.
D Matte-surface mirror (the matte side of aluminum foil, or even a piece of white paper) with a rectangular hole is similar in effect to a ringlight, but can be smaller and nearer to the lens axis. This method is suitable for color photography (fluorescent lighting is not), but generally provides less light intensity than a ringlight.

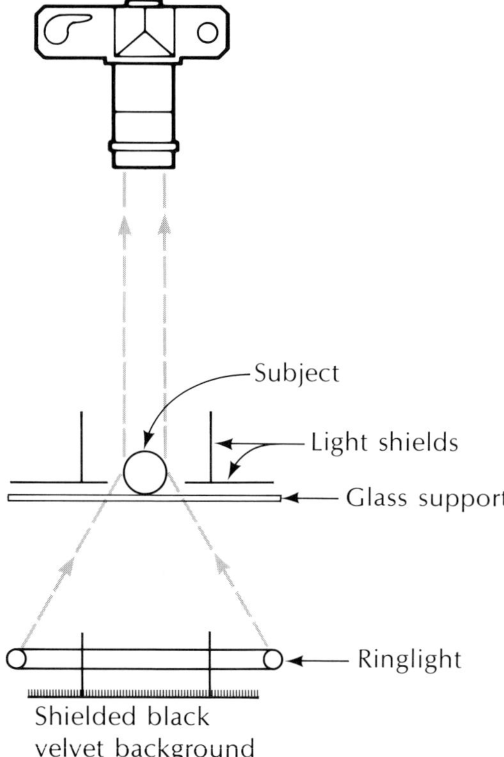

FIGURE 25
Dark-field lighting with a ringlight. The horizontal shield on the glass support protects the lens from the direct light of the ringlight. A vertical circular shield keeps light off the background material. A second vertical shield keeps ambient light off the surface of the subject. The only light reaching the lens is that refracted by the subject. (See Plate 7, parts B and C.)

effect (by placing one eye at the camera lens position and adjusting the lamp-to-subject distance), then only that light that is refracted or scattered toward the lens by the subject will be recorded. The setup is then functionally analogous to a microscope. See Plates 7 and 33B for illustrations of these effects.

By using this method, along with some carefully balanced top lighting (either direct or reflector-diffuser illumination), one can reveal normally visible surface detail and difficult-to-show edge effects, such as hairs, concurrently. Care must be taken to balance the two sources correctly so that neither is so intense as to dominate and thereby overwhelm the effects of the other. (With color films, beware of mixing

PLATE 7 ▶

Basic Lighting Methods: Dark-Field.

Dark-field light is a special form of transmitted light in which the light beam is a hollow cone that would not normally enter the lens at all. Only that portion of it that is refracted or scattered by the subject, and is thereby redirected, reaches the camera lens.

A Rotifers and protozoans swimming freely and rapidly in a water cell (×20). The light source was a high speed electronic flash ringlight placed below the subject container, and shielded so that no direct light reached the camera lens. No composition or true focus of the image was possible, so zone focusing was used and a number of randomly timed exposures were made. This one is representative. (Originally photographed for C. W. Birky.)
B Ouchterlony plate (×1.6), photographed by dark-field lighting, using a 12-inch-diameter fluorescent ringlight. Note the visible presence of lint and other contaminants in the culture medium. Though sterile, and thus not usually detrimental to the culture, these contaminants adversely affect the appearance of the photograph. They could be removed from the print by retouching, but it would be better to strain the culture medium during preparation.
C A smear culture (×1.6), photographed similarly. The culture medium has been strained and is much cleaner.

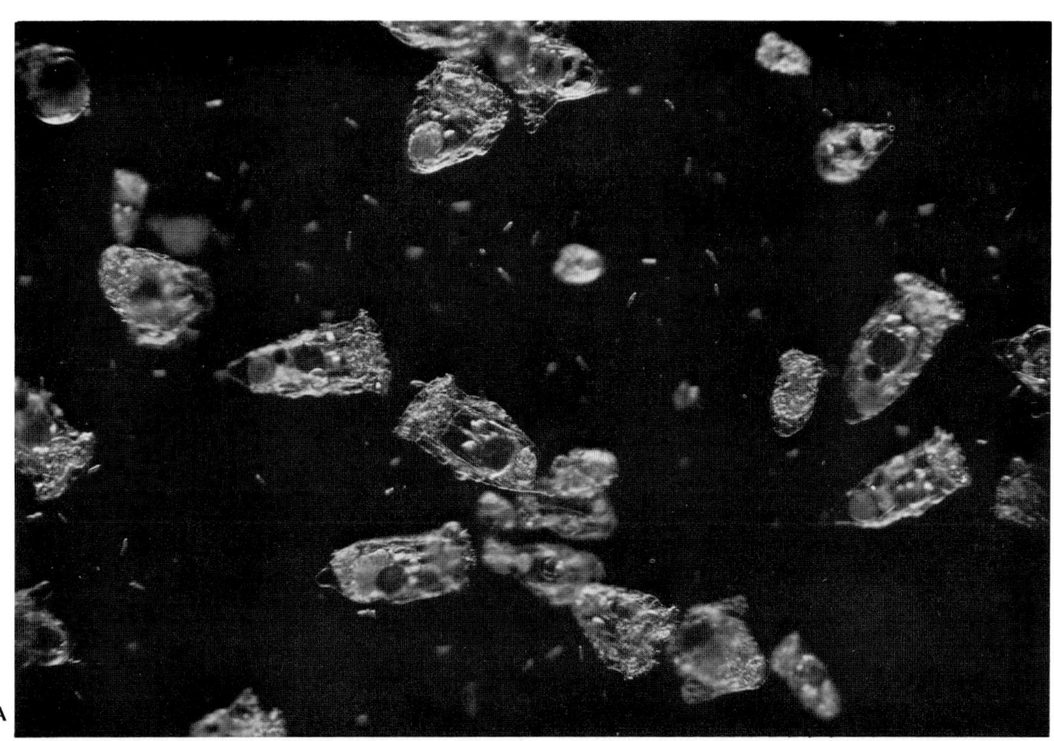
A

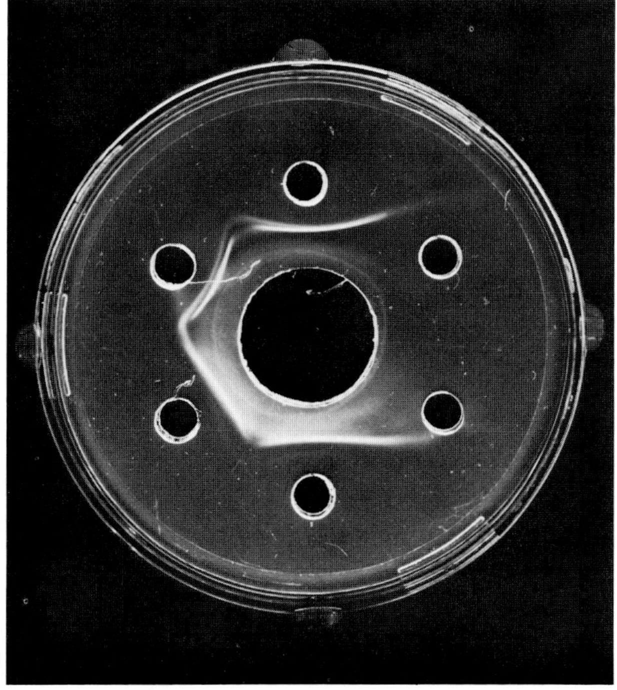
B

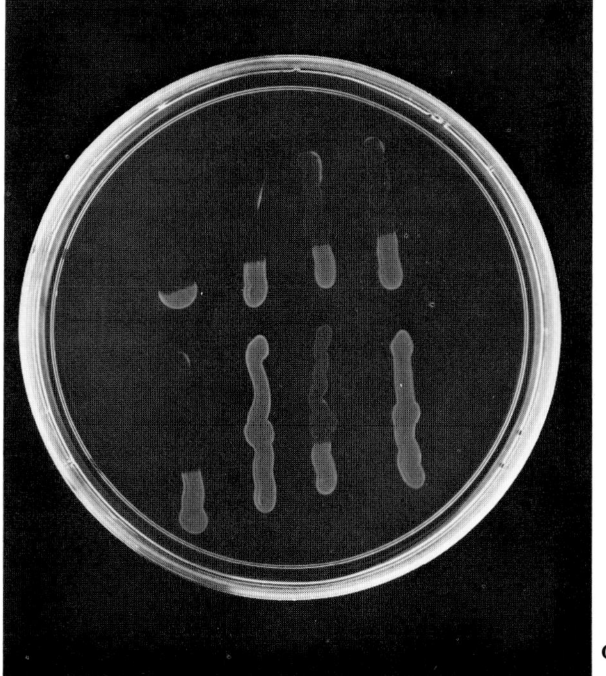
C

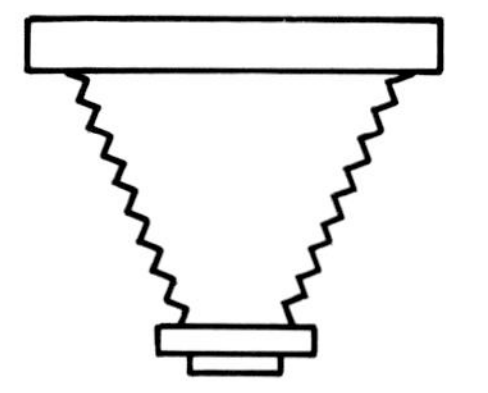

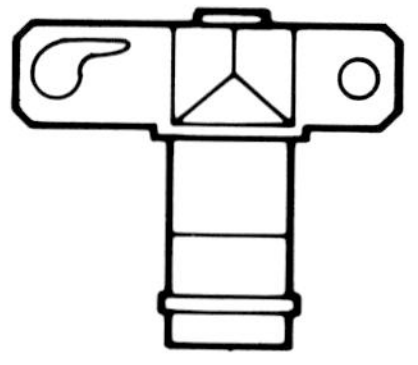

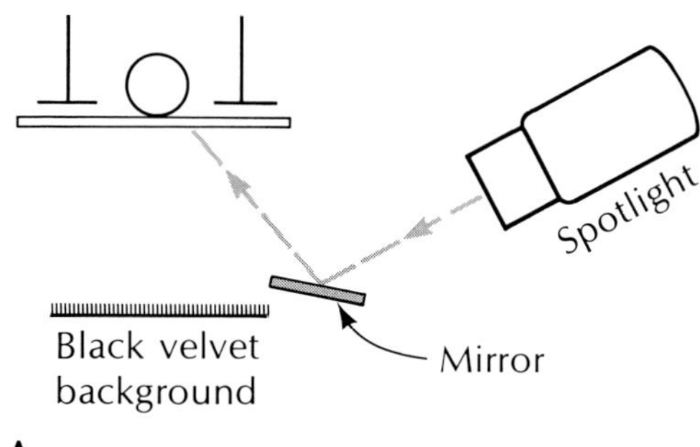

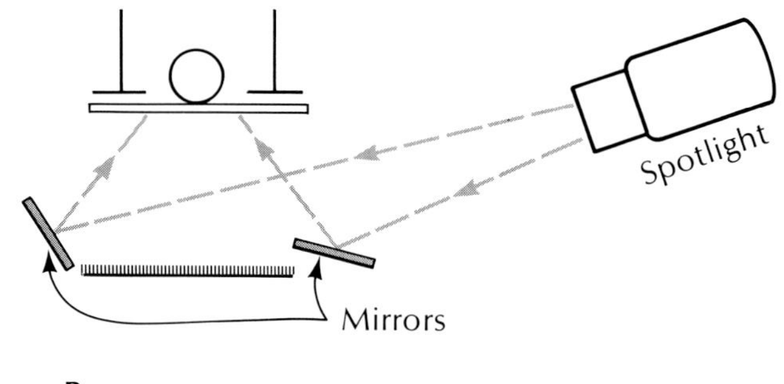

FIGURE 26
Directional dark-field lighting with mirrors.

A Unidirectional dark-field lighting, using only one mirror. (See Plate 20, parts B and C, and Plate 28A.)
B Multidirectional dark-field lighting, using two or more mirrors, makes it possible to show linear effects in more than one subject axis. Two lamps at 90°, each with its own set of mirrors, provide crossed lighting angles. If different color filters are used on each lamp, color film can be used to differentiate these axes in the picture. (As the drawings show, any type of camera can be used.)

light from a fluorescent ringlight with light from normal tungsten sources, as the color effects may be unpredictable.) See Plates 8 and 28A for some examples of dark-field lighting combined with top lighting.

Another variation of dark-field lighting allows directional effects to be achieved. Instead of using a ringlight behind or below the subject, a mirror is placed below and to one side of the subject. A beam of light is directed onto the

PLATE 8 ▶

Basic Lighting Methods: Dark-Field plus Top Lighting.

Dismantled flower (×2), photographed by fluorescent-ringlight dark-field lighting, coupled with balanced-intensity direct lighting on the top surface of the parts, from the direction of the picture top. There is reflector fill opposite the toplight. (Originally photographed for L. R. Heckard.)

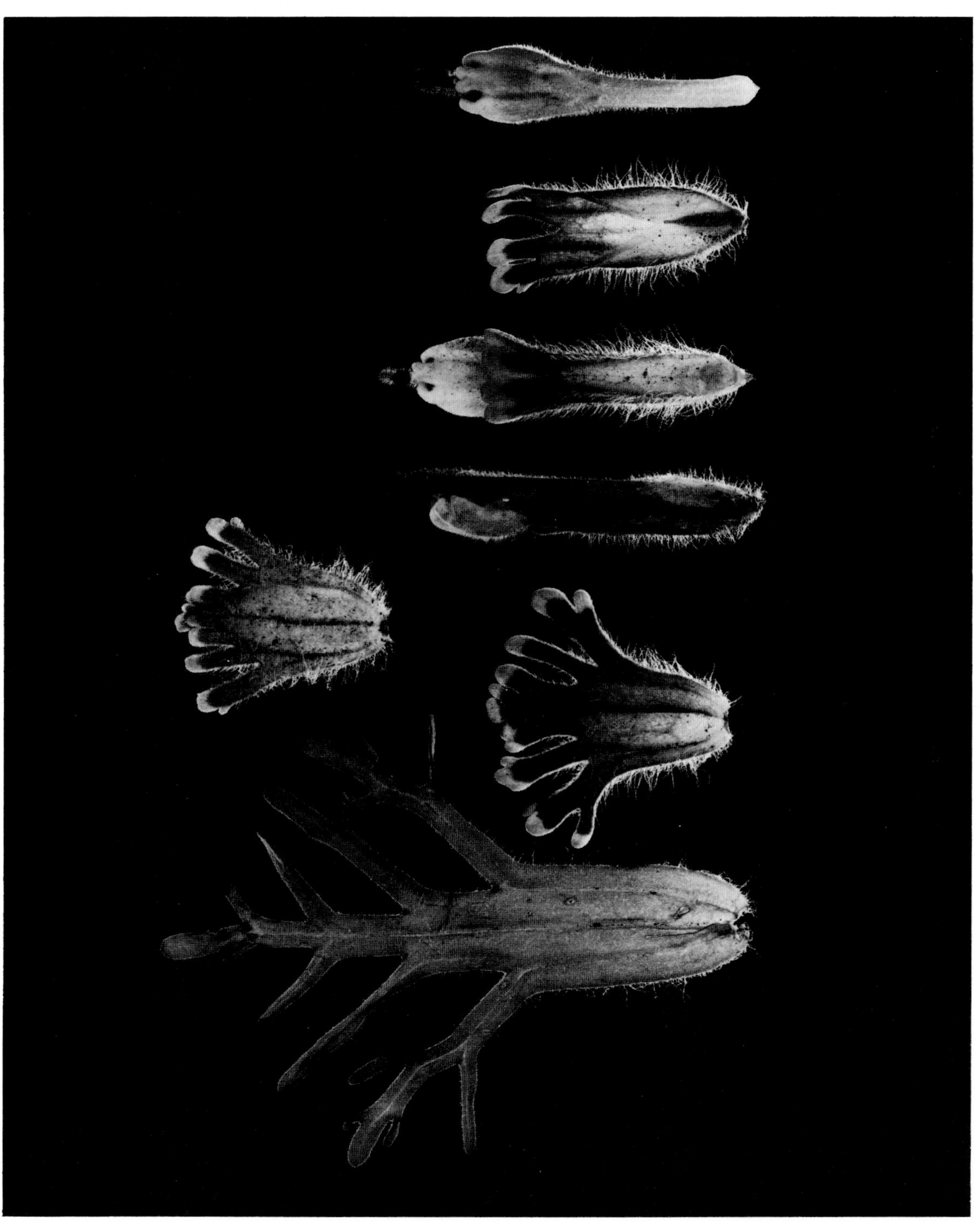

mirror and is then reflected up to the subject (Figure 26A). By turning the subject with respect to the light, one can control the directionality completely, and thereby show effects that could not otherwise be seen. The technique is particularly useful with some types of geological thin sections. Used with care, this setup can also provide the effect of a dark field, or a combination of dark field and top light, for color work.

More complex effects can be obtained by using two mirrors, arranged as shown in Figure 26B. This provides directional dark-field lighting from opposite ends of the subject, both reinforcing the effect and evening it out, while still avoiding any such light from the sides. If desired, an all-around effect similar to a ringlight, but without the undesirable color effects of a fluorescent ringlight, can be had by using two such double-mirror setups, each with its own lamp, set up at 90° to each other.

In addition to the generalized types of lighting setups described in this chapter, there are specialized setups peculiar to certain situations. These will be described where applicable later in the text.

CHAPTER 5

Filters in Black-and-White Photography

The use of filters is widespread and necessary in scientific black-and-white photography. Their purpose is to alter the nature of the light that forms the image. This is done by (1) selective color filtration, (2) polarization, or (3) reduction of intensity. Only a brief summary will be given here, as the subject is well covered elsewhere in a variety of sources and the concepts are not difficult to understand.

Filters come in several forms. They can be pieces of colored glass, the colors being intrinsic properties of the glass itself. These filters are durable, easily handled, and easily cleaned, but some are subject to eventual fading or color change.

Filters can also be made by depositing a molecular film on one side of a sheet of clear glass. The glass serves solely as a support for the molecular film, the purpose of which is usually to diminish the amount of light transmitted without otherwise altering it. Among these filters are *neutral-density filters,* which come in a variety of carefully graded and labeled densities. Neutral-density filters are without discernible color effect (hence the word *neutral*). Many beam-splitter mirrors are also of this type of construction; any silvering or other reflective coating is just such a molecular deposit, but some of them are colored (see Chapter 4 for a discussion of beam-splitters).

A third method of filter construction is to put a sheet of colored gelatin between two sheets of glass; the glass supports and protects the gelatin. Many high-quality color filters are made this way. Polarizing filters are often similarly constructed, with a sheet of polarizing material between two glass sheets.

Optically, the best type of filter is the unprotected gelatin itself, because it is extremely thin. Although subject to damage from scratching and finger marking, such filters are cheap enough that one can own a sizable variety and replace them easily. Carefully handled, they can last a surprisingly long time. If the need arises they can be cut to special shapes and sizes with scissors. Polarizing material can also be had in sheets and rolls.

Glass or glass-mounted filters can be very detrimental to image sharpness if they are of poor optical quality or if they are not accurately mounted, perpendicular to the optical axis of the lens. Neutral-density filters, some types of which are designed primarily for use at the light source rather than at the lens, should be watched particularly closely for optical defects. Final focusing with glass-mounted filters on cameras that allow ground-glass viewing should be done with the filter in place, since it may make a slight difference in the focus. This is especially true if the filter is mounted inside the camera, as is commonly done with view cameras. In high-magnification work it is best, where practical, to filter the light at its source rather than at the lens, in order to avoid any such difficulties.

TYPES OF FILTERS

Color Filters

In scientific black-and-white photography it is often necessary to differentiate colors that, when photographed on panchromatic films, will be reproduced as similar shades of grey because of their approximately equal brightnesses. For color differentiation on black-and-white films, the need will be to either darken or lighten a given color in the subject, relative to adjoining colors. See Plates 9 (opposite) and 11 (page 127).

All filters act by removing some of the light that strikes them. Color filters do this by absorbing (or, in a few special types, reflecting) certain of the wavelengths of light. In physical terms, what we call white light is made up of a mixture of all visible wavelengths, or colors, of light. In color filtering it can be described as consisting of three basic colors: blue, green, and red. A yellow filter absorbs blue, and transmits green and red. A red filter absorbs blue and green, and

PLATE 9 ▶

Filters in Black-and-White Photography.

A leaf (×1.5) lit by direct light from the direction of the leaf tip, with reflective fill opposite. Panchromatic film was used to show the effect of color filtering in the differentiation of colors as tones. The outer portion of the leaf was bright red, and the center portion seen as a light area in part C was a medium green.

A No filter used.
B A Wratten 29 deep red filter was used.
C A Wratten 58 deep green filter was used. This picture most clearly gives the impression seen by the eye.

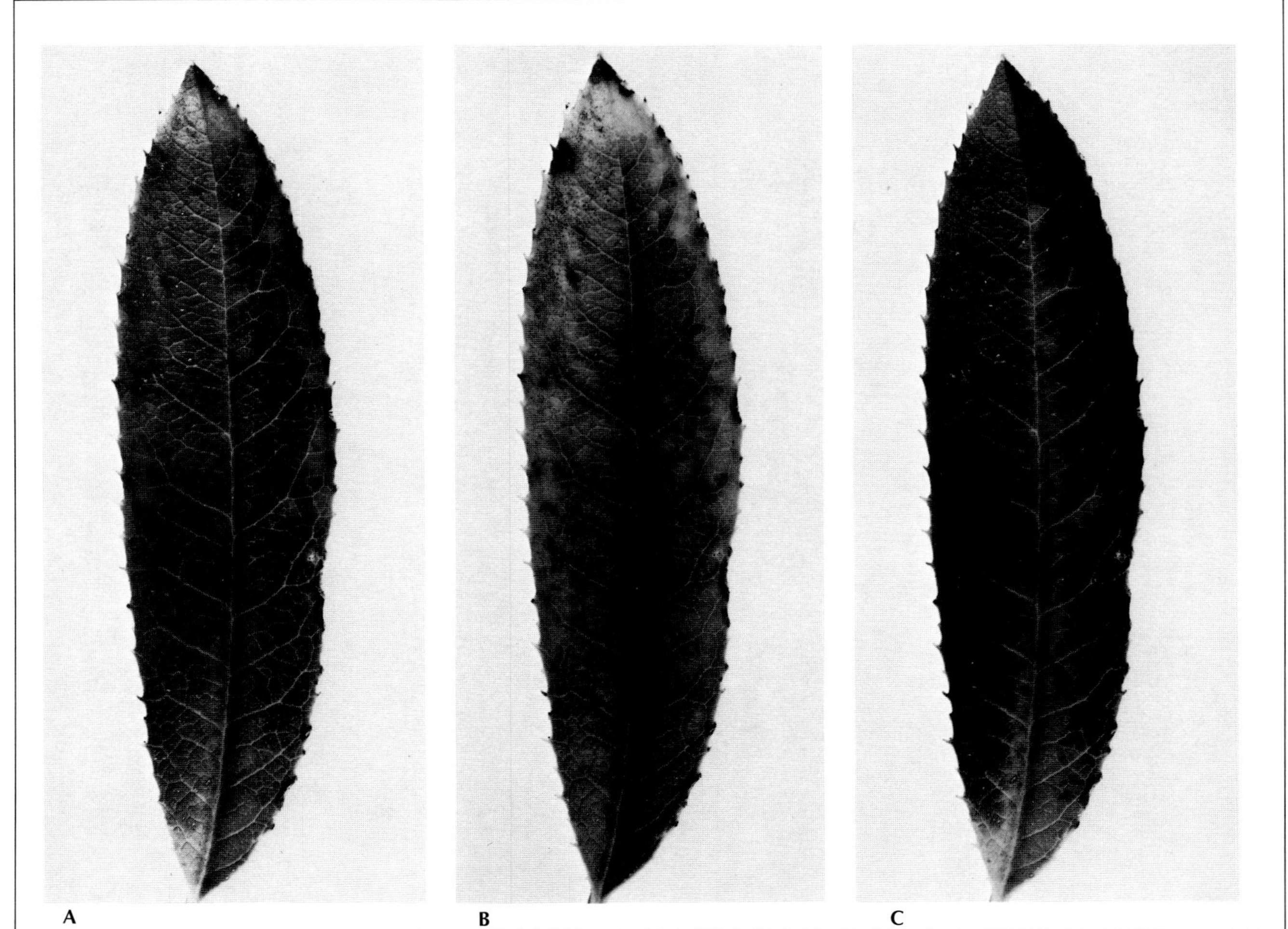
A
B
C

transmits red. And so on. However, this gives the novice only a poor idea of how to choose a color filter for tone differentiation in black-and-white photography.

Although incorrect in strictly physical terms, there is a very useful rule of thumb based upon the complementary color wheel we all learned about in school. The color wheel is a description of what happens in an additive system, where *pigments* are mixed, whereas the use of color filters is a subtractive system having to do with the mixing of *light*.

Nevertheless, it happens that if you look through a color filter the color tones will darken or lighten with respect to one another in approximate accord with a color wheel (see Figure 27). Thus, the rule of thumb is simple: to darken a color, use a filter of the complementary color; to lighten a color, use a filter of the same color. A deeper or lighter hue of the filter will provide a correspondingly greater or lesser filter effect.

Looking at the subject through a filter in this manner will give you a fairly good idea of how it will affect the image as recorded on panchromatic film. You will see a monochromatic scene, with the relative brightnesses similar to those of the final print. Although it will be seen in shades of the color of the filter, rather than in shades of grey, as in the print, a little practice will allow you to predict the final results reasonably well.

Using the color wheel as a system for choosing which filter to use fails primarily when you look for a violet filter: there is no suitable filter in that spectral region. So you must use either a red or, more likely, a blue filter to modify the tones that would be affected by a violet filter, according to the wheel.

There is a second failure of the color-wheel system that becomes important when you are photographing broad-leaved green vegetation. It arises from a peculiarity of the internal structure of such leaves that causes them to reflect strongly in the red and infrared regions of the spectrum. Thus, the use of a red filter with panchromatic film (or of infrared films and filters) will result not in the expected darkening of the greens, but of a lightening instead. (In infrared photography, such vegetation prints as very light or even white. The effect is called the Wood Effect, after its discoverer, R. W. Wood.)

Fortunately, the failures of the color wheel become obvious when you view through the filter after making an initial choice. If you are aware of these drawbacks they do not pose real problems. Although this system of choosing a

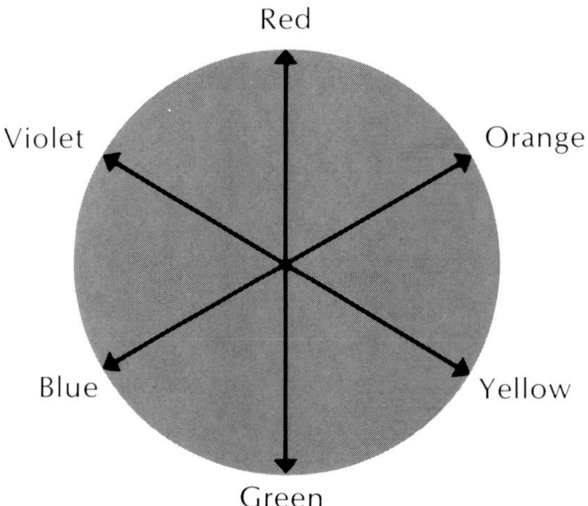

FIGURE 27
Filter-choice color wheel. In black-and-white photography, it is usually safe to assume that a color filter will lighten its own color in the subject and darken its complementary color, relative to a standard grey in the scene. Filters with a deep hue have a greater effect than lighter ones of the same color. *Note:* This method does not accord with subtractive color theory, but approximates the actual effects on the film well enough to serve as a rough guide, except in photography of broad-leaved green vegetation, where the Wood Effect with red filters lightens green vegetation instead of darkening it.

filter is somewhat inexact, it is a very useful way to start looking for the correct filter in any given situation.

Whole books have been written about the use of color filters, but the essential practical principle is that described here; such books serve to elaborate on it.

With color films, color filters are not used for the purpose or by the method stated above. Color differentiation is inherent in the film itself, and a color filter only imparts its own color to the entire image. Certain pale color filters do have uses in color photography, though, and will be discussed later, in Chapter 11.

Polarizing Filters

Polarization is one of the effects of the wave nature of light. Briefly, it is sufficient to say that unpolarized light behaves like waves in all planes about the axis of the light beam. A simple analogy is a length of rope fastened at one end and handheld at the other. The rope represents the axis of a light beam. By rapidly raising and lowering the rope end, a wave action is set up along its length. If this wave action is seen as taking place in *all* planes about the rope "beam axis," the analogy is complete. In polarization filtering the effect is that of the rope's being passed through a gap in a picket fence a foot or so from the handheld end. The wave action along the beam axis parallel to the gap in the fence is not affected, but wave action in all other planes is restricted. The result of filtering is a plane-polarized beam of light, which has a number of uses in photography (see Figure 28). The analogy here is oversimplified, and there are many other types and uses of polarization, but this explanation seems adequate for the present purposes.

There are three sources of polarized light that are photographically useful: (1) Light from the clear blue sky, partially polarized through the scattering of sunlight by air molecules and other atmospheric particles; the polarization is strongest at 90° from the position of the sun and zero in the direction of or opposite to the direction of the sun. (2) Light that has been reflected from most types of nonmetallic smooth surfaces; here the polarization is strongest at an angle of about 35° from the reflecting surface and zero at 90° to it. (3) Light that has been passed through some form of polarizing material or device.

The polarizing filter materials most commonly used are Polaroid, produced by the firm of the same name, and similar materials now produced by other firms. They are the only means of achieving polarized light artificially that will be discussed here. (Polarizing methods using Nicol or Glan-Thompson prisms, tourmaline or other naturally polarizing minerals, bundles of obliquely placed glass plates, Nörremberg doublers, and others, are not in everyday photographic use; persons desiring information on such methods are referred to the books by Strong, 1958, and Shurcliff and Ballard, 1964.)

In practical application, polarizing filters can be used in three ways. The first use applies to the polarized light that comes from the clear blue sky (see Figure 29). A polarizing filter placed at the camera lens will, when rotated correctly, deepen the blue tones of the sky without altering other color values in the picture. The degree of deepening depends upon the angle of the sun's position with respect to the camera axis and is also related to the clarity of the atmosphere. Very thick haze, by rescattering the light, may diminish the effect, although under most circumstances the haze obscuring distant land areas can itself be penetrated by the use of polarizers.

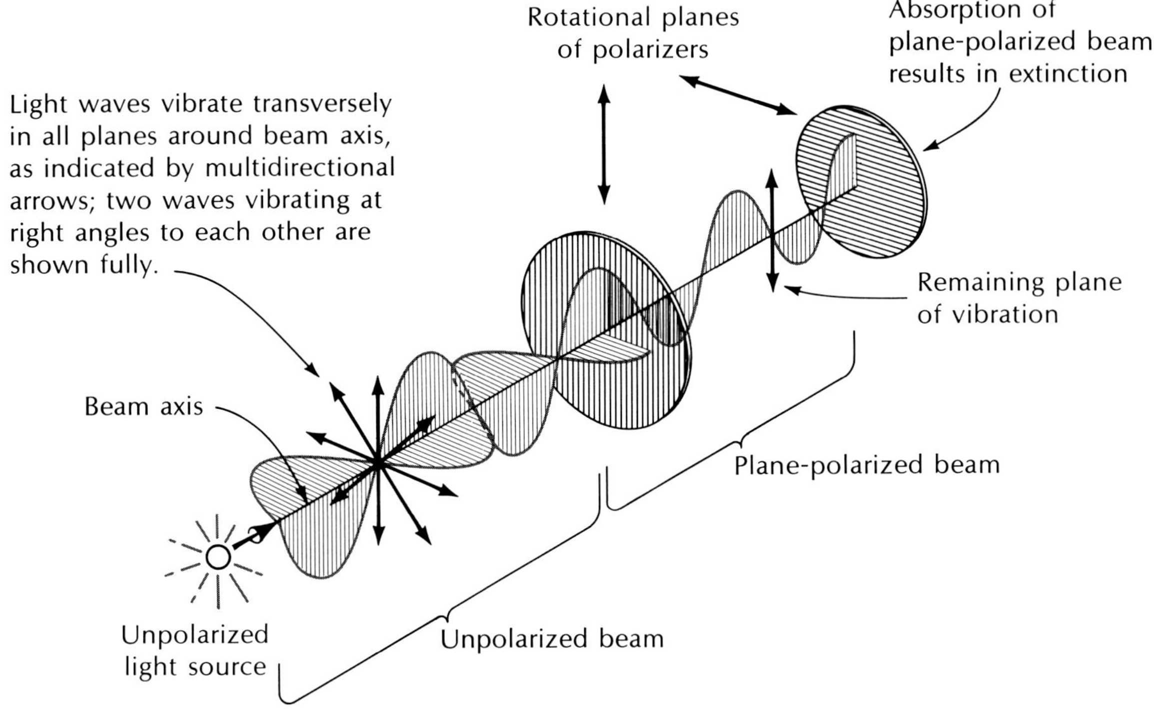

FIGURE 28
Polarization of light by a polarizing substance.

The effect of sky darkening (and of haze penetration) is useful in both color and black-and-white photography; it is almost the only way by which skies can be darkened with color films. With black-and-white films the normal practice is to use yellow, orange, or red filters to darken skies, but this sometimes results in unfortunate changes elsewhere in the picture. A warning is in order when a polarizing filter is used: watch out for any secondary effects the reduction of reflections may have on your picture.

This brings us to the second use of polarizing filters, namely, the control and suppression of reflections from surfaces. A useful degree of control can be had by suitably rotating a polarizing filter at the camera lens if the camera axis is at an angle of about 35° to the reflecting surface. At this angle, called the *polarization angle,* such reflections are most strongly polarized (see Figure 30). At greater or lesser angles, suppression will be less complete but may still be useful. If, however, two surfaces at right angles to each other are both reflecting, this method can completely suppress only one of the reflections at a time. The plane of polarization of such reflections is parallel to the reflecting surface; hence two surfaces at 90° to each other and both at about 35° to the camera axis will produce reflections whose polarization planes are at 90° to each other. Here the best that can be done overall is equal partial suppression of both reflections.

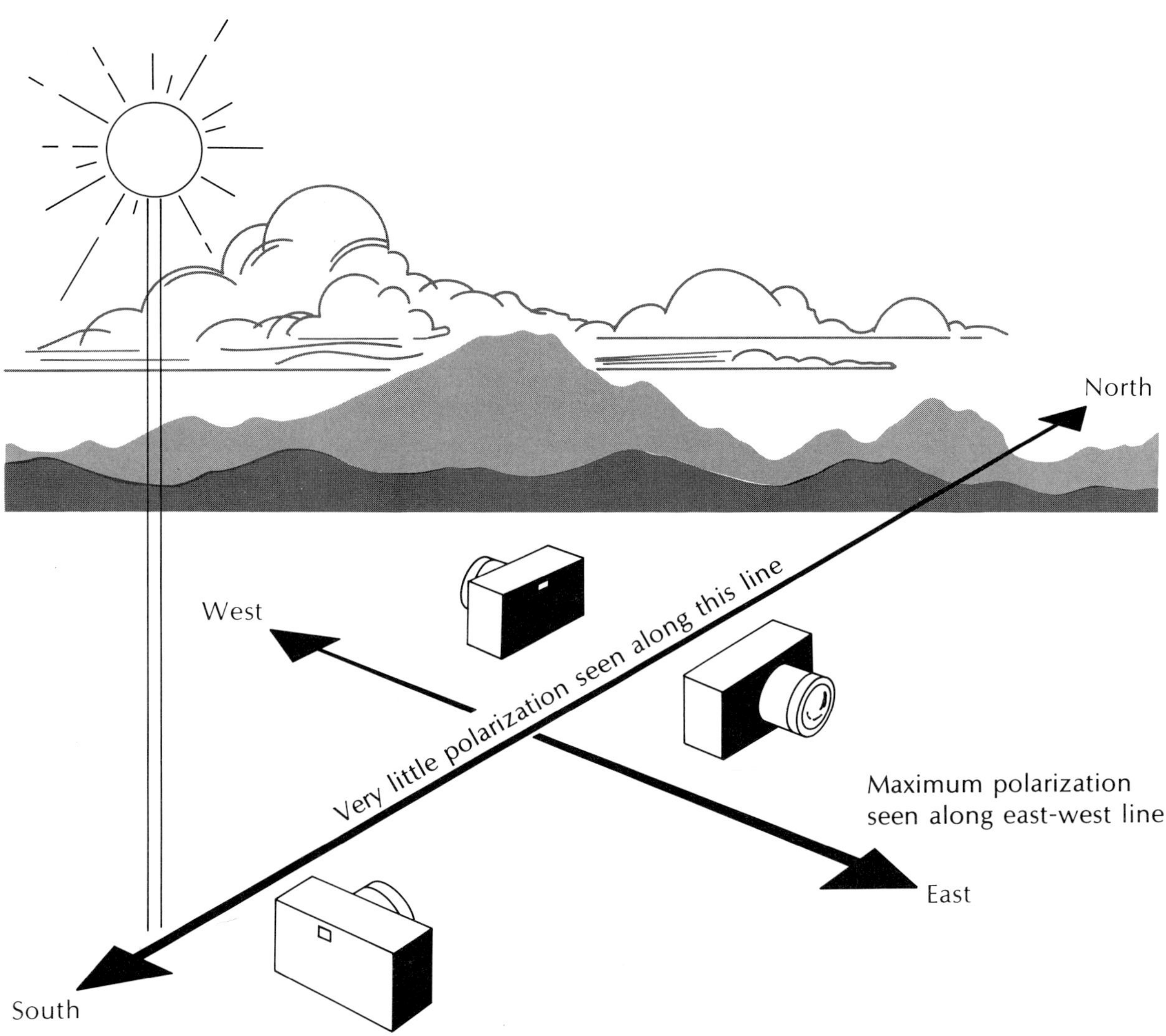

FIGURE 29
Idealization of noon-sky polarization effects. When polarizing filters are used on generally clear days, the effect on sky tones is not equal everywhere. The degree of sky darkening depends upon the relative angles of the sun and the camera. Polarization effects are more noticeable on slightly hazy days than on clear days, because of the increased polarization through particulate scattering.

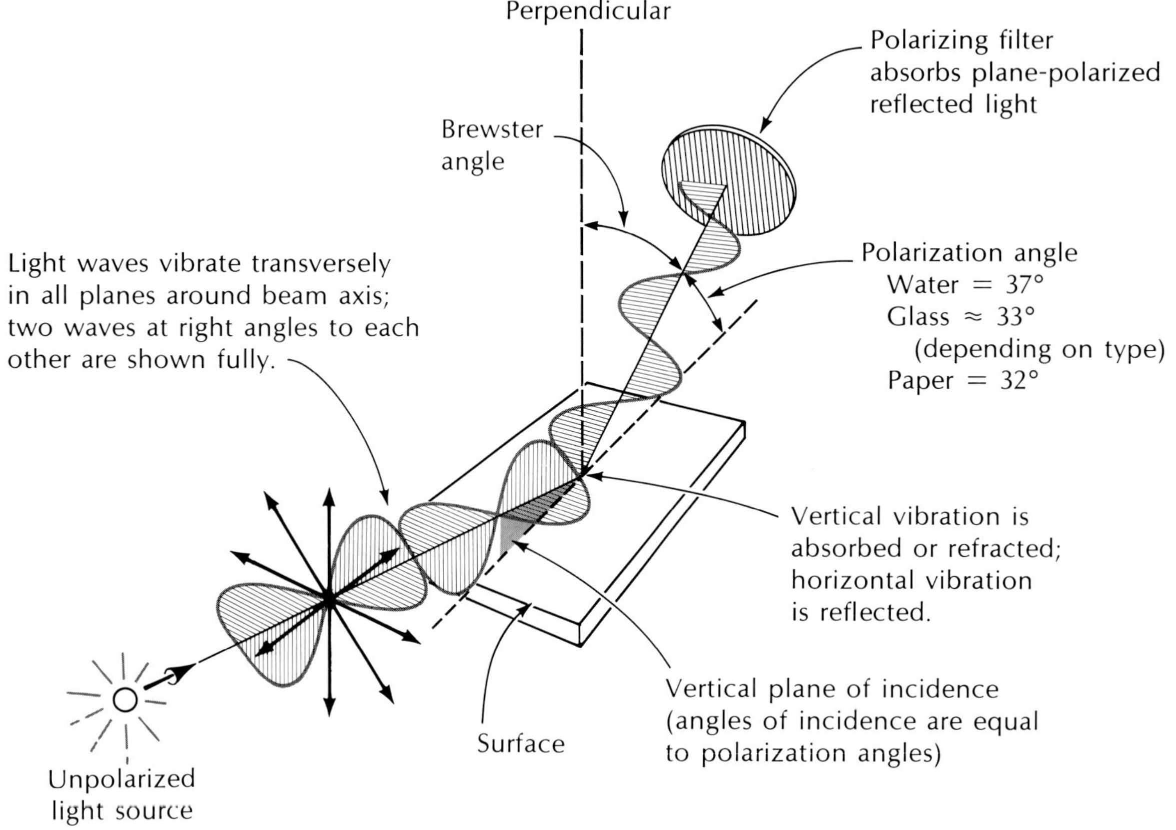

FIGURE 30
Polarization by reflection. The polarization angle is the angle of reflection that gives the maximum polarization; the complement of this angle is called the Brewster angle. The control of surface reflections by the use of polarizing filters requires an understanding of how such reflections arise. Two reflecting surfaces at an angle to each other will show opposite effects when seen through the filter; as one reflection is diminished by rotating the filter, the other increases in visibility.

If complete suppression of all reflections is desired, the most practical approach is to use artificial light. Place a polarizing sheet before each light source, and put a polarizing filter on the lens of the camera. While observing through the lens filter (itself not to be rotated), have each lamp polarizer rotated until the reflections disappear. Adjust each polarizer separately, then turn off that lamp while doing the next. Only when all the lamp polarizers are correctly positioned with respect to the lens filter will the effect be complete. Then all the lights can be turned on together, the exposure calculated (see the section on filter factors at the end of this chapter), and the picture taken. In such a setup all the light striking the subject is already polarized, so the camera angle is immaterial.

In controlling reflections you must remember that metallic surfaces, owing to a fundamental difference in their physical properties, do not produce reflections that are polarized. However, it is often forgotten that, just as they do not produce polarization, they do not remove it either. That is, a beam of light that is already plane-polarized when it strikes a metallic surface will still be plane-polarized when it is reflected. You can verify this by observing the reflection of the sky from a chromed auto bumper, rotating a polarizing filter as you look through it. Thus, you can control reflections from a metallic surface if the light striking it is already polarized, either naturally or by your own actions.

The third use of polarizing filters is to take advantage of the effects of polarized light on certain types of animal, mineral, and vegetable structures. This is a normal procedure with mounted microscope slides viewed by transmitted light, but polarization effects in plastic materials or other larger specimens can also be photographed by similar means. Briefly, the subject is placed between two polarizing filters; different effects are achieved by rotating one of the filters or by rotating the subject between them.

When transmitted light is passed through polarizers in this manner, the light passage is unrestricted (except, of course, for the normal absorption of all waves not at the polarization angle), as long as the polarizing axes of the two filters are parallel. However, when one filter is rotated with respect to the other, the light is gradually diminished until, at 90° rotation, very little light is passed at all. Reverting to our previous analogy with the picket fence, the effect is as though there were two layers of fence. If one layer is rotated with respect to the other, the wave action along the rope "beam axis" will be gradually restricted until, at 90° rotation, no waves can pass through the second fence at all. Thus, in filtering, the beam is said to be extinct, and no significant amount of light gets through the second filter. However, certain types of substances (called *anisotropic* substances) affect the polarized beam passed by the first filter in such a way that some light does actually pass through the second filter, causing great visual changes in the image at the film plane. And, if the subject is rotated between the two filters at any stage, yet other visual effects take place. Polarization in microscopy will be discussed further in Chapter 9 (see Figure 42 there). (For more detailed coverage of the physics of light in general and polarization in particular, see the books by Strong, 1958, and Shurcliff and Ballard, 1964.)

Neutral-Density Filters

Little discussion of neutral-density filters is needed here. As noted earlier, the function of this type of filter is solely to reduce light intensities. In the kinds of work discussed here, light intensities more often need increasing. But if these filters are used, they should be placed at the light source rather than at the lens. The risk of impairing the image sharpness is too great otherwise, since many neutral-density filters are not designed to be used at the lens.

Probably the primary use of neutral-density filters in scientific photography is in the practice of film-speed equalization. In photographing patients in hospitals it is often desirable to make

TABLE 3
Color filters for black-and-white films.

COLOR	WRATTEN NUMBER	LETTER EQUIVALENT[a]	FILTER FACTOR[b]			
			PAN FILM		ORTHO FILM	
			DAYLIGHT	TUNGSTEN	DAYLIGHT	TUNGSTEN
Deep red	29	F	10	8	—[c]	—
Medium red	25	A	8	5	—[c]	—
Red-orange	23A	—	6	3	—[c]	—
Orange	22	E	4	2.5	—[c]	—
Light yellow	6	K-1	1.5	1.5	2	1.5
Medium yellow	8	K-2	2	1.5	2.5	2
Deep yellow	12	—	2	1.5	3	2.5
Very deep yellow	15	G	2.5	1.5	5	3
Yellow-green	11	X-1	4	4	—[d]	—
Medium green	13	X-2	5	4	—[d]	—
Deep green	58	B	6	6	8	5
Light blue	80B[e]	—	3	3	1.5	1.5
Light blue	38	—	4	4	1.2	1.2
Deep blue	47	C-5	6	12	3	4
Blue-green (ortho)	44A	—	10	10	—[d]	—

[a]Although the Kodak Wratten numbering system is approaching industry-wide acceptance as the standard nomenclature, some people may prefer to use the older letter designations, so they are provided where they exist.

[b]Derived from standard tables in most cases—otherwise the result of my own tests with individual filters.

[c]Filter factors are not given for red filters because orthochromatic films are insensitive to red light; the use of red filters will result in little or no exposure.

[d]No factors are given here because ortho films are insensitive to the colors that these filters absorb; hence these filters serve no purpose here.

[e]This is a color-conversion filter designed for color film use, but I like to put it to double service as a very useful pale color filter for black-and-white work.

a series of photographs that are identical except for the wavelengths being recorded. Thus, you may wish to photograph a skin ailment by ultraviolet radiation, by one or more wavelengths of visible light, and by infrared radiation. This can be done by varying the type of film and the filters used. Clearly, it is usually best to work very rapidly in patient photography, but this introduces the risk of error. The best way of preventing exposure error is to make all photographs with the same lens aperture and shutter speed, which requires that the film speeds be the same. Film speeds can be effectively equalized through the selective use of neutral-density filters, in conjunction with color filters or other filters as needed.

Some studio photographers make extensive use of film-speed equalization when using Polaroid Land films to determine the lighting arrangements and correct exposure for complex pictures that will be finally photographed on conventional films; the speed equivalence is again used to avoid error. (A complete description of the technique of film-speed equalization is given in Eisendrath's article, "Polaroid Land 4," 1972.)

FILTER FACTORS

Filters of all types act by removing some of the incident light. It is therefore obvious that if filters are used exposures must be increased to compensate for the loss of light. The amount of increase needed varies with the color and density of the filter. A set of tables for color filters, exposure increases, polarizing filter materials, and neutral-density filters is given here as Tables 3, 4, 5, and 6.

Standard tables of filter factors are available from filter manufacturers. Some such information is also provided on the data sheet packed with each package of film. It should be emphasized that the exposure increases to compensate for the light loss in filtering are mandatory if underexposure of films is to be avoided. Such underexposure can be very great: some filters require that the exposure be increased to as much as ten times the normal calculated exposure time.

Filter recommendations for color films will be given later, in Chapter 11. No information on filtering as it applies to ultraviolet and infrared radiation will be supplied in this book, because the subject is so well covered elsewhere in easily available sources (see Kodak publications M-27 and M-28, which are standard works on these subjects; for field applications, see Blaker, *Field Photography,* 1976).

TABLE 4
Exposure increases for common filter factors.

FILTER FACTOR	NUMBER OF STOPS EXPOSURE INCREASE[a]	FILTER FACTOR	NUMBER OF STOPS EXPOSURE INCREASE
1.2	1/3	6	2 2/3
1.5	2/3	8	3
2	1	10	3 1/3
2.5	1 1/3	12	3 2/3
3	1 2/3	16	4
4	2	20	4 1/3
5	2 1/3		

[a]Adjustments of less than a full stop should be made by approximating positions between *f*-number markings. Not all camera shutters will work correctly if set between speed markings.

TABLE 5
Exposure information for polarizing filter materials.[a]

MATERIAL	MAXIMUM LIGHT TRANSMISSION, PERCENT		FILTER FACTOR[b]		NUMBER OF STOPS EXPOSURE INCREASE	
	SINGLY	PAIRED[c]	SINGLY	PAIRED	SINGLY	PAIRED
Photographic filters[d]						
Polaroid	40	16	2.5	6	1⅓	2⅔
Hoya	25	6.25	4	16	2	4
Polaroid sheet						
HN-22	22	5	4.5	20	2¼	4⅓
HN-32	32	10	3	10	1⅔	3⅓
HN-38	38	14	2.5	8	1⅓	3

[a]Polarizing filters and sheet stock are available, in a variety of densities, from various sources.
[b]Approximate figures, suitable for photographic exposure purposes.
[c]Used, as discussed on page 76, for reflection control; or, with polarizing axes parallel, as described on page 77, for maximum light transmission (if the axes are not parallel, the light transmission must be measured). It is assumed that paired filters are identical.
[d]Most, but not all, photographic filters approximate one of these two sets of figures. See the manufacturer's data sheet.

TABLE 6
Exposure information for common neutral-density filters.

DENSITY	PERCENT TRANSMISSION	FILTER FACTOR[a]	NUMBER OF STOPS EXPOSURE INCREASE[a]
0.15	75	1.5	½
0.3	50	2	1
0.5	32	3	1½
0.6	25	4	2
0.7	20	5	2½
0.9	13	8	3
1.2	6.3	16	4

[a]Approximate figures, suitable for photographic exposure purposes.
SOURCE: Compiled from information given in Kodak publication P-114, *Kodak Neutral Density Attenuators,* and from Clauss and Meusel, *Filter Practice,* 1964.

CHAPTER 6

Small-Object Photography

There are many ways of doing photography of small subjects. Some are simple but limited in capabilities, others are versatile but complex, and yet others require exceptionally specialized equipment. The purpose of this chapter is to provide the reader with two methods—one for doing closeup photography and the other covering most of the needs for photomacrography. The methods described provide for versatility of approach, simplicity of technique, and the use of equipment common to general photography.

The closeup technique entails the use of small single lens reflex cameras and features rapid, flexible, high-quality photography of either static or moving subjects at rather low image magnifications. The photomacrographic technique can be done with any of a variety of camera types and sizes, but is most conveniently done with a bellows-type camera of 4 × 5-inch or 5 × 7-inch film size (or their metric equivalents). It features rapid, high-quality photography, at image magnifications on the negative ranging from ×1 up to ×40 or more, of subjects that are either static or confinable within fixed bounds.

Those readers who would like to explore a wider range of techniques in this subject area, especially with reference to field work, are referred to Blaker, *Field Photography,* 1976.

CLOSEUP FLASH PHOTOGRAPHY

Almost every scientific photographer, whether working in the field or in the laboratory, will sooner or later need a good means of photographing moderately small subjects, in the image-magnification range from about one-quarter actual size (×¼) up to several times that size (about ×3 to ×6).

The technique called *closeup flash* is the simplest and most versatile general method known to me. There are other ways of doing essentially similar work, but none is as quickly and easily adapted to changing needs as this one. Basically, it is a two-handed method of operation in which a 35 mm single lens reflex camera, or a larger but still reasonably compact one, is held in the right hand (most cameras are so constructed that left-handed operation is impractical) and a small electronic flash unit is held in the left hand, the two devices being connected only by the flash-synchronization cord. The camera is set for the desired image magnification through the use of automatic-diaphragm extension tubes, and is focused by moving the whole assembly back and forth along the viewing axis. Once set for the desired magnification, the focusing mechanism of a camera cannot be operated without changing the image size. For examples of closeup flash photography, see Plates 10 and 40, and Color Plates I, IIA, and VIIIB. (This method was pioneered by E. S. Ross—see his book, *Insects Close Up,* 1953.)

The best lenses to use are the macro-type lenses, such as those made by Nikon, Canon, and a number of other manufacturers. These give very sharp images with low distortion and a flat image plane. They have built-in extended focusing ranges, and their apertures usually close down to about *f*/32, for greater than normal depth of field. Although their widest apertures are not as fast as those of most lenses of similar focal length, this is unimportant in most closeup work. And this very feature tends to increase the overall quality of the lens in other respects.

Versatility and speed of operation are fostered by not using a tripod and by not fastening the flash unit to the camera. The camera is kept safe from dropping by using a neckstrap at all times. The extremely short flash duration provides the necessary image sharpness, tending to stop the motion of both subject and camera. Since the flash unit is placed very close to the subject, the light available will be very bright—a consequence of the inverse-square law. Thus, a small lens aperture can be used to obtain maximum depth of field. Since the camera is hand-held, you can follow a moving subject (e.g., a walking insect or a flower waving in the breeze) and change the camera angle quickly at will. The unattached flash unit enables you to change the lighting angle instantaneously, to suit changing subject orientations. Best of all, the technique can be learned quickly and easily, and can be applied to almost any small subject, whether in the field, in the laboratory, or even in the operating room.

The following sections will break down the basic technique into steps to be followed in sequence. This is followed by a brief summary of the procedures and some suggestions for increasing the image magnification.

Magnification

In this method of closeup photography, image magnification is obtained by bringing the lens closer to the subject than is usual. Most normal lenses can focus as close as about 2 to 3 feet

(0.5 to 1 meter). Here we will go down to 2 to 3 inches (50 to 75 mm). The ordinary focusing range built into the lens mount is augmented by using metal extension tubes to extend the lens further from the camera body than is usual (with macro-type lenses, part or all of this extra extension is built into the lens mount). The amount of extension used, in conjunction with the focal length of the lens, determines the image magnification attained. Bellows extensions can also be used to gain magnification, but they tend to make the assembly front-heavy and their construction usually prevents the necessary one-handed use of the camera.

The extension tubes that are used, whether a part of the macro lens assembly or simply a separate set of varying lengths of tubes, must have an internal linkage that retains the automatic operation of the lens diaphragm. An auto-diaphragm, a fixture in most 35 mm camera lenses currently sold, allows you to focus with the lens aperture wide open, thus giving plenty of light to focus by and increasing the focusing accuracy, while providing for instant automatic closing to a pre-selected aperture setting at the moment of exposure—all this without requiring a third hand to perform the adjustment. Automatic tubes are essential if you are to work without an assistant. Although they are somewhat more expensive than simple "manual" tubes, the extra expense is well worthwhile.

If your equipment is not provided with an *accurate* table of setups for producing known image magnifications, you should prepare one yourself. In scientific work it is most practical to work at exactly known magnifications, each a multiple of the others, and only a few setups are needed. I recommend working out basic setups for $\times\frac{1}{4}$, $\times\frac{1}{2}$, $\times\frac{3}{4}$, and $\times 1$. The easiest method is to first determine the exact dimensions of the viewing screen of the camera (it is nominally 24 $\times$ 36 mm—about 1 $\times$ $1\frac{1}{2}$ inches—but may be a little less in some models). Then you focus the camera on a ruler while changing the focusing mechanism and/or the lengths of extension tubes used, in order to obtain the desired image magnifications. If, for example, your screen is 35 mm long, an image magnification of $\times\frac{1}{4}$ will allow you to see just 140 mm of ruler over its length. At $\times\frac{1}{2}$ you will see 70 mm, and at $\times 1$, of course, you will see exactly 35 mm. Upon working out the focusing setting and extension-tube combinations needed, record these facts in tabular form, for future reference.

Once you make up a table of magnifications as described above, it is simplicity itself to decide what magnification to use in a given situation. Just measure, or closely estimate, the size of the subject, and then refer to the table to get the necessary setup information.

Lens Aperture

There are two aspects to the choice of the lens aperture to use in closeup flash photography: depth of field and effective aperture.

Depth of field is the degree of overall sharpness of focus apparent in a picture. When you focus the lens of a camera, the sharply focused image represents only a single plane through the subject, called the *principal plane of focus.* This is readily apparent when you look at the image formed by a fast lens set at a wide aperture. However, when you close down the lens aperture (i.e., use a higher *f*-number) the depth of field increases. This effect is shown, for a single point of light in an image, in Figure 31. Because of spherical aberration, no lens can focus the light from a single subject point to an infinitely small image point; instead, it reproduces the subject point as a circle of finite size,

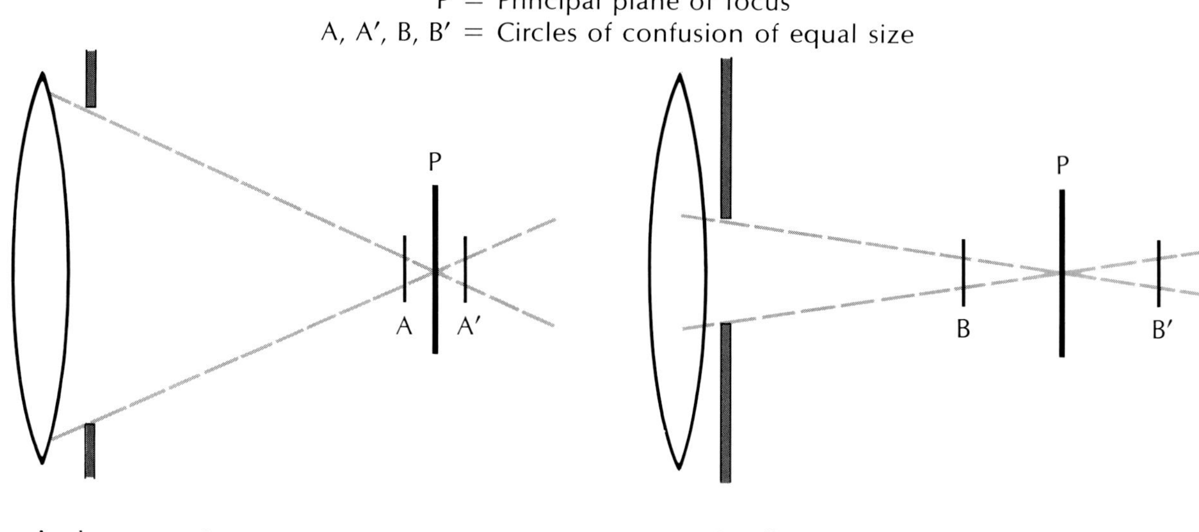

FIGURE 31
Depth of field is the amount of fore-and-aft subject matter seen in the image as acceptably sharp around a given plane of focus; it depends on the lens aperture and the image magnification. The cone of rays recording a single subject point is shown in these diagrams.

A Large-aperture effect: the depth of field is slight.
B Small-aperture effect: the depth of field is increased.

but with an indefinite boundary. This blurred circular image, the size of which is the primary determinant of the image resolution, is called the *circle of confusion* (or the circle of least confusion).

The depth of field in a picture is related primarily to two factors: the image magnification and the *f*-number. In most scientific closeup photography, the depth of field should be as great as possible in order to record as much information as possible. So, unless you are deliberately trying to isolate a certain subject plane through the use of wide apertures, the choice here is easy. You just use the smallest *f*-setting available on your lens mount. Any slight loss of image sharpness through the effects of diffraction (which is discussed in greater detail in the later section on photomacrography) is more than made up for by the greater overall pictorial detail.

In order to go further it is necessary to define the terms relating to lens apertures. In photographic parlance, the terms lens aperture, diaphragm opening, relative aperture, and *f*-number all pertain to the same basic function. The focal length of a lens (assuming the optical ideal of the "thin" lens—one having no thickness) is the distance from the center of the lens to the image plane when the lens is focused on a subject at "infinite" distance (called *infinity*). The lens aperture is the usable transparent opening through a lens; it is usually set by an adjustable iris diaphragm—the diaphragm opening. The *f*-number, or relative aperture, of a given lens opening is determined by dividing the focal length of the lens by the diameter of that opening, and is one of the basic considerations in the calculation of correct photographic exposure. For example, if a lens has a focal length of 50 mm and its widest aperture has a diameter of 25 mm, it is said to be an *f*/2 lens, since lenses are always specified in terms of their widest apertures. For depth-of-field purposes this lens might be closed down to an aperture whose diameter was only 3.1 mm. This would then be described as an aperture of *f*/16, since 50/3.1= 16. This term is a convenient way of relating the aperture size to its exposure effects.

When doing closeup photography, exposure calculation is complicated by the fact that focusing on a subject closer than infinity (functionally, to 50 feet or less) requires moving the lens away from the image plane, and thus away from the film. This movement is slight, and therefore not important in exposure calculation, within the normal range of focus of most camera lenses. At very short camera-to-subject distances, however, the amount of lens extension required is substantially greater, and necessitates an application of the inverse-square law for calculation of the correct exposure. Almost always in such closer focusing (there are a very few lenses that feature coupled focusing and diaphragm mechanisms), when you do focus closer the diameter of the lens aperture remains unchanged while the lens-to-film distance is increased. The *f*-number marked on the lens mount is a measure of the aperture *relative* to that distance when the lens is focused at infinity. Thus, when the relative aperture is changed by a gross change in focus, the corrected calculation (the *new* lens-to-film distance divided by the diameter of the opening) is called the *effective aperture;* one must know this number in order to calculate the correct exposure in closeup photography and in photomacrography. Although we will provide a formula (Formula 4) for this purpose in the later section on photomacrography, it will be sufficient for our present discussion of closeup photography simply to use a short table for determining the effective aperture. This is given here as Table 7.

It is essential to understand that the aperture itself has not changed in size, but is simply *relatively* smaller because the lens-to-film distance is longer. And the effective aperture is not engraved on the lens mount. The effective aperture is the figure that *is* so engraved, corrected for the amount of lens extension that is being used.

With modern cameras equipped with through-the-lens metering systems it is not

TABLE 7
Effective apertures for closeup photography.

IMAGE MAGNIFICATION	EFFECTIVE APERTURE IS *SMALLER* THAN THE MARKED APERTURE BY:	EFFECTIVE APERTURE AT A MARKED APERTURE OF:		
		f/16	*f*/22	*f*/32
×¼	½ stop	*f*/20	*f*/27	*f*/40
×½	1 stop	*f*/22	*f*/32	*f*/45
×¾	1½ stops	*f*/27	*f*/38	*f*/56
×1	2 stops	*f*/32	*f*/45	*f*/64

necessary to know any of this in order to do closeup photography by existing light, as long as the lens and meter are properly coupled and the manufacturer's instructions are followed. However, in flash photography the metering system is bypassed and thus rendered irrelevant, in return for stopping motion and gaining depth of field. You must, then, make use of the effective aperture to obtain the correct closeup flash exposure.

Flash-to-Subject Distance

Having found the effective aperture, we must now find the correct flash-to-subject distance. This is done by reversing the standard flash-exposure formula (Formula 1) shown on page 10, with "effective aperture" substituted for "*f*-number." The new formula is shown here as Formula 2. The distance, in feet, between the flash unit and the subject is found by dividing the guide number by the effective aperture. (The actual distance will be not more than several feet; with most small flash units, it will be as little as a few tenths of a foot.) Note the additional change in Formula 2, related to the guide number of the flash unit. Recall that you can use the dial calculator on a flash unit to determine an unknown guide number (one for a film that is not so rated in the instruction booklet), by setting the dial to the ASA film speed and then multiplying the *f*-number found opposite the 10-foot mark by 10. This guide number would be correct if the flash unit were to be used at the normal 4-to-15-foot distances. But here it will not be correct.

For the best picture quality you must use relatively slow films, which have correspondingly low guide numbers. Couple this with effective apertures based upon very small lens apertures and you will get flash distances well shorter than normal. And at very short distances most flash units (and virtually all small ones) lose light efficiency because they are being used outside their design parameters. Fortunately, this problem is easily solved. Over the years I and my students have tested many small electronic flash units and have found that in nearly all of them the efficiency of the reflector/condenser system is approximately halved when flash distances are less than 1 foot. So all you do is *divide the normal guide number by 2* in order to get a usable effective guide number. There is a distinct advantage in using small flash units for closeup flash. The very short flash distances tend to place the flash unit at about the same distance from the subject as the camera. If you use a large, powerful unit you are likely to find yourself really straining—stretching one arm behind you to hold the flash unit far enough from the subject to avoid a massive overexposure.

FORMULA 2
Closeup flash-to-subject-distance formula.

$$\text{Flash-to-subject distance (feet)} = \frac{\text{guide number (effective)}}{\text{effective aperture}}$$

$$D = \frac{GN_{\text{eff}}}{EA}$$

As an illustrative example of the foregoing material, let us assume that we are going to make a picture at an image magnification of ×1, using a lens with a minimum aperture of *f*/22, a film rated at ASA 25, and a flash unit having a normal guide number of 32 for that film. Table 7 tells us that at ×1 the effective aperture will be *f*/45. If we halve the guide number we obtain an effective guide number, for closeup purposes, of 16. Dividing that by the effective aperture of *f*/45, we get a flash distance of 0.35 foot, or 4.2 inches. We find that using a flash distance of about 4 inches will yield a correct exposure.

With static subjects the distance can be measured, but with moving insects and the like, you will have to estimate it. Many people new to this technique have found it useful to cut a stick to the length of the desired flash distance, and then use it solely as a visual reference for help in estimating the distance (you just place it—or perhaps the ruler itself—where you can easily see it while working).

Synchronization

If the timing of the flash does not coincide with the opening of the shutter, the picture will be either incomplete or nonexistent. Any kind of shutter can give flash-synchronization problems, but the focal-plane shutters common in small single lens reflex cameras have special problems that must be taken into account. Most such shutters consist of a moving curtain. The opening of the shutter is a complex action in which a slit in the curtain moves across the front of the film, the width of the slit being the major factor in determining the "speed" of the shutter. However, the use of electronic flash, with its very short flash duration, requires that the entire film be uncovered to receive light, all at the same instant. With such curtain-type shutters the slit is fully open only at relatively slow shutter speeds, usually not faster than 1/60 second. A few focal-plane shutters have a rectangular pattern of moving leaves, and most of these have a maximum electronic-flash synch speed of 1/125 second. With either kind, a faster speed results in only part of a picture, on that part of the film that is behind the opening.

To assure proper flash synchronization, read the instruction booklet for your camera. Note two basic points: (1) there will be some sort of setting device, or perhaps a separate connector point for the flash-synch cord, marked "X," which serves to set the correct time delay for electronic flash (connectors for disposable flashbulbs will be variously marked "M," "FP," or something else, but "X" always refers to electronic flash), and (2) there is the matter of which shutter speed to use.

With electronic flash, the opening and closing of the shutter serves simply to limit the effect of ambient light upon the film, with the flash duration actually determining the exposure time (releasing the shutter, of course, also closes a contact that fires the flash). It is best to use the highest shutter speed at which a full exposure can be obtained, in order to minimize the possibility of "ghost" images from ambient light.

Be sure that the flash-synchronization cord has a good electrical contact. If the cord is not wired directly into the flash unit (I prefer detachable cords, for easy replacement), I make sure that it fits tightly into its socket and then tape it in place so that it can't readily come loose or get lost. Most 35 mm camera flash-synch connectors are of the "PC" type. The end of the coaxial synch cord has a split metal sheath that fits into the socket on the camera body. To ensure a tight fit and good electrical contact, I make it a practice to slightly crimp this end sheath on any new cord, and I periodically check to make sure that it is not working itself loose.

The only problem likely to arise then is an occasional minor buildup of corrosion in the connector points. This is countered by twisting the connector several times as you put it in, to scrub the internal surfaces clean. After all this, if the ready light of the flash unit glows but there is no flash when the shutter is released, the first place to look for a fault is in the cord itself. You can check by disconnecting the cord from the flash unit and then shorting the contact on the flash unit with a pencil tip or any metal object. If the flash fires then, you probably have a broken wire in the synch cord. I always keep one or more spare cords about the premises or in my camera bag.

Color Correction

A good proportion of photographs made by the closeup flash technique will require color slide films. One of the anomalies you might notice in color flash photography is that, although virtually all electronic flash units are described by their manufacturers as having "daylight" color qualities, the film manufacturers all recommend that for critical color photography a color filter be used with electronic flash.

The truth is that many such flash units need it. An unfiltered electronic flash unit emits light that is somewhat too blue to match the balance of daylight-type color films (other types of color film are *very* far off the needed balance, and should not be used here). It is increasingly common (but far from universal) for manufacturers to build some form of yellow filtering into their units, either by coloring the tube envelope itself or by providing a built-in yellow filter capping the reflector. It is safe to say that, if the flash tube or its transparent cover plate are not definitely yellow, the unit will need corrective filtering to match it to the color qualities of daylight-type color films. This is, of course, irrelevant in black-and-white photography.

Manufacturers of color films usually recommend the use of a Wratten 81A or 81B straw-colored filter, or the equivalent in other filtering systems. My own tests show that this filtering is often not sufficiently yellow if adjoining film frames are to be made of the same subject, one by actual sunlight and the next by electronic flash. These tests show that a very good correction is achieved with a CC20Y Color-Correction filter. It is usually most convenient to simply Scotch-tape a piece cut from a suitable gelatin filter directly over the flash head. This lasts indefinitely. It is quite simple to test whether all this applies to your own flash equipment.

Using a filter applied to the flash unit will reduce the effective guide number, since all filters act by removing some light. (Remember that, once permanently filtered, a flash unit will have a reduced guide number for *any* film used—color *or* black-and-white.) Each of the filters specified above will require an exposure increase of one-third stop. Going back to the example given on page 87, the corrected guide number there was 16. If you add a correction for the filter, the effective guide number would be further reduced to about 13, and the corrected flash distance would be 0.28 foot, or 3.4 inches. Such very short flash distances are quite practical.

Summary of Procedure

Assuming that you have absorbed the foregoing material, it will be useful to have a brief summary of the procedure to be followed in doing closeup flash photography, as a reminder:

1. Determine the desired image magnification, either by measurement or by estimation, and set the camera to achieve it.
2. Maximize the depth of field by setting the lens diaphragm to its smallest opening. (If selective focus is wanted, on the other hand, find the correct aperture by observing the image on the camera's viewing screen.)
3. Determine the effective aperture (see Table 7).
4. Calculate the correct flash-to-subject distance, using Formula 2.
5. Choose the best camera angle, and from that the required lighting angle (depending upon what features of the subject you wish to emphasize—a good rule is to hold the flash unit near the lens axis and above its center, with more exact positioning according to need).
6. Hold the flash unit (connected to the camera only by the synch cord) in your left hand, at the correct distance and angle. Do not move it while attending to step 7.
7. Hold the camera in your right hand; focus and compose the image by moving the camera as a whole.
8. Expose by *squeezing* the shutter release while slowly moving the camera toward the subject: with the slack taken up, continue squeezing to release the shutter just as the intended point of prime focus becomes sharp.

Do not try to come to a focus and then hold the camera still while exposing. Your hand will become unsteady and will introduce lateral movement that can destroy the image sharpness as well as the accuracy of the composition. Instead, expose while still moving the camera in. If you miss the timing, retreat and try again. This minor longitudinal movement will be very slight during the actual exposure, and it will tend to prevent the more destructive lateral movement. Do not jerk the shutter release—just apply slight additional pressure after all the slack is taken up.

The most common error made by beginners is a tendency to move the flash unit forward and/or outward while focusing the camera. This will cause grossly inaccurate exposures. A little practice while being observed by an associate will rapidly correct any such tendency.

Increasing the Magnification

There are many subjects for which the magnification range described earlier in this section is appropriate. However, after an initial period of fascinated use of the technique, there comes the realization that there are many things of interest that could be shown better if only the image magnification were a little greater.

There are various ways of getting this greater image size. The most obvious one is simply to use more extension tubes, but doing so introduces serious problems of camera balance and diaphragm linkage, if the gain in size is to amount to much. In addition, you will find that, as the magnification increases, the lens-to-subject distance quickly decreases to the point where it is difficult to achieve a good lighting angle. And the chance of scaring living subject matter through this close approach also increases. There is a better solution: the *tele-converter.*

A tele-converter is a piece of tubing containing a multi-element lens of negative power (a lens that, by itself, shows a reduced image if you look through it). Placed between a lens and a camera body, it expands the cone of rays that make up the image, and the image becomes larger. That it does this without changing the distance between the front of the prime lens and the subject is quite important in closeup work. Tele-converters to fit most small single lens reflex cameras are available and are advertised for use in the telephotography of distant subjects. However, they are at least equally useful in closeup work because they will enlarge the image produced by *any* camera lens that is in front. Examples of tele-converter closeups are shown in Plate 40A and in Color Plate IIA.

Let us say that you have set up your camera to do photography at a magnification of ×1 and then find that the subject matter would be shown better if the image were at ×2 or more. You just remove the whole lens/extension-tube assembly and insert one or more tele-converters between it and the camera body. The image magnification will then be increased by the power of the converter. Thus, a 2× converter used behind a basic ×1 lens setup will produce an image at ×2. A 3× converter will give ×3, and a combination of a 2× and a 3× converter, stacked, will give ×6. Surprisingly, the image quality will be entirely satisfactory if the prime lens is of good quality, even for substantial subsequent enlargement in printing or for projecting on a screen as a slide. The basic factor controlling the image sharpness is the quality of that prime lens, as virtually no loss is attributable to the converter itself, beyond the effects due to its expansion of the cone of rays.

Motion control does become important, because the effects of both camera and subject movement are increased to the same degree as the magnification. Control is aided by using a flash unit of shorter than normal flash duration (for this purpose I use a unit with a flash duration of $1/_{3000}$ second instead of the usual $1/_{1000}$ second; these are readily available at low cost). It also helps to use one or more fingers of the hand that holds the flash unit to steady the front of the lens mount.

Since the image size is increased by the expansion of the cone of rays inside the camera, there is a loss of light energy in using the tele-converter. Whenever a given cone of light is expanded so as to cover a larger area, the light intensity falls off, by the inverse-square law. Therefore, an exposure compensation is needed. It amounts to a number of stops equal to the power of the converter. You must increase the exposure by two stops with a 2× converter, by three stops with a 3× converter, and by five stops when a 2× is combined with a 3×. (Note that when converters are stacked the magnification factor is the *product* of their powers, but the number of additional stops of exposure is the *sum* of their powers.)

There is a choice of methods for making this exposure correction in closeup flash photography. You can simply open the prime-lens aperture the required number of stops, you can decrease the flash-to-subject distance, or you can combine the two. I recommend that when using a 2× tele-converter you just cut the flash distance in half, thereby achieving the necessary two-stop correction via the inverse-square law. With a 3× converter I usually halve the flash distance and then open the diaphragm one stop, thus getting an aggregate of three stops correction. And with 2× and 3× converters stacked, it is usually a good compromise to cut the flash distance to one-third normal and then open up two stops, to get the needed five stops.

You might ask why the diaphragm should be opened at all, since as the magnification increases, the depth of field decreases, and I have previously recommended going for all the depth you can get in closeups. When image magnification is increased substantially beyond ×1, the use of small lens openings introduces diffraction effects owing to the reduction of the relative aperture (as will be further noted in the section on photomacrography). The exposure increase required when using tele-converters is a consequence of this relative-aperture reduction. If your lens is set at *f*/22 and thus has an effective aperture of *f*/45 at ×1, the new relative aperture will be *f*/90 when you add a 2× converter, *f*/128 with a 3× converter, or *f*/256 if you stack the two. It is therefore a good idea to get some of the needed exposure correction by opening up the prime-lens aperture. Doing this also avoids having to shorten the flash distance to a ridiculous extent (though distances as short as one inch are practical).

Aside from the diffraction effects, which occur at these very tiny relative apertures no matter what the system, the use of tele-converters has remarkably little adverse effect upon the quality of the image achieved in closeup use. (Even stacking the converters works well, though I do not recommend it when using them for telephoto effects.) This is because nearly all high-quality prime lenses, especially the macro-type lenses that are commonly used for 35 mm closeup photography, can resolve more image detail than the films in general use are capable of recording. And so the loss of resolution resulting from the expansion of the cone of rays (almost all the loss there is) is offset by the new detail that is brought above the threshold of the film's resolution ability. You can demonstrate this yourself quite easily. (For further detail see Blaker, *Field Photography,* 1976, which contains numerous additional references; see also the article by Keeling, 1972.)

PHOTOMACROGRAPHY

Photomacrography can be described as photography at image magnifications greater than actual size that is done without the use of a compound microscope. The preceding section, on increasing the image magnification in closeup photography, dealt with a form of photomacrography. In this section I will describe the techniques of conventional photomacrography, with methods that produce magnifications as high as ×40 or more. Pictorial examples are shown in Plates 3D, 5C, 6C, 7A, 26, 28A,C,D, 34, 36, 37, 39B, 43B, 44B,C, 47B,C, and 48, and in Color Plates IIB, III, VI, VII, and VIIIA.

Photographic work at magnifications may at first seem difficult and mysterious. Actually it is neither more nor less so than any other branch of the craft. No matter what the field, things are difficult and mysterious only to those who do not understand them. Doing good work at magnifications does indeed require care and some special equipment and knowledge. The choice of equipment will be left up to the individual worker. Here I will make only general remarks.

Although quite adequate work can often be done using normal camera lenses, a great increase in flatness of field and some increase in resolution can be had by using lenses specially designed for photomacrography. If a normal camera lens must be used, you should determine its optical design. A lens that is optically symmetrical can be used as is, but one that is optically asymmetrical will usually perform better at magnifications if it is reversed so that the element normally turned toward the film faces the subject instead.

A relatively recent development in 35 mm cameras was the introduction of a number of so-called macro and micro lenses (such as Macro-Rokkor and Micro-Nikkor lenses) built for use with specific cameras. (Many such lenses are not correctly named, in the sense of having been designed specifically for photography at high magnifications, but are simply very good general-purpose lenses in extended-range focusing mounts.) These lenses have been fully appraised and discussed in the photographic press, the general conclusion being that they all seem excellent for use in the low to intermediate magnification range—from ×1 to about ×10. (I have seen no discussions of uses for these lenses at higher magnifications, nor have I so used them myself.) Most of them are capable of an unusually long focusing range, built into the lens mount to allow an approach to ×1 without extra extensions such as tubes or bellows. Automatic or semiautomatic diaphragm action and an aid of some sort in calculating exposures in this low magnification range are normally built into the lens housing. These devices are handy indeed in this range, but beyond ×1 they seem to offer little advantage over other types of macro or micro lenses that are adaptable to any camera. If they fit your equipment and needs, by all means use them. They are excellent where the need is to approach the subject to within 2 feet down to several inches, as in following live insects. Their use at these lower magnifications was covered earlier in this chapter.

For the same low to intermediate range of magnifications—from ×1 to around ×10—there is another type of lens that is quite widely used. This is the process lens of 4-to-6-inch focal length. These lenses, the best-known first-class examples being the Goerz Artars, are designed to produce a high degree of color correction, field flatness, and resolution, combined with great freedom from linear and other distortions. They are, however, quite expensive. They normally come in barrel mounts but can be had mounted in shutters. Custom mounting in any available shutter can be done, or shutters can be dispensed with completely if motion need not be stopped, the exposures then being made by using the lens cap or a piece of black card to control the time. Process lenses are designed primarily for graphic arts reproduction work, but their design makes them very useful in photomacrography. One noticeable feature of these lenses is their relative slowness, their widest aperture usually being *f*/9 to *f*/11. This is seldom a disadvantage, since most work to be discussed here requires stopping down beyond that level anyway in order to obtain sufficient depth of field. These lenses require a long bellows for magnification work, because of their relatively long focal lengths.

For work in all ranges from ×1 to about ×80 there was available for many years a series of lenses produced by Zeiss and by Bausch & Lomb called Micro-Tessars. If you can still find them, you will see that they are quite good; they are of shorter focal lengths than the process lenses and therefore require less bellows length for a given magnification. They were barrel-mounted and must be adapted to one's equipment, which is usually a simple matter.

Representative of the best lenses currently available for use in the range from ×1 to ×80 are the Zeiss Luminars, available in five focal lengths: 16, 25, 40, 63, and 100 mm. Other manufacturers, including Leitz and Nikon, make comparable lines of lenses. These lenses produce images that are very sharp, flat in field, and free of distortion, being about equal to process lenses but designed for use at higher magnifications. They are sharpest when the diaphragm is wide open. (No lens is equally sharp at all openings; usually a lens is sharpest when set about three stops smaller than the widest opening.) Excellent sharpness prevails until the very smallest stops are reached, but there is a definite deterioration of the image in the last couple of stops, thereby limiting the enlargement possibilities for any negative made when the lens was fully stopped down. (I do not intend to downgrade these fine lenses by mentioning the above facts, but rather to provide detailed knowledge of a group of lenses that are the most highly recommended for this type of work. No lenses known to me are superior to these.) In addition to being of high optical quality, these lenses are quite reasonable in price and are much faster than process lenses. Although the diaphragm is graduated in a nonstandard fashion—1, 2, 4, 8, . . . instead of *f*/4, 5.6, 8, 11, . . . —the widest opening is *f*/3.5 to *f*/4.5, depending upon the focal length used. The difference between stops is the standard 100%, as the stop-numbering system implies. Luminars and similar lenses are barrel-mounted, having a standard microscope objective thread on the base, except for the 100-mm size, which is larger. They can thus be used on a photographic microscope, with suitable condensers, for translucent subjects. No ocular is required. Adaptation to camera use is simple. A set of such lenses of at least the four shorter focal lengths is highly recommended for anyone intending to do much work at medium to high magnifications.

Very good photomacrography can also be done with cine camera lenses, if they are of fixed focal length (*not* zoom lenses) and if they are used reversed. Use lenses of focal lengths that would be normal for their intended cine film size; wideangle and telephoto lenses are too asymmetrical in design.

Those workers preferring to use 35 mm single lens reflex cameras for this sort of work are encouraged to do so, particularly if the subjects are alive and moving. Where the subject moves little or not at all, however, one would be well advised to use a larger camera, thereby avoiding problems in printing. At high magnifications one is often at the limit of resolution capabilities, especially when stopped down for reasons of depth of field. Enlarging from negatives made under these conditions may well result in mainly empty magnifications (i.e., making the image larger without revealing more information). Viewing, composing, lighting, and exposure calculation may all be found easier with a larger ground glass. As always, equipment choice must be left to the individual worker, who can give due consideration to his own needs. Chapter 7 describes techniques that maximize photographic quality when it is desirable or necessary to use 35 mm equipment.

For work at magnifications, by far the best setup is usually the vertically mounted camera. This allows maximum convenience in handling the subject and the lighting fixtures.

Obtaining Known Magnifications

In photomacrography the first problem is, of course, to determine how much magnification is necessary. While it may seem obvious to say so, this is best determined by measuring the subject and then dividing the size of the desired picture by this figure. Many workers are used to computing magnifications by multiplying the dissecting-scope ocular and objective values. This is fine for visual work, but often leads to inaccuracy in estimating the magnification required for photography.

In photography the image magnification is directly related to the focal length of the lens used. It is calculated by dividing the distance between lens and film by the focal length, and subtracting 1. This is shown in Formula 3. In using this formula, note that the units of measure for *d* and *F* must both be the same, e.g., millimeters or inches. At ×1 (actual size) the lens-to-film distance is two focal lengths; at ×2 it is three focal lengths; at ×10 it is eleven focal lengths, etc.

FORMULA 3
Photomacrographic magnification formula.

$$\text{Magnification} = \frac{\text{lens-to-film distance}}{\text{focal length}} - 1$$

$$m = \frac{d}{F} - 1$$

As an example of the use of Formula 3, if you have a lens with a focal length of 16 mm and you are using a bellows camera with an extension that allows a maximum lens-to-film distance of 176 mm, the maximum magnification that can be obtained is ×10 (176/16 = 11; subtract 1 and the image magnification is ×10).

Formula 3 will suffice for rough work. The position of the film is known, of course, and one assumes that the diaphragm ring is at the center of the lens and that the lens center is the place to measure from. Unfortunately, this is not always true. Many lenses are optically asymmetrical, and many diaphragms are not located exactly centrally. Where a particular magnification is not needed precisely but the final dimensions must be known, the above calculations can be used and the picture made; then a good scale or scale micrometer is either photographed or measured on the ground glass under identical conditions and the exact magnification thereby determined directly.

Exact precalculation of the magnification is necessary wherever one wishes to render a given subject at a given final image size. This is best done by putting a scale in the subject position and then adjusting the lens-to-film distance until measurement, with another scale, of the ground-glass image yields the correct magnification. With small cameras—including reflexes—where there is no ground glass or it is not accessible for direct measurement, the best method is to open the camera back and place a small piece of fine ground glass in the film position, *ground side toward the lens.* And if the negative is subsequently enlarged, the magnification must be recalculated by multiplying the camera-set magnification by the enlargement factor.

If one does much work of this sort, it is a great time saver to calibrate the camera. Two arbitrary points on the camera are chosen, one at the front and one at the back. Then the camera is set up serially throughout the entire range of magnifications to be used, and measurements between the two points are made and recorded at each magnification. A chart can then be made up, indicating the exact measurement between the points for any desired magnification. This must be done separately for each lens to be used, of course. It may be found convenient to fasten a steel tape to one end of the camera and simply draw it out each time to a single chosen point at the other end of the camera.

Principal Plane of Focus

When a lens is focused on a subject, only a single plane through that subject is truly in focus, as noted earlier. (This effect is especially noticeable when working at magnifications.) This plane is called the *principal plane of focus.*

A point worth noting here is that, with three-dimensional objects, the magnification will be exact only at the principal plane of focus. If the focus is at the top of the subject, the edge-to-edge distance in the picture will be different than if the focus is at the center or bottom. Where overall dimensions are important—that is, if measurements of overall size are to be made directly from the final print—the principal plane of focus must be at the widest part of the subject (see Figure 32).

Preserving Magnification while Adjusting

Once an exact magnification has been calculated and set up, it must be preserved while focusing up and down. If the lens or camera back is moved to correct the focus, the magnification will change, so focusing must be done either by moving the camera as a whole or by moving the subject. This should be taken into account with any photomacrographic setup that is to be used much. Moving the subject can be done by placing it on a lab jack, a square-platform scissors-type jack designed for this type of manipulation. But any significant vertical movement will require readjustment of the lighting.

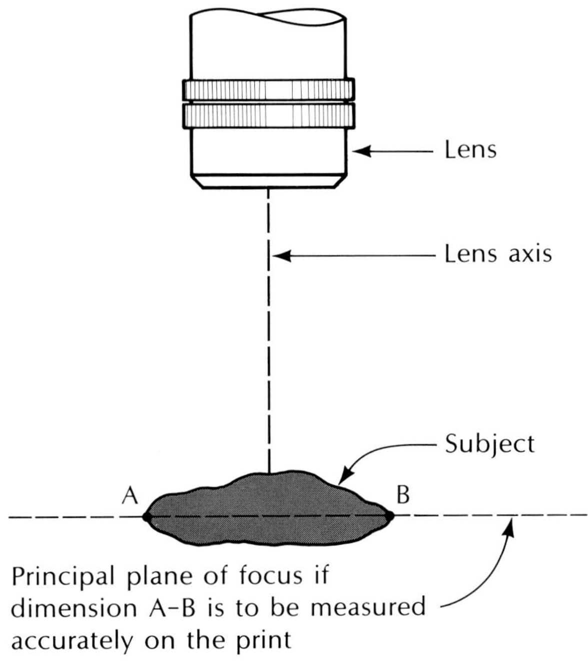

FIGURE 32
The principal plane of focus is that plane through the subject on which the lens is specifically focused.

Maximum convenience and speed of operation can be obtained by mounting the camera on a screw-driven or rack-and-pinion-driven base that will easily and accurately move the whole camera up and down while preserving the rigidity of its mounting. If construction of such a device is undesirable or impractical, one can use as a camera one of several available photographic enlargers that have camera backs available as accessories; these permit the enlargers to be used also as copy cameras. The construction of the enlarger incorporates a means for focusing the camera portion as a whole, as well as a provision for varying the lens-to-film distance. Choose one with a bellows as long as possible, to allow maximum magnification without additional accessories. One or two such enlarger cameras on the market even have both fine and coarse adjustments, and at least one (made by Beseler) has the coarse adjustment electrically driven.

Depth of Field

One of the functions of the lens diaphragm is to provide a degree of control over the apparent thickness of the principal plane of focus; this apparent thickness is called the *depth of field.*

Focusing is normally done with the diaphragm wide open, for accuracy and maximum image brightness. If the diaphragm is then closed down to a smaller opening, parts of the subject on both sides of the principal plane of focus will appear sharp also, and this effect increases as the diaphragm is closed down further. This is the method for increasing depth of field, and its intelligent use allows you to control with great accuracy just what will or will not be shown sharply in the final picture. The basic principle of depth of field was mentioned earlier in this chapter, and Figure 31 should aid you in understanding it.

To achieve the greatest control of the depth of field in normal photography you should usually focus about one-third of the way into the region you wish to have sharp, because the depth of field extends farther behind the principal plane of focus than it does before it, in the normal range of focus. This factor is not a constant, however. At ×1 magnification, for example, depth of field is approximately equal on both sides of the principal plane; above that magnification it extends farther forward than it does behind.

There are limits, of course, to what can be done. With any given iris diaphragm the mechanical limitations will allow you to stop down only so far, and a thick subject at high magnification may not be entirely in focus even at the end of the scale. A second limitation is that all lenses are sharpest at one particular aperture, but at just which one depends on the lens. The Luminar-type lenses are sharpest when wide open, but most camera lenses are sharpest about three stops down from their widest opening. This is because they have residual aberrations that are corrected by closing down the aperture; at several stops below wide open, however, further increase in sharpness is prevented by the onset of diffraction effects, which are a consequence of the wave nature of light.

Diffraction is a distortion of the light that produces the image, caused by the interference of the light waves as they pass by the edges of the iris diaphragm; it is least at the widest apertures and becomes greater as the size of the aperture diminishes. When recording fine image detail at high magnifications, a point may be reached where further increase in the depth of field is valueless because of the overall image degradation caused by diffraction. I have seen cases where important fine detail was lost by closing down a single stop from the maximum opening (for example, this occurred once when I was using a 16 mm Luminar at a magnification of ×40 to photograph very fine striations on a portion of an insect). Thus, when you are working at high magnifications you must watch for this image degradation carefully. A good magnifier should be used to examine the image detail while the aperture is being closed down, so as to determine the best compromise between sharpness and depth of field.

One of the most common misconceptions about depth of field is that it is greater with short-focal-length lenses than with long ones. This is not so. There are only two main factors that affect depth of field: *Depth of field is a function of the relationship between the diaphragm opening and the image magnification.* Thus, you can *increase* depth of field by closing down the diaphragm or by decreasing the image magnification. You can *decrease* depth of field by opening up the diaphragm or by increasing the image magnification. The misconception arises because, *for a given camera-to-subject distance,* a short-focal-length lens gives less image magnification and consequently more depth of field at a given aperture. The depth comes from the decreased image size, not from the shorter focal length of the lens. If the images produced by two lenses have the same magnification and the *f*-stops are identical, then the depths of field are identical, regardless of focal length. Thus you gain nothing in depth of field by changing to a shorter-focal-length lens and then decreasing the camera-to-subject distance to retain image size.

Working Distance

Another factor in photomacrography is *working distance*. This is the distance between the lens and the subject when the camera is focused. It is a figure that must be known beforehand, at least approximately, if a setup is not to require an inordinate amount of time and cause considerable frustration.

At high magnifications you must be near to a correct focus even to be able to see the subject on the ground glass at all. The working distance, like the lens-to-film distance, is related to the focal length of the lens being used. At ×1 it is the same as the lens-to-film distance—that is, twice the focal length of the lens (assuming the use of a theoretical "thin lens"; with actual lenses the measurements will vary somewhat, according to lens design). As the magnification increases, the working distance decreases rapidly until, at around ×3 to ×4, it approaches the focal length of the lens. Thereafter, it slowly approaches this value ever more closely, but never quite reaches it (see Figure 33). Thus, for practical purposes, by ×3 you simply set the camera position so that the front of the lens is at about its own focal length from the subject. Then, watching the image on the ground glass, the camera is moved to bring it into exact focus.

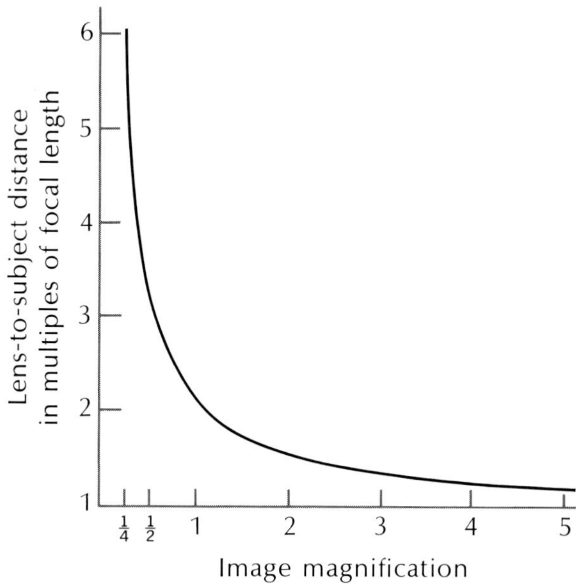

FIGURE 33
Working distance is the distance between the front of the lens and the nearest part of the subject. It is related to the focal length of the lens and to the image magnification. In the photography of small subjects, where there is no recognizable image until the lens is almost in correct focus, it is difficult to know how closely to approach the subject, unless this relationship is understood. Move too close and you may damage the subject (or scare it, if it's alive); stay too far away and you will be unable to locate the subject by looking through the camera.

Perspective

In working at magnifications it is desirable to choose a lens of the correct focal length, if possible. The matter is quite simply put, and for simple reasons. Figuring from the desired magnification and from how much lens-to-film distance is possible with your equipment (that is, how long a bellows or other extension is available), you use the lens of longest possible focal length.

A long-focal-length lens gives a longer working distance, with less apparent image distortion of three-dimensional objects, i.e., better perspective. As Figure 34 shows, the longer lens gives a truer picture of the actual size and outline of the subject. The shorter the lens, the more likely it is to depict the nearest portion of the subject as unrealistically large compared

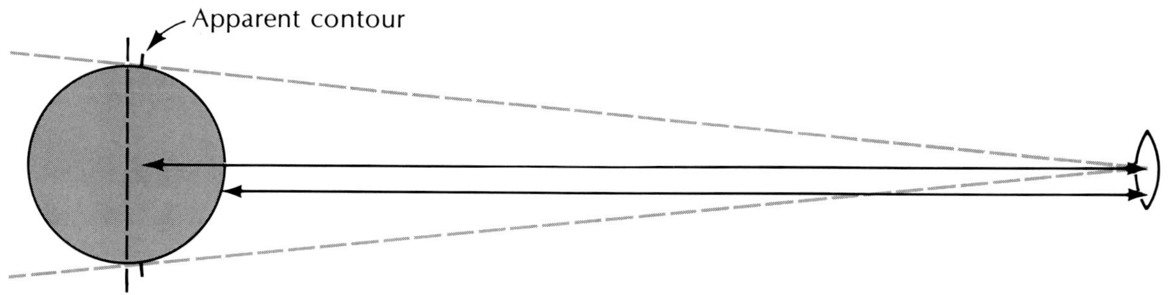

A Long-focal-length lens

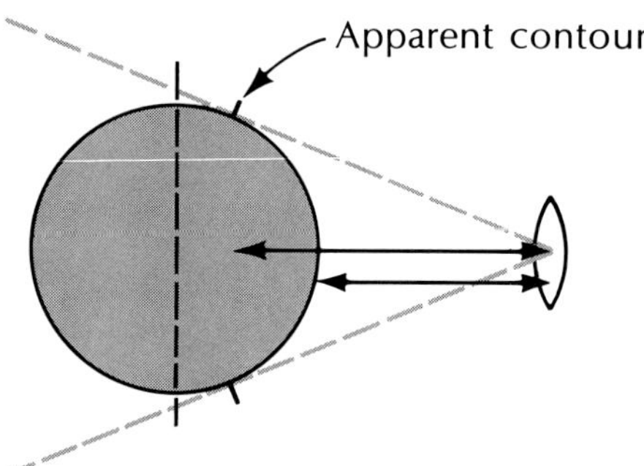

B Short-focal-length lens

FIGURE 34
Perspective effects vary with the focal length of the camera lens and with the relative image magnification. If the working distance is kept the same, the perspective will be similar but the image will be larger with a longer-focal-length lens. If the image magnification is kept the same, the perspective and the apparent contour will change.

A With this long-focal-length lens, the near and far focusing distances are nearly equal (the short distance is 92% of the long), so the image sizes of different subject parts will be close to equal. The apparent contour is close to the actual one.
B With this short-focal-length lens—with image magnification in the principal plane of focus held constant—these distances are quite different (the short distance is only 73% of the long), so the image sizes of different subject parts will differ noticeably. In addition, the apparent contour is quite different from the actual one.

to the further portions, since with a short lens the lens-to-subject (or working) distance is likely to be very short also. And when the working distance is that short, the lens cannot see as far around the contours.

The second reason for using the longest possible lens is to exploit the resulting longer working distance to provide ample room for the proper placing of lights, diffusers, and other fixtures of the setup.

Lighting

In the course of making small things large through photography, one runs into lighting difficulties. Actually, the methods of lighting described earlier are as applicable here as they are elsewhere. But since the subject is small, so must the fixtures be small. If reflectors and diffusers are overly large they may, especially if badly angled, produce too much light scatter, with consequent flare inside the camera. This will tend to lower contrasts and give generally poor results. There are no hard-and-fast rules here, but the possibility of such effects should be considered when setting up the equipment. Some setups, such as light tenting, demand fixtures that are large compared to the subject.

More than in other types of photography, the intensity of light required here is of great importance. According to the inverse-square law, the light intensity falls off as the square of the distance. For example, a light source will throw only one-fourth as much light on the subject if the lamp-to-subject distance is doubled. This law also holds inside the camera. When a camera is focused at infinity, the lens-to-film distance equals the focal length of the lens. At ×1 this distance is twice the focal length; hence the inverse-square law states that only one-fourth as much light actually gets from the lens to the film. If exposure time is to be kept within reason, one of two things must be done: (1) the diaphragm must be opened up an additional two full stops, or (2) the light intensity on the subject must be quadrupled. But we have just seen that increasing the magnification of the image also decreases the depth of field, at any given *f*-stop. Therefore, if any significant flexibility in depth of field is to be retained and the exposure time still kept within practical limits, one *must* raise the light level. It is by now obvious that by the time the ×40 to ×80 range is reached, the problem can reach formidable proportions, and time exposures (up to 30 to 60 seconds) will be the rule rather than the exception.

A subsidiary problem in light falloff through magnification is that the ground-glass image can become very dim, especially when the diaphragm is stopped down to the working level. A magnifier of about ×6 to ×10 power is useful here, not only in checking the accuracy of focus at the ground glass, but also to serve as a light gatherer and thus to aid the eye in observing the degree of depth of field gained by stopping down.

As described earlier (and illustrated in Figure 15), the simplest remedy is to use a high-intensity source such as a spotlight, place it as close to the subject as is practical, place a magnifier before it to concentrate the beam further, and be *sure* to place a water cell somewhere between the lamp and the subject to cool the beam so that the subject will not suddenly shrivel and disappear in a little blue cloud of smoke. Even after all this, it may be necessary, at extreme magnifications or with active subjects, to use a faster film than desired. This will be especially likely if color film is being used, and fairly short exposures are needed to avoid color shifts due to reciprocity failure.

A hand magnifier mounted on a common lab stand can be used to concentrate the light

FORMULA 4
Effective-aperture formula.

Effective aperture = indicated aperture × (magnification + 1)

$$EA = I \times (m + 1)$$

beam. Or, one of the readily available plastic Fresnel lenses can be taped to the subject side of the water cell (it, too, may need protection from the heat). All necessary reflectors, diffusers, mirrors, and other equipment can be used with this high-intensity beam just as with less concentrated sources of light. It is obvious that no light-concentrating lens can increase the intensity of a light source, but it is equally obvious that such a lens can greatly increase the intensity of the beam from the source, by causing the rays to converge. Thus the *effective* intensity of the source is increased.

Calculation of Exposure

Another difficulty now arises—that of calculating the correct exposure. The problem is twofold: (1) the light falloff inside the camera is not taken into consideration by the standard light meters, and (2) the small size of the subject and the cramped nature of the setup may make normal measurements difficult or impossible with systems using either reflected or incident light.

As was pointed out earlier, in the section on closeup flash photography, it is necessary to find the effective aperture of the diaphragm opening in order to determine the correct exposure for photography at greater than normal magnification. Table 7 gave corrected figures for very low image magnifications. Here we must be more general, because the possible and probable circumstances are much more varied.

There is a standard formula for determining the effective aperture for image magnifications greater than actual size. It is shown here as Formula 4. For example, suppose the image magnification is to be ×9 and it is necessary to use an indicated aperture of *f*/16 to obtain sufficient depth of field. In order to obtain the effective aperture you multiply 16 by 10 (the magnification plus 1, which is the number of lens focal lengths needed to get that magnification, as shown in Formula 3). The result is an effective aperture of *f*/160. Once you know this figure you can use a light meter to obtain the correct exposure time. If your meter lacks *f*-number markings that high, just note that *f*/160 is 6⅔ stops above the *f*/16 you started with. You can work this out from Table 8, which gives an extended list of *f*-numbers for this purpose. The difference between any two successive entries in Table 8 is one stop, and the exposure time would double with each increase of one stop in the *f*-number (e.g., from *f*/32 to *f*/45). If, in the example above, you had calculated a correct exposure of 3 seconds at *f*/16, the new exposure time, for *f*/160, would be 320 seconds, or a little

TABLE 8
Extended *f*-number scale for photomacrographic effective apertures.

f/16	*f*/45	*f*/128	*f*/360
f/22	*f*/64	*f*/180	*f*/512
f/32	*f*/90	*f*/256	*f*/720

over 5 minutes. This is an unusually long exposure, not likely to be needed unless the lighting were quite dim and a very slow film were being used. However, I have used longer exposures than that upon occasion.

At these very long exposures you will encounter reciprocity failure, which was discussed in Chapter 1. Instructions for countering this difficulty were given there. In this particular example, you should first of all consider using a faster film and increasing the light intensity.

The foregoing method of calculating exposures is fine if the magnification is such as to allow a light meter to be used in the normal way to determine the exposure in the first place. For those with suitable equipment, however, there is a better and simpler means of reading the exposure, which eliminates all secondary calculations except that of possible additional exposure time to compensate for reciprocity failure. With small cameras equipped with through-the-lens metering systems one can simply read the exposure directly in many cases. This is especially practical with meters using the so-called "stop-down" system, but most other systems can be used, too. See your camera's instruction booklet for details, as the technique is specific to the make of camera.

If you are using a sheet-film camera there are other alternative methods, each of which gives the effective aperture automatically by simply reading the light directly at the film plane, where the image will be formed. Image-plane metering has obvious advantages, since it eliminates the need to consider such factors as the light-transmission efficiency of the lens, the accuracy and placing of aperture settings, and the light losses through image magnification or the use of lens attachments. If the metering system has been checked and found free of any anomalies in spectral sensitivity, you can even forget about filter factors. All you will be determining is the exposure time itself.

A number of firms make exposure meters that fit into the larger cameras like sheet-film holders. Some of these, such as those made by Gossen and Hoffman, incorporate a movable probe that allows you to take a spot reading at any place on the image. Others, such as the Calumet meter, read the whole image area. See your photo dealer for details.

Actually, any sufficiently sensitive meter, such as any of the Gossen Luna-series meters, can be calibrated to read directly on the ground glass, without any special attachments, and the readings will be just as accurate as those of the devices mentioned in the preceding paragraph. Calibration consists of determining which *f*-number on the circular dial of the meter to look opposite, in order to find the correct exposure time. There may be some variation from model to model, and even from meter to meter for a given model, but I can list some suggested starting points with the Gossen meters (the only make I have tested extensively). On the Lunasix Model I, look opposite *f*/1.4; on the Lunasix Model II, try *f*/2; and on the Lunapro, use *f*/1. These recommendations should be used as starting points for exposure tests.

To use the method, place the reflection-reading light-sensitive cell of the meter against the ground glass of the camera at the image point that you wish to read, shielding the ground glass and the end of the meter from ambient light. Read that portion of the image that contains the darkest area where you wish to record just barely visible detail (Zone II, if you are using the Ansel Adams Zone System of exposure determination). Press the low-light button on the meter and hold it down for a count of ten, to allow time for the needle to settle. Accuracy is improved if the meter needle is made to swing to the opposite end of the scale from where you expect it to fall in the reading, by momentarily exposing the cell to somewhat brighter light. The long return swing overcomes inertial effects that might be encountered if there were only a short swing. The meter reading is transferred to the circular dial calculator in the normal way. But instead of having an array of shutter-speed/diaphragm-opening combinations to choose from, there will be a single choice, opposite the *f*-number that has been determined by test to yield a good exposure.

You do have to take into account the effect of colors in the subject, or of any filter being used. Most very sensitive meters are of the cadmium sulfide (CdS) type. These do not have the same spectral sensitivity as either the human eye or panchromatic or color films. The direction of the reading error can vary even in meters of the same design, depending upon the batch of sensors used in their construction, so testing is necessary. With the Luna-series meters that I have tested, it was necessary to add one-half stop of exposure if the color being read was orange, and a full stop if the color was red. Otherwise, there were no color errors.

There is one further problem that can easily arise: some subjects have virtually no dark areas. An example is a white insect pupa being photographed against a black background. If you read the background there will be a gross overexposure. And if you read the subject, which is virtually all "highlight," there will be an enormous underexposure. The best solution is to make use of an aspect of the Adams Zone System. The lightest areas should be Zone VIII in the print. To achieve this, take a reading of the subject as described above, and then expose six stops (about 64 times) longer than is indicated as correct.

For further information on both image-plane exposure reading and the application of the Adams Zone System (and variants of it) to scientific subjects, see Blaker, *Field Photography*, 1976.

Flash Lighting

Where flash exposure is necessary in working at magnifications, some special problems arise. Two of these are due to the probable necessity of placing the lamp or lamps closer than normal to the subject.

The first problem is the sudden blast of heat that accompanies the flash. A water cell between flash and subject may be needed to avoid overheating and possibly destroying the subject. This is not likely to be a significant problem with electronic flash, but at high magnifications you may find that your flash unit is too weak. Your only option may be flashbulbs, which have a much longer flash duration (thus allowing time for the subject mass to heat up). They emit much more light than any but the largest electronic flash units. To take maximum advantage of this light output, use the *open-flash* method—that is, do not use fast shutter speeds, but rather a speed slow enough that the full output of the bulb is used.

The second problem lies in the fact (as noted earlier, in the section on closeup flash photography) that flash-unit reflectors are designed to provide an even beam of light at average distances. Used closer up, this beam pattern may be very different—perhaps distinctly uneven or not well related to the normal guide number. Use of reflectors and diffusers at the subject will even out the beam pattern, but testing to establish the guide number is a good idea.

Yet a third difficulty arises in the calculation of exposure, even after testing the guide number. Since you must work at a given *f*-number in order to achieve the best balance between maximum depth of field and minimum diffraction, you cannot use the standard method of flash-exposure calculation, but must instead compute for the flash-to-subject distance. This method has already been described fully on page 86. In Formula 2, shown there, you must use the effective aperture as calculated by Formula 4, on page 100.

Control of Movement and Vibration

Another special problem in photography at magnifications is movement or vibration. A camera can be imagined as a sort of optical lever, with the subject at one end, the lens as the fulcrum, and the image at the other end. Under normal photographic conditions, the lens-to-image distance is very short compared to the lens-to-subject distance. Thus conditions are favorable. But at magnifications over ×1 this relationship is reversed. Consequently, movements of the subject or of the camera itself become greatly magnified in the image, because of the unfavorable "lever action." Sometimes control can be exercised by using short exposure times to minimize image movement. In extreme cases, only the use of electronic flash, with a flash duration of $1/_{1000}$ second or less, will save the situation. Using disposable flashbulbs with the open-flash method will give effective exposure times averaging about $1/_{50}$ second (the approximate flash duration of most bulbs). This is not as good as electronic flash, but a whole lot better than a time exposure.

Where time exposures are needed—where, of course, the subject moves not at all—it is of primary importance that all parts of the photographic setup either are very rigid or are not moved during the exposure. In extremely delicate cases, the shutter is not even used, for fear of introducing vibration; it is kept open, and the exposure is timed by interrupting the light beam with a card. The workroom must be moderately dark to prevent the recording of stray light. Vibration, whether in the room itself or in the camera and its parts, is a great and common problem in this work, and all practical steps must be taken to avoid it and eliminate it. In areas where heavy motor traffic causes building vibration, it may be necessary to work only during hours when traffic is lightest.

Indicators of Scale

A final consideration in work at magnifications is the need for a scale indicator to be included in the picture. This is by no means always needed, but is often desirable, particularly where the final picture may be reduced or enlarged for publication. The scale indicator can be photographed together with the subject (where it must be placed at the principal plane of focus to be accurate), or it can be added to the negative or print later. If photographed with the subject, it can be an actual scale—usually metric—or some common object of known and standard size (do not use articles of variable size, such as paper clips). If the magnification is relatively high, beware the use of actual scales, as they are seldom good enough to stand much enlargement without showing irregularities in the graduations.

In work at high magnifications, adding the scale later is best. The work is done at a known magnification. A line of the correct length can then be drawn or scored on the negative; for ×40, for instance, a line 40 mm long will represent 1 mm. If the background is to print black, the negative will be transparent there, and a line can be drawn on it with India ink, or a narrow strip of opaque tape can be applied. Either way, the result will be a white line on the print. If the background is to print white, it will be opaque in the negative, and a knife point can be used to score a line in the emulsion. This will print black. Alternatively, suitable lines can simply be drawn on the final print itself. Further remarks on indicators of scale will follow where applicable in the text, particularly in Chapter 17.

A

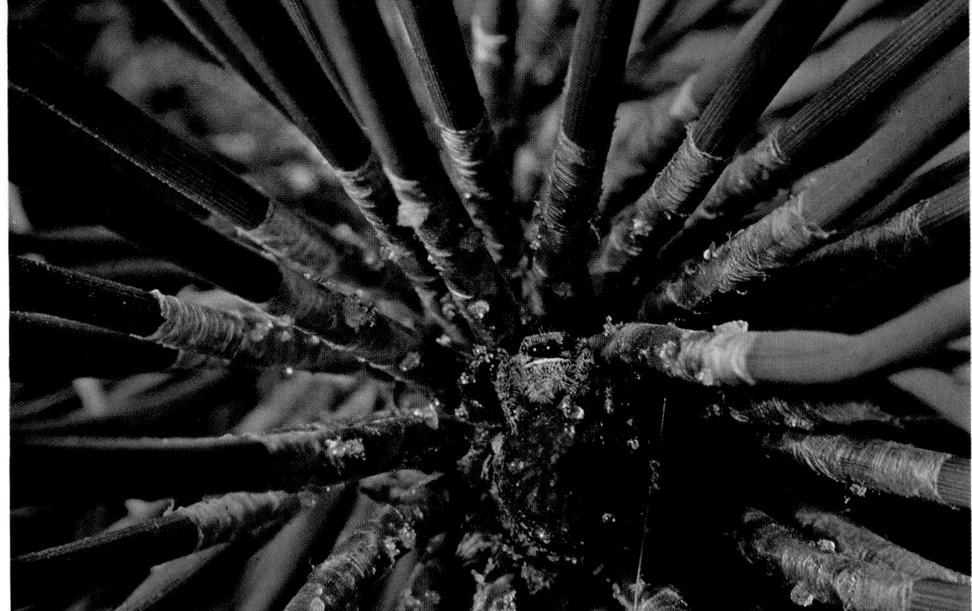

B

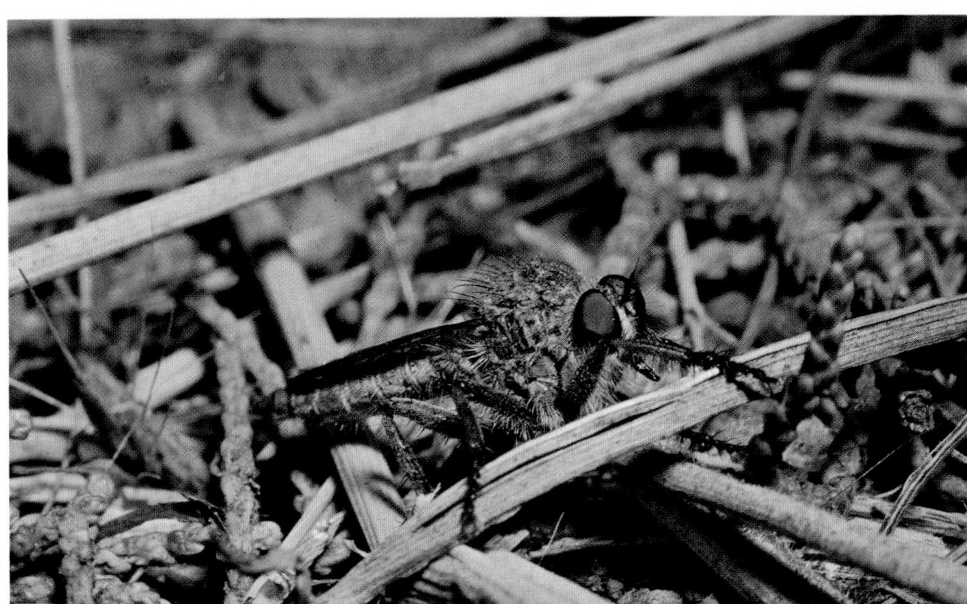

PLATE I

Closeup Flash Photography

The ability to photograph small living creatures in their natural habitats or in the laboratory is greatly enhanced by using the closeup flash technique. Speedy operation, the stopping of subject motion, the achievement of maximum depth of field, the ability to use slow, high-resolution films, and the constant control of lighting effects are all combined in one versatile photographic method.

A Jumping Spider (Salticidae) on pine tip (×3.6). These spiders have excellent binocular vision, can jump surprising distances for their small size, and are wary of any close approach. This one was cornered, and had turned at bay.

B Robber Fly (Asilidae) in dry grass (×3.6). It was photographed at ×1, as was the spider, and enlarged in reproduction.

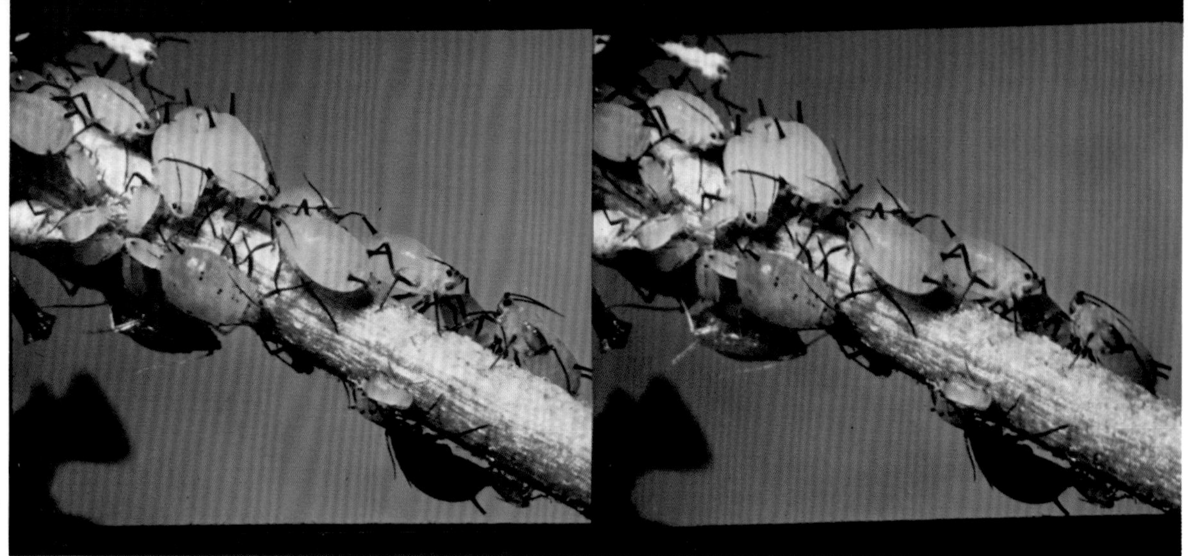

A

PLATE II
Stereo Photography

A Yellow aphids on a milkweed stem (×9). This is casual stereo, being two separately made closeup flash pictures. Exact alignment of the film frames is unlikely in casual stereo, as this pair shows. The stereo effect is imperfect because a few aphids moved, but is better than no stereo at all. The original ×3 magnification was obtained with a ×1 setup and a 3× tele-converter. The color slides were copied and brought to ×9 in my enlarger, using 4 × 5-inch Polacolor 2 sheet film (see pages 165–167). The enlarger lamp was a tungsten source, but daylight-type film was used; color correction with a Wratten 80B filter was therefore required.
B Moth egg (×40), photographed directly on Polacolor film in a photomacrographic stereo setup (see pages 117–119). The pictures were focused at slightly different levels to increase the apparent depth of field.

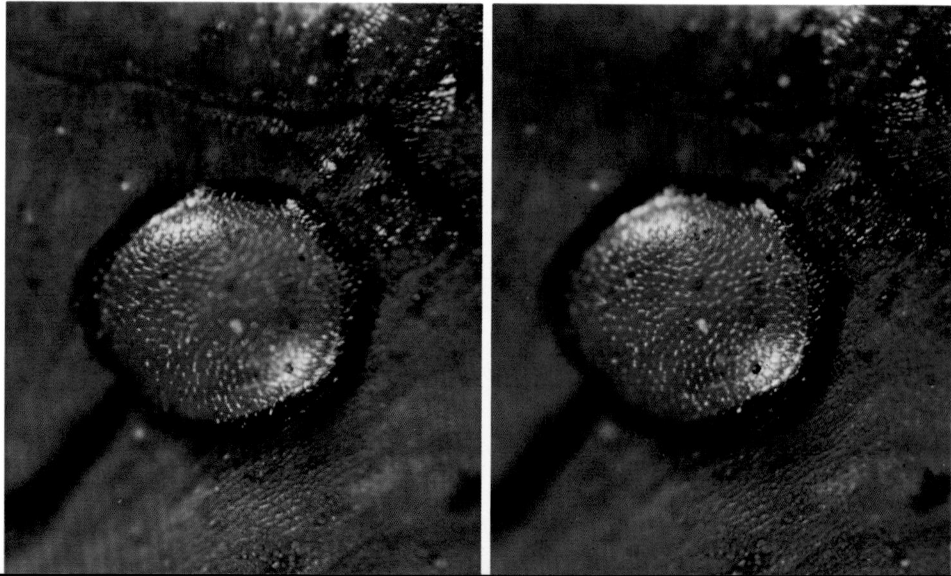

B

PLATE III
Background Effects

A tiny wasp (photographed at ×12 and enlarged in reproduction to ×18), shown here to illustrate the profound effects that can result from a mere change of background. The lighting and photographic technique were identical in both pictures; only the background was changed.

A A chip of white card was placed below the subject to get the normal white background effect. It was sized in proportion to the subject to avoid excessive optical flare.

B A piece of black velvet was substituted as a background. Note the enhancement of the iridescence in the wings, and the increased brilliance of the colors elsewhere. The picture even looks sharper at a casual glance, though careful examination will show that it is not.

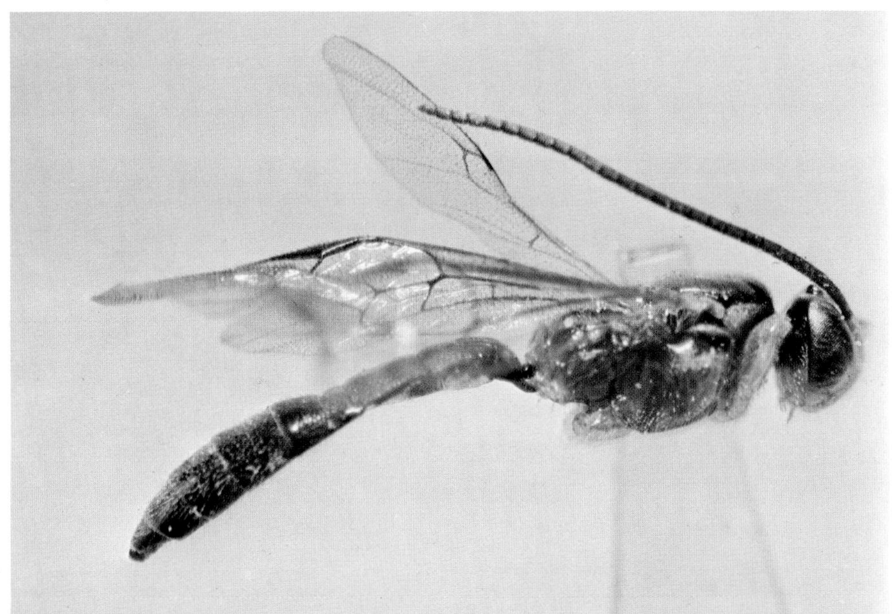

A

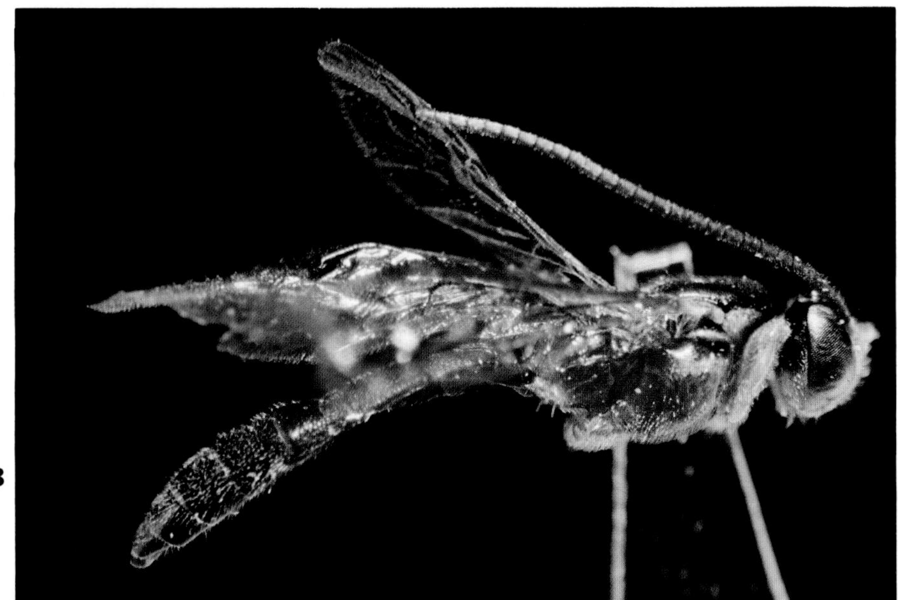

B

A

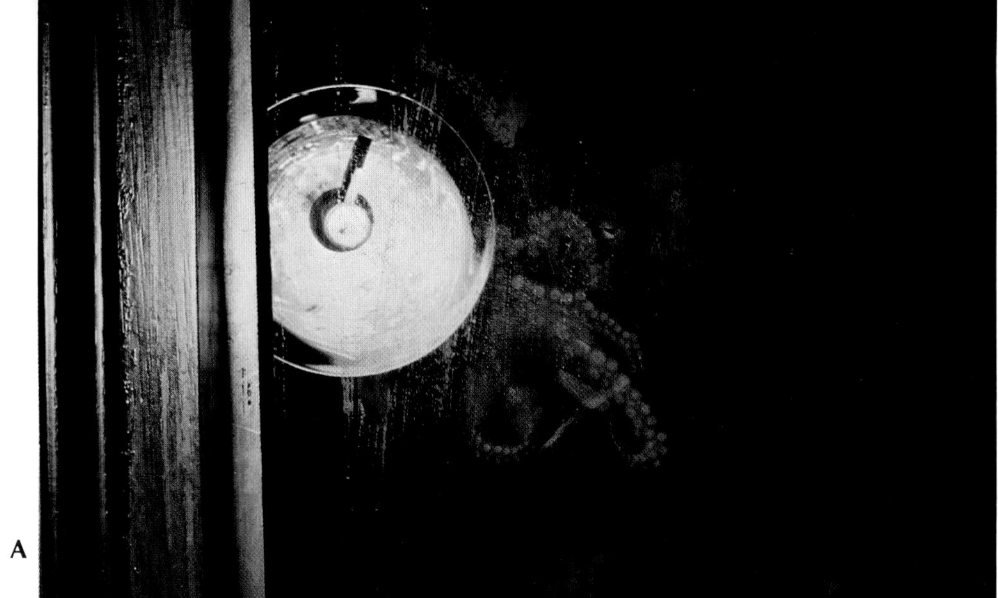

B

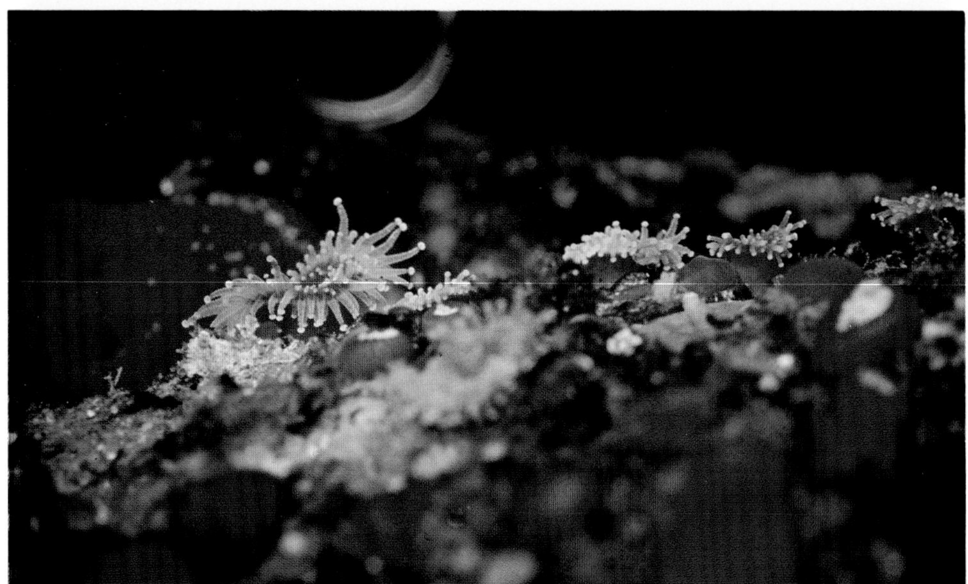

PLATE IV

Aquarium Photography by Flash

The low levels of existing light in wall-mounted aquaria, and the rapid subject motion, may require the use of flash. The technique, which is described on pages 190–191 and illustrated in Figure 49, is not as straightforward as it may at first seem.

A With the flash mounted on the camera—a common error in this situation—the result is usually a picture of the flash unit, reflected from the aquarium glass. This photograph of an octopus failed for that reason. Because most of the light is reflected by the glass, that portion of the octopus that is visible is underexposed.

B After considering the law of reflection and thereby solving the problem of the flash angle, you may still have a reflection of the front of the camera lens mount, as seen in this photograph of sea anemones (photographed at ×0.5 and enlarged in reproduction to ×1.8), unless you take the appropriate steps to avoid it.

PLATE V
Subjects in Glass Containers

A Fungus culture *(Clitocybe)* grown in a flask (photographed at ×0.62 and enlarged in reproduction to ×1.0). The problem of reflections was avoided here by the simple expedient of breaking the flask. However, there is a risk of damaging the subject when this is done. And, of course, this cannot be done with some types of subject matter. (Originally photographed for R. D. Raabe.) Similar material is shown photographed in the flask in Plate 30B.
B Algae being cultured in flasks. Here the recommended method of using a single lamp high in front of the flasks was used. There are no significant reflections in the area of the actual subject material.

A

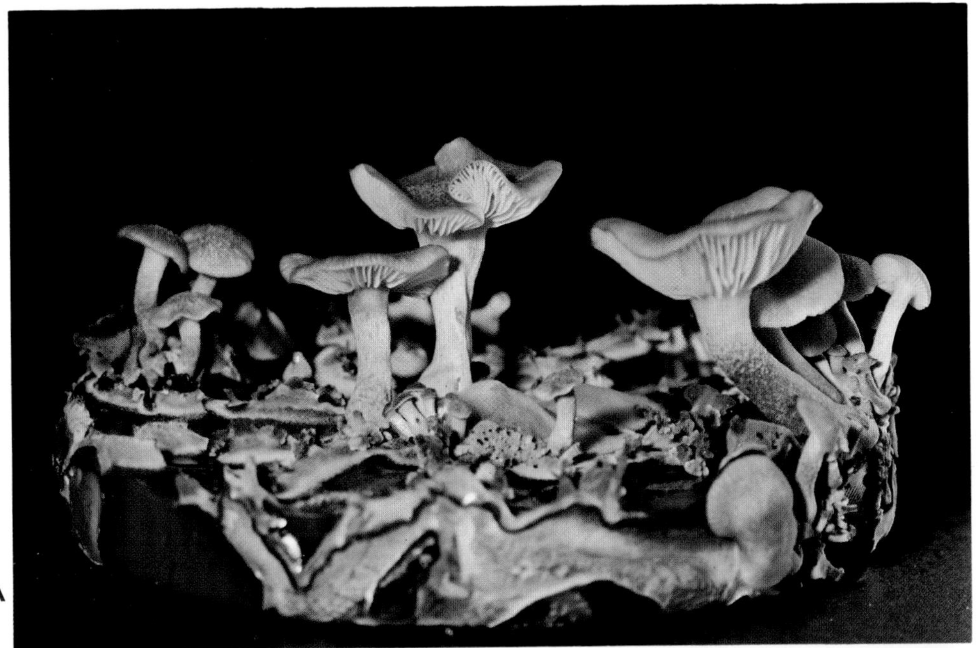

B

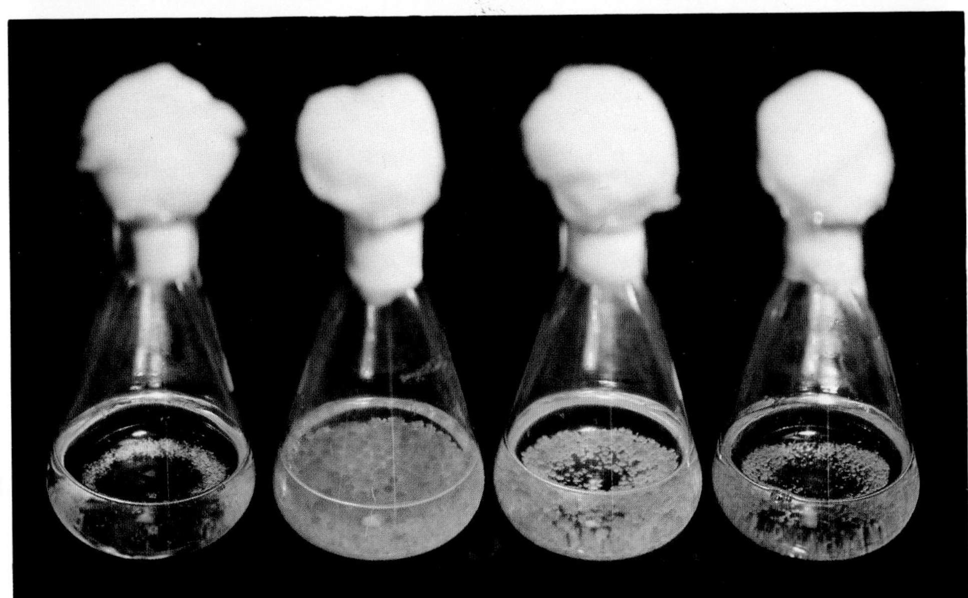

PLATE VI
Colors as Artifacts

Not every color that appears in a photograph is correctly representative of the subject. There are a number of ways in which unavoidable color artifacts can enter into photography, and these artifacts should be recognized as such.

A Insect (Diptera: Cecidomyiidae) in amber (photographed at ×25 and enlarged in reproduction to ×42). The overall orange color is that of the amber, and of course gives no clue as to the color of the insect remains. (Originally photographed for P. Hurd.)
B Shrimp stomach (photographed at ×6 and enlarged in reproduction to ×10). The brownish and yellow tones are really present in the subject, but the overall blue cast is the result of light scattering in the translucent tissue. This is the same phenomenon (Rayleigh scattering) that causes the blue of the sky. The blue here could be removed only with distortion of the other colors.

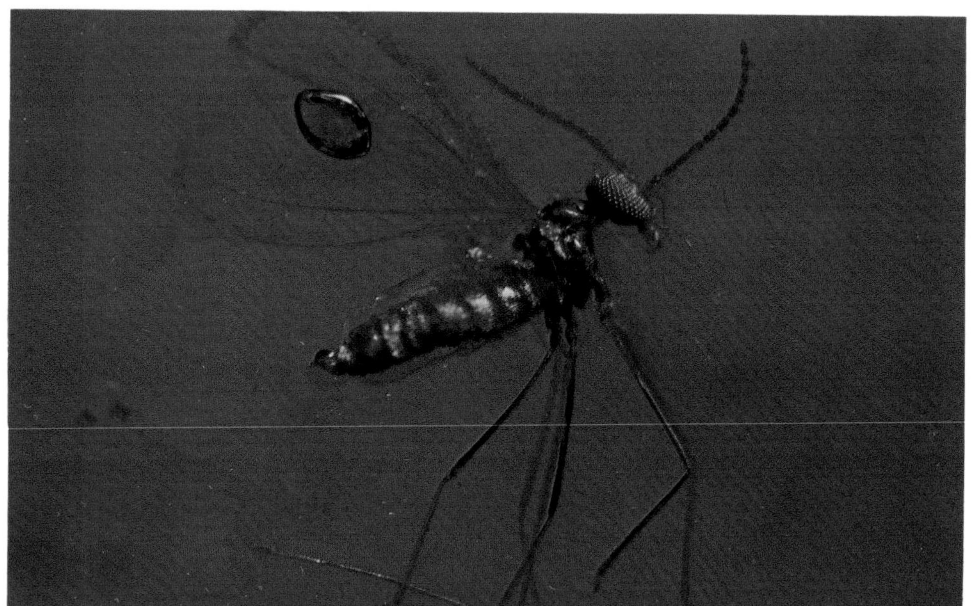
A

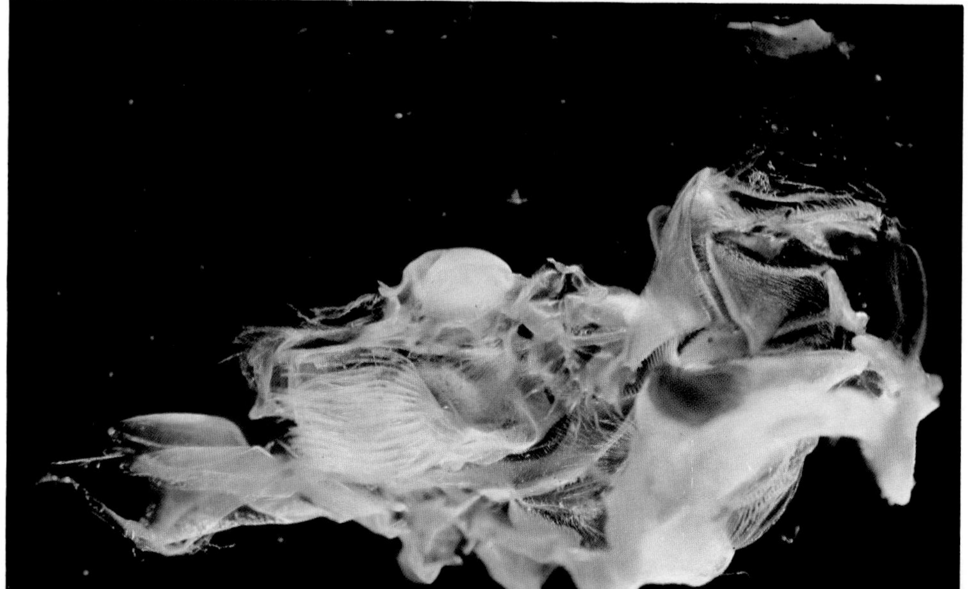
B

A

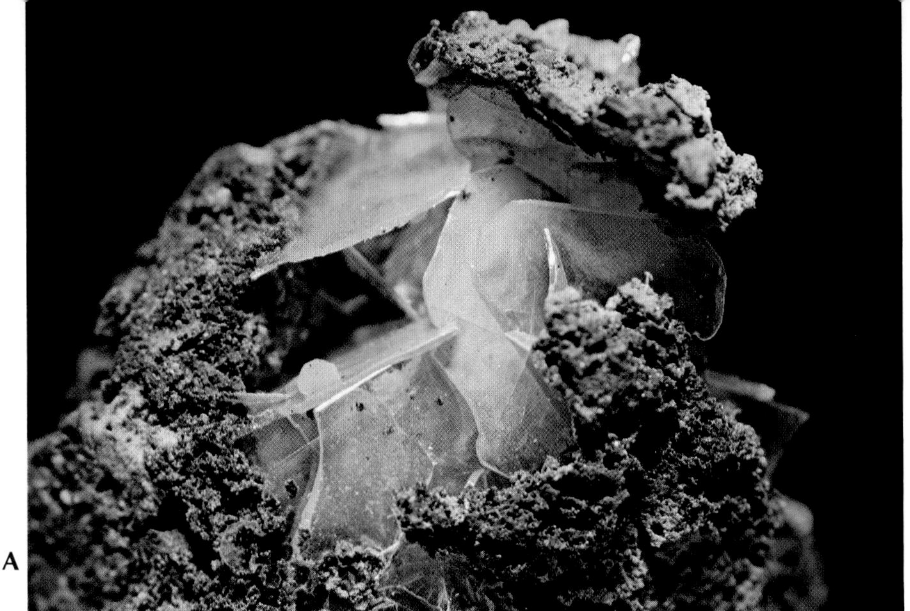

B

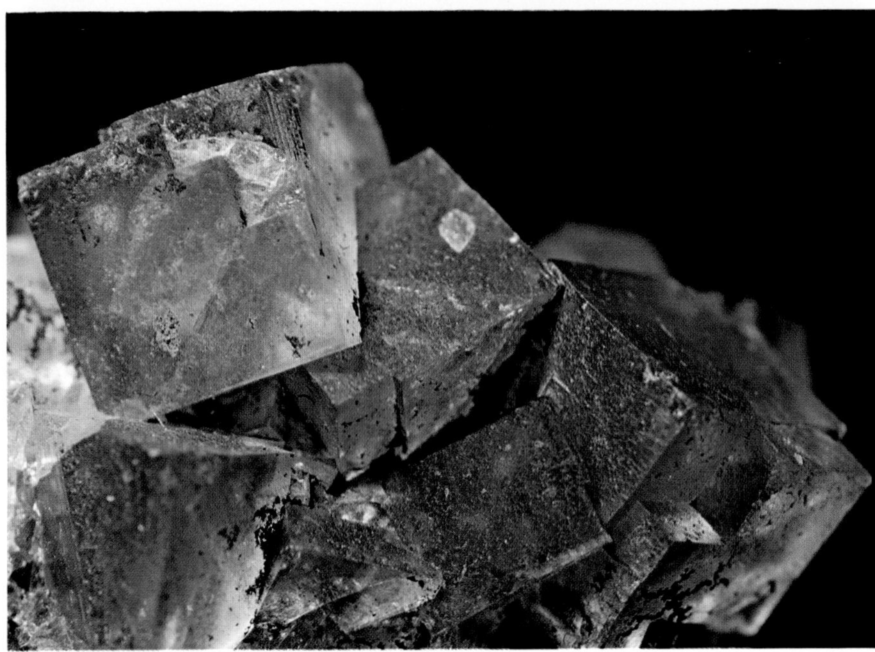

PLATE VII
Crystals

These photographs were made using the technique described on pages 221–222. The specimens were quite small, and the backgrounds were black velvet.

A Wulfenite and selenite, from Arizona (photographed at ×4 and enlarged in reproduction to ×6).
B Fluorite, from Mexico (also photographed at ×4 and enlarged in reproduction to ×6).

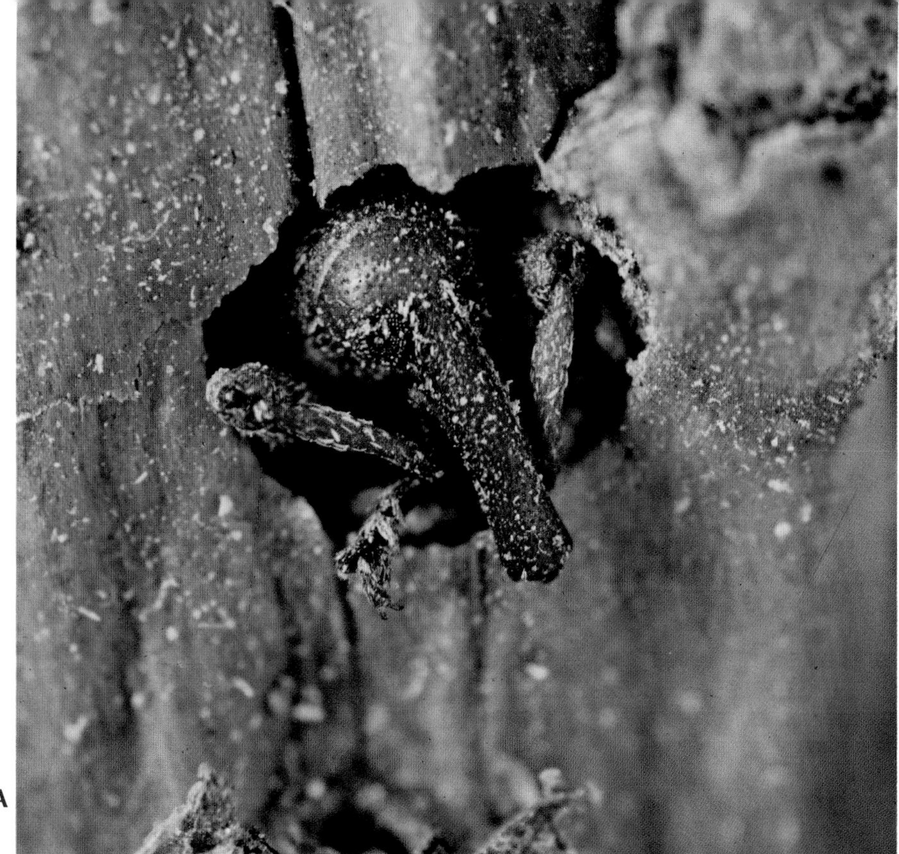

A

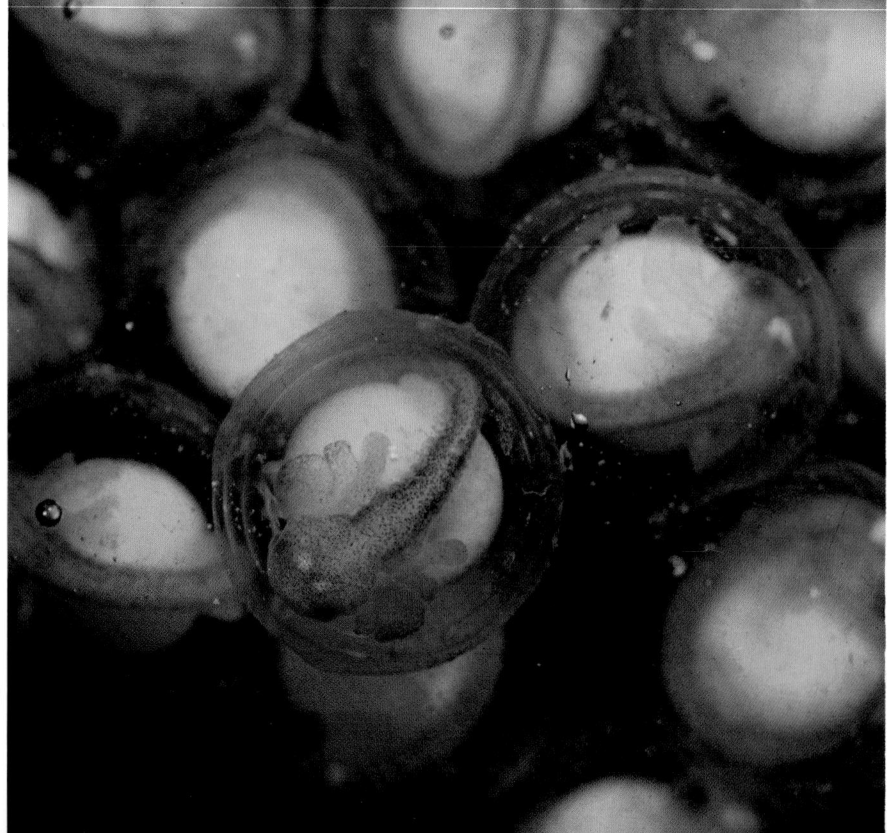

B

PLATE VIII
Insects; Living Animals

A Weevil (Curculionidae), deceased, photographed at ×24 and enlarged in reproduction to ×53. This was a photomacrographic subject lit by the reflector-diffuser method. Flash was used to keep the exposure short enough to avoid color shifts due to reciprocity failure. (Originally photographed for B. Barr.)

B Eggs of the salamander Ensatina *(Ensatina eschscholtzi),* photographed by the closeup flash technique at about ×2 and enlarged in reproduction to about ×4.4. The embryos were in slow but constant motion, circling within the egg membranes, but the flash easily stopped this motion. The winglike processes are gill structures.

CHAPTER 7

High-Resolution 35 mm Photography

With even the best of general-use films, 35 mm black-and-white photography does not provide the quality of, for example, an 8 × 10-inch negative that is contact-printed. The grain structure of the negative degrades the image to the extent that fine subject detail is not visible; this limitation appears even in whole-negative prints no larger than 5 × 7 or 8 × 10 inches. This level of quality is entirely satisfactory for most purposes, but when you need to make a very large print for wall display (where it may receive close and critical examination) or when you must enlarge a small portion of a negative to normal print size without loss of image resolution, you must take extraordinary measures. With appropriate equipment, films, and developers it is possible to do 35 mm photography that, in black-and-white print form, can rival the quality of good large-negative photography. Technique must be impeccable throughout, but the potential is there.

If the camera equipment is of excellent quality, if the films and developer are well chosen and correctly used, and if the enlargement is made using careful technique and a superior lens, you can make prints of surprising size that can readily stand comparison with a large contact print. Whole-negative prints can be made as large as 4 × 6 *feet,* or a portion of a negative as small as ⅛ inch across can be enlarged to 8 × 10-inch print size, while retaining grain and resolution characteristics at least equal to those of a whole-negative print of 8 × 10 inches made from a general-use, fine-grained, 35 mm film such as Panatomic-X. See Plates 10 and 40C.

This kind of work is not especially difficult, but you must take great care in all steps to ensure optimum quality. It is not necessary, or even desirable, to use the method regularly, but you should know how to go about it if the need arises.

CAMERA EQUIPMENT

Cameras

Any reasonably well-made 35 mm camera will serve, if the film lies flat and if the focusing mechanism is accurately adjusted. The accuracy of adjustment of the rangefinder linkage in rangefinder cameras should be checked by measurement. Single lens reflex cameras should be examined to assure that the image plane of the viewfinder screen coincides with the film plane. The infinity focus of lenses should be verified by test. Many lenses can be focused past infinity, especially lenses that make use of adapters to fit a number of makes of camera bodies. The mechanical stop on the focusing mechanism should be located so as to stop any further turning of the mechanism exactly when the infinity focus is reached. If this is not so, you must know about it and take it into account in order to do sharp photography at the infinity focus.

Lenses

High-resolution photography can be done only with the best of lenses, but it should be realized that most good lenses in use today can resolve substantially finer detail than general-use films can record.

For photography at or approaching the infinity focus, you should use a lens of normal focal length that is not excessively fast. Lenses faster than about *f*/2 sacrifice flatness of field and certain other characteristics in order to

PLATE 10 ▶

High-Resolution 35 mm Technique.

The choice of film is the first consideration in high-resolution 35 mm photography. Even "fine-grain" films intended for general use do not resolve as much fine detail as commonly available high-quality camera lenses.

A Haltere and leg joints of a crane fly photographed at ×1 with a Nikon F camera and a 55 mm *f*/3.5 Auto Micro-Nikkor lens, and subsequently enlarged to ×14. The film used was Kodak Panatomic-X, developed in Microdol-X developer that was diluted 1:3 and used at 75°F. Even at this relatively low enlargement factor, equivalent to a full-negative 14 × 20-inch print, image structure is visibly breaking up in the barely discernible film grain.
B Same subject, photographed identically but on H & W VTE Ultra Pan film, processed as directed in H & W Control 4.5 developer. Note the superior rendering of the fine hairs.
C Head of the subject (taken from the same 8 × 10-inch print as part A). Note the loss of fine detail in the eye and in the hairs on the mouth parts.
D Same area (taken from the same 8 × 10-inch print as part B). There is noticeable improvement. Greater printing enlargement would reveal progressively greater differences in quality.

A good 35 mm negative made with high-resolution film can be enlarged to as much as 4 × 6 *feet* before showing the amount of grain structure visible in a full-negative 11 × 14-inch print from films comparable to Panatomic-X. These latter films are entirely satisfactory for normal photography, but when the needs are extreme the other films show their worth.

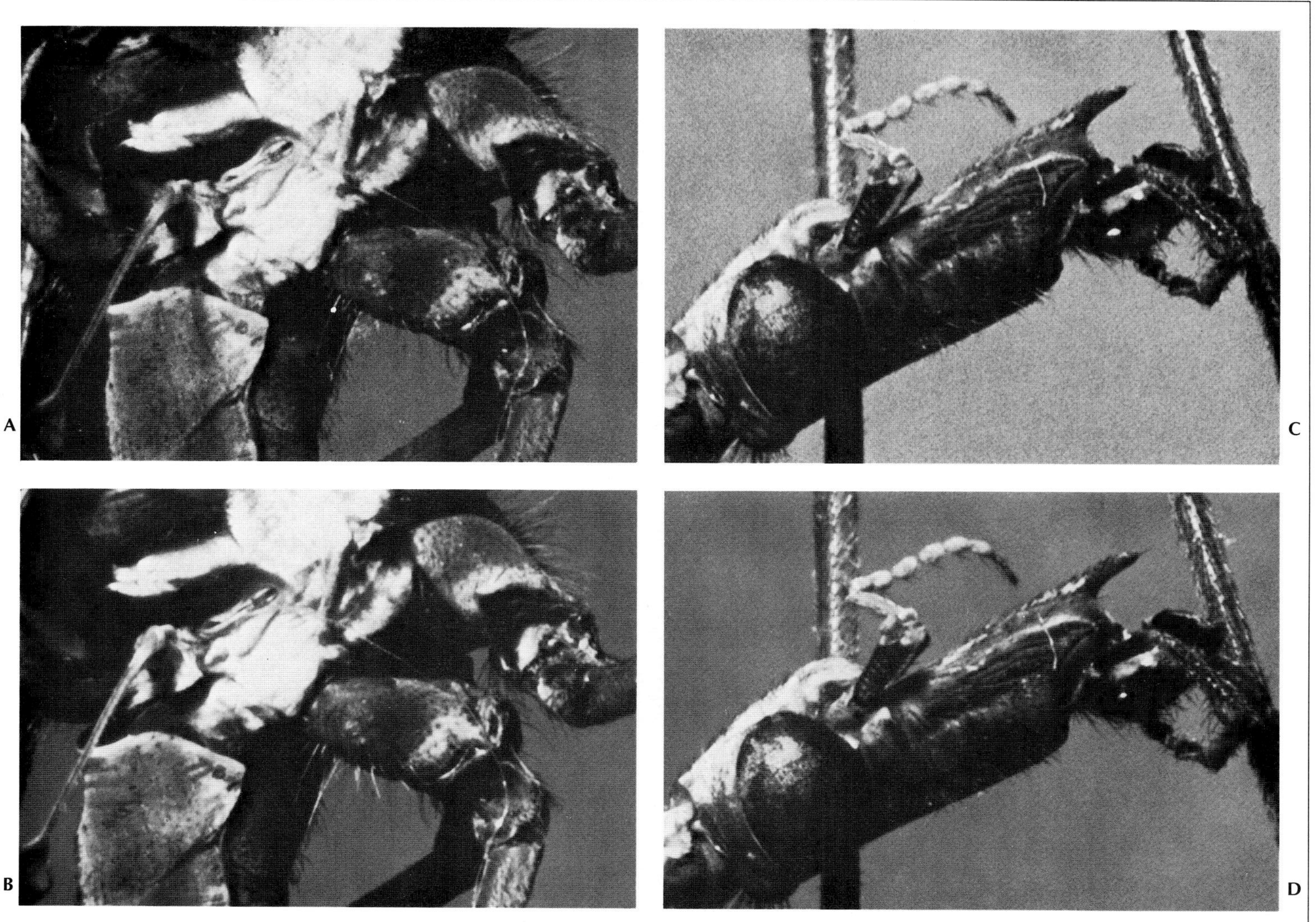
A
C
B
D

achieve their speed. For high-resolution work I prefer to use a lens with a maximum aperture not faster than about *f*/3.5, other factors being equal. The otherwise very fine macro-type lenses are not especially suitable for high-resolution infinity-focus work (though they are quite satisfactory for normal photography), because they are designed for optimum performance at an object/image ratio of about 1:10 (that is, about $\times \frac{1}{10}$).

Fast wideangle lenses are notorious for their considerable curvature of field and image distortion, as well as other aberrations. I prefer to use wideangle lenses with maximum apertures of about *f*/3.5. If such lenses are shifted off center, as some designs allow, great care must be taken in focusing.

Closeup photography of the highest quality usually requires using one of the widely available macro-type lenses. These are now made to fit virtually all types of small single lens reflex cameras, and offer very good image resolution, freedom from image distortion, excellent flatness of field, and general freedom from noticeable optical aberrations.

Telephoto lenses of moderate focal lengths—say, from 85 mm to about 135 mm—should be tested. Even with a big-name manufacturer, it is worthwhile to test three or four samples of a given lens before purchasing one. If you can't do that, test a new lens carefully immediately after purchase and get a replacement right away if it doesn't meet your needs.

Telephoto lenses and mirror optics of very long focal lengths may not be too satisfactory for laboratory work, because they are designed to perform best at long subject distances. Even when they are so used, atmospheric disturbances and the general difficulty of handling them can easily prevent high-resolution results—a point worth remembering for someone who usually works in a laboratory but is planning to undertake a field excursion requiring telephotography (see Blaker, *Field Photography,* 1976, for details of telephotography and related field practices).

CAMERA HANDLING

You cannot do high-resolution photography unless you give careful attention to the use of the camera.

Motion Control

The primary cause of unsharp pictures is camera motion. This comes from two main sources: actual movement of the camera, as when handholding it, and jars and vibrations occurring in the mechanism.

Avoid handholding the camera if at all possible. Put it on a sturdy tripod, simply set it on a bench, or—best of all—bed it down on a sandbag. But get it out of your hands. Use a cable release, with slack left in the cable, to release the shutter. Do not use a stiff, armored cable release if you can get a nice, weak, flexible one. The nearer it resembles limp spaghetti, the better it will insulate the camera from the movements of your hand. I buy the cheapest cable releases I can get, keeping spares around in case of breakage—which actually occurs rather seldom.

Camera vibrations are of two basic types: steady grinding effects from the mechanism that operates the focal-plane shutter, and abrupt jerks from the inertial effects of the moving mirror in a single lens reflex camera, often called *mirror flop.* Internal vibrations are best controlled by a two-way approach: test your camera and shutter to see which shutter speeds, if any, give particular problems, and avoid those speeds (for example, my Nikon is almost unusable at $\frac{1}{15}$ second, but quite trouble-free elsewhere); then use a sandbag to absorb jars and vibrations whenever you can. Some camera designs allow you to lock the mirror up after focusing, to avoid mirror flop. This, of course, is useful only when photographing static subjects.

When the camera must be handheld, as in closeup flash photography of live insects, do all that you can to steady your hands. For example, rest your elbows on a supporting surface, or press against the side of the lens mount with one or more fingers of the hand that holds the flash unit, to steady the front of the camera. Finally, consider using a flash unit of unusually short flash duration. I use a small, inexpensive unit that has a duration of $\frac{1}{3000}$ second.

Exposure Accuracy

It is essential in high-resolution photography to achieve accuracy of exposure, because the films used have virtually no exposure latitude. Whenever practical, make a series of exposures in half-stop increments, straddling the calculated correct exposure with one or two increments on either side. This can be done by changing the exposure time, by changing the *f*-setting, or, in flash photography, by varying the flash-to-subject distance.

FILMS AND PROCESSING

Films

The best films for 35 mm high-resolution photography are the panchromatic films designed for document copying. These include Kodak High Contrast Copy film, Fuji and Agfa-Gevaert microfilms, and H & W Control VTE Pan and VTE Ultra Pan (the VTE Pan is also available in 120-sized roll film). These films all have basically similar characteristics. In the present context, all can be speed-rated at an *exposure index* (EI) of 10, except for H & W Control VTE Pan, which should be exposed at an EI of about 40 for best results. (These are not the ASA speeds, as specified by the manufacturers, but are equivalents that I recommend for laboratory photography requiring exceptionally full dark-area detail. They apply *when the films are processed in the manner prescribed in the following section.*)

These films are panchromatic; that is, they respond to a reasonable degree to all of the visible wavelengths of electromagnetic radiation. Their grain structure is exceptionally fine, allowing enlargement in printing to at least 50 to 60 times before the film grain has any noticeable effect on the image. Typically, these document-copy films are very high in contrast. In order to use them for photographing general subjects, this contrast must be lowered to usable levels through special processing techniques. When processed as recommended, these films can record a normally full range of tones, with good highlight separation and quite open shadows.

The first noticeable appearance of film grain in general-use 35 mm films usually occurs in the middle tones, this being especially obvious in the less textured greys and in out-of-focus areas. With high-resolution films these areas typically show a smooth, creamy look that is normally characteristic of contact prints made from large negatives. Because of this freedom from apparent film grain, the image structure carried by the lens is reproduced to a high degree of accuracy.

Processing

Any of several formulations, mostly using the Ilford-produced chemical Phenidone®, can be used to develop high-contrast/high-resolution films to a normal contrast range. However, there is one readily available commercial product that does a particularly fine job: H & W Control 4.5 developer (I do not usually specify brands in this manner, but in this case it is desirable because of the product's unique qualities). This product comes as a liquid concentrate and is diluted with water *immediately before use.* Once diluted, it has a very short active life, although an unopened bottle is still good after a year of storage. It is available in several container sizes, but I prefer to get it in the form of six-packs of small bottles, each of which contains, premeasured, the correct amount of concentrate for processing one roll of film.

This developer is a bit tricky to use, because of its affinity for oxygen. If not used immediately upon dilution, it will oxidize in a few minutes to the point where serious underdevelopment will occur (if you use some from one of the larger bottles, you must decant the remainder into a smaller container, or exclude air from it in some other way, for further storage). Therefore, you should fully prepare for processing by stabilizing the temperature of water and fixer, loading the film reels, etc., *before* diluting the stock solution. Then dilute and process exactly as prescribed by the manufacturer.

The sequence and times for normal processing are summarized below. See the manufacturer's instructions for further details, including time recommendations for processing at other temperatures, compensation for developer age, etc.

1. Development: H & W Control 4.5 developer, mixed 1:21.5 with water (10½ ml to 225 ml of water); develop for 4½ minutes at 68°F (20°C). Agitate gently by inversion for 10 seconds continuously at the start, and thereafter for 6 seconds every 30 seconds. Discard the developer after use.
2. Rinse: plain water (listed as optional by the manufacturer, but it reduces contamination of the fixer).
3. Fixation: ordinary acid fixer (hypo), for 2 minutes maximum.
4. Wash: running water, for 10 to 20 minutes.
5. Postwash rinse: wetting agent (e.g., Kodak Photo-Flo or equivalent), diluted as directed, preferably in distilled water.

Note that all solutions, including the wash water, should be stabilized to the same temperature, to avoid reticulation in the film.

PRINTING

Printing high-resolution negatives is basically similar to printing in normal 35 mm work; however, there are fine points of technique that are useful at each step.

Enlargers and Lenses

Any ordinary 35 mm enlarger can be used with reasonable success if the lamphouse does not overheat the negative to the point of flexing it during printing and if any condensers in it are properly aligned so as to provide even lighting. Because high-resolution films are thin, flexing during printing is a real possibility, and should be watched for. Some enlargers do very well, whereas others—apparently of similar design—overheat.

Most enlarger lenses, even those of purportedly good quality and undeniably high price, are no better than fair when it comes to high-magnification, high-resolution photography. I have found that by far the best readily available lenses for this work are the macro-type camera lenses. I use my Nikon 55 mm Micro-Nikkor for most such work, with perfect satisfaction. Adapters for attaching camera lenses to enlargers are commercially available at little cost, for many of the more common makes. Regardless of what some camera-store employees may tell you, camera lenses will not be damaged by heat from the enlarger.

Macro-type lenses are corrected for optimum performance in just the image-magnification ranges that are normally used in printing, and the images projected will be flat, without distortion, and free of any detectable optical aberrations.

If you need more image magnification than you can get with these normal-focal-length lenses, try using a high-quality, not-too-fast wideangle camera lens. For instance, my 35 mm PC-Nikkor, centered, does very well indeed. I am told on good authority that certain of the Leitz camera lenses are also very satisfactory here (for many years, Leitz enlargers have made provision for the use of camera lenses in printing).

Choice of Negative

It is here that the practice of making straddling exposures in the original photography pays off. Generally speaking, but particularly in laboratory photography, if you have a choice of otherwise identical negatives that vary in exposure level, you should choose the one that shows the most dark-area detail, consistent with the retention of good light-area contrast. Overexposure may cause light-area contrasts to drop, thus making them look muddy in the print. If this happens, reprint using the next lighter negative of the series. If the dark areas are deficient in detail, reprint using the next darker negative. And if you cannot encompass both areas well in one print, the negative was too high in contrast. In laboratory photography, where you control the lighting, the most likely cause of excessive contrast is improper lighting, assuming that you have processed the film correctly. Take better care the next time. Few things teach one as well as a properly diagnosed failure.

The Negative Carrier

The ordinary glassless negative carriers found in enlargers will suffice unless the negative is overheated by the lamphouse during the exposure. When a negative overheats, it expands and flexes, and thus "pops" in and out of focus. If this occurs, you must use a glass carrier in order to do whole-negative printing, i.e., the negative must be sandwiched between two sheets of glass. If you don't have a glass carrier, you can improvise by placing the film between two 1 × 3-inch or 2 × 3-inch microscope slides. The difficulty here is that you must keep all six surfaces scrupulously clean, as every trace of dirt or lint will show glaringly on the print. Remember that doing clean work takes less time and energy than "spotting" the prints later.

Small portions of negatives can be printed without the need for glass negative carriers. My preferred method is to use ordinary negative carriers designed for subminiature films, such as 8 mm and 16 mm sizes. You can remove any inconveniently placed locating pins, being careful to smooth off any burrs around the remaining holes, and then center that portion of the negative that you wish to print over the opening in the carrier. If such small carriers are not available to you, you can make them from paired pieces of aluminum or heavy cardboard (preferably the type called chipboard). Reducing the size of the hole in the negative carrier also reduces the area of the negative that can flex, and thus the amount of popping that it can do.

Focusing the Image

At high magnifications it is necessary to use a special magnifying device, usually called a *grain focuser,* for accurately focusing the image on the printing paper. Good models are available at surprisingly low prices. Although the name implies that you will be focusing on the film grain, the grain in high-resolution films is so minute as to prevent this in most cases. Therefore, you should buy one that has a built-in grid in the viewing system. This allows *parallax focusing,* a method in which you come to a best visual focus and then move your head slightly while observing the image. If the image moves relative to the grid, the focus is not exact. So you change the focus until you find a position where there is no relative motion. The method is easy to learn, and is actually quicker and easier than focusing on fine grain. It is very accurate.

Beware of problems stemming from flexing of the enlarger itself during and after focusing. Also, many enlargers have rather coarse gear mechanisms that make accurate focusing difficult. Most people have a tendency to put weight on the focusing knob unconsciously while trying to get the focus accurate. Then when they let go of it, the enlarger lifts a little and the image is left slightly out of focus. By using, on the enlarger, a camera lens of the type that has a built-in focusing mechanism, you can solve both of these problems at once. Use the focusing knob on the enlarger for a coarse adjustment, and then do the fine focus by turning the appropriate ring on the lens mount. It is difficult and quite unnatural to put excessive weight on the lens mount, because of its construction. An accurate fine focus is thus very easily achieved.

Vibration

Printing times are typically time exposures. Keep in mind that any vibration during the exposure will make your prints appear unsharp. Hold still during the exposure, so that your body movements do not cause vibrations. Watch for the effects of nearby equipment motors, the footsteps of passers-by, or the rumble of vehicles outside your building. Vibration effects can be detected quite easily during focusing by closely watching the image in the grain focuser.

CHAPTER 8

Stereo Photography

Stereo photography is the making of pictures that can be viewed so as to appear three-dimensional, by optically fusing two separate pictures in the viewer's mind. There has always been a definite value in the stereo photography of objects of scientific study, since it is such a convenient means of communicating spatial relations. Unfortunately, this value is frequently overlooked. See Color Plate II for examples of stereo photos.

The recent development of the scanning electron microscope (SEM), in which the subject can be viewed only indirectly as a two-dimensional representation on a viewing screen or as a photographic print, has done much to stimulate the interest of scientists in stereo viewing. It is only by this means that the spatial relations in SEM subjects can be accurately determined, and failure to do so can easily result in substantial misinterpretation of visual information. Some scientists and scientific photographers are coming to realize that similar misinterpretations can also occur in other contexts.

The use of stereo photographs in scientific publication has been limited somewhat by misunderstandings of the basic principles of stereo photography and of the practical methods of viewing. The following text should clear up most of these problems. It is assumed that you will be photographing subjects that are essentially static. Moving subjects require the use of optical stereo attachments, special stereo cameras, or linked double cameras. Greater flexibility of approach is possible when the pictures are made using sequential single exposures, or when two cameras are used in a manner that allows variation of the separation between them.

BASIC PRINCIPLES

It is not my intention here to present a definitive text on all aspects of stereo photography, or to describe its application to problems of measurement, as in the science of photogrammetry. However, studying the material to follow will enable you to do stereo photography well enough to communicate very accurately the three-dimensional shape of the subject and the way in which portions of it may overlap and underlie one another. For deeper study of the method and for other applications, see the books by Blaker, 1976, McKay, 1953, and Valyus, 1966.

Base Separation

The basis of stereo photography is the making of two similar but not identical photographs from lens positions, relative to the subject, so spaced as to simulate the separation of your two eyes. The actual spacing used is related to the intended appearance of the subject; the technical term for this spacing is *base separation*. Ideally, the axes of these two lens positions should be parallel, though "toeing-in" can be successful if it is not overdone (in fact, in SEM work it is the normal technique, because of limitations inherent in the instrument). Excessive convergence of the lens axes will result in a noticeable change of image magnification across the picture; this change proceeds in opposite directions in the two prints. Only parallel-axis techniques will be discussed here.

In normal stereo photography, the base separation should approximately equal the distance between your two eyes. Conventionally, a distance of 65 mm is usually considered a normal separation for stereo photography (though wider and narrower separations between people's eyes are common; my own are 75 mm apart). Unusually distant subjects, which will not receive further attention here, require abnormally wide base separation if a good stereo depth effect is to be achieved. Closeup photography and photomacrography both require bringing the lens unusually close to a rather small subject, and thus require an abnormally narrow base separation.

There is a formula, shown here as Formula 5, for calculating any of the four variables in stereo photography. To solve for any one unknown, knowing the other three variables, just multiply the two diagonally opposite knowns and then divide that product by the third known. This will yield the unknown value. Note that all four distances in this formula must be given in the same units of measure. The formula represents a simple proportional relationship.

FORMULA 5
General formula for stereo photography.

$$\frac{\text{Normal eye separation}}{\text{Apparent subject distance}} = \frac{\text{base separation}}{\text{lens-to-subject distance}}$$

$$\frac{N}{D} = \frac{B}{d}$$

FORMULA 6
Stereo base-separation formula.

$$\text{Base separation} = \frac{\text{normal eye separation} \times \text{lens-to-subject distance}}{\text{apparent subject distance}}$$

$$B = \frac{N \times d}{D}$$

If you know the values of N, D, and d, as you normally would in laboratory work, you will be solving for the value of B, the base separation. This is shown in Formula 6, which is identical to Formula 5 except for the rearrangement of terms. Thus, if $N = 65$ mm, $d = 2000$ mm, and D is to be 1000 mm, the correct base separation is 130 mm.

Calculating the correct base separation requires that you understand the nature of the factor D, the apparent subject distance. In normal stereo photography you simply want distances and sizes to appear as they do to the unaided eye. Therefore, D should equal d, the lens-to-subject distance. If it does, then B will obviously be equal to N. A question arises when you do unusually close photography: What should be the value of D when the lens-to-subject distance is drastically shortened? This is answered by realizing that the magnified image will appear in the picture like an enlarged model of the subject. Therefore, it seems reasonable that the apparent subject distance should be a close normal viewing distance, as though you were actually viewing a model. A reasonable value for D, then, would be about 16 inches, or 400 mm, for all stereo photography where the camera lens is closer than normal to the subject, as in closeup photography and photomacrography.

Axis Alignment

In order to view a pair of stereo photographs without difficulty, they must be accurately aligned in both the original photography and in mounting the prints. If the pair is made by taking two successive pictures with the same camera (or with two unlinked cameras), as will be assumed in this book, the equipment must be set up so that there is a common horizontal baseline, perpendicular to the lens axes. If this is not done, the tops and bottoms of the two pictures will be stepped, or the two will be rotationally misaligned, as shown in Figure 35. Only the subject matter in the centers of the pictures will be correctly related. Thus, there will be no stereo depth effect in those portions of each picture that are not also included within the bounds of the other.

The two prints must be mounted (or at least carefully laid out) so that this horizontal axis is maintained. If the two pictures were photographed in correct alignment, but are mounted either stepped (one slightly above the other) or with one rotated slightly, it will be difficult to fuse the two images visually. Most people can accommodate their vision to slight errors in alignment, but some few cannot tolerate any misalignment at all.

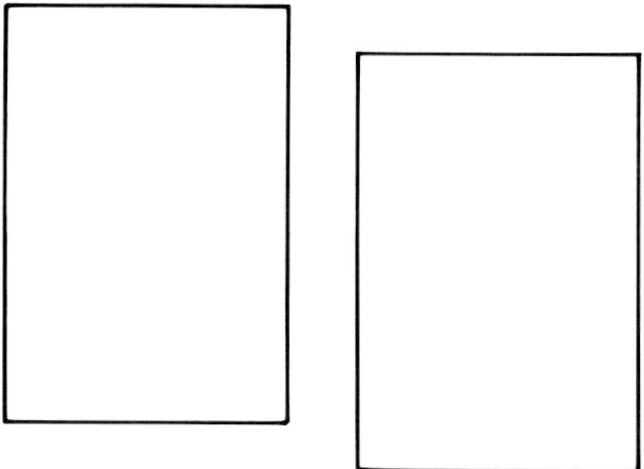

A Vertical misalignment

B Rotational misalignment

FIGURE 35
Misalignment of stereo pairs. If stereo pairs of photographs are not properly aligned it will be difficult to visually blend the two into a three-dimensional view.

A third factor related to axis alignment is the correct left/right placement of the two pictures. The essence of stereo photography is that the lens axes of the two pictures—whether exposed simultaneously or sequentially—are displaced left and right in analogy with human eyes. In order to obtain a correct impression of the spatial relations, the two prints must be mounted in the correct left/right order. If they are reversed, the depth impression will be reversed also: nearer portions of the subject will appear to recede, and farther portions will jut forward. In photographs of familiar subjects the error will be immediately obvious, but in science there are many subjects whose relief effects are not so easily perceptible—and these are where the stereo depth impression will be the most important. Therefore, you must keep careful account of which picture is which.

If you know for sure whether the overall shape of the subject is convex or concave, all is not lost if you lose track of the left/right orientation in handling the photographs before mounting. You need only remember that the right eye will see further around the right side of the subject than the left, and vice versa. Careful examination of the two photographs will then reveal the correct placement. However, if you are at all uncertain about the overall shape, you must go back and redo the photography, this time keeping better track of the pictures.

TECHNIQUES

In this section it is assumed that you are making sequential exposures, with either the camera or the subject shifted between them so as to achieve the desired base separation. If you use a commercial stereo camera, the accompanying instruction booklet will provide all the guidance you need.

Casual Stereo

With all the talk here about base separations, axis alignments, and the like, you should not forget that these matters simply rationalize the process of stereo photography. Actually, it is possible to achieve a usable three-dimensional viewing effect with almost any two closely similar but not identical photographs of the same subject. Thus, for instance, if you use a handheld camera to make a series of closeup flash photographs of a small, immobile subject, all at the same magnification, chances are good that you have the raw material for a stereo pair, should you later feel the need for it.

Handheld operation of a camera, as in normal closeup flash photography, virtually assures that no two pictures will have quite the same lens axis. Therefore, you will have a good chance of achieving a stereo depth effect by mounting any two similar views in the correct left/right alignment (which must usually be determined by examining the pictures, as noted above). Obviously, there would be no calculation of base separation, nor would the horizontal baselines or rotational alignments be likely to coincide exactly. However, with suitable trimming or masking, a stereo pair usable for limited purposes could probably be made. For an example of casual stereo photography, see Color Plate IIA.

I don't particularly recommend doing such casual stereo photography, but you should keep the possibility in mind in case a change in circumstances should develop after the fact—it could be beneficial to your ends. And there might be times when, although the expected subject motion would appear to preclude stereo photography, the subject might actually hold still long enough to allow a quick second shot.

Normal Stereo

Doing normal stereo photography of laboratory subjects is quite simple. You just make two well-aligned photographs in which the base separation is equal to the normal distance between human eyes, about 65 mm. Lens-to-subject distances here would include anything over about 16 inches, up to any distance your space allows. (For telephotography of distant subjects in stereo, see Blaker, *Field Photography*, 1976.)

Closeup Stereo

In closeup photography, with lens-to-subject distances less than about 16 inches but with image magnifications not much exceeding actual size, Table 9 will assist your work. It is based on Formula 6, and assumes a normal eye separation of 65 mm, a lens focal length of 55 mm, and an apparent subject distance of 400 mm.

Photomacrographic Stereo

In photomacrography using large film sizes (or, for that matter, in large-negative photography through the microscope), it is often more practical to move the subject, rather than the camera, to achieve base separation. The details of this method are a little different, but it is both convenient and effective.

The first requirement is that the film used be somewhat larger than the picture area needed (it is assumed that the negative will be contact-printed, if it is not on Polaroid Land film). About the smallest practical size is the 3¼ × 4¼-inch size of the standard Polaroid films. Although conventional films are entirely practical, the rapid access to both black-and-white and color Polaroid prints is very useful here, as the stereo effect achieved can be checked at once. For the first picture, you compose the desired 65-mm width of subject matter on one side of center of the camera's viewing screen, and make your

TABLE 9
Suggested base separations for closeup stereo photography.

IMAGE MAGNIFICATION	LENS-TO-SUBJECT DISTANCE, mm[a]	BASE SEPARATION, mm[b]
×0.2	330	54
×0.25	275	45
×0.33	220	36
×0.50	165	27
×0.75	128	21
×1	110	18
×2	82	13
×3	73	12

[a]Calculated as for a "thin lens" of 55 mm focal length, a normal eye separation of 65 mm, and an apparent subject distance of 400 mm.
[b]In the ×2 and ×3 magnifications, the suggested separations are appropriate regardless of the method used (i.e., bellows extension or tele-converter) to get the image size.

exposure. The second picture is composed with the subject shifted to the opposite side of the viewing screen, and is made on another sheet of film.

The second requirement arises in mounting the prints for viewing. After the excess, non-duplicated print area is trimmed away, you mount the prints *in the reverse order:* the left exposure is placed on the right side, and vice versa. The reason for this reversal is simple. When the subject was shifted to the *left* of the lens axis, it was seen by the camera *as though by your right eye,* and vice versa. If this reversal of print position is not done, the relief effect will be opposite to normal, with "hills" appearing to be "valleys."

TABLE 10
Suggested base separations for photomacrographic stereo.

IMAGE MAGNIFICATION	LENS FOCAL LENGTH, mm[a]	LENS-TO-SUBJECT DISTANCE, mm[b]	BASE SEPARATION, mm[c]
×5	40	48	8
×8–15	25	28	4.5
×20–50	16	16.5	3

[a]Focal lengths shown are for readily available photomacrographic lenses, and are those regarded as most likely to be used for the magnifications listed, considering the lengths of common bellows.
[b]At magnifications much above ×1, lens-to-subject distance changes very little as magnification is increased further (see Figure 33); therefore, these are average figures. They are based on "thin lens" calculations, but are adequate for the purpose.
[c]These are close approximations, adequate for the need.

A tabulation of suggested base separations is offered here as Table 10. The apparent subject distance is again standardized at 400 mm, and the eye separation at 65 mm.

Depth of field is always a problem in photomacrography because of the limitations that diffraction effects impose on the use of small lens apertures. In stereo photomacrography I have found that it helps to focus at slightly different levels for the two exposures; if not carried to excess, this tends to expand the apparent depth of field without sacrificing the stereo depth effect. The slight magnification anomalies that result are easily accommodated visually. See Color Plate IIB.

It is possible to make stereo photographs through the oculars of dissecting microscopes that use doubled objective lenses, using special commercially available cameras, but I don't recommend this practice as a rule. There is no control over depth of field, and in some such microscopes the optics—though adequate for visual observation—are inferior for photographic purposes. You can probably get substantially better results by other methods. In any case, it is useless to attempt it with binocular research microscopes: these have only one objective lens, so there will be no stereo effect. The use of stereo technique in photomicrography will be discussed in Chapter 9.

Exaggerated Stereo

When photographing subjects of low relief or with closely set overlapping structures, it is often useful to exaggerate the stereo depth effect for purposes of easier analysis. It is quite simple to do so: just use a wider base separation than would ordinarily be recommended for the circumstances.

VIEWING METHODS

Much of the resistance to the use of stereo photographs in publication is due to a failure to realize the simplicity of several of the methods of viewing them. There are a number of methods and devices used for viewing stereo pairs. Three of the simplest will be described here.

Although the base separation in the original photography should generally comply with the standards described earlier, the prints for viewing need not do so if the viewing method does not demand it. The compact viewers that operate on a principle similar to that of the old parlor stereoscopes require a center-to-center distance—and thus a maximum print width—of 65 mm. But some devices or methods allow you to view larger sizes of prints.

Optical Viewers

User-generated stereo pairs are most commonly viewed with the aid of a double-lens optical viewer of the type shown in Figure 36. These devices are readily available, very satisfactory, and inexpensive. They do limit the print width to about 65 mm, but the prints can be of any reasonable length.

Larger prints, usually up to about 10 inches in width, can be viewed with the rather more complex and considerably more costly laterally adjustable viewers intended for use primarily in the interpretation of aerial photographs. If you do a lot of stereo work and do not want to be limited to small print sizes, one of these viewers may be just the thing.

Tube Viewing

Probably the simplest and cheapest device for viewing either large or small stereo pairs (with

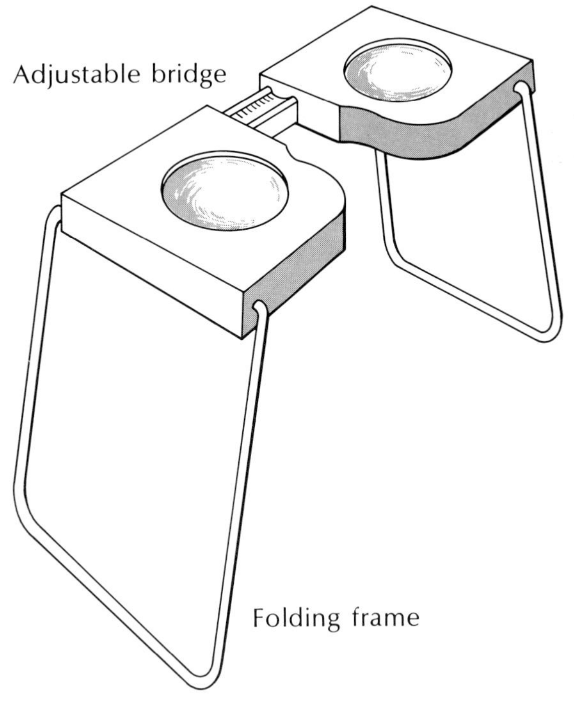

FIGURE 36
Typical stereo viewer, a folding pocket model that adjusts to the viewer's eye separation.

no limits on size, and practical for viewing pairs as small as 35 mm color slides) is a pair of paper or cardboard tubes about 1½ inches in diameter and about 4½ inches long—ordinary toilet-paper tubes do nicely. See Figure 37.

To view by this method, lay the prints out in good alignment and then hold the tubes like binoculars in front of your eyes. Adjust their positions so that the vision of each eye is restricted to the appropriate print of the pair. This way you can easily fuse the two images visually, to obtain the full stereo depth effect.

Direct Viewing

With a little practice, most people can learn to visually fuse stereo pairs without any viewing device at all. This method, of course, places no upper limits on the print size.

Once you have laid out or mounted the prints in correct alignment, you look "through" them by letting your eyes focus at infinity. The pictures are then out of focus, but the eye axes are parallel. After doing this for a moment you should see a third out-of-focus image appear between the two pictures. The trick lies in focusing your eyes on this center image without converging them, as would be normal at close focus. If you let your eyes converge, the center image immediately disappears, and you find yourself looking at one of the prints. But focusing on the center image without convergence immediately results in a stereo effect with all of the depth discernible by any other method of viewing. The technique does take some concentration and a little practice, but it is very convenient.

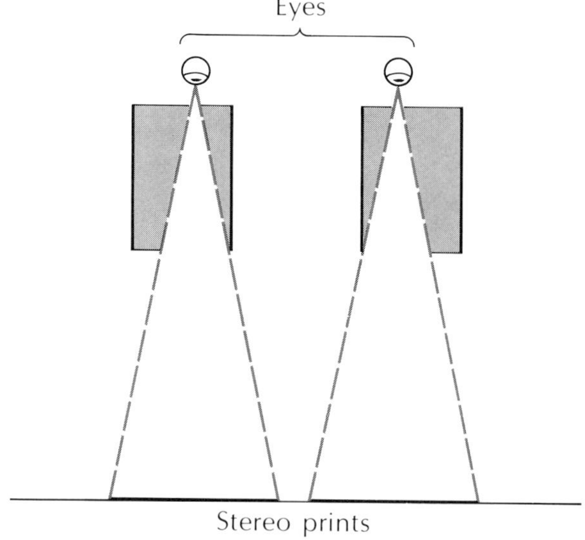

FIGURE 37
Tube viewing of stereo prints. Two paper tubes can be handheld so that each eye can see only the appropriate picture of the stereo pair. This is a quick and easy method of viewing unmounted stereo prints or color slides.

Some smug individuals can do direct stereo viewing quickly and at will, while others seem quite unable to do it at all. I can do it quite easily most of the time, but if I am tired it comes hard or not at all. If I find it difficult, or if I just don't feel like concentrating, I have found it practical to employ a variation of the tube method in which I cup my fingers around my eyes, binocular fashion. It works quickly and without strain, even when I am tired. Once you do establish the depth effect you can take your hands down and view indefinitely without losing the stereo effect and without strain.

Any feeling of eyestrain that develops during tube or direct viewing is usually due to misalignment of the two pictures—particularly when they are simply laid out rather than carefully mounted—or from having your head rotated slightly off-axis. In the latter case, just move your head appropriately and the problem ceases. If two loose pictures are out of alignment, let your eyes go to infinity focus, and you will see the main blocks of light and dark of the two pictures. Any misalignment will be obvious if you look for it, and you can move one of the prints as needed. When the alignment is correct, the third image usually appears right away, and you can then slip into strain-free stereo viewing.

CHAPTER 9

Photomicrography

Photography through the compound microscope is called photomicrography, and is a technique that many people in science must sooner or later use. It can be done at many levels of finesse, starting with the combination of the simplest of box cameras with a student microscope, and progressing through the use of semiautomated integrated-design photomicroscopes, to the sophisticated use of research-grade microscopes for the definitive photography of difficult subjects.

The purpose of this chapter is to provide sufficient basic information to allow the accomplishment of photomicrography good enough for the illustration of anything from high school science projects to professional research papers. The emphasis will be on the techniques that can be used with ordinarily available basic equipment. There will be no discussion of the phase-contrast or interference-phase techniques, because they are equipment-specific. The best source of information for those techniques is the instruction booklet supplied with the equipment. But, since those techniques, as well as various other esoteric practices, are based squarely on standard methods of microscopy, the material here should aid you in understanding them.

I will also not discuss the operation of commercial integrated-design photomicroscopes, because they too are equipment-specific. See the appropriate instruction booklet for details. Automated and semiautomated devices are capable of producing fine results, if they are well designed and kept in good adjustment. Unfortunately, they are often—perhaps even usually—out of proper adjustment, in my experience; worse yet, many of them have design limitations that tend to reduce their capabilities. They do give the impression of speed and ease of operation; however, this is an illusion, since their correct operation requires precisely the same technical method as that used for an ordinary camera placed on a good standard microscope. The one method is no harder or easier than the other. The integrated devices tend to be needlessly expensive, and one of the latest and most grand-looking models, for instance, is almost impossible to clean without major dismantling. If you are already a user of such equipment, however, this chapter should enhance your understanding of it.

It is possible to make publication-grade photomicrographs using surprisingly simple equipment and setups. The basis of good image quality is the quality of the microscope optics and the care used in the lighting. The type and quality of the camera are close to irrelevant, if it is used carefully and correctly.

COMPOUND MICROSCOPES

A compound microscope is an instrument in which two lenses in train—the objective and the ocular—produce a highly magnified image by a stepped and optically corrected method. (Objectives and oculars will be discussed in detail shortly.) There are several types of compound microscopes. Those most commonly used in photomicrography are appraised below.

Dissecting Microscopes

One type of microscope likely to be encountered early in one's education is the dissecting microscope, which is typically a double-objective, binocular instrument of low power. It is used primarily for the study of small three-dimensional objects, and provides a full stereo image.

Although it is possible to do either stereo or two-dimensional photomicrography through a dissecting microscope, I do not generally recommend it. The optics of many such instruments, though entirely satisfactory for visual observation, are inferior for photographic purposes. Furthermore, such low-power work commonly requires a degree of control of the depth of field that is impractical or impossible without a lens diaphragm. Therefore I believe that this sort of work can be done better, and usually easier, using the techniques for photomacrography and stereo photography described earlier in this book.

Student Microscopes

The relatively inexpensive microscopes generally provided for student use in high schools and colleges are quite suitable for certain types of photomicrography. Typically, these are monocular or binocular instruments, and have either no *substage condenser* (a light-concentrating lens system placed just below the microscope stage) or only a rudimentary one. Often, the only provision for concentrating the light is the swiveling substage mirror. One side is flat and is used simply to change the direction of the illuminating beam, but the other is concave and can act to focus the beam. The *substage diaphragm* (properly a part of the substage condenser assembly, and used to control depth of field, image contrast, and image diffraction) may be absent, or present only as a rotating metal disk with holes of different sizes in it.

With all their limitations, however, most student microscopes have adequate optics and can be carefully used so as to yield photomicrographs that are sufficiently good for many publication purposes. Well handled, they are at least the equal of a poorly handled high-quality instrument.

Research Microscopes

A typical full-scale research microscope of recent design is of the trinocular type. There is the usual angled binocular apparatus for comfortable visual observation, and a straight-through, third ocular position for convenient photomicrography.

Most research microscopes have a focusable substage condenser with a built-in iris diaphragm. An illuminator may or may not be built into the base. Those that *are* built in feature a certain degree of adjustability of the lamp position, a lamp or field condenser lens, and an iris field diaphragm. (Although the two systems work together, the field condenser and diaphragm primarily control what is called the *field of illumination,* while the substage condenser and diaphragm are used mostly to control the depth of field, image contrast, and image diffraction, as noted above.)

These instruments are capable of quite sophisticated photomicrography; if flat-field optics are mounted, you may not need anything more, unless high-grade photography is a major concern in your work.

Photo Microscopes

Essentially, a first-class photo microscope is an unusually fine research instrument with a large-diameter tube. This tube allows a larger image spread for the objective lens, and its size tends to prevent internal reflections. The objective and ocular lenses are matched to each other to provide a maximum degree of optical correction and a flat-field image projection. The objective lens mounts should provide for mechanical centering of the lenses.

The main stage has a two-dimensionally adjustable mechanical stage mounted on it, and the main stage itself should rotate. The substage condenser can be focused, centered, and rotated, and has a built-in iris diaphragm and a provision for mounting filters, center stops, and other light modifiers. There may be two interchangeable condensers, matched to different objective lenses, for maximum control of the lighting. Technical descriptions of the use of these fixtures follow later in this chapter.

LENSES

Top-quality photomicrography requires that the objective and the ocular be matched, as noted above, for best image correction; in particular, they must be matched to provide a flat field in the projected image so that it will coincide with the plane of the film. If flat-field oculars are not used, you will be able to focus sharply only in the center; the edges of the picture cannot be focused sharply at the same time because the projected image will be a portion of a sphere. Poorer lenses may also exhibit substantial optical aberrations in the off-axis image areas, which grow progressively worse with increasing distance from the center. Your eyes can compensate for these defects to a degree, but the film cannot.

Objectives

The lens that is nearest to the subject and does the initial magnification is called the *objective*. There are a number of variable attributes in objective lenses. First of all, one must understand the meanings of the figures engraved on the objective lens mounts; reference to Figure 38 will help.

As an example, the first line in the lens shown in part A begins with the manufacturer's designation of the lens type: "Plan" (a contraction of a trade name) means that it is a planachromat, or flat-field achromat. Such markings vary widely because there are many lens designs by a good number of makers. The figure "40" means that the initial magnification is ×40. The figure "0.65" after the slash denotes a numerical aperture of 0.65. (Numerical aperture is a figure that indicates, among other things, the resolution capability of the lens. We will consider some of the implications of numerical aperture later—see page 150.)

The second line begins with the notation "160," which means that the distance between the seat of the objective and that of the ocular—known as the tube length—should be 160 mm. The figure "0.17" after the slash means that this lens is corrected for a cover-glass thickness (on the microscope slide) of 0.17 mm. Some

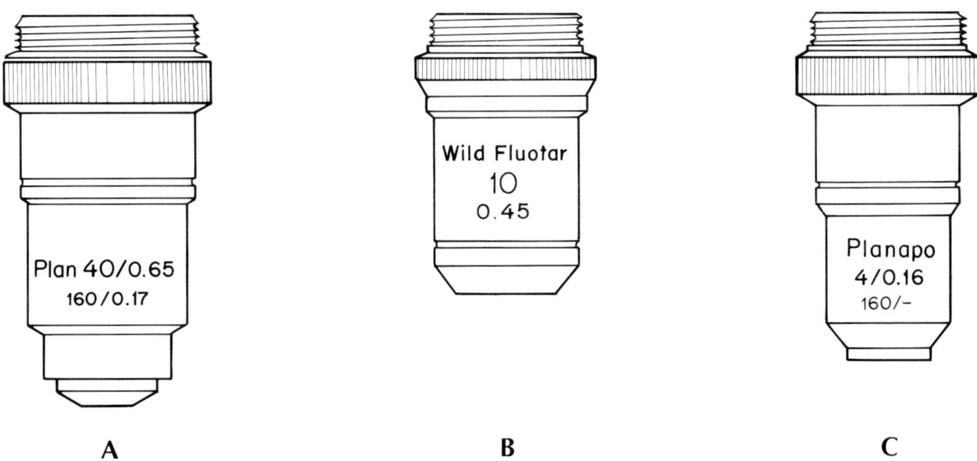

FIGURE 38
Examples of engraving on typical microscope objective lenses.

A A Zeiss lens of ×40 magnification and a numerical aperture of 0.65. It requires a microscope tube length of 160 mm, and is corrected for a cover-slip thickness of 0.17 mm.
B A Wild lens of ×10 magnification and a numerical aperture of 0.45. (No tube length or cover-slip thickness is specified.)
C A Zeiss lens of ×4 magnification and a numerical aperture of 0.16. It is designed for a tube length of 160 mm. (Cover-slip thickness is not specified.)

Note that, as the magnification decreases, so does the numerical aperture (though there is some variation in each magnification range).

lenses are corrected for use without a cover slip, and others for glasses of differing thicknesses. For best results, of course, you should use lenses corrected for the thickness of the glass you use, or vice versa. (The engravings on the objectives shown in parts B and C of Figure 38 are interpreted in the figure legend.)

Oculars

The eyepiece of a microscope is called the *ocular.* Its functions are to provide secondary magnification of the initial image formed within the microscope tube by the objective, and to correct certain optical effects so that the final image will be substantially free of aberrations. Under specified standard conditions, the final image magnification will be equal to that of the objective multiplied by that of the ocular; thus, a ×40 objective used with a ×10 ocular will produce a ×400 image, at a plane 10 inches (254 mm) above the eyepoint of the ocular (see pages 145–146). In photomicrographic practice this particular distance is not always used, however.

For photomicrographic purposes, the ocular should be matched to the objective by make and type. It is, for example, a poor idea to use a Leitz objective with a Zeiss ocular, because they are not likely to be of optically matched designs. See your dealer for recommendations within your chosen line of equipment.

ILLUMINATORS

The lamps designed for use with microscopes are generally called *illuminators,* and come in a variety of forms. I will not discuss those that are built into certain microscopes, as they are equipment-specific. For such items, direct any questions to your supplier.

The illuminators provided to students, or otherwise used for casual microscopy, are generally quite simple. Some are merely an ordinary frosted household light bulb enclosed in a shaded holder. Even these can be used for successful photomicrography if the image-resolution demands are not too great.

An illuminator that can assist in the formation of images of the highest quality, as in Köhler-system imaging (which is discussed later in this chapter), must be of quite complex design. The bulb will typically burn at low voltage, and may be of almost any basic filament design (the once almost universal ribbon filaments are not needed with Köhler lighting, as almost any reasonably compact filament will suffice). It will be two-dimensionally centerable, and either it or the condenser lens on the lamphouse will be focusable. The condenser, called the *field condenser,*

PLATE 11 ▶

Photomicrography: Filtering in Black-and-White. (See page 136.)

In photomicrography of stained slides, subject detail is generally shown most clearly by using black-and-white panchromatic films in conjunction with color filters. Color photography, though perhaps prettier, is seldom as satisfactory for tissue differentiation. The subject here is a triple-stained leafhopper salivary-gland preparation, photographed at ×325. (Originally photographed for D. D. Jensen and J. Richardson.)

A A Wratten 45 deep blue-green filter serves to show the cell nuclei clearly.
B A Wratten 8 medium yellow filter fails to show the nuclei at all, though it does differentiate certain other structures more plainly.

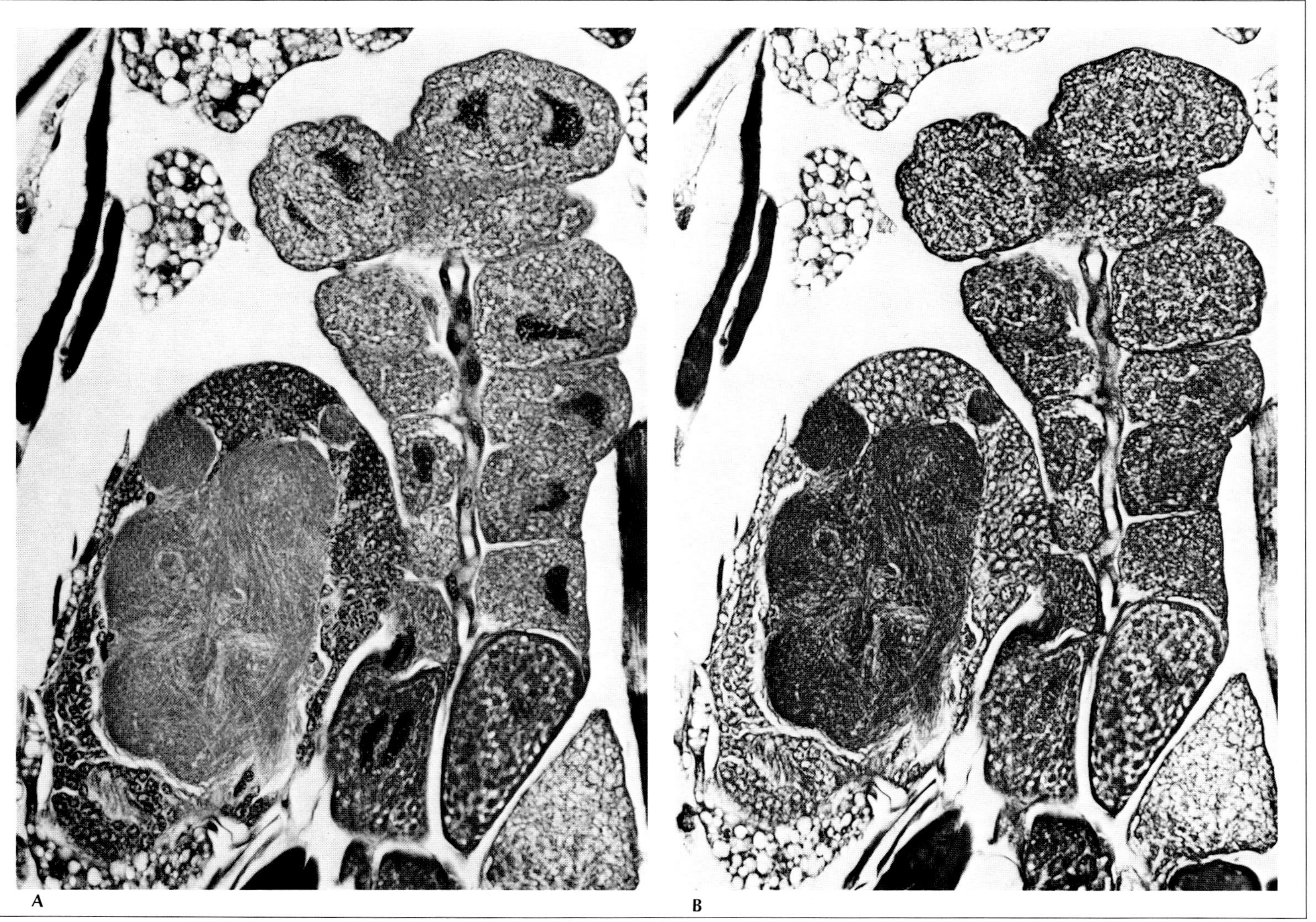
A
B

will be a single-element or multiple-element lens and will have a built-in iris diaphragm called the *field diaphragm.*

Good microscope illuminators tend to be quite costly, but they do contribute substantially to both image quality and ease of operation. In some the incandescent source is supplemented by an electronic flash tube, for stopping subject motion in photography; its use may also tend to standardize the color balance, when color films are used.

CAMERAS

Any camera at all can be used for photomicrography. A simple box camera, ranging from the large rectangular models of a few years ago to the current miniature designs typified by the Kodak Instamatic, can yield quite good photomicrographs, if the microscope itself is good and is well handled. However, the larger film sizes are to be preferred, in order to avoid overenlargement of very small negatives.

Complex small cameras such as the modern 35 mm models can yield good pictures, but there are two potential drawbacks. First, if the lens cannot be removed, as with most rangefinder models, it may yield a poorer image than that obtained with a simple box camera, because the very complexity of the lens may be optically detrimental to the system as a whole. Most single lens reflex cameras permit the removal of the lens, which is good, but mirror flop and the action of the focal-plane shutter may introduce unwelcome vibrations that will reduce image sharpness. It is therefore a good practice to avoid these problems; how to do it will be explained later. Second, the small film sizes with such cameras may be a disadvantage in ways quite aside from that of possible overenlargement, as will be seen when numerical aperture is discussed later.

In terms of image quality and general ease of operation, the best cameras for most photomicrography are the large press or view cameras, when suitably mounted (or, perhaps better yet, one of the old large-film-size cameras mounted on an optical bench—check your departmental attic). Such large cameras are always used with their own lenses removed. It is a distinct advantage to avoid the need for enlargement in the printing of photomicrographs.

Any camera used in conjunction with a microscope should be mounted separately, in such a way that there is no direct contact between it and the microscope. The space between them can be spanned with a baffled light trap, or you can simply wrap it with opaque black cloth.

PLATE 12 ▶

Photomicrography: Substage Diaphragm Setting. (See page 150.)

The degree of opening of the substage diaphragm of a microscope controls both depth of field and contrast. Although too small an opening will introduce diffraction effects, a moderate closure usually improves the appearance and clarity of the image. The subject here is tissue of the Oriental conifer *Gnetum gnemon,* photographed at ×221 with a Wratten 11 yellow-green filter. The original plate was labeled as for journal publication, prior to printing here. (Originally photographed for R. Rodin.)

A The full opening of the substage diaphragm was 30 mm in diameter, and for this picture it was closed to 20 mm.

B Here the diaphragm was closed further to 11 mm, to gain depth of field and contrast. Note the increase in visibility and sharpness of the points indicated by the arrows.

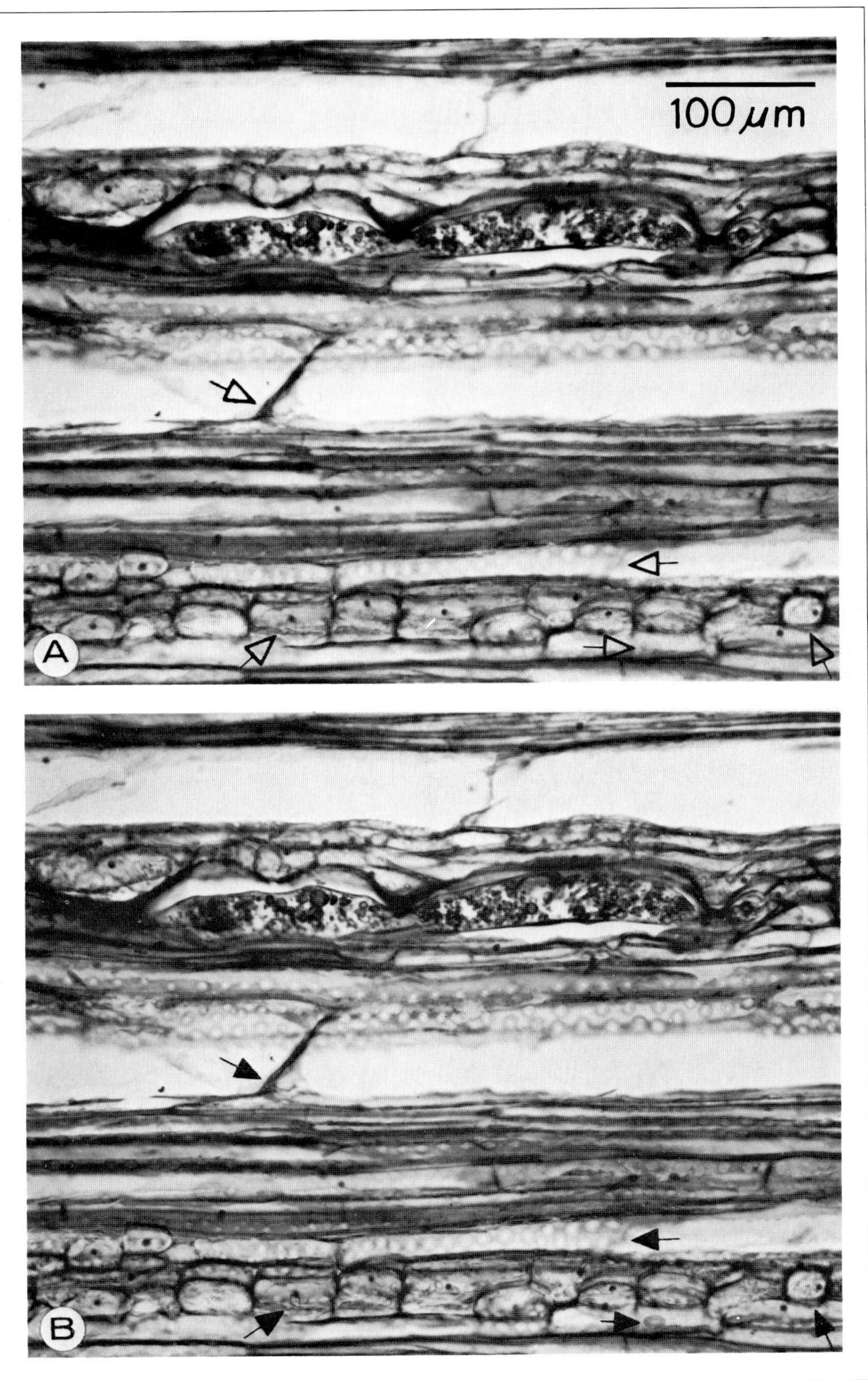
100 μm
A
B

This will prevent the transmission of any camera vibrations to the microscope. It is also a poor practice to use a mounting system that places the weight of the camera on the focusing mechanism of the microscope. The focus may tend to creep under the pressure; in any case, it causes undesirable wear.

FILMS

Any film that is appropriate for general photography can be used for photomicrography, but certain types offer special advantages at times.

Panchromatic Films

The commonly used panchromatic black-and-white films are very widely applicable in photomicrography because they record all of the visible wavelengths of light well. Since the dyes used to stain micrographic subjects come in many hues, the use of panchromatic films in conjunction with color filters provides a great degree of control in differentiating tissues and structures. Film grain is no part of the desired subject matter, so fine-grained films are especially needed in the smaller film sizes.

Orthochromatic Films

When the wavelengths to be recorded are in the blue and green regions of the spectrum, orthochromatic films are especially useful. The filtering required with panchromatic films in such circumstances may require inordinate increases in exposure time; this is particularly a problem with live subjects or those that have Brownian motion. Ortho films are easily obtainable in sheet-film sizes, but are rare in roll form.

PLATE 13 ▸

Photomicrography: Numerical Aperture and Magnification, I. (See pages 150–154.)

This series of photomicrographs reveals the effect of using various objective lenses, as seen in prints made to the same final magnification. Not all the effects shown are directly attributable to the different numerical apertures, but these results are typical of careful work designed to achieve maximum comparability. It was not possible to make prints precisely matched in overall contrast, because of differences in the image structure.

A Objective: 16 mm Zeiss Luminar, designed for use in low-power micrography without an ocular. It is a lens of tested fine quality, and was used at its maximum resolution aperture (wide open): the #1 aperture, equivalent to *f*/3.5. Original photography was at ×62, enlarged to ×510.
B Objective: ×4 Carl Zeiss Planapo N.A. 0.16. Ocular: Zeiss Kpl 8. Original photography was at ×62, enlarged to ×510.
C Objective: ×10 Carl Zeiss Planapo N.A. 0.32. Ocular: Zeiss Kpl 8. Original photography was at ×192, enlarged to ×510.
D Objective: ×25 Carl Zeiss Planapo N.A. 0.63. Ocular: Zeiss Kpl 8. Original photography was at ×510, and this is a contact print.

It would not be normal to print parts A and B at such great enlargement, but projection slides might commonly be made from them. Clearly, slides from these equal subject areas would deliver widely different amounts of information to the screen, depending upon which objective was used. Color slides *were* made under identical conditions, and showed comparable results.

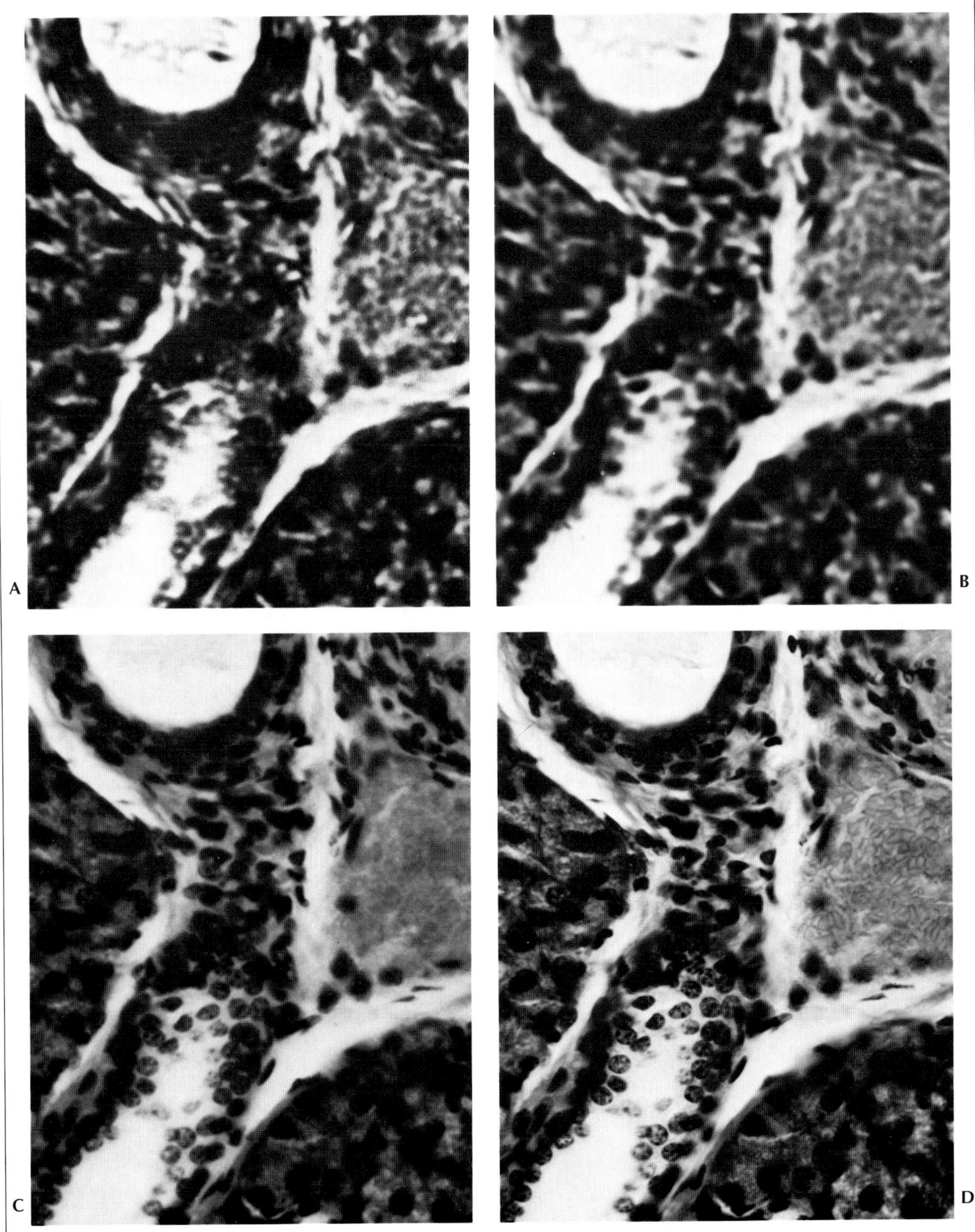
A
B
C
D

High-Contrast Films

Slides that are stained lightly or not at all, or that stain to very low visual contrast, are a special problem. For these you should consider using such films as Kodak Contrast Process Pan or Contrast Process Ortho, when using sheet films. Those using 35 mm cameras can get similar effects with the high-contrast panchromatic films intended for document copying, such as Kodak High Contrast Copy film, or H & W Control VTE Pan and VTE Ultra Pan. (These films have exceptionally fine grain and can, if necessary, be processed to normal contrasts; see Chapter 7.)

Color Films

Color transparency films are often used to make slides, "to wake up the audience" with their colors. Although the use of color film is fully justified wherever it genuinely contributes to the information content of a photomicrograph, it should be realized that in most cases the use of color filters with black-and-white films will considerably increase the clarity with which structures can be seen. Color used for its own sake is seldom a good idea in photomicrography, where the color in the subject is usually an artifact intended simply to differentiate the structures.

Kodak has a color transparency film specifically for photomicrography, called Photomicrography Color Film 2483; it offers better than normal color separation, relatively high contrast, and very fine grain.

Color negative films are generally not a good idea for photomicrography, if someone else is to do the printing. Commercial printers, or anyone else not familiar with the particular subject slide, will have no idea of the correct colors of the subject. Any accuracy in the color reproduction will therefore be largely accidental. If color prints are needed, it would be better to use color transparency film and have color prints made later. The transparency itself then serves as a guide to the correct colors.

Polaroid Land Films

The rapid-access Polaroid Land films, in both black-and-white and color, have obvious uses in photomicrography. The P/N-type black-and-white films, in which both a positive print and

---

PLATE 14 ▶

Photomicrography: Numerical Aperture and Magnification, II. (See pages 150–154.)

Contact prints from the negatives used in Plate 13 are shown here to reveal that there is nothing wrong with the lenses being compared, but only that their use must be carefully considered.

A Contact print of the negative used in Plate 13A.
B Contact print of the negative used in Plate 13B.
C Contact print of the negative used in Plate 13C.

Plate 13D was already a contact print, and is not repeated here. To show the possibilities inherent in large-negative photomicrography, the following are offered:

D Center portion of a contact print from an 11 × 14-inch negative made under conditions similar to those of Plate 13D. The setup and magnification are the same, but a different slide was used.
E Lower right corner of the same print as that from which part D was taken. It is slightly darker, owing to light falloff, but is otherwise optically about equal.

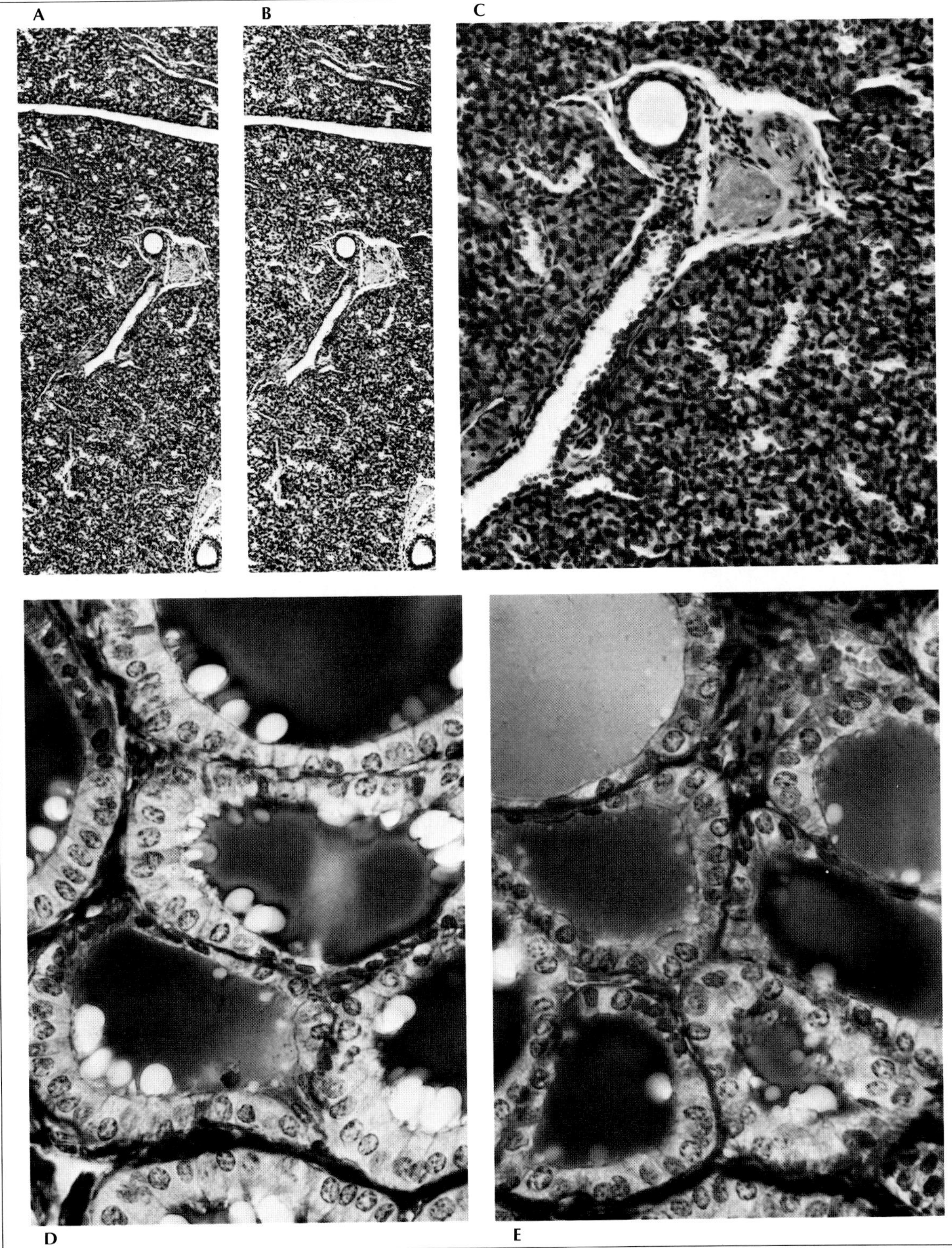
A
B
C
D
E

a high-quality negative are produced, are especially good.

The improved Polacolor 2 film is much better than the earlier form in its color qualities, and is a good way of getting prints with controlled color. Any corrective filtering can be done in the original photography, with immediate determination of the need for and the correctness of the filter choices. Although previously available only in a $3\frac{1}{4} \times 4\frac{1}{4}$-inch format, it has just been introduced in an 8×10-inch format.

The Polaroid Land SX-70 color film, which has very good color saturation, can be used in photomicrography by adapting the SX-70 camera to a microscope. The format is small ($3\frac{1}{8}$ inches square), but the prints are unusually durable and colorfast.

Special-Purpose Films

Various manufacturers make a variety of special-purpose films that can be used for photomicrography. See your local representative if you feel the need for something unusual.

FILTERS

There are a couple of misunderstandings about filters that seem to be prevalent among the more casual users of photomicrographic apparatus.

As part of the equipment normally supplied with certain microscope illuminators, there is a light blue "daylight" filter. Its intended purpose is to decrease glare and give a more "natural" color rendering in visual observation. In fact, it does neither to any important degree. It should not be used routinely in all photomicrography, as some people do, but it does have some minor utility as a color filter in black-and-white photography.

A deep green or blue-green filter is often sold as a "high-resolution" filter for photomicrography, on the grounds that it transmits light in the region where wavelengths are short and where the lenses are maximally corrected. A surprising number of people use it for all photomicrography, because they have come to believe that without it their pictures will not be

---

PLATE 15 ▶

Photomicrography: Oil-Immersion vs. High-Dry. (See page 152.)

Certain photomicrography, in the higher magnification ranges, is best done using oil-immersion of the objective lens, and perhaps of the substage condenser (often only the former is oiled to the subject slide, as was true here). This plate compares the results of oil-immersion and so-called high-dry photomicrography of a slide showing a neuron of a Goby fish, photographed at ×754 using a Wratten 15 deep yellow filter. The original plate was labeled as for journal publication, prior to printing here. (Originally photographed for D. Zambrono.)

A Oil-immersion photomicrography using a Carl Zeiss Jena Apochromat ×35 N.A. 0.85 oil objective, a Carl Zeiss Kpl 12.5 ocular, and an eyepoint-to-film distance of 40 cm. Sharpness is very good (the unsharpness of the right edge area is due to a minor wrinkle in the tissue on the subject slide).
B High-dry photomicrography using a Carl Zeiss Planapo ×25 N.A. 0.63 dry objective, a Carl Zeiss Kpl 8 ocular, and a distance of 88 cm—a length generally considered to be too long. This unusually long camera extension is too much for this lens combination (though it might be entirely satisfactory for others), and produces an unsharp image (empty magnification).

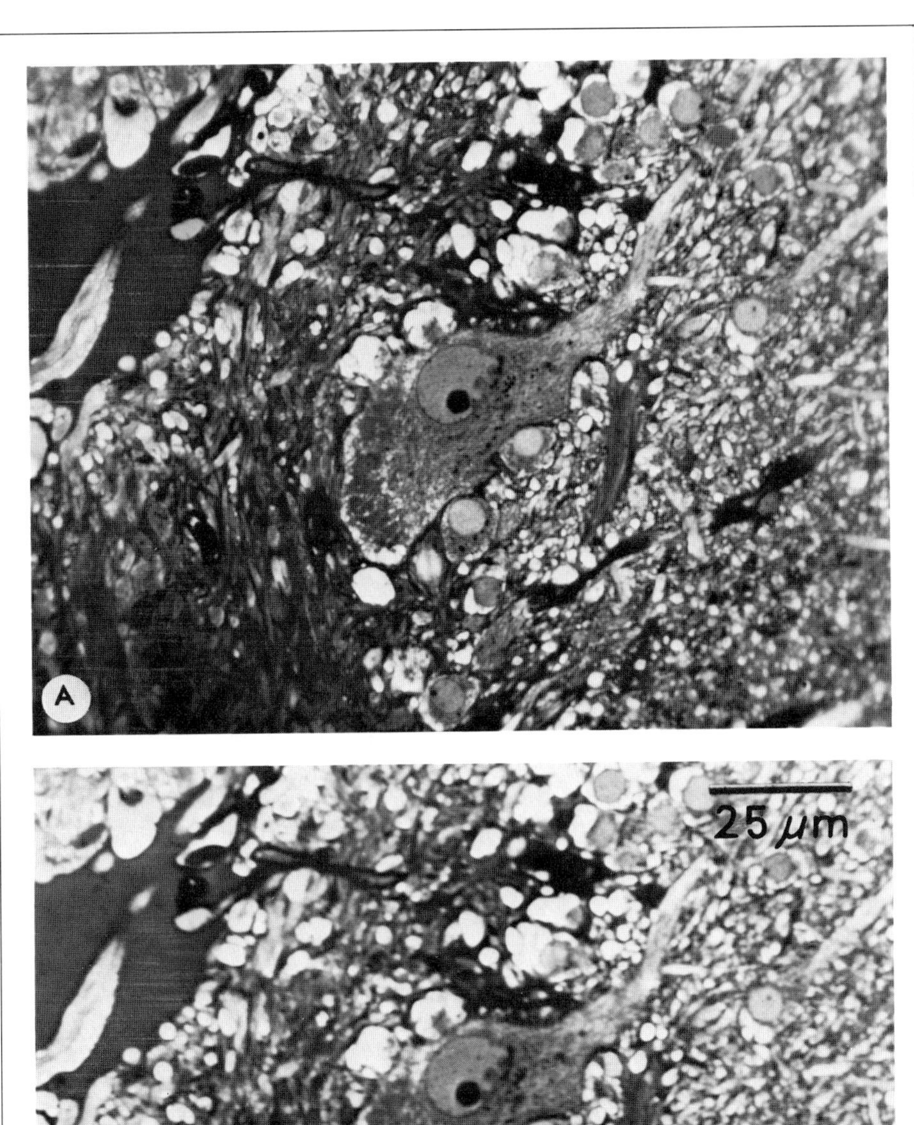

A
B
25 μm

sharp. The claim regarding the resolution is basically true, but has little importance in most photomicrography. Many stains are in some shade of red, and the use of a green filter results in black print images that carry little or no information. Use color filters according to the recommendations in the following section and you will be better off.

Color Filters

The use of color filters with black-and-white panchromatic films is the most widely practical way of differentiating stained tissues in photomicrography. See Plate 11.

One can select a suitable filter by comparing the wavelength bands of absorption and transmission of the various filters with the known characteristics of the common biological stains (this is well explained in Kodak publication P-2). However, although it has a certain theoretical elegance, this method does not take into account the degree of staining and of the resultant contrasts in particular slides. I have usually found it more useful to employ the method of filter choice described earlier in this book, on page 72.

Do not overlook the possibility of combining two filters, for special advantage in some few cases where only a combination of filters will provide a sharp enough cutoff of wavelengths.

Color-Conversion and Color-Correction Filters

When color films are used in conjunction with various artificial light sources, the film must be balanced to the source. If films are used with light sources other than those for which they were designed, you must use filters to balance the light to the sensitivity range of the film. Much photomicrography is done with incandescent projection bulbs that radiate at a color temperature (see Chapter 11) of about 3200 to 3400°K, and these require the use of Type A or Type B color films (see the instruction sheets enclosed in the film packages for further information). If these are used, no filters are required. However, it is often desirable or necessary to use a daylight-type film, such as Polacolor 2.

PLATE 16 ▸

Photomicrography: Deliberately Uneven Lighting. (See page 157.)

In some photomicrography, particularly of unstained living tissue, the visibility of inconspicuous subject features can be increased without loss of resolution through the deliberate use of uneven lighting. The basic setup is the Köhler system, but a sector of the cone of light is blocked at the substage diaphragm plane. This produces a visual effect similar to three-dimensionality, and somewhat resembles Nomarski differential-interference results. The subject shown here is a slightly dried smear (with cell distortion beginning) of the internal fluid of the mudworm *Urechis campo,* showing small-nucleated red blood cells and large oocytes. The original plate was labeled as for journal publication, prior to printing here. GV is a germinal vesicle, and N is a nucleus. The magnification was ×250, and no filters were used. (Originally photographed for F. Davis, Jr.)

A Appearance with normal Köhler-system lighting, with the substage diaphragm closed down quite far to increase the contrast.
B Here a quarter-section of the light cone was interrupted with the corner of a piece of black tape; nothing else was changed. Note the greatly increased clarity of the image, especially in the fine detail.

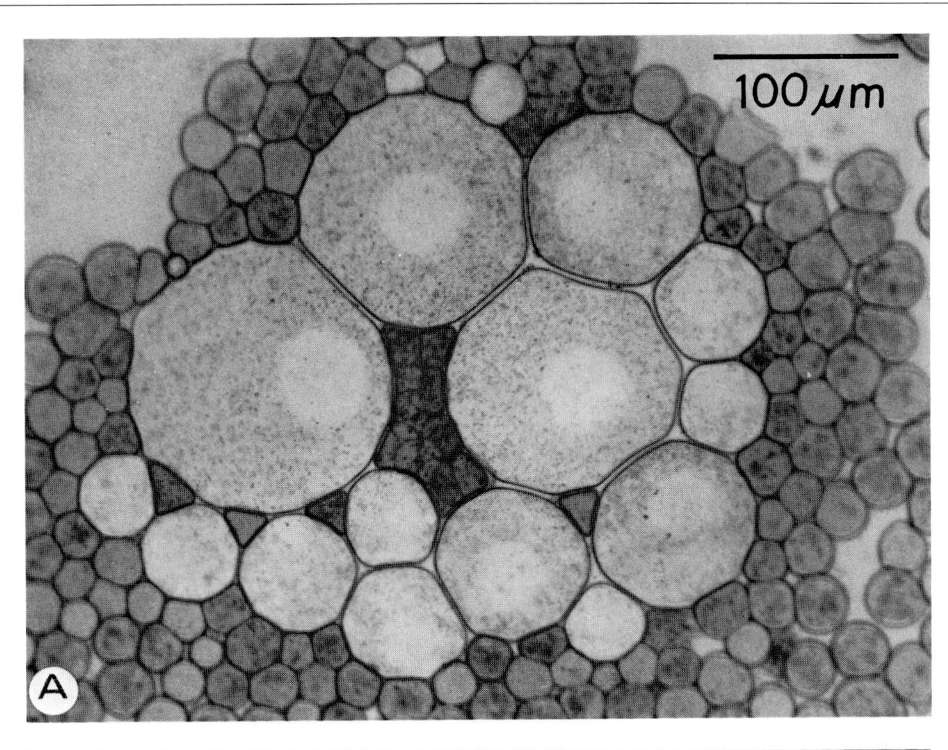
100 μm
A

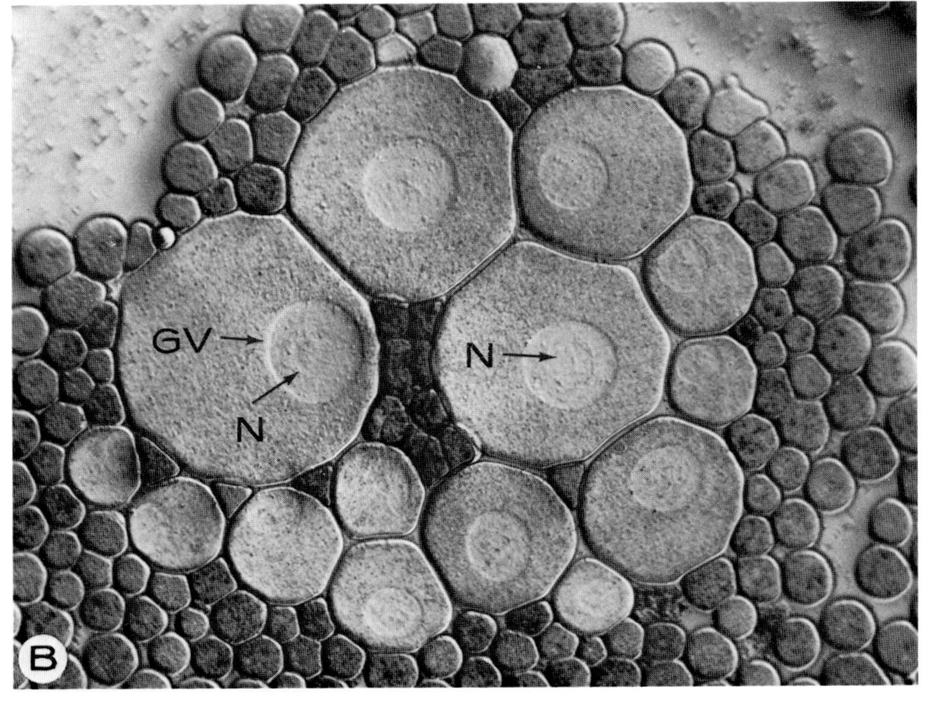
GV
N
N
B

Here the standard correction filter would be the color-conversion filter designated as Wratten 80B, or the Tiffen 820 or 840 filters.

The foregoing recommendation is valid only if the bulb is burned at its rated voltage. Lowering or raising the voltage, as for control of light intensity, would change the color of the light so as to make it appear more orange or blue, respectively. It is therefore generally a poor practice to control the light intensity by varying the voltage (even with black-and-white films, this would have an effect similar to that of using filters of those colors, which might well be detrimental to tone differentiation). See the section on neutral-density filters, below, for a better method of control.

Another correction problem arises when color photomicrographs are made at different magnifications but are to be compared directly in presentation. Because of varying optical factors, the exposure times will not be the same. In time exposures this may result in color variations due to differences in reciprocity failure. It is best, therefore, to standardize the exposure times of all pictures in a series, preferably to a time that does not cause reciprocity failure (see page 140).

If for some reason it is not practical to standardize the exposure times, it is feasible but rather tedious to work out a table for the use of color-correction (CC) filters, for fine-tuning the color balance. CC filters are pale filters of varying strengths that are colored in the basic red, yellow, blue, green, magenta, and cyan hues. (See Kodak publication B-3 for details of the use of CC filters.)

Didymium Glass Filter

In color photomicrography of sections stained with hematoxylin and eosin (the common H & E staining agents), there is some benefit to be derived from using the pinkish-colored didymium glass filter, which has qualities that improve the coincidence between eosin stain and the color layering of color films. Often the effect will not be great, but in important work the filter should be used (see the article by Koster, 1964, for technical details).

Neutral-Density Filters

Since shutters can so readily cause troublesome vibrations, I have found it best to avoid their use in the photomicrography of stained slides

PLATE 17 ▶

Photomicrography: Plant-Tissue Examples, Compound Microscope.

Plant material looks more "organized" than animal material, at the microscopic level, because of the more clearly delineated cell walls. However, there is great diversity in the ways in which such material is presented in photomicrographs, depending on the nature of the subject and its preparation.

A An embryo—sectioned—of a bellflower (*Campanula*), photographed at ×350, with a Wratten 58 deep green filter used to differentiate stained tissues. (Originally photographed for D. Kaplan.)

B A mature specimen of *Helodromyces elegans,* a microscopic fungus, also photographed at ×350 with a Wratten 58 filter. The substage diaphragm was closed down unusually far in order to render the nearly invisible cell walls clearly, for taxonomic purposes. There is some diffraction, but not enough to be detrimental. (Originally photographed for E. Tavares.)

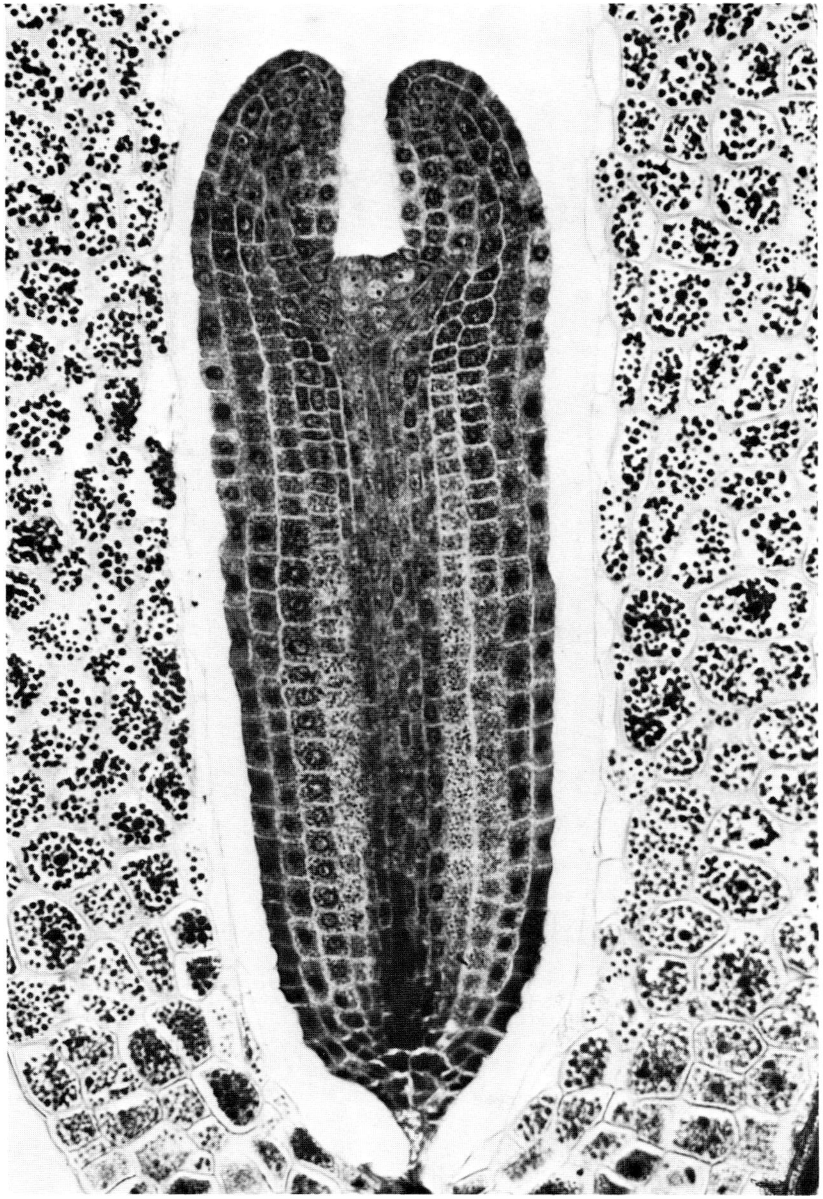

A

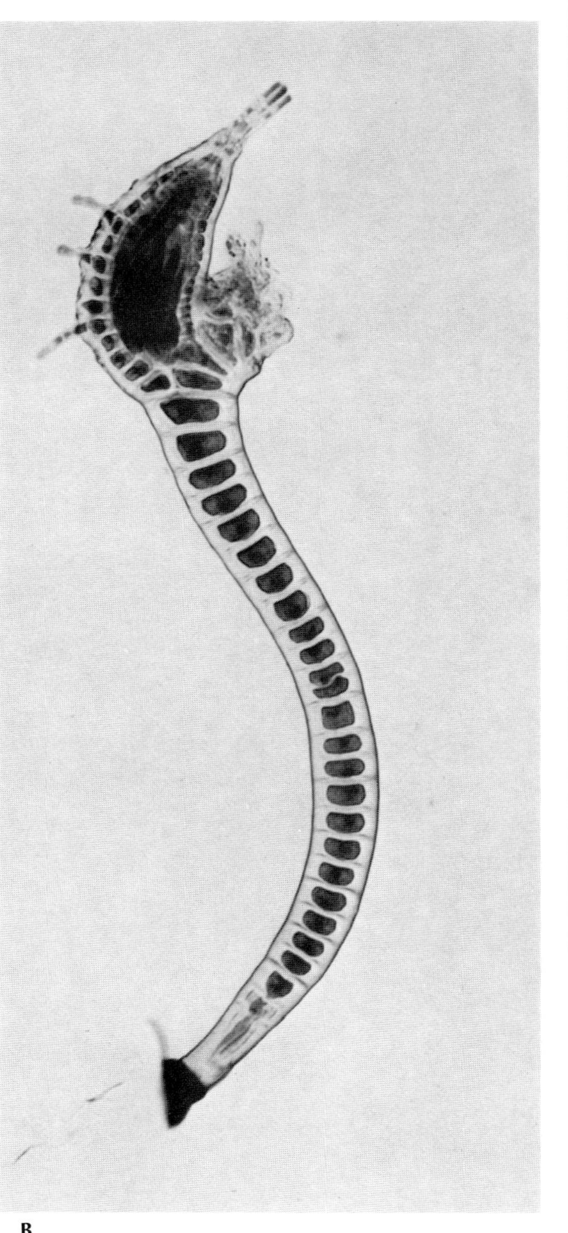

B

and other nonmotile subjects, particularly in black-and-white photography. The simplest alternative is to use neutral-density (ND) filters, at the light source, to attenuate the intensity of the beam so that you can use time exposures of preselected length. The exposure time is controlled with a card "shutter" placed in the light beam just before the camera shutter is opened, or, with sheet films, before the film-holder dark slide is withdrawn. When all vibration has ceased, the card is carefully lifted out of the beam for the requisite time, and then replaced. (This is called the Duran Neverfail Shutter, after my original tutor in this field, Victor G. Duran.)

In color photography, similar but less strong filtering is done to bring all exposures to a common time base, to control the effects of reciprocity failure upon color balance, as stated earlier. The time chosen is either one that is fast enough to eliminate the problem, or one for which you have tested to determine the necessary filter correction.

Neutral-density filters are colorless in the sense that they absorb all visible wavelengths of light similarly, and look grey to the eye. Thus, they attenuate light without changing its color. Commercial neutral-density filters are graded to standard calibrations. For example, a filter labeled ND 0.3 will absorb precisely one stop of light (i.e., 50% of it). Common ND filters are listed according to their effect on exposure in Table 6 (page 80).

EXPOSURE DETERMINATION

Determining the correct exposure for photomicrographs requires an understanding of two factors: what it is that constitutes "correct" exposure, and how to measure the light.

Most general black-and-white photography is considered a success if the deepest shadows of a subject are represented in a negative by areas with barely printable detail. The areas of greatest interest are almost always found in the middle tones and highlights. Photomicrographic subjects, however, do not have shadows and highlights—they have areas of more or less density, and a photomicrograph is a record of these relative densities. Furthermore, there is generally little of interest in the lightest areas (often consisting only of blank backgrounds or undetailed lumens). The real subject is the material making up the middle and dark tones. Therefore—and this is often not realized—a good photomicrograph should routinely receive more exposure than would a general photograph of a subject that registered a similar meter reading. A large proportion of all the nonprofessional photomicrographs that I have seen were basically underexposed.

There now comes the question of how much additional exposure to give. In general, it is appropriate to expose 50 to 100% longer than

PLATE 18 ▶

Photomicrography: Animal-Tissue Examples, Compound Microscope.

Like plant tissues, animal tissues are extremely diverse in their appearance at the microscopic level.

A Cross section of a spider's eye, photographed at ×334 with a Wratten 15 deep yellow filter. The structural features of this "simple" eye are vividly apparent. (Originally photographed for R. Eakin.)
B Section of skin from a small desert rodent, photographed at ×132 with a Wratten 8 medium yellow filter. (Originally photographed for W. B. Quay.)

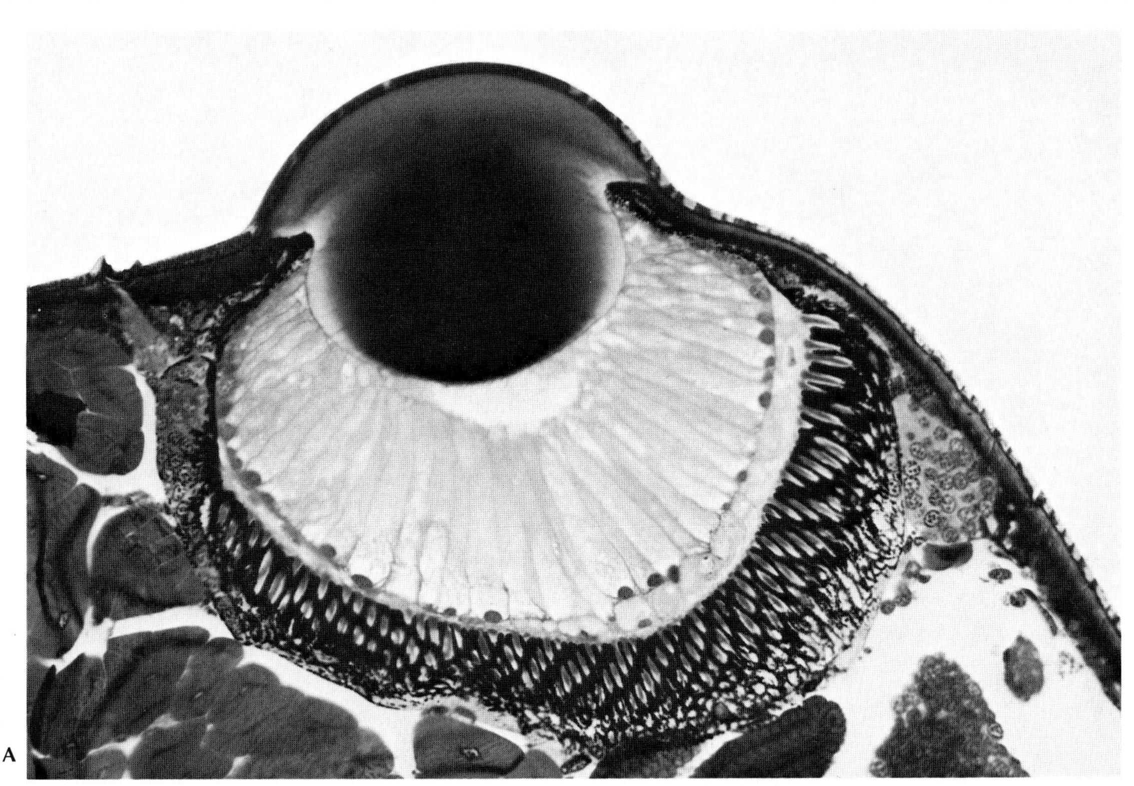
A

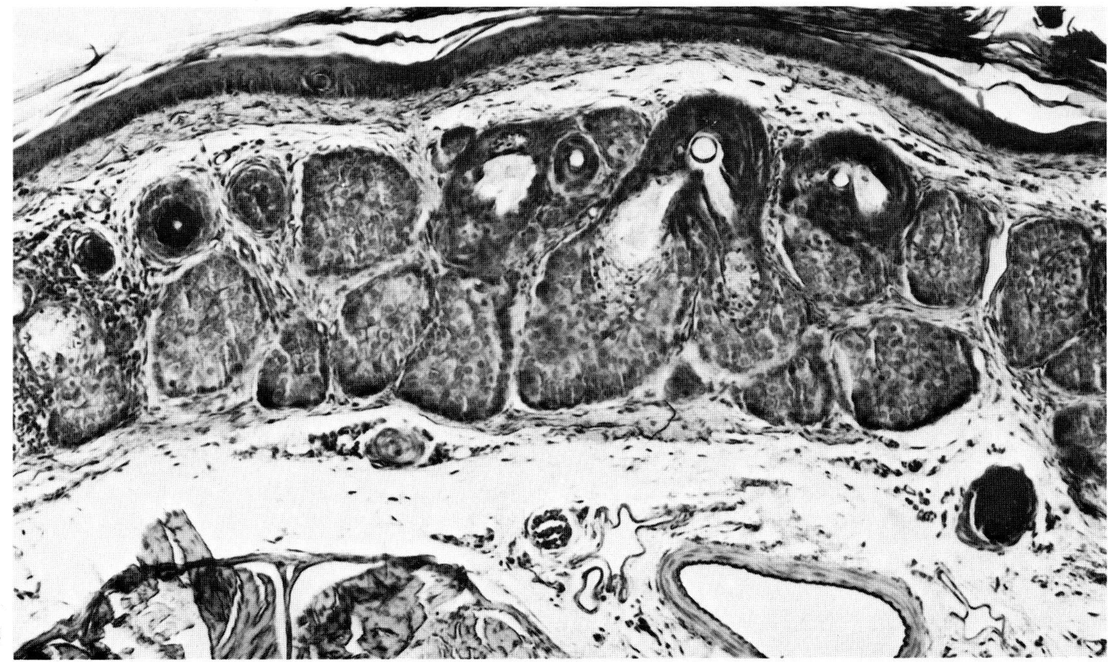
B

normal, depending upon what the particular photograph is to show. This brings out the dark-area detail while tending to lower the contrast in the light areas—a desirable feature because it reduces the visibility of minor background artifacts such as irregularities in the transparent mounting medium that surrounds a subject. (This does not apply to color transparency films, which generally need no exposure correction.)

By far the most practical method of exposure metering is reading at the image plane. Those using small cameras with built-in through-the-lens meters should simply use them according to the instruction manual, giving such excess exposure as is needed. Those using sheet-film cameras should see the instructions for image-plane reading on pages 101–102. With box cameras, you place a piece of ground glass at the film plane, with the camera open before you load the film, and read in this same manner. Those who use Polaroid Land P/N films should keep in mind that the best negative will result when the print looks decidedly too light.

COMMON PROBLEMS IN PHOTOMICROGRAPHY

Vibration has already been mentioned as a problem in photomicrography, but it deserves particular emphasis. The high image magnification, the need for image sharpness, and the fact that you are usually operating at the limits of optical resolution all require that no unnecessary loss of quality be sustained. The situation is complicated by the fact that small vibration effects look, on the negative, like general unsharpness from other causes.

Vibration can originate in nearby machinery, your own body movements, the camera mechanisms, or passing foot or motor traffic. Constant vibration can be detected most easily by observing the ground-glass image with a Sherlock Holmes-type magnifier, with which you need not touch any part of the camera. You will see the image vibrating with respect to the static grain of the ground glass. Intermittent jars and bumps can usually be anticipated and thus prevented from affecting the picture.

PLATE 19 ▸

Photomicrography: Simple vs. Compound Microscope. (See page 160.)

A compound microscope uses both an objective lens and an ocular lens to achieve high image magnifications; a simple microscope has only an objective lens, and operates at lower magnifications. Low-power photomicrographs—made with the simple microscope—are often made as "survey" pictures, to locate features and indicate relations within a subject slide. They are combined with higher-magnification photographs of details, to provide fuller visual explanations. The subject here is a mounted specimen of an aphid.

A The subject was photographed through a simple microscope with a 16 mm Zeiss Luminar objective lens at a magnification of ×28. A Wratten 47 deep blue filter was used to increase the contrast in this very pale yellow subject.
B The same subject, photographed through a compound microscope at ×100, using the same filter, to show details of parts of the head. Although the substage diaphragm was closed down so far that some diffraction appears, there is still insufficient depth of field at this higher magnification to provide sharp images of the eyes and the mouth parts simultaneously. But the eyes and the antenna mounts are shown quite well. Enlargement in printing of the picture in part A would have provided more depth of field, but the image quality in general would have been greatly inferior if enlarged to this level.

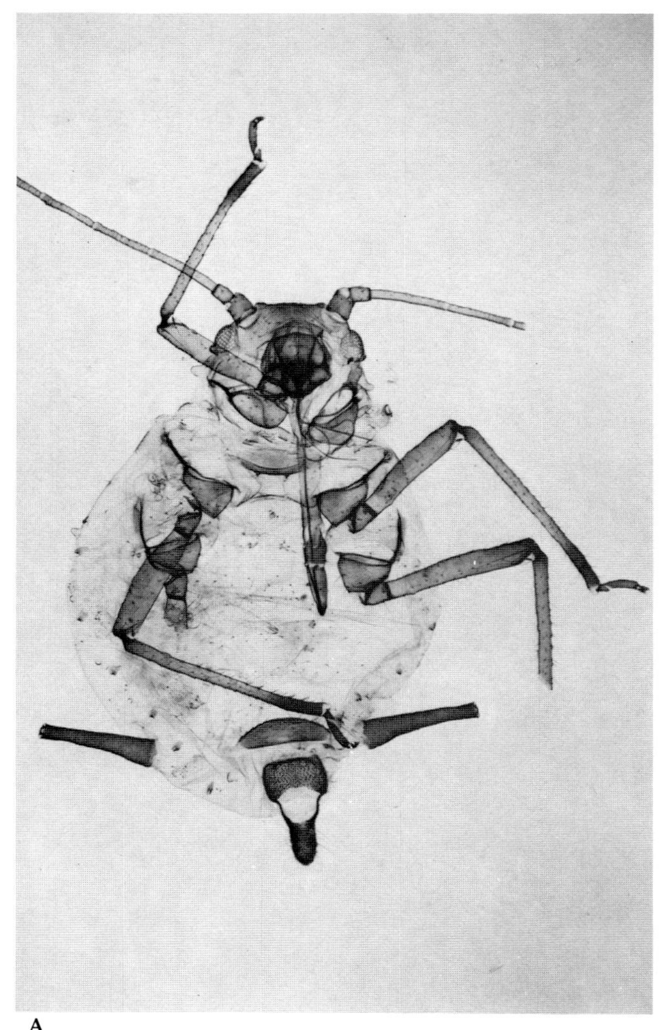

A

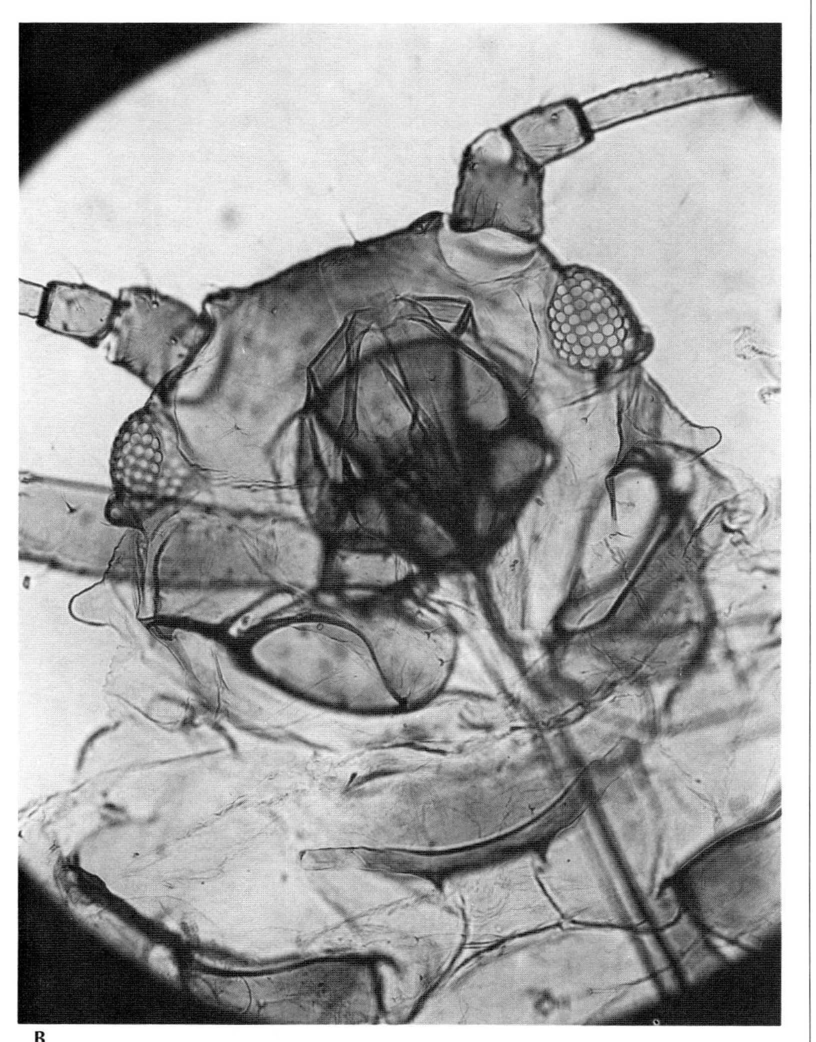

B

Dirt in the optical system is a constant problem in photomicrography. The most likely place to find dirt is on the subject slide. Both top and bottom must be cleaned, using small amounts of water or xylene on a soft cloth or lens tissue. The most critical area, of course, is the surface of the cover slip, particularly that part of it directly over the immediate subject area. If the slide is newly made, be very careful not to bear down too hard while polishing it, or the subject will be damaged. Fresh mounting medium may also be carried from the edge of the cover slip onto its surface during cleaning. Water mounts cannot be cleaned, so the cover slip must be especially carefully cleaned before placement.

A fingerprint or other foreign presence on the objective or ocular lens will reduce the image sharpness and contrast. A dust speck or a piece of lint on the ocular or on the field condenser will show as a large shadow on the image. To determine its location, throw the substage condenser out of focus while watching the image. If the shadow disappears, the problem lies with the field condenser, and you must clean it. Should the field condenser be scratched (such damage is sometimes caused by bumping it against the light bulb, in focusing the light beam), defocus the substage condenser *slightly,* and *toward the lamp* (moving it toward the microscope slide is likely to introduce unwanted color effects into the image).

Shadows that remain on the image when you defocus the substage condenser may come from lint on that condenser. Test for it by rotating the condenser. If the shadow rotates with it, clean the condenser. If it does not rotate, the next place to look is the top or bottom surface of the ocular. Again, test by rotation, and if the shadow turns, clean the ocular.

The best method for cleaning lenses is sometimes a point of controversy. Properly, it is a simple process that follows an order of priorities. You first blow off any surface dust and lint. Always blow at an angle to the surface, not directly on it. Pressurized cans of gas, such as Omit or Dust-Off, are very handy because you can aim their tiny jet so as to get a short burst of high-pressure gas right on the target. Do not tilt the can while using it, or it may spray liquefield gas on the lens. Freon-type gases are environmentally less desirable than dry, compressed air. Easiest to use, but least controllable, is your own breath.

The next step is to breathe gently on the lens so that a film of distilled water condenses on its surface. Before it evaporates, polish lightly with a soft, lint-free cloth or lens-cleaning tissue to remove most other dirt or minor fingerprints. (Commercial cleansing tissues leave lint.)

Greasy substances may require a more effective solvent than water, but it should be used sparingly and only when actually needed. Slight amounts of ether or benzene will remove most such substances; the former is preferable because it leaves less residue. Immersion oil can be removed effectively with a soft cloth lightly dampened with xylene. *Do not use alcohol* as a cleaning solvent, as it may tend to dissolve the lens cement. After using any organic solvent, finish up by removing solvent residues with distilled water, in the manner described above.

The most likely damage to a dropped optical component is a partial or complete separation of two cemented lens elements. Checking them from both front and rear with a magnifier lens will immediately reveal such a separation. The lens must then be sent to the manufacturer for repair. It is not just a question of more cement—recentering is also needed. Other likely damage includes simple decentering of lens groups, and actual bending of the lens mount. All require factory repair.

Prevent damage to optical components by handling them carefully. When a lens is dismounted or otherwise handled, keep a cupped hand under it, to catch it in case of a drop. Sit, don't stand, at a bench while cleaning lenses. Damage to lenses is far more easily prevented than repaired.

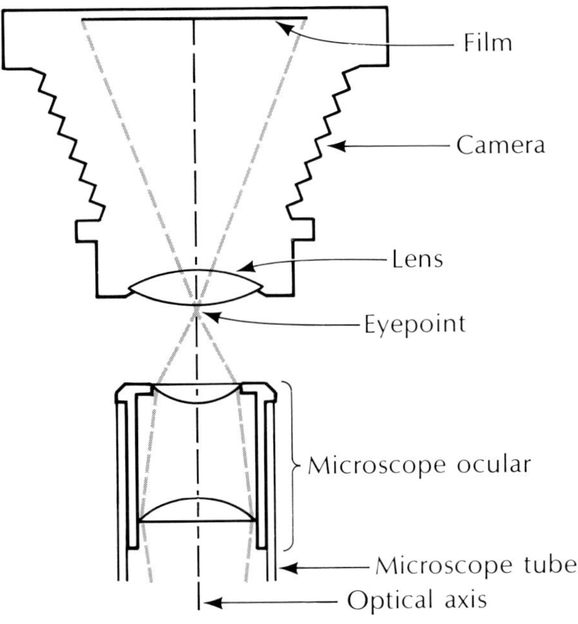

FIGURE 39
The eyepoint of a microscope ocular in photomicrography. When using a camera with its own lens, the front glass element of the lens should be at or slightly above the eyepoint (the point where the cone of light rays emerging from the ocular converges to the smallest diameter).

PHOTOMICROGRAPHY WITH SIMPLE EQUIPMENT

Camera Lens On

Any camera can be used. Optical quality may be best with a very simple box camera mounting a single-element lens, but exposure reading is simpler with through-the-lens metering. Follow these steps:

1. Adjust the microscope so that the image appears sharp; then adjust the lamp and substage mirror until the lighting is even across the whole field of view. It helps to remove the ocular and look down the tube with your head well above the instrument. The most even lighting is achieved when the bright spot of light is seen to be centered in the back of the objective.
2. Determine the position of the *eyepoint* (that point at which a thin paper held above the ocular shows the cone of light rays emerging from the lens as a spot of light of the smallest diameter—see Figure 39).
3. Place the camera lens, *focused at or as near as possible to infinity and with the lens aperture wide open,* so that the surface of the front element is at the eyepoint. Image quality deteriorates if the lens is not accurately placed, but does so more rapidly when the lens surface is below the eyepoint. Therefore, any error should be *upward.* The camera lens aperture should be kept wide open, or the image-field size will be reduced ("vignetted"). The camera-lens axis must be coaxial with the microscope axis for best results.

4. Lighttight the space between the camera lens and the top of the microscope. The simplest method is to wrap the space with opaque black cloth, held in place with a spring clip. Special microscope adapters are not needed, and if used, they may transmit vibrations from the camera to the microscope.

5. Determine the correct exposure time, and make the picture; use color filters, as needed, to differentiate tones and colors in the image.

The approximate magnification of the visual image in a microscope is usually obtained by multiplying the objective-lens magnification by the ocular magnification, but in photomicrography this is based on a standard 10-inch eyepoint-to-film distance (see page 126). With short cameras (virtually *all* roll-film cameras), divide the magnification figure so obtained by the distance between the front of the camera lens and the film plane. If the negative is enlarged in printing, you must multiply *this* figure by the enlargement factor, to obtain the final correct image magnification. It is probably simpler just to photograph a stage micrometer, if you have one, at each setting. Then you need only measure its image on the negative and multiply the calculated magnification by the printing enlargement factor.

A common problem in this sort of photography is the presence of a bright spot in the center of the picture (a dark spot on the negative). It is due to internal reflections (inside the microscope tube) being brought near to focus at the film plane. The effect may vary when the microscope objective lens is changed, because of differences in the diameter of the projected initial image. And it may not be especially apparent to the eye when observing through a single lens reflex camera, because viewfinder screens normally appear somewhat brighter in the center anyway. To solve the problem, remove the ocular and insert a rolled piece of black paper or other light-absorbing material into the tube. It should be just long enough to span the distance between the top of the objective and the bottom of the ocular. When the

---

PLATE 20 ▶

Low-Power Photomicrography: Prism Photomacrography. (See pages 162–163.)

A substage prism that can be rotated to vary the lighting effects in low-power photomicrography (more properly called photomacrography when the subject is three-dimensional) is a very useful device. Similar effects can be obtained with mirrors, but a prism gives better control of the light.

A A bright-field photograph of the male genital apparatus of the Milkweed Bug, *Oncopeltus fasciatus* (×19). (Originally photographed for A. P. Economopoulos and H. T. Gordon.)
B The same subject, with the substage prism rotated to provide a directional form of dark-field lighting. Different features are shown best in the two versions, so the pictures complement each other well.
C Cockroach ganglion (×38), by prism dark-field lighting. (Originally photographed for A. Bonhag.)
D Megaspore of the water fern *Marsilea vestita* (×38), with the substage prism rotated to provide a marginal effect between dark- and bright-field lighting. The surrounding cloudlike envelope is invisible under most lighting conditions, and can be seen clearly only in this transitional type of lighting. It is an important structure connected with the fertilization by the smaller sperm, one of which is seen at right center. This megaspore has already been fertilized, and has started to develop. (Originally photographed for L. Machlis.)

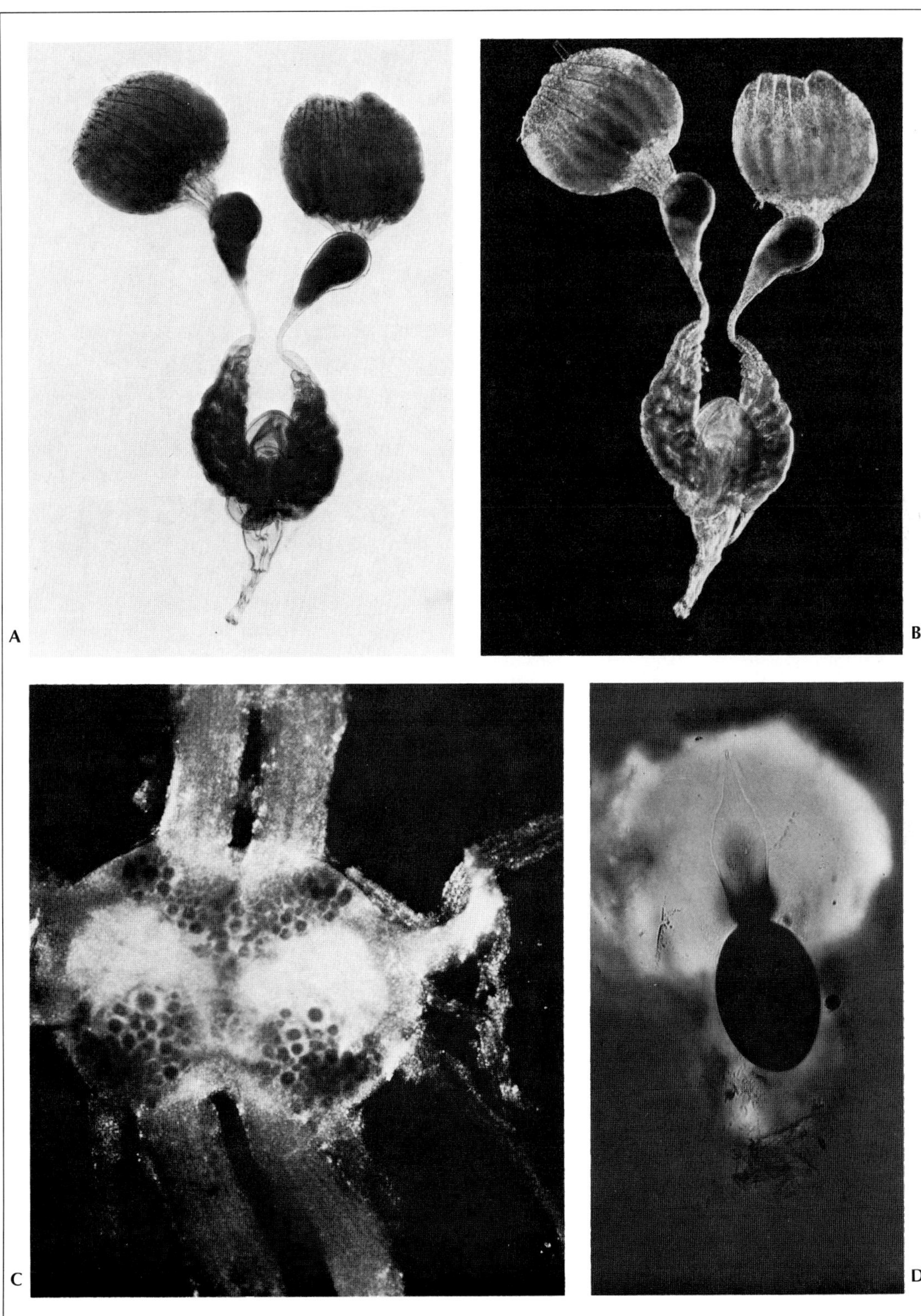
A
B
C
D

ocular is replaced there should be no further problem. The use of a large-diameter microscope tube, as in professional photo microscopes, usually prevents such reflections.

Camera Lens Off

Here the microscope can be used as described above. However, the camera can be placed so that the film plane is at any height above the ocular of the microscope. Thus, it can be placed at the standard 10 inches above the eyepoint, or magnification can be varied at will—within limits—by placing it above or below that point. It is thus possible to have an ocular-to-film distance as short as perhaps 5 inches, or as long as 25–30 inches, without significant change in the quality of the projected image. The size of the image circle will expand or contract according to the increase or decrease in magnification; however, the amount of subject seen within that circle will remain constant.

The camera can be as simple as an old camera back, held horizontal above the microscope by a stand, with the space between it and the top of the microscope swathed with opaque black cloth; or you can use a press or view camera, or an enlarger that is convertible to a camera (see your dealer for makes and types). If a shutter is used, it is best to mount a leaf-type shutter, without a lens, so that the leaves of the shutter intersect the cone of rays precisely at the eyepoint. Should the shutter be mounted too high in the cone, a shadow of the leaves may be projected upon the image during the exposure, thus spoiling the picture. The shutter should not be connected to the microscope, but should be fastened to the camera front or to the stand supporting the camera. Again, light-tighting can be done by wrapping opaque black cloth around the space between the camera and the microscope.

At the longer ocular-to-film distances, it is not a good idea to enlarge the picture in printing, since the lens resolution is already strained. But the probable reason for using such long distances in the first place is to use a large film. With long bellows lengths, one can use film sizes as large as 11 × 14 inches without visible loss of image quality, if flat-field optics are used (see the section on numerical aperture, below, and see Plate 14, parts D and E).

KÖHLER-SYSTEM PHOTOMICROGRAPHY

Regardless of the camera being used, the best image quality will result only when the microscope is of fine quality and the lighting is set up to assure maximum image resolution. There have been other systems used for photomicrographic imaging, but the best and most versatile is the so-called *Köhler system,* named after its inventor. It requires that one understand the relations among the parts of the setup and follow a particular sequence of adjustment steps. Figure 40 is a diagram of a basic photomicrographic setup with all major parts identified (any particular setup can be arranged either horizontally or vertically—the principle is the same for either).

The adjustment procedure is as follows. If a given step is performed out of sequence, or is left out, seemingly inexplicable things will happen in the image. If you get lost, start over again.

1. Make a rough setup, and focus the image of your subject slide on the ground glass of your viewing screen.

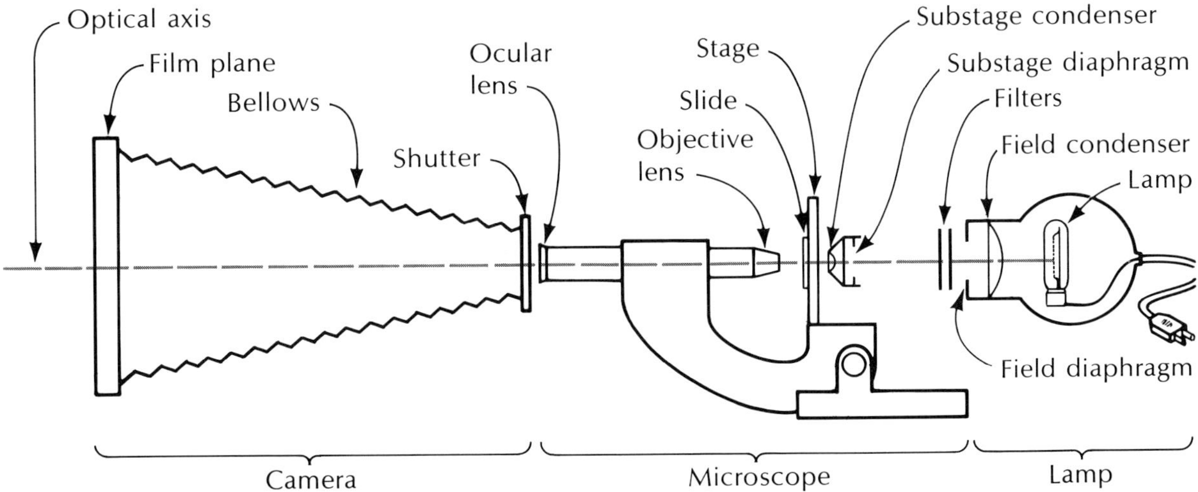

FIGURE 40
Köhler-system photomicrographic setup (horizontal form). The camera, microscope, and lamp are carefully aligned on a common optical axis. The lamp filament is imaged in the plane of the substage diaphragm to yield an even and efficient field of light in the subject plane.

2. Close the substage and field diaphragms.
3. Move the lamp within its housing, or focus the lamp condenser, until an in-focus image of the lamp filament appears on the surface of the substage diaphragm. Move the lamp so as to center that image.
4. Open both diaphragms fully.
5. While observing the ground-glass image, close the field diaphragm until a circular shadow surrounds the lighted subject area of the image. At this point the edge of the shadow may be very diffuse, and the circle may be so far off center that it runs off the screen.
6. Focus the substage condenser until the edge of the shadow is as sharp as you can get it. Then center it on the screen by turning the centering screws on the substage condenser. At this point both the image and its surrounding shadow-edge look reasonably sharp.
7. Open the field diaphragm until the edge of the circular shadow (the image of the field diaphragm) slightly more than clears the corners of the viewfinder screen, if possible. With a short eyepoint-to-film distance the image may be circular even with the field diaphragm wide open. And when a camera lens is left on, its diaphragm—even wide open—may limit the size of the image circle to less than the dimensions of the film. But if the film corners are cleared, stop opening the field diaphragm. Too wide a spread will cause internal reflections within the camera, and these will lower the image contrast.
8. Make final adjustments at the microscope stage to place and center the subject as you want it on the film.

9. Close the substage diaphragm until you have the best compromise between depth of field and image diffraction. With the diaphragm wide open there is excessive glare. Theoretically, the best resolution occurs at about a 90% open position, but practical considerations of depth of field and contrast usually require a smaller opening, often roughly a 50% position (see Plate 12). As the substage diaphragm is closed, the depth of field increases (as when you close the diaphragm of your camera lens). At the same time, the image-detail contrast tends to increase. However, diffraction of light by the edge of the diaphragm increasingly impairs the image resolution until the image becomes "rotten." A rotten image has one or more diffraction rings (alternating light and dark lines) around the edges of a subject. A magnifier will reveal that there is no true sharpness, and that it is hard to tell whether you are seeing subject detail or diffraction effects. Usually the best method for establishing the compromise is to deliberately close the substage diaphragm until the image is obviously rotten, and then to open it until the diffraction effects disappear. It is especially necessary to be careful at this point if the photographic image is to be enlarged in printing. See Plate 13, parts A and B, for examples of rotten images.

10. Decide upon and insert the necessary filters, to differentiate tones and colors in the image. Filters can be mounted in front of the field condenser, on the lamp; or they can be placed next to the substage diaphragm. Rarely, they are placed just above the microscope ocular (as with the analyzer of a polarizing setup, or with the didymium glass filter).

11. Do a very careful final focus.

12. Determine the exposure, and make the picture. Be very careful to avoid vibration or jarring at this stage.

NUMERICAL APERTURE AND FILM SIZE

There are distinct advantages in photomicrography in using large film sizes, despite the emphasis in the publications of the past forty years on the virtues of small films and cameras. Among these advantages are the speed and ease with which you can process sheet films, the speed and ease of contact printing compared to projection printing, the fact that there are more types of films available in sheet form (and that you can, if you wish, make series of exposures in which each one is on a different emulsion), and the fact that you can work to the limits of

---

PLATE 21 ►

Low-Power Photomicrography: Dark-Field. (See page 163.)

Dark-field photomicrography using a center stop next to the substage condenser is just as practical at low magnifications as in high-power work with the compound microscope.

A Section of Red Gum wood (×57), using a 16 mm Zeiss Luminar and a 20 mm condenser for a bright-field effect.
B The same subject and setup, with a center stop introduced next to the condenser to produce the dark-field effect. Certain fine structure is seen more clearly. Dark-field lighting is more commonly used with unstained animate subjects, but can be worthwhile in other work, too.

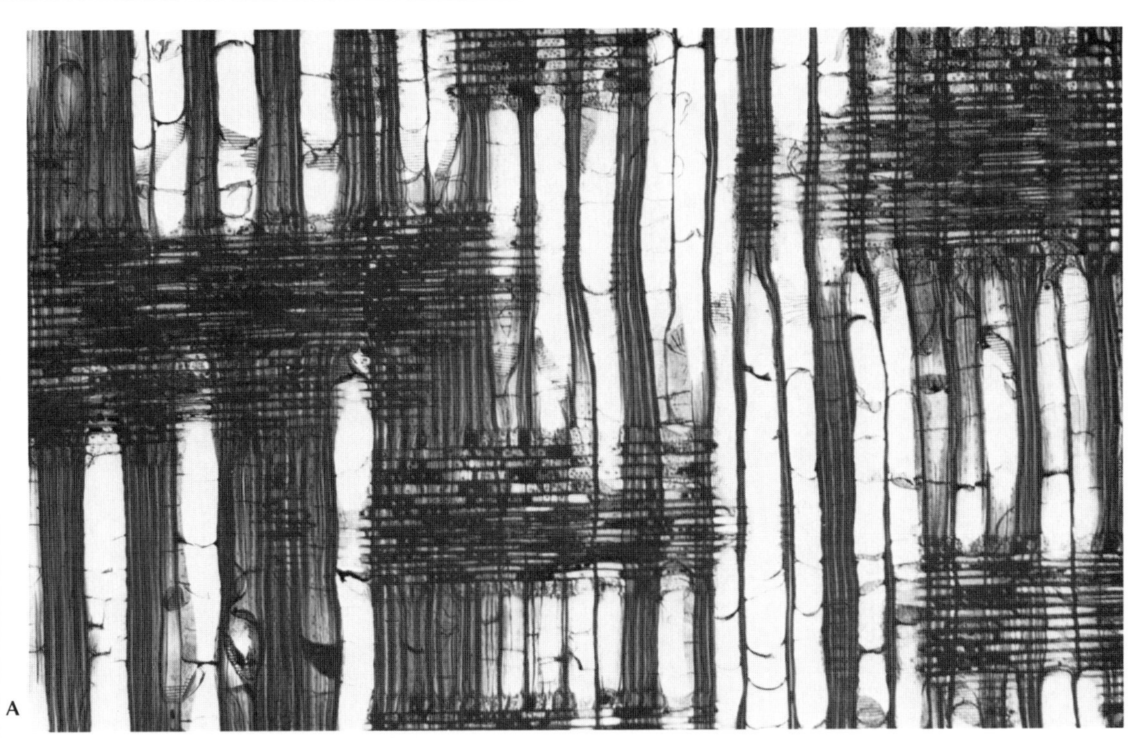
A

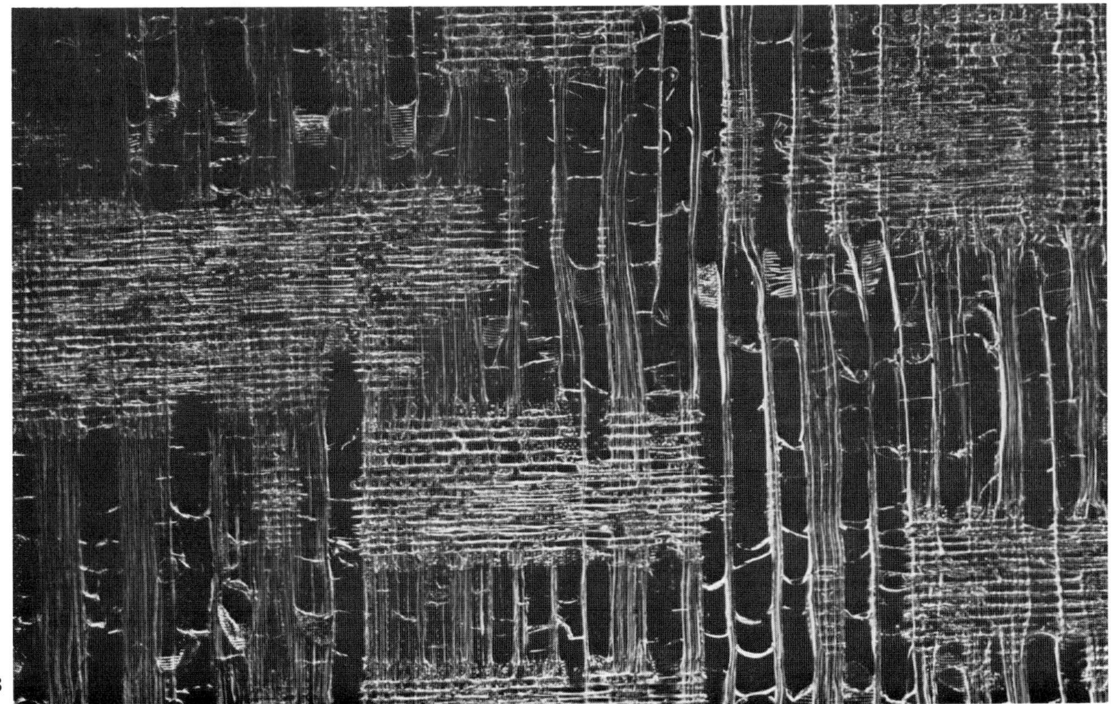
B

optical resolution on the film without regard for the effect of enlargement in printing upon the image quality.

Often overlooked, however, are the relations among the numerical aperture, the objective lens, the image resolution, and the film size. *Numerical aperture* (N.A.) in the objective lens is, among other things, an indicator of the maximum magnification capability of the lens. Resolution varies somewhat with the wavelength of the light making up the image, and with the type of lens used (achromat vs. apochromat, etc.). A rule of thumb often employed, however, states that the numerical aperture multiplied by 1000 equals the highest useful magnification that can be achieved with the lens in question. Thus, a lens of N.A. 0.30 could be used, with a suitable ocular, to obtain a maximum magnification of about ×300, before the onset of empty magnification (image enlargement without the revelation of new detail); a lens of N.A. 0.65 could go up to about ×650. The figures may not prove to be exact in practice, but the N.A. does indicate the proportional capability.

To a considerable degree, numerical aperture is linked to the initial magnification of an objective lens. Thus, ×4 objectives have a range of N.A. from 0.10 to 0.20; ×10 objectives range from about N.A. 0.22 to 0.40; ×20 objectives range from N.A. 0.45 to about 0.65; and ×100 objectives (all used with oil immersion, or the like) range from about N.A. 1.00 to 1.40. The point is that, when small films are used to photograph a given subject area, you must use relatively lower-power objective lenses, or image magnification may be too great for the film to encompass. So, with any but the very smallest of subjects, you cannot get as much resolution in a picture as you could if you photographed *the same subject area* on a larger film, using an objective lens of higher numerical aperture. These effects are illustrated in Plates 13 and 14. Plate 15 illustrates the difference in resolution between oil-immersion and high-dry photomicrography.

This principle is of particular interest when your goal is to produce a projection slide. If you start with a 35 mm film, the image on the wall screen will be rather unsharp, at best. But if, say, you use an 8 × 10-inch film to make the negative, the image on that film can have almost seven times as much linear magnification. If a ×10 objective of N.A. 0.30 (the most common figure) and a ×10 ocular were used with the 35 mm film to fill the film frame, the standard magnification would be ×100. Using a longer bellows would tend to decrease the resolution undesirably. But if you changed to

---

PLATE 22 ▸

Low-Power Photomicrography: Polarization. (See page 165.)

Many subjects—animal, mineral, and vegetable—show birefringence and other effects when photographed between polarizers. These effects are often most appropriately photographed at relatively low image magnifications.

A A mineral thin section photographed at ×38 by plane-polarized light (in this case the visual effect would be similar if the light were not polarized at all).

B The same subject, with the polarizers crossed. In many cases the different shades of grey seen here would represent a wide variety of spectral colors. Here the subject colors were in shades of grey except for the central rectangular feature, which was in varying shades of brown and tan.

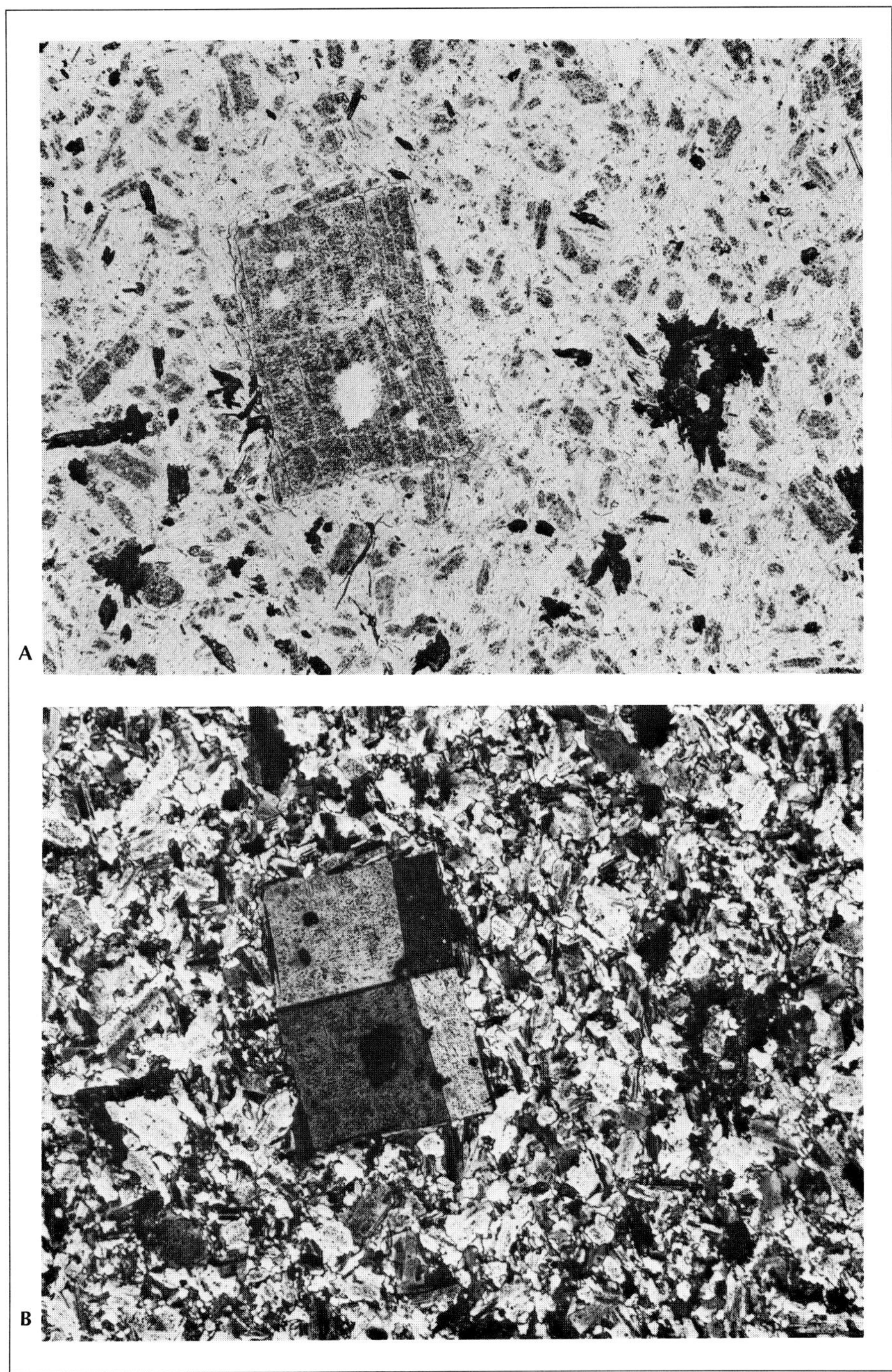
A
B

an 8 × 10-inch film you could fill the film frame using an objective of ×20 initial magnification and an N.A. of 0.65, and the same ocular, but with a longer bellows used without loss of resolution. With a 30-inch bellows, image magnification would be about ×600—at least double the best performance of the lower-power objective, and well within the numerical-aperture capability of this lens. When optically reduced onto a film size appropriate to your slide requirement, this gives a very much sharper slide. Try it—you may surprise yourself. And the financial outlay to employ this method need not be great.

SUBSIDIARY TECHNIQUES

Köhler-system imaging is the basis for several other methods used in photomicrography. Although I will not go into these equipment-specific techniques here, both phase-contrast and interference-phase microscopy can be thought of as variants of the method, with special equipment added. Some other, simpler variant methods will be described, however. In each of these, the microscope is first set up according to the Köhler method; then further steps are taken to augment the system and make it more versatile.

Also to be presented in this section are several working methods that can be applied to any photomicrographic technique.

Dark-Field Lighting

In dark-field photomicrography the basic method is Köhler-system imaging, which produces a cone-shaped pattern of illumination through the subject slide as one of its characteristics. To produce the dark-field effect in its simplest form, you must introduce into the plane of the substage diaphragm a center stop, which intercepts the middle of the entering beam of light so that when the cone of rays leaves the condenser it will be hollow. The center stop, which is a metal disk surrounded by open space (see Figure 41A), allows only the peripheral rays to pass.

When the equipment is properly set up, with the right size of center stop, the peripheral rays of light do not enter the objective lens unless they have been refracted or scattered by the subject. The visual effect is that of a black background with a bright subject on it. The method is most useful with unstained, perhaps living, subjects, but can be used to some degree with most slides. At present, the dark-field method tends to be neglected in favor of the phase-contrast method, but much can be done with it

PLATE 23 ▶

Low-Power Photomicrography: Polarization Examples. (See page 165.)

Mineral thin sections can exhibit a great variety of striking visual effects in polarization microscopy. These examples are offered to give some idea of what can be encountered.

A A section that exhibits grey-tone changes across a line of differentiation (×50). (Originally photographed for H.-R. Wenk.)
B An example of granulations that show on the viewing screen of the camera as varied brilliant colors (×11).
C A "basket-weave" effect that has much visual appeal as well as scientific interest (×37). (Originally photographed for L. E. Weiss.)

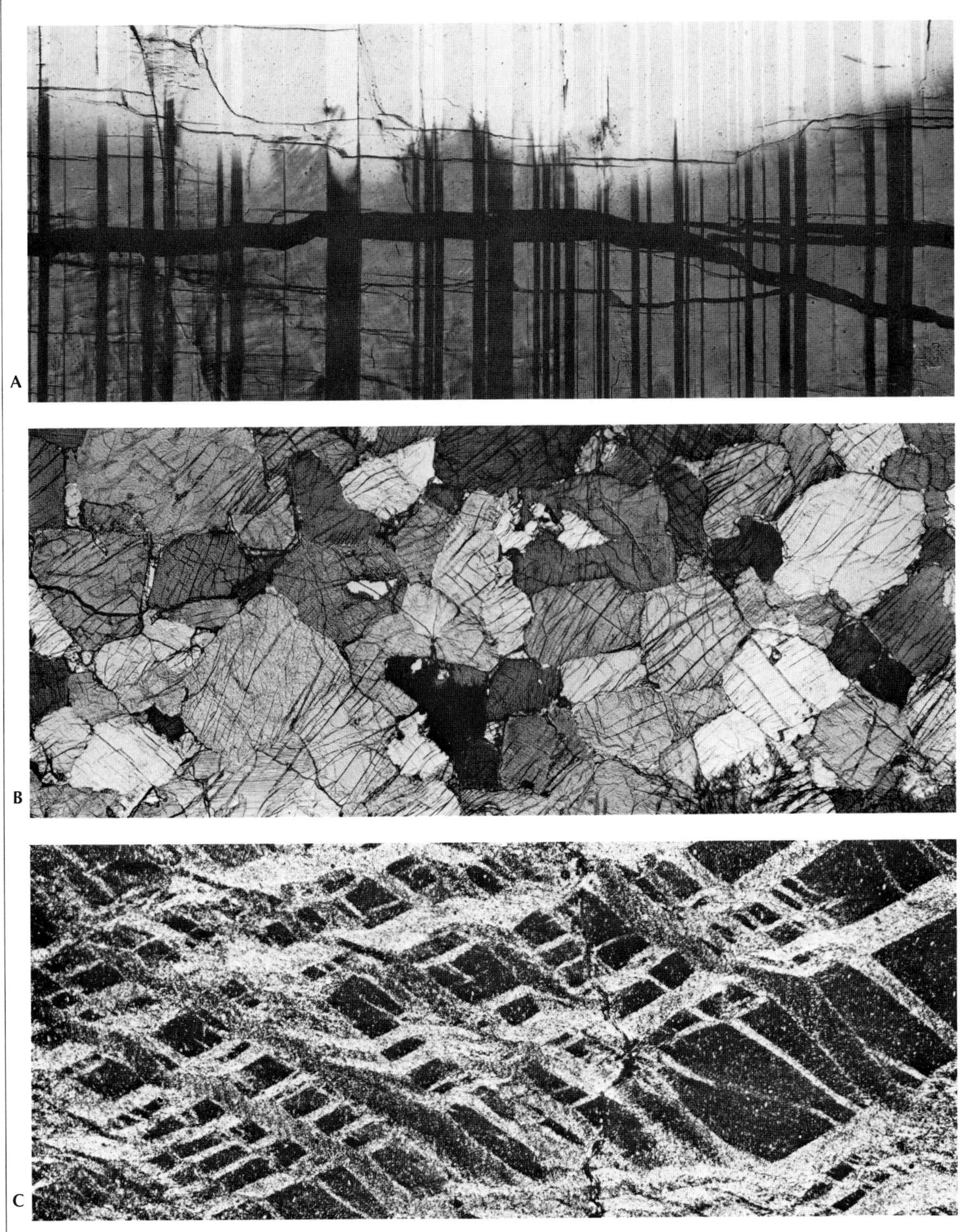
A
B
C

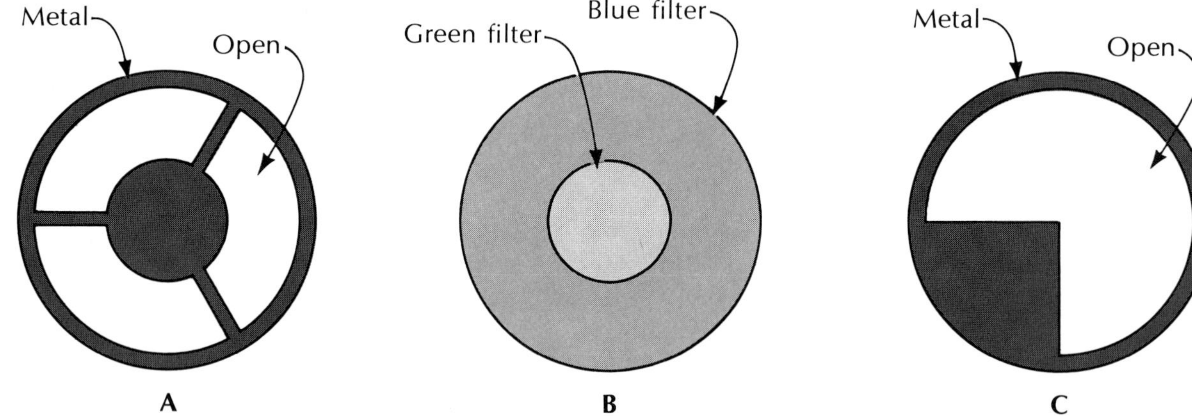

FIGURE 41
Substage diaphragm fixtures.

A Center stop, for dark-field lighting.
B Rheinberg filter, for "optical staining" of living or otherwise unstained subjects (this version produces a blue image of the subject on a green background).
C Pie-shaped diaphragm stop, for "shadowing" an unstained subject through deliberately uneven lighting. (See Plate 16.)

without the equipment expense of the latter. Although the two methods are dissimilar in their theory and practice, certain of the visual effects achieved are similar in both.

It should be remembered that, with a center stop in place, the substage diaphragm cannot be closed down to any great degree to gain depth of field, or the subject image will suddenly disappear.

Rheinberg Lighting

Another very useful method of photomicrography of living or other unstained subjects is "optical staining" through the use of Rheinberg filters. The method was invented in 1896 by Julius Rheinberg, and is a special combination of Köhler-system imaging, dark-field technique, and color filtering. In this method the center stop is a colored transparent filter and is surrounded by a second, concentric filter of a contrasting color (see Figure 41B). Thus, the center of the cone of light, which would be completely interrupted in dark-field lighting, is colored by the center filter, while the peripheral rays are contrastingly colored by the outer filter. The visual effect, which can be quite striking, is of a background the color of the center filter, with the subject on it largely in the color of the peripheral filter. (Because the background is passing light, there are some of the usual silhouette effects in the subject, also.) The method has been used with particular success in making photomicrographs of protozoans, small multicelled creatures, algae, and the like.

A variation of Rheinberg lighting can be done in which only one area—usually the background

—is colored, or in which neither is colored. In the former method the center rays are colored by a filter but the peripheral rays are left white. In the latter method there is a neutral-density center filter but again no peripheral filter. The visual effect is then of a grey background—the shade depending upon the strength of the ND filter—with the subject seen against it in white or light greys, with some silhouette effects.

At one time, Rheinberg filters were commercially available from Wratten, but this is no longer so. Fortunately, they are quite easily made by cutting out gelatin filter stock (see the articles by Vetter, 1963, and Delly, 1976). Although the method has largely fallen into disuse with the introduction of the newer (though much more expensive) technique of interference-phase microscopy, which can produce a variety of often visually similar effects, Rheinberg lighting has not lost its utility. In fact, it is rediscovered every year or so by younger workers. It is well worth a try, for many purposes. As with dark-field lighting, the substage diaphragm cannot be closed down unduly to gain depth of field, or the essential peripheral rays will be lost.

Deliberately Uneven Lighting

Yet another variant of Köhler-system imaging produces a visual effect of shadowed three-dimensionality similar to that produced in certain forms of the interference-phase technique. The additional equipment required can be as simple as your thumb or a piece of opaque tape.

The basis of the method is to introduce a particular form of uneven lighting in the Köhler method, by interrupting one segment of the cone of rays produced by the substage condenser. To appear more professional, you could make and use a pie-shaped opaque stop (see Figure 41C), to be placed at the substage diaphragm; but your thumb, or the corner of a piece of black tape, judiciously inserted into the light beam at the base of the substage condenser housing, will do just as well.

Although the effect of shadowing is often attractive to the eye, the real beauty of the method is that it increases the contrast of unstained subjects without the diffraction effects that would accompany excessive closing down of the substage diaphragm. It makes minute detail much more visible without introducing artifacts that would distort the information carried by the picture. The effect produced can be very subtle or it can be obvious, depending upon how large a segment of the cone is interrupted. I have used the technique with great success upon occasion. See Plate 16 for illustrations.

Polarization Technique

Polarization photomicrography is a very useful method for the study and analysis of birefringence (double refraction) and related physical phenomena occurring in many types of subjects. It is perhaps most widely used in mineralogy, but also has many applications in the biological sciences.

For nonanalytical photomicrography, the Köhler system of imaging is used, with the addition of two polarizing filters: one fitted below the substage condenser as a polarizer for the entering light beam, and the other placed either just above the objective lens or immediately above the ocular, as an analyzer. When the two are crossed, little or no light is passed unless the subject is *optically anisotropic*. (An anisotropic substance both rotates the plane of polarization of an incident plane-polarized beam and alters its nature in other, more complex ways so as to produce a beam that is said to be elliptically polarized.) If the subject in such a setup with crossed polarizers *is* anisotropic, the polarized beam passing through it will be rotated and otherwise affected so that some light passes through the analyzer to the film plane. See Figure 42 for a greatly simplified illustration of this effect (see also Figure 28, page 74, for other aspects of polarization that apply here).

Once the subject slide has been put in place on the microscope stage, a variety of visual effects can be observed. Some occur when the polarizer or analyzer are rotated; others, quite different, occur when the subject is rotated between them. (Understanding and analysis of the results will be aided by referring to Phillips, *Mineral Optics*, 1971.)

Stereo Photomicrography

It is quite possible to obtain useful three-dimensional viewing effects with stereo pairs of photomicrographs. In my experience, the most practical method is the shifting-subject method, as described for photomacrography on page 117. One need not be especially concerned about base separation here, since the very thinness of the sections makes it desirable to gain all the depth effect possible. I have simply used a 5 × 7-inch or 8 × 10-inch film and accepted as much separation as the circumstances allowed. Mechanical and spatial limitations will stop you well before the stereo depth effect becomes too great for practicality.

Rolling Focus

When working with whole-mount microscope slides or with very thick sections, such as may be made for the study of nerve synapses, depth of field becomes a real problem. Microscope objectives have been made with built-in diaphragms for depth-of-field control, but diffraction limitations severely restrict their value. The depth of field obtainable by closing down the substage diaphragm is similarly diffraction-limited. The most practical technique for increasing depth of field is "rolling" the focus, or changing it during the exposure.

The focus can be changed during a single time exposure, or two or three exposures can be made at different focus settings on the same film. Both methods rely upon the presence of numbered calibration marks on the microscope fine-adjustment knob. By looking at the ground-glass image (the method is impractical with cameras that do not have a through-the-lens viewfinder), the top and bottom limits of focus are determined, and the corresponding numbers on the knob are noted. In the single-exposure method, the fine-focus knob is turned constantly during the exposure. The exposure time should be about half again the amount calculated as correct for a normal exposure. In the multiple-exposure method, two or three positions are selected (more than three is impractical) that, in combination, encompass the full depth of the subject. Each exposure is about two-thirds the normal length. Thus, a two-exposure negative will have received about 1⅓ times the normal exposure time, and a three-exposure negative will have received about twice the normal exposure time.

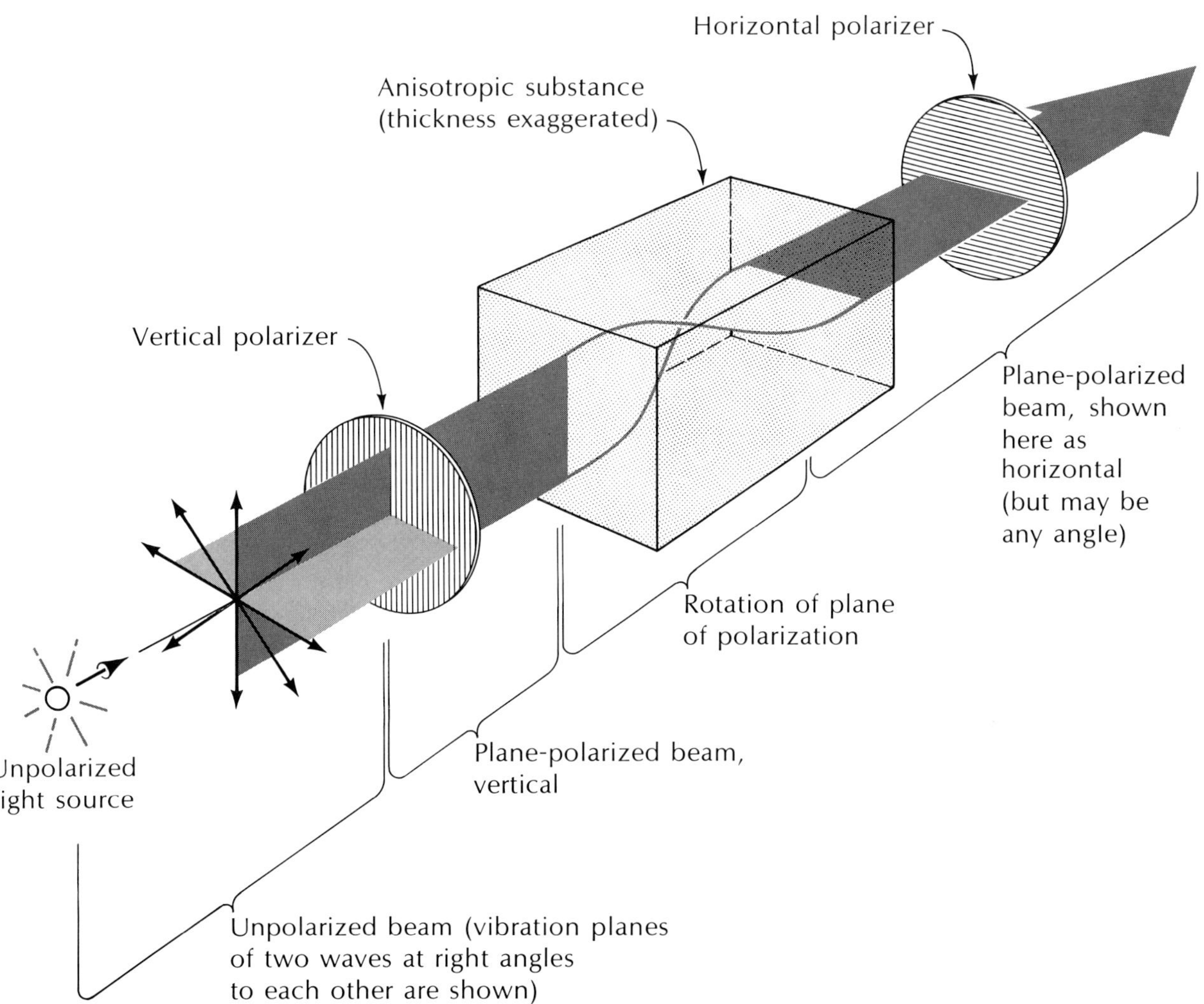

FIGURE 42
The rotation of a plane-polarized beam by an anisotropic substance. The direction and amount of rotation are not the same for all substances. (This greatly simplified drawing is intended as a visual aid for understanding one aspect of the phenomenon in question; in reality, the beam undergoes a much more complex transformation than can be shown here.)

The reason for giving extra time is that out-of-focus subject elements are not visible, so enough time is required at each level to assure a good image. The negatives will appear surprisingly good, if vibrations are avoided. I prefer the multiple-exposure method to minimize the possibility of vibration. (Both of these methods, and those using separate negatives, either printed together or printed separately and then joined afterward, are described in the article by McComb, 1961.)

For other useful information on photomicrographic techniques in general, see particularly Kodak publications P-2 and P-39, and Loveland's two-volume *Photomicrography: A Comprehensive Treatise,* 1970. Plates 17 and 18 are typical of photographs made with the compound microscope, and illustrate some of the differences between plant and animal tissues.

LOW-POWER PHOTOMICROGRAPHY

When doing photomicrography of stained slides there is a frequent need for low-power photographs of whole sections, for survey purposes. It is not practical to make these with compound microscopes, because of the limited size of their field of view; the methods used therefore fall more properly under the heading of photomacrography. Nevertheless, these methods are discussed here because of the similarities of subject matter and lighting methods. Comparative illustrations appear in Plate 19.

For work in the magnification range from about ×10–20 to ×50–100, the most practical approach is to use a photomacrographic camera, as described earlier, but with a condensered transillumination system. Photomacrographic lenses such as the Zeiss Luminars and their like are provided with matched condensers for substage use. There are published diagrams for the use of such systems (see Kodak publication N-12B, *Photomacrography;* also Engel, *Photography for the Scientist,* 1968), but it is usually sufficient to use a more rule-of-thumb method.

For instance, if you are using a large-negative (4 × 5 inches or larger), vertically mounted camera with a 16 mm photomacrographic lens, with its matched, single-element, planoconvex condenser lens, it is practical to use a glass-topped subject table with the mounted con-

PLATE 24 ▶

Low-Power Photomicrography: Black-and-White Rheinberg Lighting. (See pages 164–165.)

A growth tip of *Ephedra chilensis* (×24), a gymnosperm native to the mountains of Chile. A Wratten 22 orange filter helped to separate the tones in this red-stained slide. (Originally photographed for A. S. Foster.)

A A normal bright-field low-power photomicrograph.
B The use of a directional form of black-and-white Rheinberg lighting—with no attempt at optical color staining—aided in the differentiation of tissues. The direction of the light beam producing the dark-field component of the lighting was down the length of the specimen, at an off-axis angle of 26°. Refraction of light in the tracheary elements in the veins, which occur as spirals with a main axis across the vein, produced the effect of a glow in those areas.

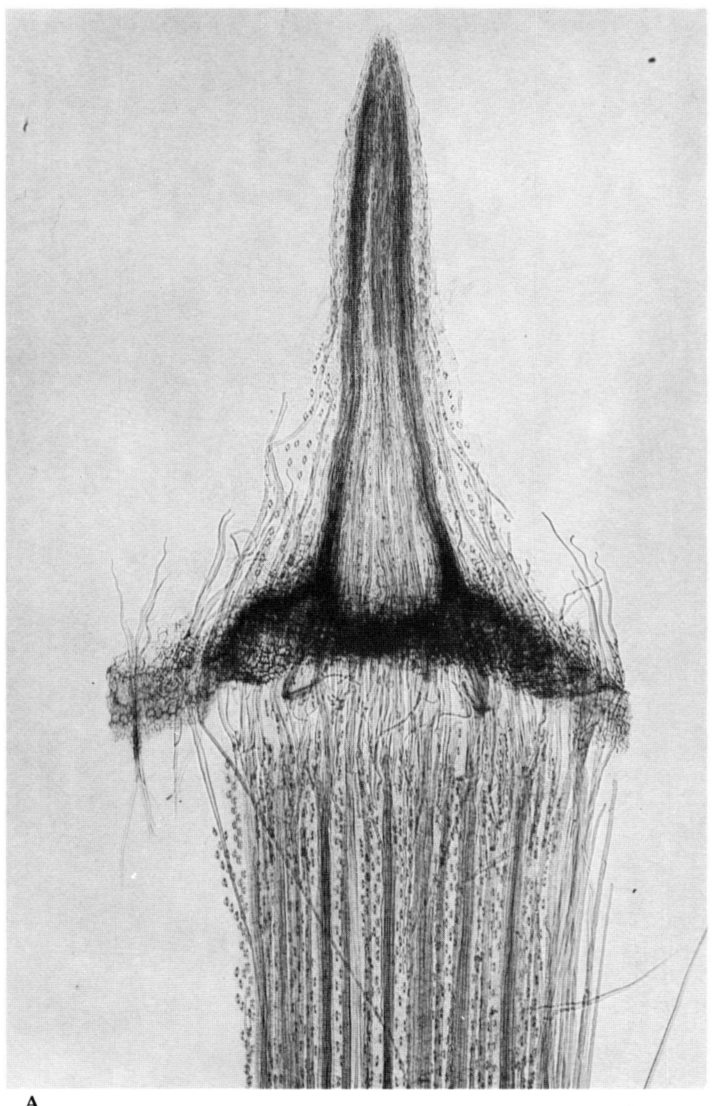

A

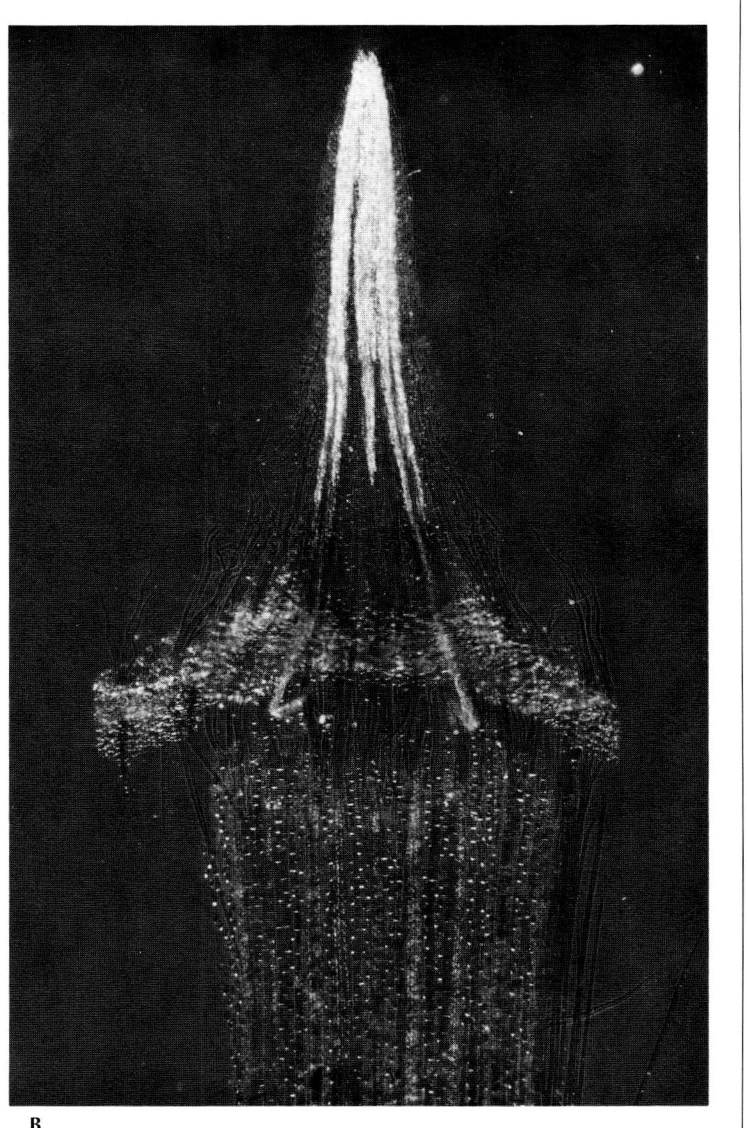

B

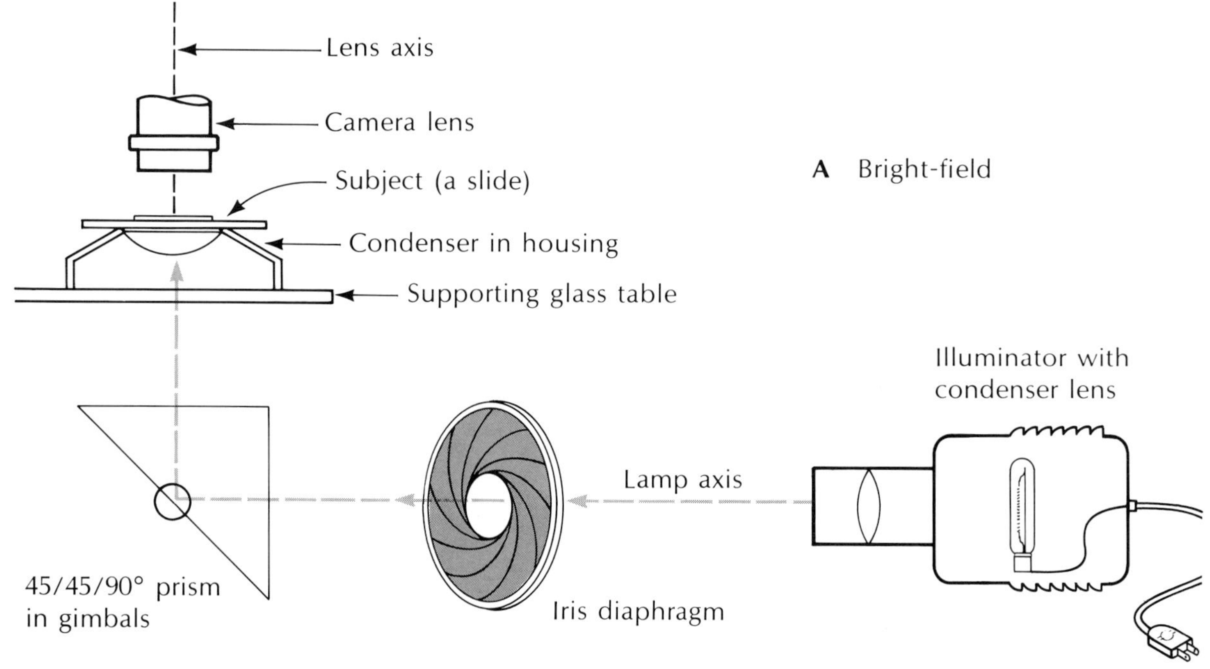

A Bright-field

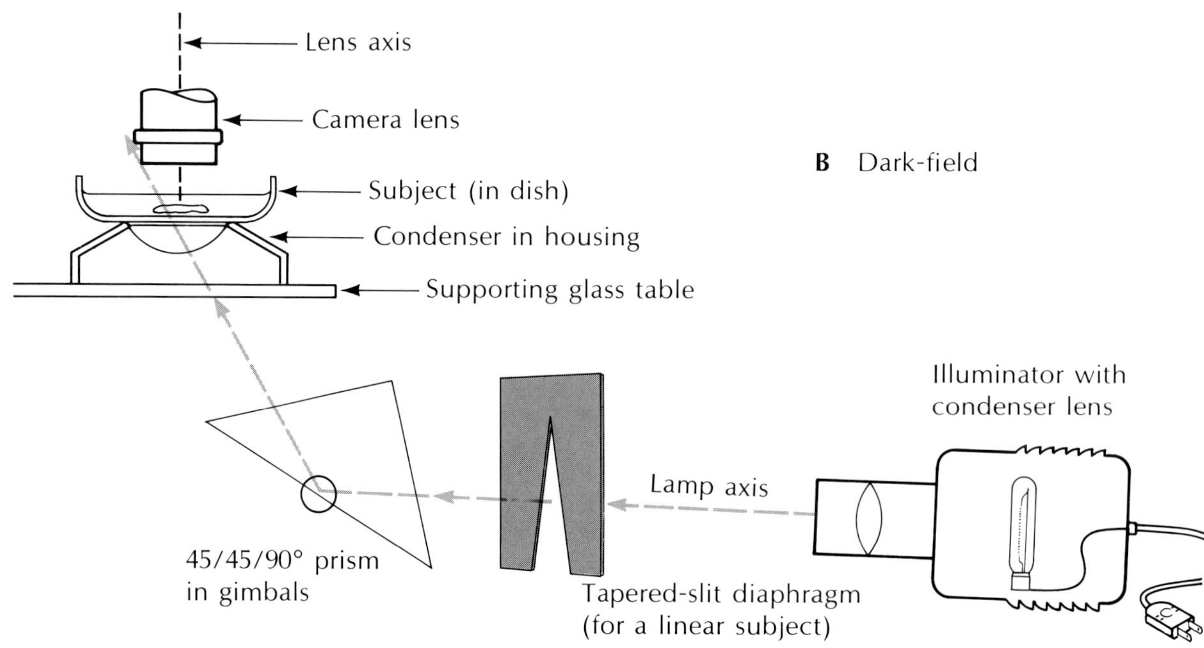

B Dark-field

denser lens set on it, flat side up. The subject slide can simply be balanced on top of the condenser housing. Beneath the table you place a gimballed 45/45/90° right-triangle prism, or a suitably large high-quality mirror, and reflect the beam of the microscope illuminator up to the camera lens (see Figure 43A). Observing the ground-glass image, you set the illuminator angle and the position and angle of the prism or mirror so that the lighting is centered behind the image of the subject. Then you adjust the focus of the field condenser, or the position of the bulb in the illuminator, until the full area of the viewing screen is evenly filled with light. The method sounds crude, but it is a pragmatic way to obtain the correct lighting. It is quick and simple, and produces images of excellent quality. See Plate 20A for an example.

A variation of this method is used with such transparent or translucent subjects as dissected-out arthropod guts, algae, etc., and provides both normal bright-field lighting and a useful form of directional dark-field lighting. (See Figure 43B). The subject is placed in a small Petri dish, immersed in a suitable liquid (e.g., distilled water, mineral oil, oil of wintergreen, etc., according to the nature of the subject). Here a prism is better than a mirror as a substage reflector. Otherwise, the setup is the same as before, if bright-field effects are wanted. To obtain directional dark-field lighting, set up as described above, and then rotate the prism until the edge of the illuminated field either passes through the centerline of the subject or passes off the edge of the viewfinder screen entirely. In the former adjustment, the visual effect is of a background graded at the center from bright to dark, with virtually invisible portions of the subject clearly revealed by the off-center lighting. The latter adjustment gives a very useful overall, but directional, dark-field effect. See Plate 20, parts B, C, and D.

In all of the foregoing setups, the lens diaphragm must remain wide open, or very close to it, or the lighting will probably become uneven. Some depth-of-field control is possible by using an aperture below the condenser. For bright-field work an iris diaphragm between the two condensers will help somewhat. In directional dark-field lighting, the axis of rotation of the prism is also the axis of directionality of the lighting, as you will see by experiment. The substage aperture should be basically linear, and tapered for adjustability of the width. For best results, the axis of this aperture should be at 90° to the axis of prism rotation. It then complements the directionality of the lighting.

It is also practical to do dark-field low-power photomicrography using a center stop just below the substage condenser, very much as

◂ **FIGURE 43**

Prism photomacrographic lighting, an improvised method of achieving efficient lighting with relatively unsophisticated equipment. (See Plate 20.)

A A setup for bright-field lighting, shown with a slide-mounted subject. (The diaphragms here and in part B are shown in perspective to illustrate their shapes.)
B A setup for directional dark-field lighting, shown with an unmounted subject immersed in liquid in a glass dish.

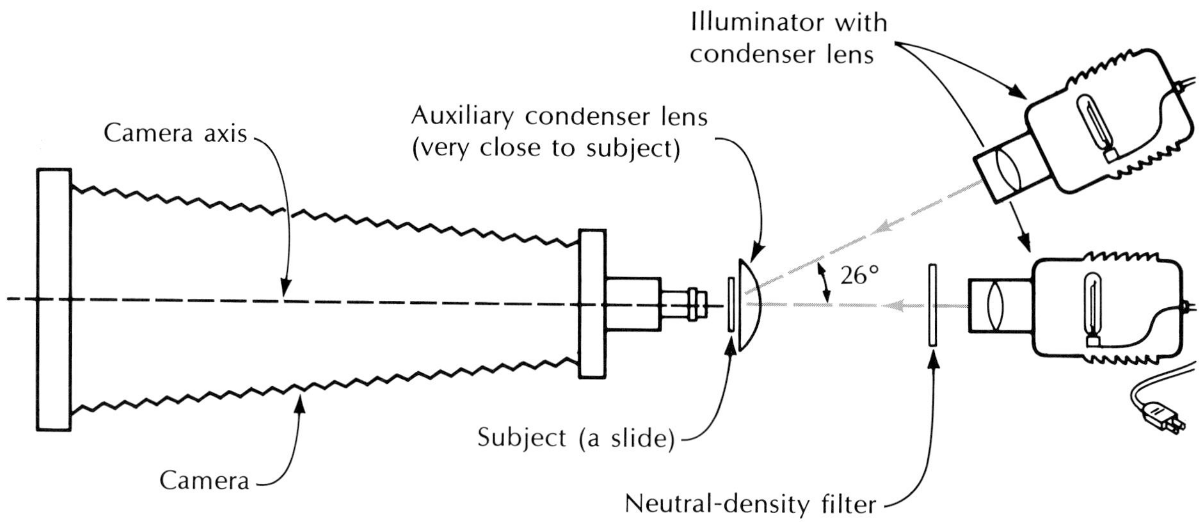

A Black-and-white setup

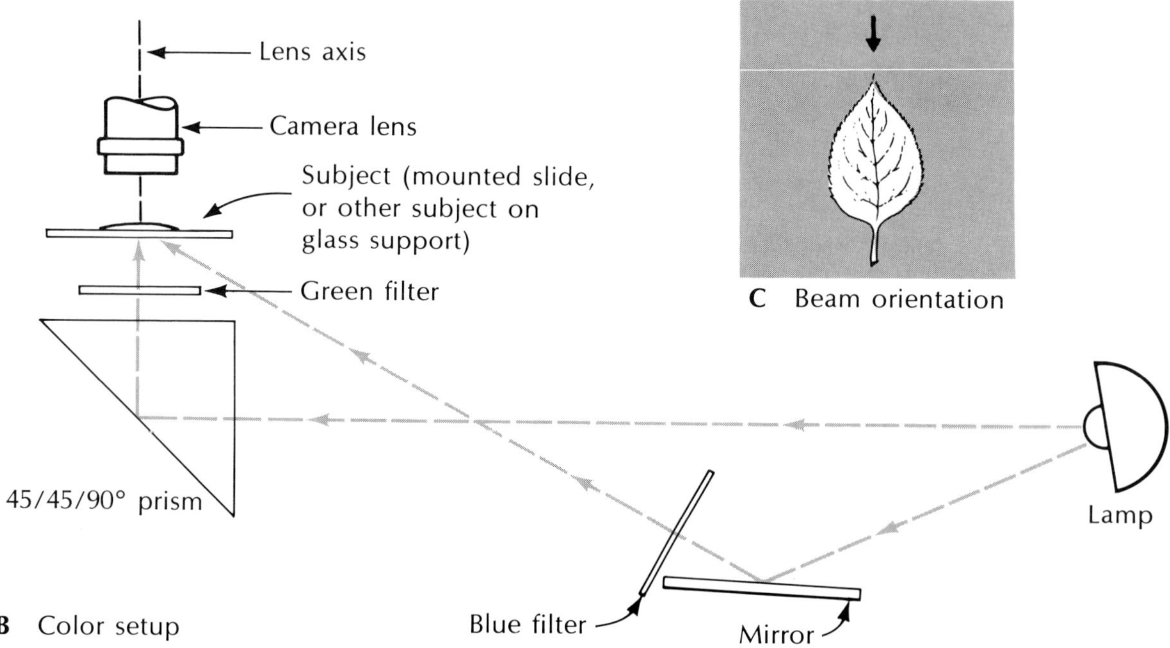

B Color setup

C Beam orientation

you would in high-power work with a compound microscope. Plate 21 illustrates one result obtainable with this method.

Another transillumination method that also works well at low magnifications makes use of polarized light. The polarizer can be placed anywhere between the light source and the bottom of the substage condenser, and the analyzer can be placed either just below or just above the camera lens. Plate 22 shows a mineral thin section photographed at low power, with plane-polarized light and with the polarizers crossed. Plate 23 illustrates some of the variety of polarization effects obtainable with mineral thin sections.

A further variation of transillumination for low-power work is a directional form of Rheinberg lighting, in which the most convenient camera setup is horizontal; it thus uses no substage prism or mirror. (See Figure 44A.) A neutral-density filter is used to attenuate the straight-through beam from the illuminator. A second illuminator is then placed about 26° off the axis of the first (I have found this angle to work best), and provides a one-sided peripheral beam. This form of directional dark-field illumination then gives a grey-backgrounded silhouette of the subject with brightly illuminated detail at 90° to the direction of the peripheral beam, emphasizing certain subject features, such as tracheary elements and the like. See Plate 24 for an example.

The needs for low-power transmitted-light photomicrography in the ×1 to ×15 magnification range can be satisfied very well by placing the subject (e.g., a whole-mount microscope slide, or a 35 mm color transparency to be copied into black-and-white or color print form) in the normal negative position of a photo-enlarger.

Good results can be achieved with either diffuser or condenser enlargers, but the condenser types usually give shorter exposure times. If a condenser enlarger is used, be sure that the bulb and the condenser are adjusted to give an even field of light. The best image quality from almost any macro system on an enlarger will be obtained with a high-quality camera lens instead of the normal enlarger lens (see the printing instructions for high-resolution 35 mm photography on pages 110–112, which also apply here).

The simplest film holder is a Polaroid Land 545 sheet-film-packet adapter, placed face up under the enlarger lens, with P/N black-and-

◂ **FIGURE 44**

Directional Rheinberg photomacrographic lighting, for subjects having transverse, translucent, linear elements (e.g., tracheary structures in a leaf vein, or banded granular material in a mineral thin section).

A A setup for black-and-white photography, shown in a horizontal position. The subject appears in light and dark tones on a grey background (see Plate 24B).
B A setup for color photography, shown in a vertical position (this setup will produce a blue image of the subject against a green background).
C Orientation of the off-center light beam with respect to transverse linear elements in the subject.

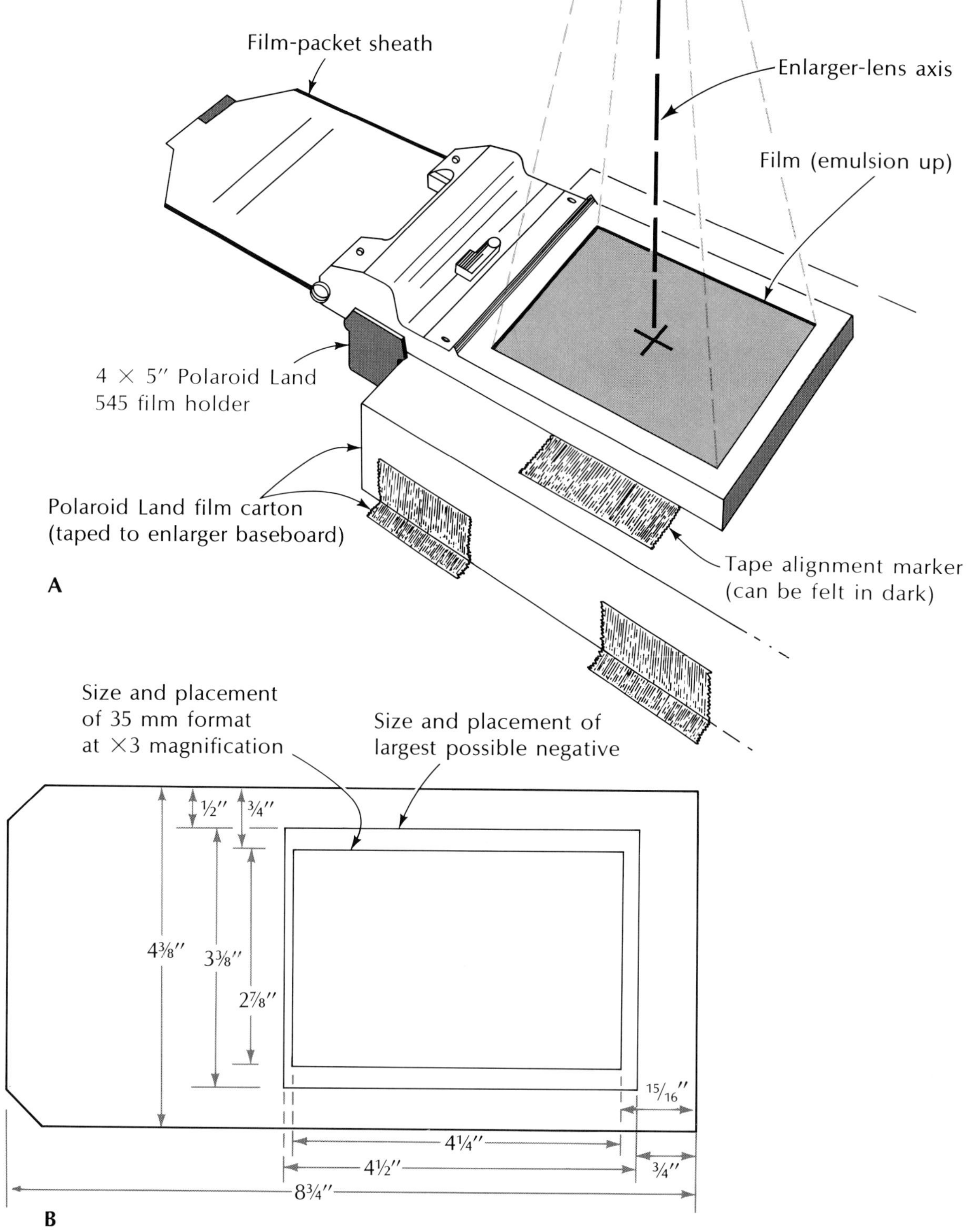
Film-packet sheath
Enlarger-lens axis
Film (emulsion up)
4 × 5″ Polaroid Land
545 film holder
Polaroid Land film carton
(taped to enlarger baseboard)
Tape alignment marker
(can be felt in dark)
A
Size and placement
of 35 mm format
at ×3 magnification
Size and placement of
largest possible negative
½″
¾″
4⅜″
3⅜″
2⅞″
15/16″
4¼″
4½″
¾″
8¾″
B

◂ **FIGURE 45**

Photomacrography and slide copying with a photo-enlarger, onto Polaroid Land film. The subject slide is in or on the negative carrier, and its image is projected onto the film plane of a Polaroid Land sheet-film holder laid face up on the enlarger baseboard. A focusing card is placed in the film holder for composition and focusing, and is replaced with a film packet for photography.

A A simple method for positioning the film holder.
B A plan for a focusing card ($\frac{1}{2}$-scale).

white film or Polacolor 2 color print film. See Figure 45 for details. A surprisingly good color print can be obtained with Polacolor 2 film, but color balancing with a Wratten 80B light-balancing filter will be needed. Some additional fine-tuning with color-correction (CC) filters may also be required. In color work, incandescent illumination gives less color-balancing problems than does a cold-light head, unless the enlarger has a cathode source intended for color printing.

It is often said that cold-light or other diffuser enlargers are unsuitable for this type of work, and that condenser enlargers—particularly point-source designs—will give sharper results. Recent experiments, however, seem to indicate that image quality is just as good with cold-light illumination, and possibly better.

Plate 25 illustrates the high degree of quality that can be achieved in the low-power photomicrography of animal and plant materials.

PLATE 25 (overleaf) ▸

Low-Power Photomicrography: Examples.

A Section of a kitten pituitary gland, in situ (×10.5). A Wratten 15 deep yellow filter aided in tissue differentiation. The soft tissues were stained in shades of red and pink, and the bony material in blue. (Originally photographed for P. Timiras and E. S. Evans.)
B A whole marine plant, *Anadyomene stellata,* photographed as an unstained whole-mount slide (×26). The background was very carefully painted out on the negative, since the subject is virtually transparent and would otherwise have appeared in low contrast against a similarly grey surrounding. (Originally photographed for J. West.)

Since the background in part B was pure white in the original print, it would have reproduced here as a light grey similar to that of the background in part A, which had also been painted out on the negative. However, the pressman removed the background in part B photomechanically so as to *keep* it white. Thus, part B here shows the same high subject/background contrast as in the original print.

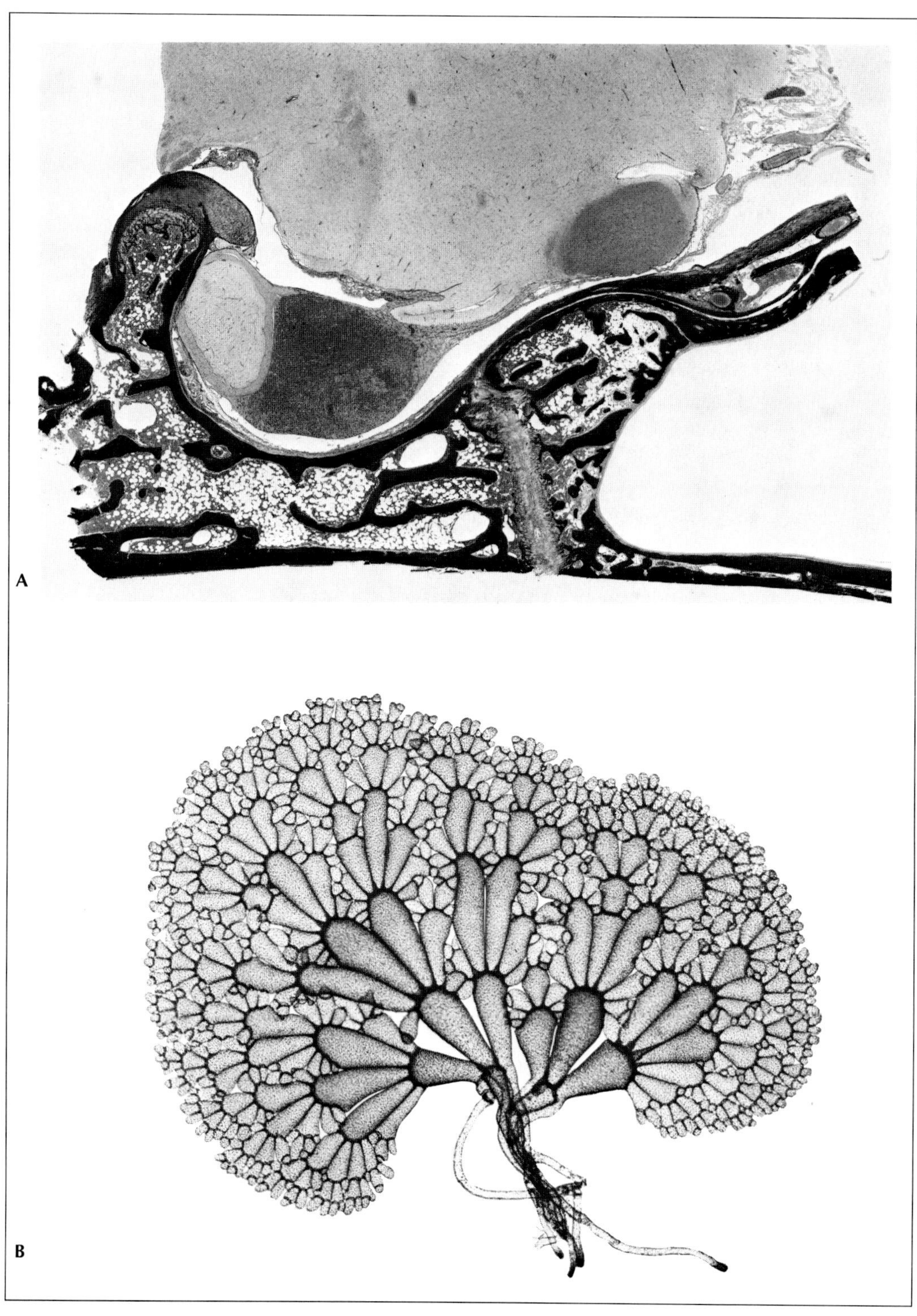
A
B

CHAPTER 10

Repairing Faults in Negatives and Prints

When it is of prime importance to present a photographic subject as clearly, succinctly, and unambiguously as possible, the intrusion of extraneous matter into the picture is intolerable. Also to be avoided are the marks and scratches that can result from accidents in film handling. There are a number of steps that can be taken, more or less readily, to remove such flaws from one's pictures, if they are there.

Before removing anything, however, first decide whether it is truly in the interest of scientific accuracy to do so. In other words, is the material to be removed actually extraneous? The answer will usually be obvious, but sometimes it is not so easy to decide where the limits lie. This chapter will attempt to provide some basis for judgment concerning these limits, as well as specific information on the methods to be used.

It should be said at once that neither the subject matter nor the resulting picture should ever be changed in such a way as to change the essential character of what is to be shown. Nor should any part of the photographic equipment or technique itself intrude on the subject matter. The purpose of a scientific photograph is to record clearly and unambiguously what is there, and not to allow the many and varied artifices of the field to be used as a means of special pleading. No reputable scientist would do so intentionally, of course, but there are times when enthusiasm or failure to consider the circumstances fully can lead one astray. Great care must be exercised to avoid unintentional misrepresentation.

TYPES OF ARTIFACTS

Dust and Lint

Dust and lint are the common contaminants in photography. Since they are airborne, they find their way everywhere. It is therefore essential to clean the interiors and exteriors of cameras, film holders, enlargers, and all other equipment, frequently and thoroughly. Any speck of dust or lint landing on a film prior to exposure throws a shadow during the exposure, and leaves on the developed negative a clear spot the size and shape of the particle. This will print as a black spot or lint mark. If a dust mote lands on the negative before or during printing, it will produce, by the shadow it throws, a white spot on the print. And if the negative image is being enlarged, such spots will be similarly enlarged. These marks can be removed from both negatives and prints, but it is both time-consuming and difficult to do well. Some such marks may be inevitable, and if they could cause any ambiguity they should be removed. But much grief can be avoided through simple cleanliness.

Another place to look for dust is on the subject matter itself, particularly if the subject is being magnified. Mounted insect specimens and other such materials that are kept for periods of time before photographing do tend to gather dust. Examination with a dissecting microscope prior to photography will reveal it, and a light touch with a good watercolor brush will remove most such particles easily. Although seemingly an obvious point, the magnification of a subject to ×30 or ×50 will render a speck invisible to the unaided eye in truly heroic proportions.

Photographically undesirable dust can also be expected in culture media. Unless especially carefully prepared (with care beyond that needed for normal research purposes), nearly any agar or similar culture medium will have minute particles of solid matter suspended in it and deposited on it. Although this material may be sterile and biologically inert (it may even be just some of the culture medium that didn't fully dissolve), it will be devastatingly visible if photographed by dark-field lighting, even at a mere ×1 magnification. For many purposes, such as the recording of precipitation bands, this sort of lighting is mandatory. A few minutes spent filtering a culture medium can save hours of retouching of prints later on. The moral is plain: if you are making cultures that will later be photographed, work carefully.

Marks on Transparent Containers

Marks on containers can cause aches in heads. Whenever a transparent container of photographic subject matter will come between the subject and the camera or will show beyond the subject (as with tube slants, Petri-dish cultures, plants grown in sterile tubes or flasks, etc.), the exterior of the container must be scrupulously cleaned before exposure.

Nor is dirt the only thing capable of degrading the picture. Scratches and irregularities in the container material itself can also do it. This can best be controlled by careful selection of the glassware or other containers at the outset of the experiment. The bottoms of glass Petri dishes commonly become extensively scratched and abraded through repeated use. If cultures are destined for eventual photography, new dishes should be used. But this still leaves the matter of the concentric rings of uneven thickness and shape found in most Petri dishes. If such rings are present or if the dish is scratched or abraded, all is not lost. Place a small quantity of clear, clean mineral oil on the glass supporting plate and float the dish on it. Through the similarity of its index of refraction to that of glass, the oil will effectively remove all such flaws from the picture. It is a bit messy, but very useful. See Plate 26A.

Disposable plastic Petri dishes are in common use, and these are usually free of scratches; however, there are often internal flaws in the bottoms. The light-piping property of the plastics used makes such flaws especially visible in dark-field lighting. If such dishes are to be used for photography you must choose them carefully.

Condensation on Glassware

Cultures or plant materials growing in contained environments present yet another problem—that of moisture condensing on the interior of the glassware, thereby distorting and partially obscuring the image of the subject.

This is best countered by gentle warming of the container, which is readily done by playing an infrared lamp or an ordinary hairdryer over it until the offending moisture evaporates. Care must be taken to avoid overheating, and thereby damaging, the culture material. All setup work and the exposure determination must be done prior to heating, since the picture must be made immediately upon the disappearance of the last traces of moisture. Prolonged heating may produce new condensation through increased metabolic activity of the plant material, and the cooling that follows any heating will produce condensation that may be temporarily greater than was there originally. Do not delay the exposure, therefore, or you may suddenly find yourself worse off than before.

RETOUCHING, SPOTTING, AND TREATING NEGATIVES AND PRINTS

The best retouching is none at all. This way, time and effort can be saved and ethical problems avoided. Much retouching results from the intrusion into the picture of matter on the subject material, the film, the negative, or the printing paper that ought not to have been there in the first place.

But there remain a few situations where some special handling will be necessary. With due regard for the ethical principles mentioned earlier, we will discuss these problems and the techniques for solving them.

Dust on the subject matter and on films and negatives has already been discussed. Similar in principle to dust is water-borne contamination, which can deposit as particles or stains during the washing of both negatives and prints. Frequent cleaning of washers and the use of fully filtered water supplies will eliminate nearly all of this type of contamination.

Such contaminants are not the only things that must be removed from pictures in order to reproduce the subject clearly and unambiguously, however. Subjects immersed in liquids during photography may slough off tiny pieces that scatter over what is intended to be a plain background, of any color; a background may print as grey when white is needed; or, after a picture is made, it may prove desirable to remove one of a group of articles in it, for some legitimate reason. All of these circumstances will be discussed in the following sections. It is obvious that working directly on negatives is practical only if the negative is fairly large. Generally speaking, 35 mm negatives are too small to allow this sort of work.

Enhancing Backgrounds

As was mentioned in Chapter 3, on backgrounds, it is often necessary to show certain subjects against a pure white background, as though they were floating in air. The method advocated there was to put the subject on a glass-topped table with a white card below it; the card could then be overexposed to produce a shadowless white background in the print. In industrial photography the same problem is often solved by placing the subject on a light box, which is internally lighted. The result is roughly the same. The method works well in most cases, and is often called *self-masking;* that is, the subject itself is used as a mask in producing the white background. However, this method cannot be used when any part of the subject is transparent or translucent. This could be true of a thin leaf, for example, and is definitely true of glassware or a transilluminated section under the microscope. So a less straightforward method must be used.

Since a background that is to be white in the print is black on the negative (or near enough to call it so), the solution is to paint the appropriate areas of the negative black. This is done with a specially prepared mixture, available in photo stores, called *opaque*. Care must be taken, of course, not to paint over the edge of the subject matter. In edging, a good method is to work with a magnifier and paint *not quite* to the edge. Then, if the background was not too dark to begin with, the remaining halo will probably not be visible in the print. If the background *was* too dark, the edge must be very accurately delineated; this requires a steady hand. Extraneous objects are simply painted over. This use of opaque is called *opaquing* or *blocking out.*

PLATE 26 ▶

Extraneous Matter in Photographs.

These parasitized insects (×4) were photographed while immersed in liquid. (Originally photographed for G. Poinar.)

A There are two primary problems in this photograph: scratches on the bottom of the glass container and bubbles of gas emerging from the subject. With a white background the scratches would not show, but the nature of the subject required a grey background, which gave them maximum visibility. They could have been eliminated from the picture by floating the container in a pool of mineral oil. The bubbling was impossible to control. It would have stopped eventually—but when?

B The major problem here was the presence of myriad particles suspended in the liquid, which is common with specimens photographed in preservative liquids. It may help to transfer the subject to a clean bath, but doing so could produce further fragmentation. It is possible to clean up the picture by "spotting" the print, and this has been done in a sector at the top center, as a demonstration. But it is a tedious and time-consuming procedure. To minimize the effort, it helps greatly to crop the print as close as possible to the subject. The area ahead of the upper wing was not spotted, but was swept clear of debris by the subject when it oscillated in the liquid during positioning under the camera.

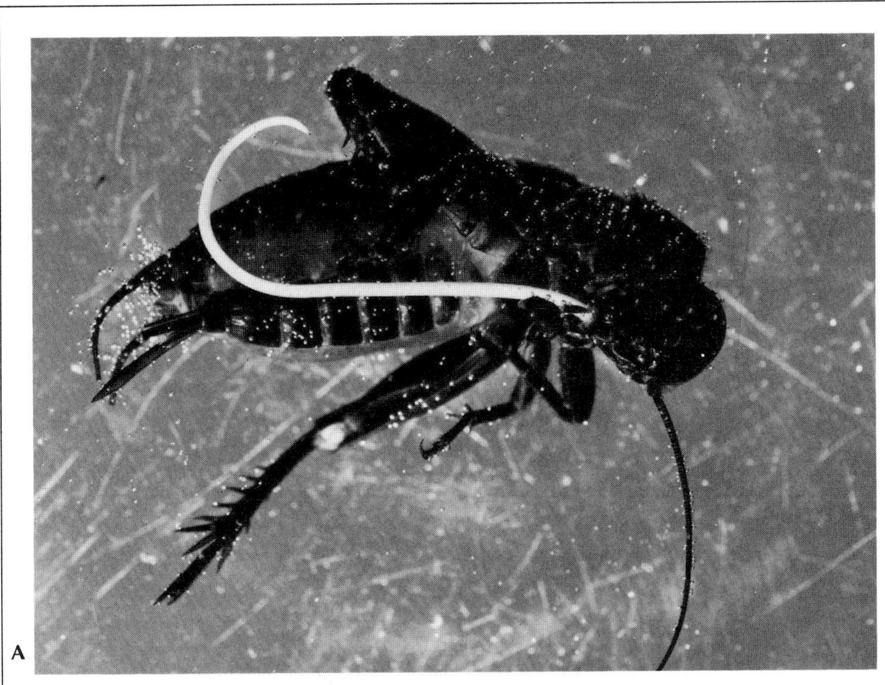

A

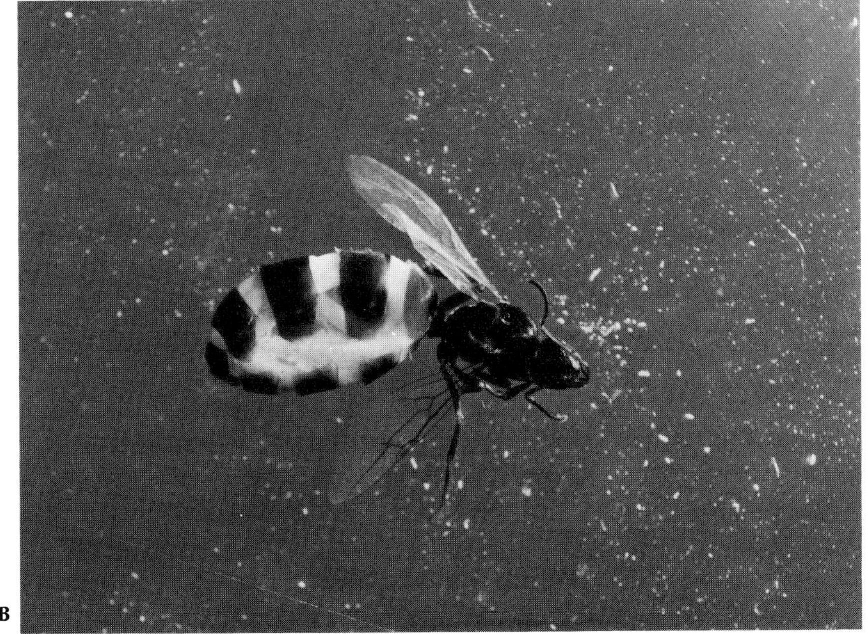

B

Microscope slides present special problems of interpretation. In painting out a background around any structure, it is possible to remove at will anything that is there. It is the obligation of the painter to be sure that material that may *seem* to be extraneous, but that is actually relevant, is not removed, since this would tend to misinform the viewer.

If a more subtle approach is desired, you can treat the *print* with a photographic reducer, such as the old reliable Farmer's reducer (a dilute solution of hypo to which a few drops of a dilute solution of potassium ferricyanide have been added; it is named after its inventor, E. Howard Farmer).* This is especially useful when you have attempted to produce a pure white background in a print but have not quite succeeded. Here a little reducer, carefully swabbed onto the offending background areas, will soon turn those portions of the print white. You must be very careful not to get any reducer on portions of the print that show subject matter. Some writers advise the use of Farmer's reducer to lighten up and thereby "brighten" highlights. I consider this a poor practice. Using a reducer can easily lead to chalky, unnatural-looking effects. Furthermore, it is hard to confine the reducer to a small area in the middle of a print, since it also tends to affect the areas it passes over while being washed off. If you need to lighten any highlight areas, the effect will be much more natural if you use the differential printing method (see Chapter 1). Any prints that *do* receive reduction must be thoroughly flushed with running water immediately following the treatment, and before fixation, if staining of the print is to be avoided.

A useful variant of Farmer's reducer can be made by preparing two stock solutions: one a saturated solution of sodium thiosulfate (hypo), and the other a saturated solution of potassium ferricyanide (*Caution:* the latter is poisonous). These solutions differ in appearance, the hypo being colorless and the ferricyanide being a deep red-orange. Pour roughly equal amounts of each into a processing tray containing water: about 50–100 ml of each in about 500 ml of water. These amounts will result in a color similar to that of cider. The strength of the mixture can be varied at will. If you wish to strengthen it after the original mixing, be sure to add approximately equal amounts of each stock solution. To use, swab the mixture onto the offending areas of the print. The reduction is not instantaneous, and should be continued until you get the desired visual effect.

With backgrounds that are intended to be black on the print (and that are therefore clear on the negative, or so light as to print as though clear), but where dust specks or objects intrude, there are two possible approaches. The most direct one is to use a knife edge to scrape the emulsion itself from the offending areas. This may make the negative look pretty bad, but if the background is to print black anyway, these marks will not show at all. The method works very well.

Again, if a more subtle approach is desired, Farmer's reducer or some variant of it can be used on the negative, to remove minor exposure effects on a background that should print totally black. It can also be used to generally

*Note that the term *reducer* is used here not in the chemical sense, but in the photographic sense of its reducing the image density in that area of the print to which it is applied. Chemically, in fact, Farmer's reducer and other photographic reducers are oxidizing agents that oxidize the silver grains in the emulsion to complex silver salts that are water-soluble and can hence be washed away.

lighten an entire negative (but not a print) that has been overexposed, but I do not recommend this practice. It is too likely to result in uneven reduction effects that will spoil the negative. If you do try it, do not swab the reducer onto the negative. Instead, immerse the negative in a weak solution of the reducer in a processing tray and agitate it very gently until the result is satisfactory.

Either negatives or prints can be reduced after initial processing and drying. You first thoroughly wet the item to be worked on by soaking it in plain water, and then use the reducer. When the treatment is complete, be sure to refix and thoroughly wash the negative or print, to stabilize it.

Even the best of us make mistakes and produce negatives that are too underexposed to print well. Normally in laboratory work, all you need to do is make a new negative. But sometimes you don't get that second chance. The answer then is a method called *intensification,* which is the opposite of reduction. There are several intensifier formulations on the market, most of which require bleaching of the negative and then redeveloping. However, there is one formulation that works directly and will salvage any negative that is not so underexposed as to have absolutely lost the necessary detail. It requires only two chemicals. To make it, dissolve 12 grams of mercuric chloride (*Caution:* poisonous) in 600 ml of water. Then dissolve 36 grams of potassium iodide in 250 ml of water. Add the second solution to the first, slowly, while stirring. The resulting solution, called Motox intensifier, is good almost indefinitely. If, after a while, crystals form in the bottom of the bottle, filter them out before use.

To use Motox, you first soak the negative in water to saturate the emulsion, if it has been dried. If it has not yet been dried, wash it after fixation before attempting the treatment. Pour the intensifier into a tray and immerse the negative in it, with very gentle agitation, for 30 seconds to 2 minutes. Then place it in a running water wash. Very little visual effect will be seen while the negative is in the intensifier, but shortly after it enters the wash the image will turn to dull shades of orange. This color has a strong effect in printing because of the roughly orthochromatic color sensitivity of the papers.

There is one pitfall: fingerprints on the base side of the film (but not on the emulsion side, fortunately) may absorb intensifier. It is therefore a good practice to lightly swab *the base side only* with fixer, part way through the wash.

The Motox formulation is especially useful for several reasons: it does not require bleaching and redeveloping, you can see the effect in the washer and re-immerse in the intensifier if needed, and the effect is reversible—up to a point. If the intensification is too strong, as seen in the washer, simply immerse the negative in a normal solution of fixer, and it can be swabbed off. Then you can rewash and try again. Once the negative has been intensified, washed, and dried, the process is no longer reversible. So make your final decision before drying the negative.

How effective is intensification? A negative that has a full range of tones, at least in trace form, but that is too underexposed to print well on even the most contrasty printing papers, can be treated so as to yield a print of normal appearance on normal grades of printing paper. The only adverse effect is that film grain size is increased significantly during the process. The method therefore is most appropriate with the larger negative sizes, which are least likely to be enlarged in printing.

Removing Spots and Scratch Marks from Negatives and Prints

It is impossible to avoid entirely some dust and lint marks on negatives. Also, scratches will occasionally be found on important negatives. These and the resulting print blemishes can be removed with one of the commercially available retouching and spotting compounds, which come either as liquids or as pigments deposited on a card. The liquid forms are used by brushing some of the liquid onto a small glass plate and allowing it to dry. The residue (or the dry pigment from a card) is then picked up in minute quantities on the tip of a finely pointed, damp brush, and appropriately deposited on the negative or print. (It may sound unsanitary, but the best solvent for these dyes and pigments is saliva; it has a viscosity effect that plain water lacks.) This is called *spotting*. Along with other, more complex forms of retouching, it requires skill for good results. The importance of spotting in cases where ambiguity can arise requires some discussion.

Enough skill at spotting to remedy most minor blemishes can be acquired with only moderate practice. For a beginner, the dry-pigment type of spotting compound is the most practical, since it forms only surface deposits on the print, and these can be readily removed in case of error. Most of the liquid forms are dyes that penetrate the surface of the print. Though they are more subtle, they are essentially unremovable, once applied. Overspotting is as bad as no spotting.

If a flaw in a negative results in a white mark on the print, it is best not to try to retouch the negative, because prints are easier to work on. And one's errors do not repeat on every print, as they do when the negative is retouched badly.

Where the flaw will print black, the easiest solution for the inexperienced is to spot it so that it will print as a white speck, and then spot that out on the print. Unskilled retouching of a negative will show blatantly on the print, whereas satisfactory work can usually be done on the final print quite readily.

Extensive retouching is commonly done by the more routine studio portraitists, but is neither desirable nor defensible in scientific work. Research reporting should be fact, not fiction. But sometimes it may help to darken or lighten an edge slightly to aid in visual differentiation. This should not be done, of course, unless the exact position and shape of that edge are already visible enough to serve as a guide, and are carefully maintained. Retouching should not be used as a late substitute for poor technique in lighting.

Spotting technique is quite simple, though it requires some finesse, particularly in handling the brush. White spots are darkened by using the tip of the spotting brush to deposit one or more tiny dark specks in the white area until it blends into its surroundings. White lines are harder to conceal than spots, so practice a bit on waste prints before tackling an irreplaceable one. The best method is to first place spots of dye at intervals along the line, so as to break it up. Then, with the brush aligned along the axis of the line, spot each short section. If you try to start at one end of a line and proceed to the other end without breaking it into a series of "dashes," you will find it much more difficult to blend the dye into the background. See Plate 26B.

The most common failure in attempting to remove a white spot is drawing a black circle around it, thus rendering it even more visible. This happens remarkably often. The cause is a persistently inaccurate aim with the brush tip.

It is more likely to occur when too much of the tip is pressed down. Use only the very tip of the brush, and aim it well. I have found it useful to employ a magnifier. There is one type that is a pair of magnifiers mounted in a sort of plastic eyeshade; it fits over eyeglasses, if you wear them, and is very convenient to use.

The strengthening of edges should be done very subtly, if at all. The brush should have less dye on it than is used for spotting. The effect is built up with repeated gentle strokes along the edge, with minor blending back from the edge. Once the edge is just visibly delineated, *stop.*

Most spotting requires a dark dye or pigment to conceal a light mark. As noted earlier, either type of spotting compound will work, but I prefer to use dyes, such as Spotone. The less common black spots, which result from dust specks on the film at the time of exposure, require a white pigment. And this requires a clean brush. Save one for this sole purpose. I have found it best to apply tiny specks of pure white pigment to cover the black spot, let it dry, and then go over it with black dye, for final blending.

CHAPTER 11

Special Considerations in Color Photography

In scientific photography, color films are used mainly to produce projection slides for use in classes or meetings, and original color illustrations for publication in journals or books. Although there will be no separate discussion of projection slides here, much of what will be said applies to them. The cost of color reproduction makes its use in journals relatively rare, but since it does occur, some discussion is appropriate.

FILMS

Color Correction

Either positive or negative film materials can be used in color photography, and for publication purposes either can be successful. But for technical reasons the use of positive color transparencies is usually to be preferred. Transparency work is simpler for most users because the accuracy of color reproduction is determined largely at the time of the original exposure; this is done by using films matched to the light sources, by using suitable filters to correct any slight imbalances in either the film-color accuracy or the color temperature of the lamps, and by using care in obtaining correct exposures. With color negative films, the color correction is done at the time of printing, and the results are more likely to be off color than on. It can be a difficult and time consuming process, particularly if great accuracy in the color is desired and if, at the time of printing, the original subject is not available for matching purposes. In commercial practice, exact color matching in prints is very expensive.

Exact color matches in transparencies are quite unlikely and rarely achieved, since the dyes presently available and used in the industry are not spectrally ideal. However, a very satisfactory job can be done if suitable precautions are taken at the outset. Color balances vary among the different makes of film and, to some extent, among different batches of the same film. This is especially apparent when paired comparisons are made of similar subject matter, or when an ongoing job is split between two batches of film. To avoid this problem, it is advisable to buy color film in moderately large lots (all of the same emulsion number), test the initial rolls or sheets under controlled conditions to determine what correction filters may be needed, and then use the remainder under similarly controlled conditions. Stock film should be stored under refrigeration to prevent, or at least inhibit, degradative chemical changes. Only in these ways can consistently comparable results be obtained.

Reciprocity Failure

With black-and-white films, correcting for reciprocity failure requires only some additional exposure. In color films the emulsion is multilayered to record all the colors and the different layers show different degrees of reciprocity failure. The result of this differential reciprocity failure is that excessively long or short exposures may produce more or less pronounced color shifts, as well as the familiar underexposure effect (see Chapter 1). At the expense of adding even more exposure time, these color shifts can usually, but not always, be corrected through the use of color-correction filters. Film data sheets should be checked for specific information on this subject. If the manufacturer says that some procedure is "not recommended," this usually means that the procedure will produce a noncorrectable color shift. This may be very important in such uses as photography at high magnifications, where light falloff through the bellows extension is significant.

Quality

For high-quality color reproduction it is necessary to use the sharpest, finest-grained films possible in the given circumstances. For 35 mm cameras the standard for comparison is, and has been ever since its introduction, Kodachrome. In recent years Kodachrome has been produced in several types and film speeds, and Kodachrome 25 is the current standard for quality. Circumstances may require the use of other films, but this will usually result in larger grain, less sharpness, less standardized processing, less accurate color rendering, or some combination of these. These factors vary from film to film, ranging from major differences to minor ones. So the needs of the job at hand must govern the choice. Kodachrome is not available for the larger cameras, so other films must be used; there are a number of excellent color films available in large formats. On any large, important, or unusual project, check the manufacturers' claims, both for color accuracy and for suitability to the job, before deciding on a film.

In any event—not counting Kodachrome, which is really exceptional in performance for most uses—quality is usually best achieved by using the largest films one has the equipment to handle. With large film sizes and suitable testing and correction, as described above, it will be found possible to obtain publication-grade results with any of the commonly available makes and types, except where special circumstances require the use of a film having specific qualities matching the conditions imposed by the subject. In such special cases, consultation with the manufacturers' representatives is suggested.

Some recent technical advances have made the Polaroid Land color films much more suitable for use in publication. The recently released Polacolor 2 is much improved over the earlier version in color fidelity and image sharpness. And the SX-70 system, using a totally new type of film and a revolutionary new type of single lens reflex camera, offers the ability to do a wide variety of professional-quality work, though in a somewhat smaller print size. (These two films measure $3\frac{1}{4} \times 4\frac{1}{4}$ inches and $3\frac{1}{8} \times 3\frac{1}{4}$ inches, respectively; Polacolor 2 has just been introduced in 8×10-inch format also.) Both types of film are especially useful in that you get the print almost immediately; you can thus make corrections for color balance as you go. Color Plate IIA was made with Polacolor 2 film; part B was made with the earlier type of Polacolor film, and the colors are muted.

With either large or small sizes of any color film, the best accuracy of exposure is obtained by straddling the calculated correct exposure with two or more additional exposures, displaced $\frac{1}{3}$ to $\frac{1}{2}$ stop on either side. It uses more film, but can be well worth it where ultimate quality is desired and the chance to try again later is not assured. And with 35 mm films the additional cost is usually negligible.

BACKGROUNDS

Colors Usable

In color photography, backgrounds offer far greater possibilities than they do in black-and-white. They can be any color desired, as well as black, white, or grey.

What, then, is the best background color for scientific reporting? As in most other photographic matters, "it all depends." For some uses, usually where a natural or seminatural effect is being attempted, colors are quite permissible; for example, a light blue card placed behind a twig or leaf grouping will simulate a sky tone. But most often, backgrounds should be in neutral tones.

For subjects where a dramatic effect is desired, and particularly where it is desirable to call attention to subtle pastels, the best background color is black—preferably the absolute black produced by using deep-nap velvet as a backing. The blackness of the background forces the viewer's attention upon the subject and, by its own total lack of color, makes it more likely that the eye will perceive all of the subject's color subtleties (see Color Plate III).

Some workers may prefer a more understated approach, just as some subjects may benefit from it, especially subjects that are themselves brightly colored. In this case a plain white backing is useful; but if the photograph is intended for projection, beware of *too* white a background, which will produce too much glare. A *very* light grey or just a trace of a suitable color may be preferable. Darker greys and darker shades of the more muted colors are appropriate where the subject is very light but where black backgrounds are undesirable or tend to create ambiguity.

Effects of Colored Backgrounds

Many writers on color photography for informational purposes suggest using brightly colored backgrounds to take advantage of the sheer visual attraction of color. For scientific purposes, however, this seems undesirable, the main reason being that here it is usually important to preserve as much accuracy as possible in the subject colors. And there is a peculiar psychological process that tends to cause an effect of color tinging to transfer from the background to the subject, if the former is the more highly colored. That there is usually no actual transfer has been determined experimentally, but the eye tends to see it as though it exists. Actual color transfer takes place, with all films, only where colored light reflects obliquely onto the subject from an overlarge background or from other colored objects in the vicinity.

It is an all too common practice to use brightly colored backgrounds behind some of the more spectacular masks and other objects found in museums of anthropology. The frequent result is that reflections appear on surfaces of the object and obscure or misrepresent the actual colors. I have seen the same effects in medical photographs of gross specimens, such as whole organs. It is part of the responsibility of the photographer to see that there is no unwitting misrepresentation of the colors. Partly because color reproduction is expensive and partly because of its intrinsic visual appeal, pictures that are presented in color tend to assume great significance. Thus, even a color cover photograph that is supposedly primarily decorative will be examined by readers and considered a part of any editorial matter that it is associated with.

LIGHTING

It is stated in several standard texts on color photography that lighting contrasts should be less for color photography than for black-and-white. In actual practice—particularly where the intended use will be projection rather than publication—it will be found that one can get away with contrasts that would be hopelessly high in black-and-white photography. Why? Because in color work one can readily distinguish differences in shadow and highlight from differences in color.

A fairly safe generalization, in accord with the techniques for scientific photography described earlier in this book, is that informationally suitable lighting for black-and-white pictures will also produce good results in color. The reverse is not necessarily true. A type of lighting that produces a quite acceptable color slide may reproduce execrably in black-and-white, or even in a color print. This point is well worth noting by those who primarily make color slides but who may wish later to convert them to black-and-white for publication.

Regardless of how the lighting is done, some types of subjects produce color effects that are not correctable. These effects must be recognized and noted as impairing the color accuracy. See Color Plate VI for examples.

FILTERS

As mentioned earlier, the strongly colored filters normally used with black-and-white films cannot be used with color films because they will simply produce an overall color cast of their own hue. With color films the use of color filters is restricted to those relatively pale ones designed to correct imbalances in the films or in the color temperatures of light sources.

Color Temperature

All color transparency films are designed to be used with light sources that are calibrated for color balance in terms of their *color temper-*

ature, measured in degrees Kelvin. (For further discussion of this system, see Kodak publication B-3.) This is the basic difference between daylight and tungsten color films. Mismatched films and lights can be paired through the use of color-conversion or light-balancing filters; the necessary information for this is given in the data sheet packed with the film. For accurate color rendition, then, one should use a film matched to the light source or filtered for correction to it. One cannot mix light of two different color temperatures (say, daylight and tungsten sources) in one picture without badly upsetting the results.

Color photography by the light of fluorescent lamps should be avoided wherever possible. These lamps are different from sunlight and incandescent lamps in that they have no true color temperature; their radiant energy is produced by a different means. Color films, being calibrated to true color temperatures, will respond unpredictably. Lists of filter corrections for various fluorescent lamps are available (see Blaker, 1976, and Kodak publications AE-3 and H-9), but it should be understood that their use requires testing under actual working conditions and can still not guarantee optimum results. Fluorescent lighting may be unavoidable in some circumstances, but for color work it is never preferred.

Types of Filters

There are three basic types of filters designed for use with color films and intended for balancing light sources to the basic sensitivity range of the film, or vice versa.

The most strongly colored (but still relatively pale) filters are called *color-conversion* filters, and are designed to allow you to use a film with a mismatched light source. For instance, you may need to do photography with daylight-type film, but using an incandescent photoflood lamp. The film is color-balanced for about 5500°K, but the lamp radiates at 3400°K. Here it is necessary to use the blue Wratten 80B filter, or its equivalent in another filtering system. This filter is a color-conversion filter. To determine the appropriate color-conversion filter for given conditions, consult the instruction sheet provided with the film.

Somewhat paler in tint are the filters that are used for balancing a film to a light source that is almost right; these are called *light-balancing* filters. For example, it might be necessary to do photography with a Type A color film, which is balanced for 3400°K, but where the light source to be used is a 200-watt household bulb that radiates at 2850°K. This would require a combination of two Wratten light-balancing filters, the 82 and 82C filters.

Palest of all are the *color-correction,* or CC, filters. These come in six colors—red, yellow, green, blue, cyan, and magenta—and there is a wide variety of densities. CC filters are used to fine-tune films to light sources with great exactness. My own most common use here is to match electronic flash sources to daylight-type color films with a CC20Y filter (a pale yellow filter calibrated to 0.20 density).

Kodak publication B-3, *Kodak Filters for Scientific and Technical Uses,* is the primary source of information concerning the use of filters related to the Wratten system. Manufacturers of other filtering systems publish similar information for their clients. The Wratten system is featured here because it is overwhelmingly the most used in the United States, and I have little experience with the Decamired, Harrison, and other systems.

Two other types of filters used in black-and-white photography are also used to some extent with color films: polarizing filters and neutral-density filters.

Polarizing filters retain their properties in color use. They are normally grey, and so impart no color casts. One primary use is to deepen sky color without affecting the subject color, except insofar as surface reflections may be eliminated and the surface color thereby deepened. There is no other way of darkening the sky and emphasizing clouds with color films. Polarizing filters are otherwise used the same as with black-and-white films for reflection control and for any other control and use of polarization effects.

Neutral-density filters, which are also grey, are used identically with either black-and-white or color films, to control exposure time.

Filter Factors

Filter factors apply to color films just as they do to black-and-white films, and this includes the very pale color-correction filters. All filters work by absorbing some of the light that strikes them. Kodak publication B-3 is an excellent source of information concerning filter factors, as well as all sorts of other information on filters. It should be part of the daily-use equipment of any photographer who uses the Wratten filtering system.

PART III

Solutions to Problems

CHAPTER 12

General Problems

Many specific photographic difficulties are more easily solved if you view them as examples of general problems. This chapter will review several of the most commonly encountered photographic difficulties, with the view that the information provided can be applied directly in a variety of circumstances.

CONTROL OF REFLECTIONS

There are two aspects to the problem of reflections from surfaces: the removal of unwanted reflections from a subject surface or from surfaces intervening between the camera and the subject, and the use of controlled reflections to reveal the shape and nature of a subject.

The Law of Reflection

The law of reflection, which states that a reflected beam departs from a surface at an angle equal to that of the incident beam, was illustrated in Figure 16, on page 49. Figure 46, shown here, reveals what happens when the position of a lamp illuminating a subject is changed even slightly. In part A the beam reflected from a particular surface has been found to enter the camera lens; in part B a minor change in the

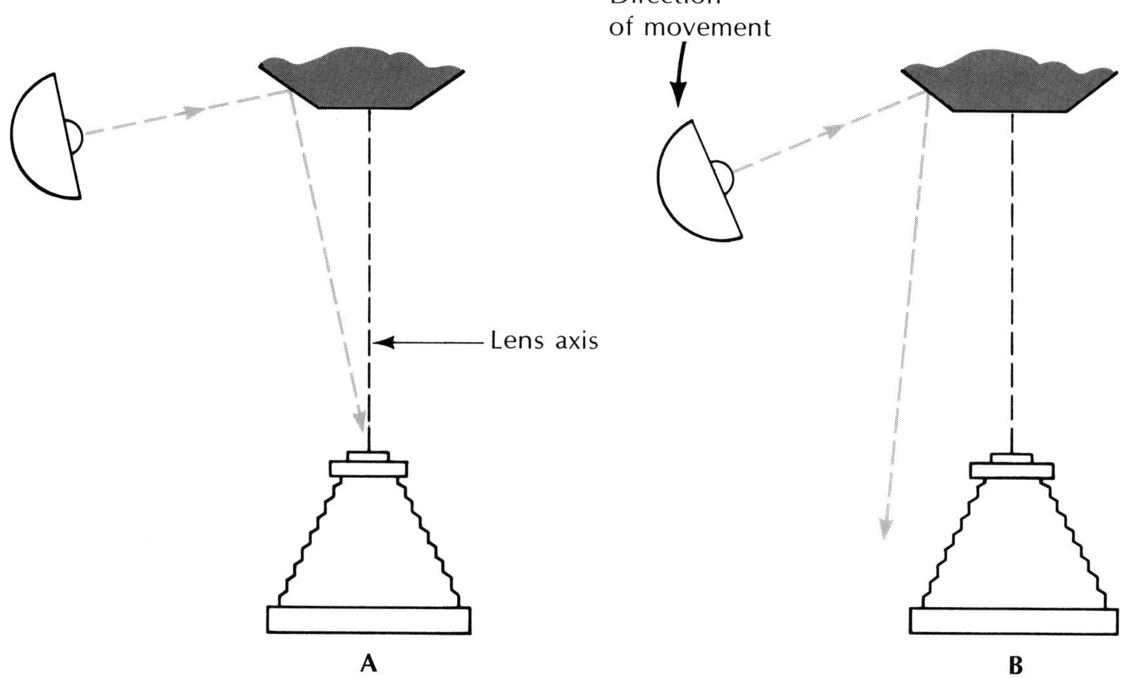

FIGURE 46
Reflection control on surfaces. By invoking the law of reflection (see Figure 16), control is simple.

A Light from a particular surface is reflected into the camera lens.
B A minor change in the lamp position directs the specularly reflected light away from the lens.

lamp's position has redirected the reflected beam away from the lens without significantly changing the general lighting effect. Whether this is desirable depends upon what the picture is to show.

Reflections on the Subject

One of the most common problems in scientific photography is the presence of unwanted reflections of the lights on the subject itself, on its container, or on some other surface between the subject and the camera. Such reflections can nearly always be eliminated or substantially reduced by one means or another.

The quickest and easiest method of controlling a reflection is by moving the light or lights until—from the camera position—the reflection is either subdued or eliminated. This works best where the reflection is on a flat surface, such as a piece of sheet metal or a glass case enclosing the subject. The required change in the position of the lamp is usually not great.

If the surface showing the reflection is irregular in shape, and changing the positions of the lamps serves only to move the reflection around, a suitable method of control—if the subject will not be damaged—is to immerse it in liquid. Useful liquids are distilled water (which does not contain the annoying air bubbles present in freshly drawn tap water), alcohol in various dilutions according to the subject, glycerin (though it has visible striations due to varying density, if it is subject to a thermal gradient), and mineral oil. This last liquid is very useful with insects embedded in amber, owing to the similarity of the indexes of refraction; this not only cuts out surface reflections but also reduces distortions introduced by irregularities in the shape of the amber. The effect of liquid immersion is to ensure that the only surface producing direct reflections of the lights is the liquid surface itself. Being flat, this surface produces reflections that can be readily controlled by the placement of the lamps.

If liquid immersion is impractical and the lights cannot be moved about (or if such movement does not suffice), there still remains a good solution: the use of polarizing filters (see Chapter 5). The main difficulty here arises through a severe loss of light, necessitating an increase in the exposure time. Where a setup is employed with incandescent light sources polarized with filters, and with a polarizing filter at the camera lens, the exposure increase needed is considerable (see Table 5, on page 80, for exposure information for several types of polarizing materials).

A secondary source of reflections, after all light-source reflections have been controlled, may be some flat surface that lies between the camera and the subject and is perpendicular to the optical axis. This can be a glass cover, the surface of the immersing liquid, and so on. The problem is the reflection of the camera or lens mount, which shows up in the center of the picture area. This reflection can usually be removed by putting the camera behind a screen of black paper or other material, with a hole cut out for the lens. This type of reflection is easily missed when setting up the camera but is very disturbing in the final picture; watch for it carefully.

Sometimes one can regard surface reflections from a subject as an advantage rather than a disadvantage. This is especially true where the subject contains several planes, as in the skull structure of certain animals or in the faceting of chipped stone artifacts.

The ability to show such subject planes well (rather than haphazardly, as is often done) depends on your understanding the law of reflection. Knowing where you want the reflection to appear, and the angle between the lens axis and the surface in question, it is a simple matter to determine where the light or lights should be placed.

Metallic apparatus of basically rectilinear form can be photographed very conveniently by this method, often using only one or two lamps aimed at the subject almost at random angles. The trick is to place white reflecting cards at suitable angles to the main planes of the subject, and then see that these cards also receive light. Undiffused light striking the subject provides metallic-looking highlights, while diffuse reflection from the cards provides overall lighting of the planes. See Figure 47 for a diagram, and Plate 29 for an illustration of these effects.

Museum-Case Photography

In photographing museum exhibits in glass cases, the control of surface reflections is both necessary and quite simple. The source of the

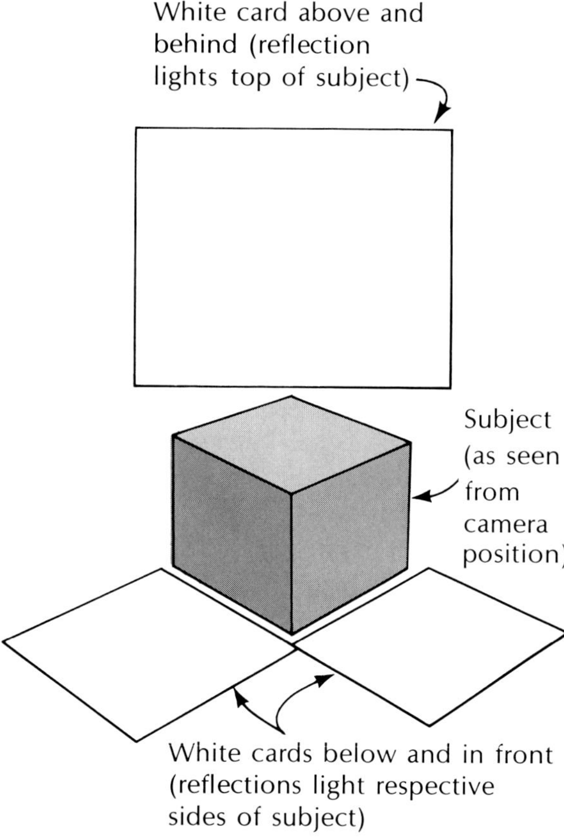

FIGURE 47
Lighting a basically rectilinear metal apparatus by reflection. Each of the three visible planes receives diffuse reflected light from the respective card, resulting in a soft overall highlight. A single flood lamp is placed so that it illuminates all three cards. How it lights the subject is irrelevant as long as there are no harsh specular reflections of the lamp—the lighting from the cards will overpower the direct lamp light if the latter is not at any of the main angles of reflection. The subject can be very complex in structure (see Plate 29).

reflections is usually the lighting fixtures in facing or adjoining cases. When the camera is aimed at an angle to the case, any reflection must come from an angle equal to that of the lens axis (see Figure 48 for an example). You need only find the source of the reflection and intercept the light from it with a black cloth. This method solves the problem nicely and avoids all the difficulties associated with the use of polarizing filters.

Aquarium Photography

A similar problem occurs in the flash photography of subjects in aquaria, the main difference being that the light source used to illuminate the subject is also the source of the surface reflection. In aquarium photography it is usually a poor practice to look through the glass at a broad angle, because of refraction effects induced by the water. Yet if you aim the camera perpendicularly to the aquarium surface, the light from an attached flash unit will be reflected directly back into the lens, and the subject will be obliterated by a massive reflection. (See Figure 49A.) The solution is to aim the camera so that the lens axis is at an angle close to the perpendicular, and then aim the flash unit from within the *acute* angle between the lens axis and the surface (Figure 49B). The reflection will then be directed away from the camera and will not affect the picture. There is a light loss, represented by the reflection itself, of about 50%, but this can be taken into account in determining the exposure, by using a lens aperture one stop wider than would otherwise be used (alternatively, the flash unit could be placed about one-third closer to the subject, to achieve a similar correction by way of the inverse-square law). You will find that the lighting of the subject will not be adversely affected by this technique. Remember that if the flash unit is placed on the obtuse side of the lens-axis angle, at least part of the reflection will enter the camera lens.

Even with a lens-axis angle that is slightly off the perpendicular, there may still be surface re-

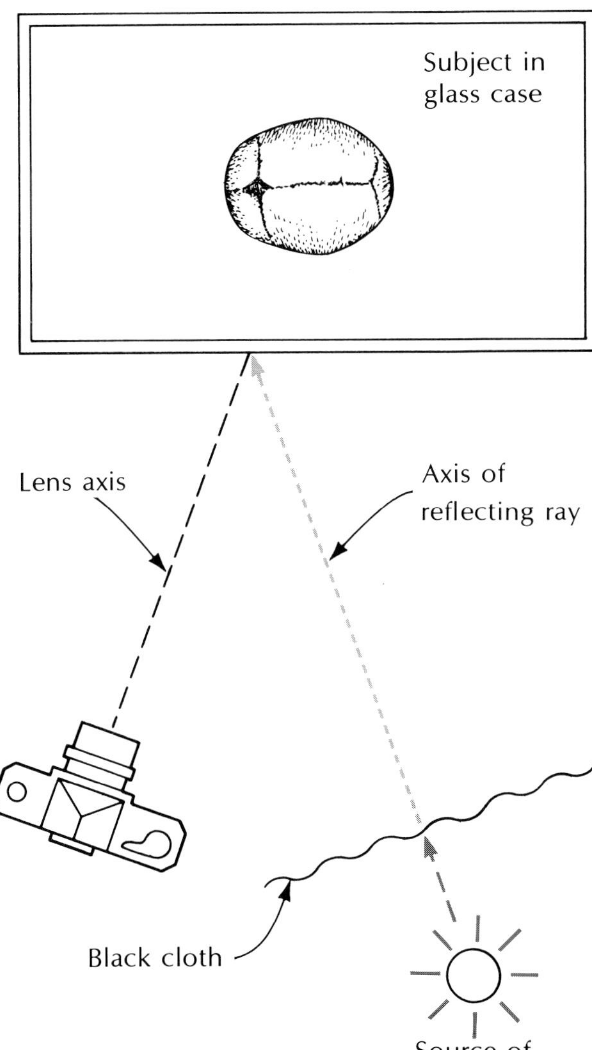

FIGURE 48
Removing reflections from museum cases. Once the source of a reflection is located, by applying the law of reflection, it can be removed with a piece of black cloth.

flections from the front of the camera. These can be prevented by covering all shiny surfaces on the camera front with black photographic tape. Do not forget the ring at the front of the lens mount. And do not forget that your own clothing can also reflect light, so wear dark clothing. See Color Plate IV.

There may be times when some reflections must be eliminated and others created, in the same picture, but if you keep the law of reflection clearly in mind you should be able to handle the job.

MOTION CONTROL

Camera Motion

Where fine detail is essential, as in scientific photography generally, the danger of loss of sharpness from camera motion can scarcely be overestimated. Almost always when the camera is handheld, the limiting factor in resolving fine detail lies not in the capabilities of the lens or film, but rather in the amount of camera motion at the moment of exposure. Only when exposures are shorter than about $1/250$ to $1/500$ second can really sharp pictures be taken with a handheld camera—other than through chance momentary stillness during the exposure interval. The *full* resolution potential of either lens or film can be realized only when the camera is firmly supported. You must determine for yourself—preferably through comparison trials—when and where you can afford to do handheld work, i.e., when and where mobility is more important than sharpness.

When mobility is a prime requisite, the obvious method of countering camera motion is to use flash lighting, particularly electronic flash with its ultra-short flash duration. If the subject is static, but of a type demanding the resolution of very fine detail, it is necessary to use a stand of some sort to do away with any possibility of

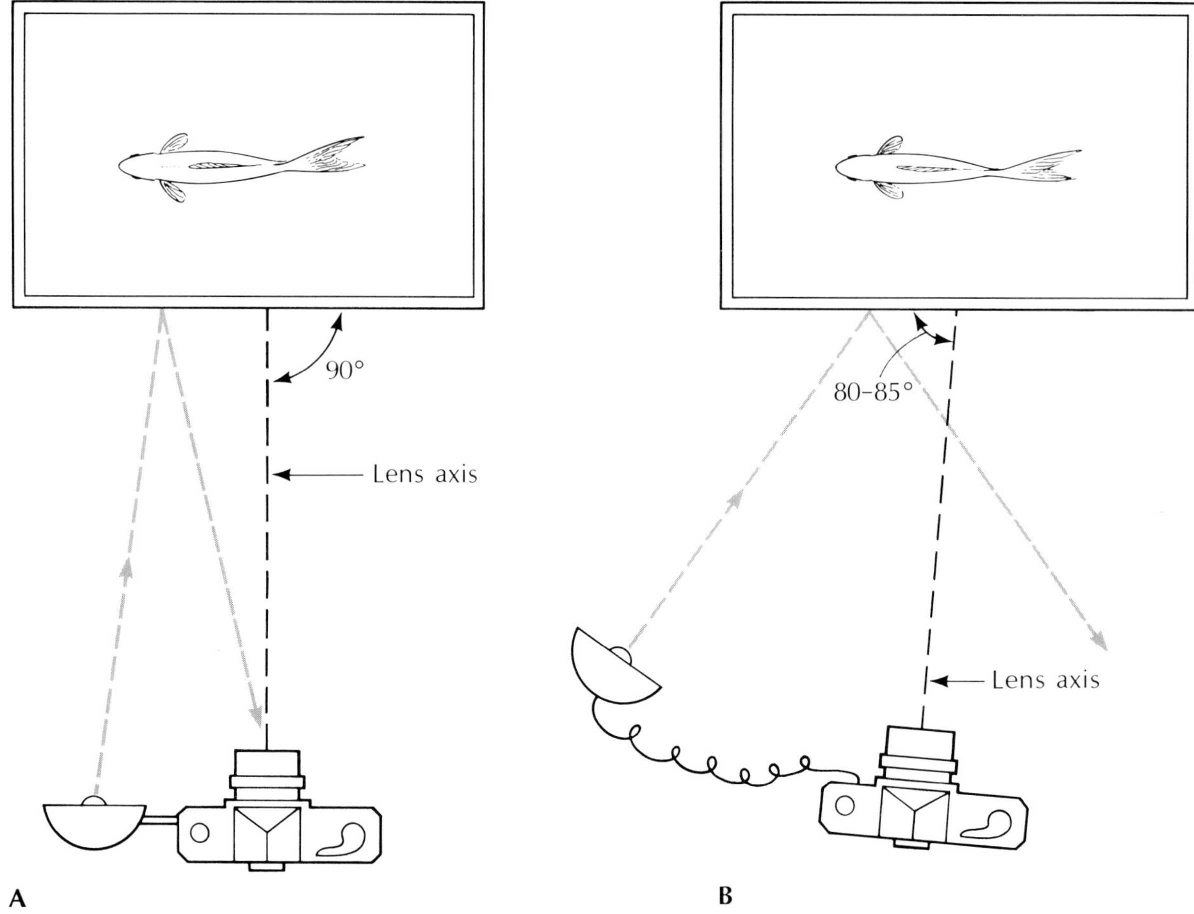

FIGURE 49
Flash photography of subjects in aquaria or in glass cases. With the flash unit on the camera and the camera perpendicular to the glass surface, the picture will be of a reflection of the flash. Placing the camera and flash as shown in part B will ensure that any reflected light from the flash will bypass the camera.

A Flash on camera (a reflection obscures the subject).
B Flash off camera, and on the acute side of the lens-axis/glass angle (the reflection is directed away from the lens—light loss is about one stop). (See Color Plate IV.)

camera motion. Sometimes the best way to immobilize the camera is to seat it firmly on a sandbag. Such a bag should properly consist of a relatively soft but very tight weave. The best filling is clean, dry sand of relatively rough-surfaced, coarse grain. Neither rice nor beans, often recommended for this purpose, have enough mass to resist camera motion, and both are too smooth to pack well. Polished grains of sand tend to slip in packing, too.

Such extreme care in camera handling is particularly necessary when using small single lens reflex cameras. The gear trains used in the shutter mechanism may set up vibrations, and the jarring of the moving mirror (mirror flop) is a well-known cause of picture unsharpness. A good sandbag will take care of both of these problems, whereas even a sturdy metal tripod may simply resonate, thereby increasing them.

Subject Motion

Motion of the subject itself is another source of difficulty, though more obvious than camera motion.

Both types of motion can be minimized by using a high shutter speed or a high-speed flash unit. And both of these control methods can be augmented by using one of the very fast films currently available.

If for some reason it becomes desirable to use time exposures with live subject matter—if, for instance, the exact lighting setup is critical and makes flash use questionable, and great depth of field is necessary—other methods can be used. Most organisms have moments or even considerable periods of natural quietude; even 20- or 30-second exposures can readily be made of many types of arthropods, if care is taken not to alarm them.

In extreme cases the subject can be cooled (as with cold-blooded animals) or anesthetized, but these methods should be used only where the form of the organism is important, not its stance or behavior. Either method can entail considerable danger to the life of the subject. Motion-stopping through the skilled use of electronic flash is a much better solution. (See Blaker, *Field Photography,* 1976, or Garrison and Gray, *Secrets of Zoo Photography,* 1972, for useful information.)

The method used to minimize the effects of camera or subject motion is not in itself important. The main thing is to realize the need for doing so, and then to devise a means suitable to the task.

SPHERICAL AND CYLINDRICAL OBJECTS

For the beginner attempting to do careful lighting, one of the more challenging subjects is anything of spherical or cylindrical shape. It is hard to show the shape without at the same time obscuring some of the detail.

A good method of lighting spherical objects is to use a variation of the reflector-diffuser setup described in Chapter 4. Here the reflector and the diffuser together completely surround the object, while close to it, inside the reflector-diffuser ring, is a ring of black paper that rises to about the midline of the object. Correctly set up, the result is a slight soft shadowing completely around the perimeter of the subject, which clearly indicates the shape without being so strong as to conceal any detail. Or, you can eliminate any suggestion of shape and show the subject as a disk (see Figure 50).

Cylindrical objects are best lit from one end, either by direct or diffuse light. Cross lighting makes shadow control difficult, and the edge nearest the light is difficult to differentiate against a light or white background. See Plate 27. With black backgrounds, of course, it is the edge *away* from the light that tends to blend with the background. An exception might be a metallic object for which a dramatic presentation is more important than detail within the object.

To show the shapes of both spheres and cylinders, it may occasionally help to place a

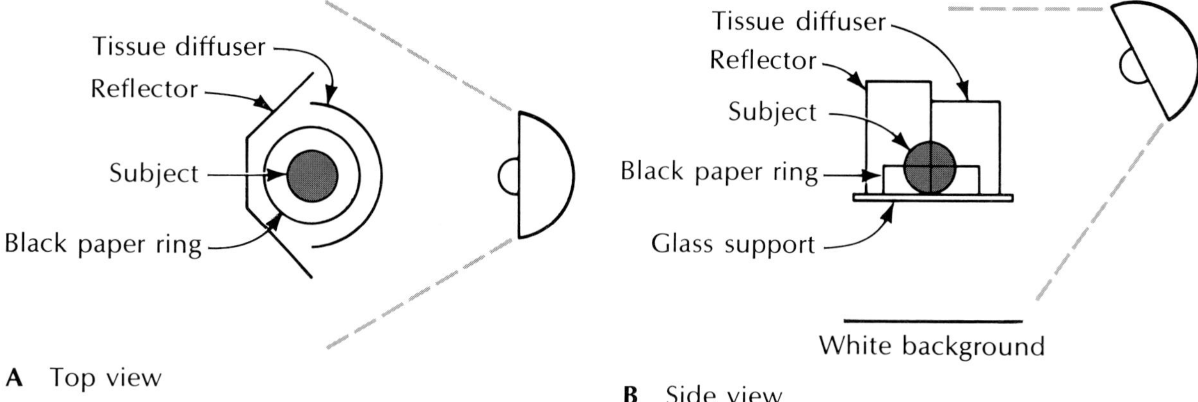

FIGURE 50
Lighting a sphere so that the shape is deemphasized and it appears to be a disk, a useful technique when color patterns are to be shown. A variation of reflector-diffuser lighting (see Figure 17) is used, but the reflector and diffuser are shaped to follow the curve of the subject. A black paper ring with a height about equal to the radius of the sphere is placed close around it, inside the reflector and diffuser, and serves to even out the lighting. The positions of the fixtures are worked out by trial and error.

single highlight somewhere on the subject. More than one, however, tends to cause confusion about the directionality of the lighting.

HAIRS AND HAIRLIKE PROCESSES

One of the more common attributes of living things, whether plant or animal, is the presence of hairs or hairlike processes, either at edges or on the surfaces. Showing these well in a photograph can present a considerable problem to the inexperienced.

Perhaps the best way of showing such structures along edges is to use the dark-field lighting methods shown in Figures 25 and 26. With care it will be found possible to exactly balance this

PLATE 27 ▸

General Problems: Lighting Cylindrical Objects.

Cylindrical objects in general share one photographic characteristic: if the lighting is across the axis of the cylinder, there will be bands of light and dark along that axis. The effect is harshest on smooth metallic surfaces, but occurs to a degree on any surface. Therefore, if surface features along the cylinder are at all important, lighting should generally be *along* the axis of the cylinder.

A Log with an insect gallery (×0.45). To show the gallery best, the lighting is from a point just to the right of the log axis—from about 1 o'clock. It is direct lighting, with some reflective fill opposite. (Originally photographed for R. Lanier.)
B Smooth twigs with lesions (×1.8). These are lit right down the twig axis by a medium-contrast version of the reflector-diffuser method. (Originally photographed for P. A. Ark.)

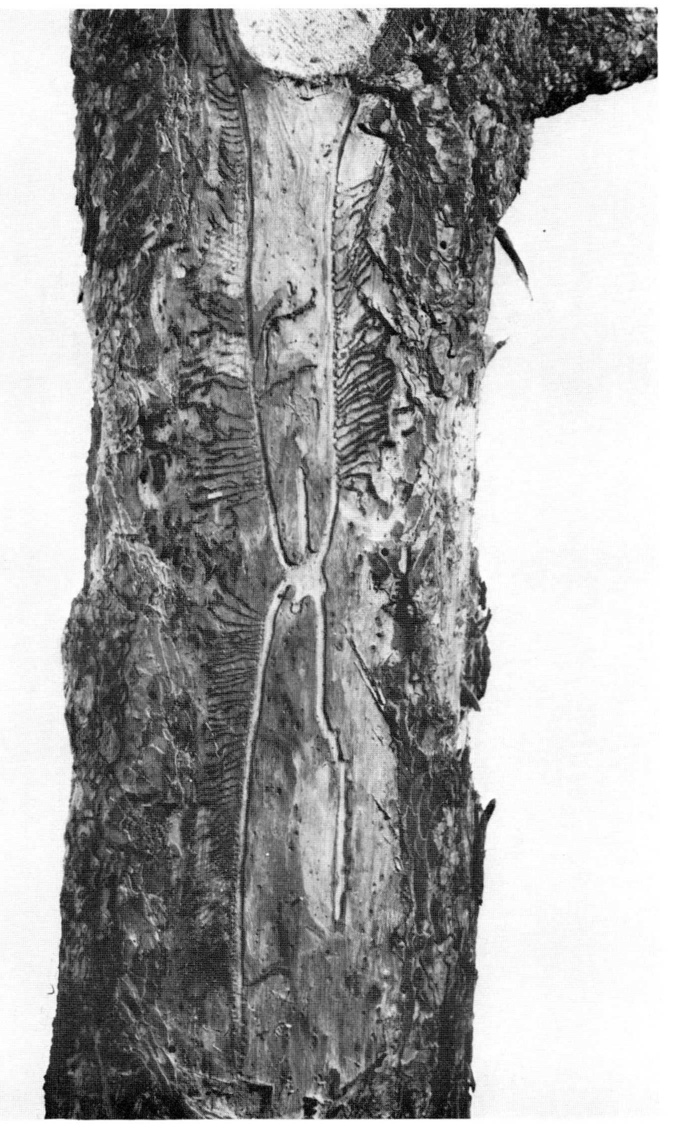

A

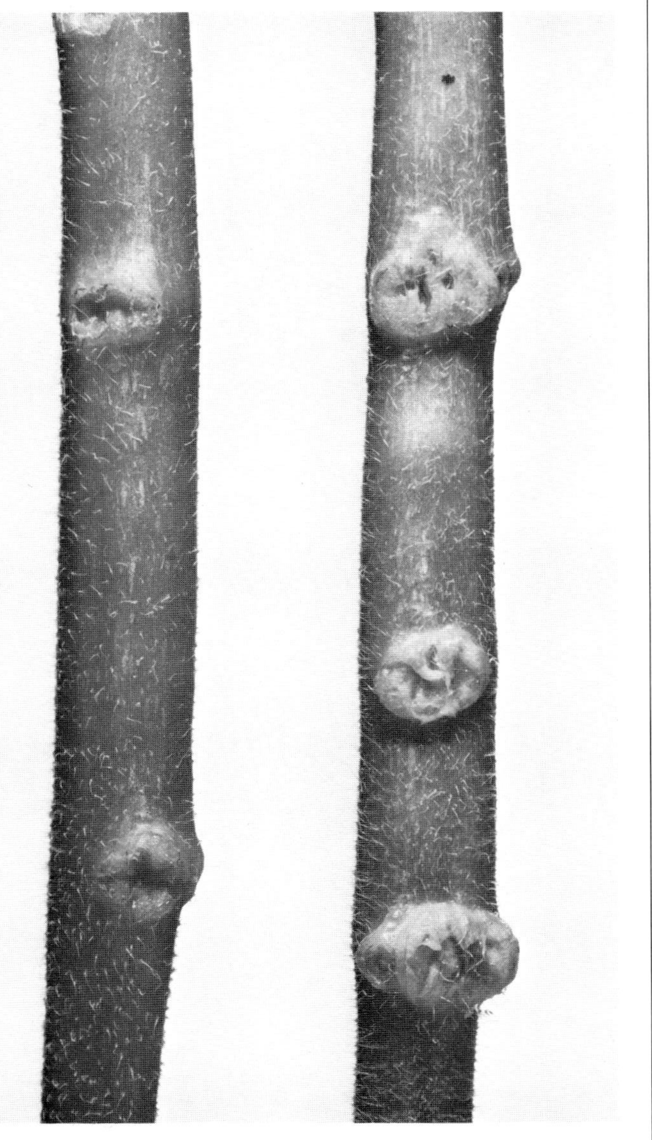

B

backlighting with ordinary top and front lighting, so that surface appearance can be shown at the same time (see Plates 8 and 28A). If only top light is used, the edge hairs will usually not show against a black background, but adding the dark-field lighting will show them brilliantly. Diffuse white backgrounds tend to obscure edge hairs. Successfully showing such edge effects against white backgrounds usually requires a collimated light beam such as is used in transmitted-light microscopy.

Surface hairs are usually best shown by throwing a direct light beam at a grazing angle across the subject (see Plate 28B).

BLACK OBJECTS

Showing objects that are of an overall dull black color requires that they be printed as grey. The best appearance is usually achieved by lighting diffusely and then printing to rather high contrast in tones up to dark greys. Moderate overexposure of the negative may help to increase the contrasts, by getting the dark main subject onto the middle, highest-contrast portion of the negative's characteristic curve (see Figure 11, on page 41).

Shiny black objects will not appear to be shiny in the picture unless a specular reflection is left somewhere on them. Thus, a direct main light source is usually desirable. In some cases it may not be practical to use a reflector opposite the main light at all, since it may result in a large, disturbing, diffuse highlight on one side of the subject. Again, printing in shades of grey may be indicated, except that the very darkest areas should be just about black. Using polarized light may sometimes help. Only experimentation with particular subjects will tell.

In this day of electronic "black boxes," a common type of subject is a box or chassis painted dull black, and either wired with white-insulated wiring or fitted with brightly polished fixtures. To show all these features well, it is advisable to light at roughly normal contrasts, overexpose about two full stops, and develop normally (that is, without compensation for the overexposure). The result will be a very dense negative having relatively high contrasts in the shadow areas (the black box) and relatively low contrasts in the highlight areas (the white wires or the shiny chrome). A negative of this nature is difficult or impossible to enlarge (the exposure time in printing would be enormous), so a large negative is necessary. Contact printing is perfectly practical, however. And such a contact

---

PLATE 28 ▶

General Problems: Hairs; Monochromatic Colors.

A Longhorn Beetle (×5), by grazing direct light from the picture top to show the surface hairs (no fill lighting), and directional dark-field lighting with mirrors to show the edge hairs. (Originally photographed for J. Chemsak.)
B Leaf (×1.5), by grazing direct light from the tip of the leaf to show the hairlike processes all over the subject, with reflector fill opposite the lamp.
C Fossil (×5), by reflector-diffuser lighting to emphasize the color staining. Normal-contrast film and development were used, but the negative was printed to very high contrast. Even so, the subject shows poorly. (Note the presence of dust and lint all over the subject, left uncleaned as a demonstration.)
D Same subject, lighting, film, and development as in part C. Overall contrasts are much improved by immersing the subject in water for the photography. There was no need for high-contrast printing. (Originally photographed for W. Berry.)

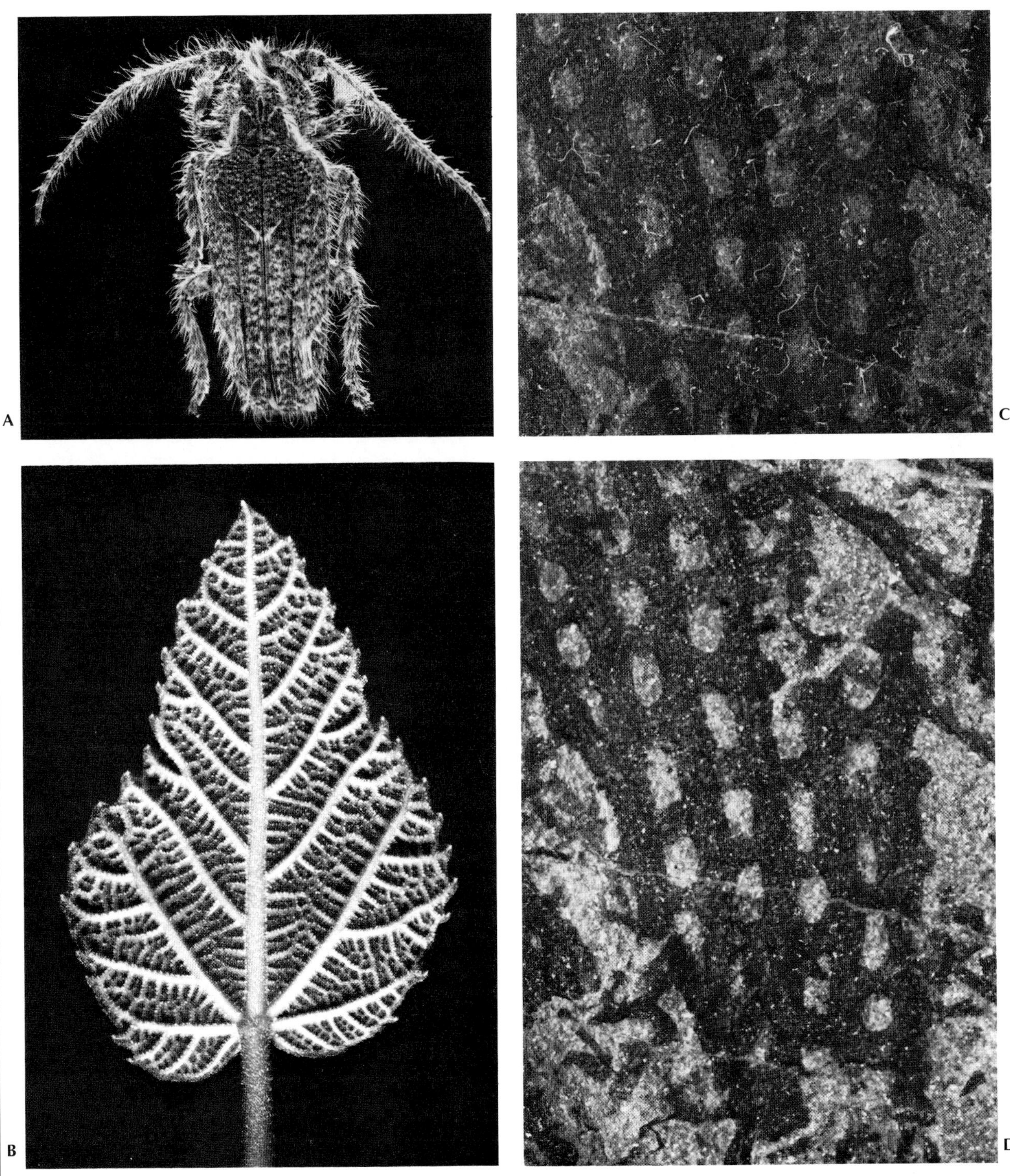
A
B
C
D

print will yield results that cannot be approached in quality by any other means known to me.

MONOCHROMATIC COLORS

Although three-dimensional objects can be clearly shown through light and shadow, and multicolored objects can be differentiated in black-and-white photography through the use of color filters, there remains one type of subject that can be difficult to handle in black-and-white and sometimes even in color: a plant or mineral specimen that is composed primarily of areas of various shades of essentially the same color.

In such cases the best approach is usually to light as low in contrast as possible, so that shape and surface texture are diminished to the vanishing point (through light tenting), and then print to high contrast.

Where this treatment is still not sufficient, and where no damage will result, immersion of the subject in distilled water will often greatly increase the color contrasts. Mineral specimens often exude air bubbles that stick to the surface of the specimen, but these can be brushed off with a watercolor brush. See Plate 28, parts C and D.

CHAPTER 13

Specific Subject Matter

The general principles of photographic usage discussed in the preceding chapters are widely applicable, and a knowledge of them will be assumed here, but some discussion of particular types of subject matter is called for. Relatively minor changes in some of the general setups can make significant differences in the results, and it is not always obvious just which general technique will be most applicable in a given situation. Without some hint it may be difficult to determine just where to start and what changes may need to be made. Although particular types of subject matter will be described here, it should be realized that the techniques described may be nicely applicable to quite different subjects as well. And these techniques may not always be the correct or most applicable ones for *some* specimens within some of the classes of subject matter covered.

LABORATORY APPARATUS AND EQUIPMENT

This category, being extremely broad by nature, involves some unusually difficult lighting situations, which are often complicated by the presence of seemingly mutually exclusive (from a lighting standpoint) factors. The discussions will necessarily be quite general.

Metal Objects

Metal objects can be lit either by the normal direct and diffuse lighting techniques applicable to any three-dimensional object, or by taking advantage of reflection principles. If the components of primary importance in a piece of

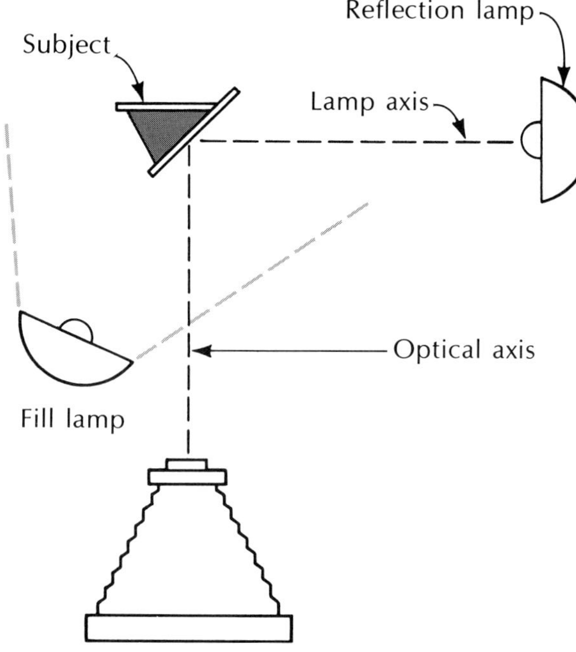

FIGURE 51
Lighting of apparatus by direct reflection, a variation of direct lighting, is based on the law of reflection (see Figures 16 and 19). It produces a bright reflection on the surface of the subject, and is useful for showing the positions of screw-heads, seams, and other incised surface details. A second lamp can be used to fill in the shadows on parts of the subject not lit by direct reflection.

apparatus or a laboratory setup are irregular in shape, the normal methods are usually by far the best. If the surfaces are shiny and this shininess tends to obscure detail, the best solution is probably extremely diffuse light, even to the point of light tenting.

Where the components of primary importance are composed largely of flat surfaces—bare metal or painted—one can exploit the reflectivity of those surfaces (even if the painting is flat black).

In Chapter 12 we considered the use of this basic technique for photographing metal apparatus as an example of the controlled use of reflection. Starting with the more generalized technique described there, we can work variations on the theme, to suit it to more specific subject matter. You first choose a camera angle that best shows what is desired. Then place a light on one side of the subject, at the same angle to the main subject plane, but from the opposite direction. This lamp, called the *reflection lamp,* will cause the surface detail to be shown very plainly, whether its texture is rough or smooth, dull or shiny, its color dark or light (see Figure 51). A *fill lamp* is usually required to light the rest of the subject; it should usually be placed on the side of the camera away from the reflection lamp and close to the optical axis, to provide direct frontal lighting and thus maximum overall light coverage with minimum shadowing. A third lamp may be required to light a background. (See Plate 29 for an example.)

PLATE 29 ▶

Subjects: Apparatus I—Metal.

Metal apparatus on a cat skull (about ×1). Overall lighting was provided by two diffused flood lamps, one on each side of the camera at about 45° off the optical axis. Detailing of the flat metal surface was by the light reflected from a white card hung vertically above and behind the subject. It was lowered until, from the camera position, its reflection appeared all over the polished surface, thereby lighting the entire surface in a fine, soft manner. The card was lit by the same lights as the subject. A direct lamp reflection from the polished surface would have been too harsh. The background was a white card curved up behind the subject; this background was opaqued on the negative so as to show better the transparent plastic support. (Originally photographed for O. T. Ellsworth.)

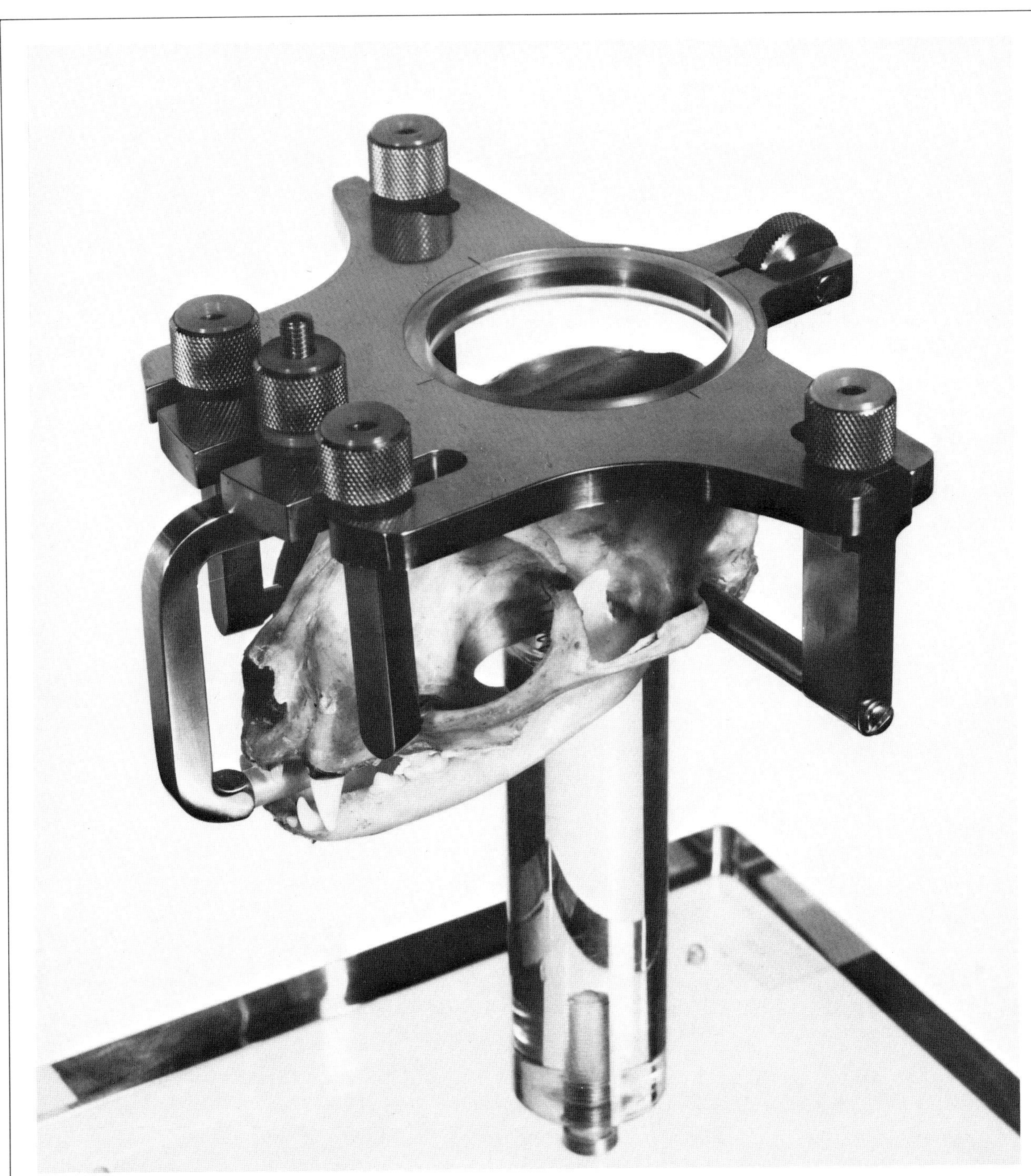

Either or both of the two main lamps may have to be diffused. Cavities in the faces of some subjects may require other lamps, to show their interiors. You can use a ringlight surrounding the lens, or, probably better, small spotlights (sometimes even an ordinary flashlight will do), each placed very close to the camera and adjusted for distance until its light level balances with the overall level while illuminating any cavities. This kind of work requires close reasoning and lots of experimentation.

There is a simple way to photograph moderate-sized equipment (e.g., antique microscopes, or perfusion chambers) in laboratories with large, boxed, fluorescent ceiling lights. The subject is set on a curved white-card background on a table (as in Figure 54). With the table set against a wall, the ceiling lights will provide a soft, diffuse lighting from in front and above. No other lights will be needed. The background should be relatively large to avoid unduly large, dark edge reflections on the subject.

Glass

Most discussions of the photography of glassware describe how to make it as conspicuous and glamorous as possible. If this effect is needed, it can usually be achieved by using a black background and lighting from the edges all around, or from such particular directions as best delineate the subject. Another commonly used method is to silhouette the subject against a white background, which is lit either evenly or unevenly according to aesthetic preference. Small specular reflections are often created to increase the appearance of "glassiness."

In scientific photography, however, the need is generally for lighting that will render the glassware inconspicuous while suitably illuminating its contents. Laboratory glassware is of importance primarily as containers. The lighting can be done with either black or white backgrounds.

With a black background, the usual method is to light the subject from above with a direct lamp. With the proper setup, the glass container will now be virtually invisible. Then white cards, usually quite narrow, are so placed on both sides of the container that they provide edge reflections that indicate its shape. If correctly placed, they also serve to fill in the shadows of the main subject, by reflection (see Figure 52).

With white backgrounds the method is similar, except that the background should be quite large for the size of the subject matter and may need a separate and brighter light, and the edge-reflection cards should be black instead of white. The result will be to show the whole container as an even, very light grey, which the black cards will provide with a thin black outline. In most cases it will help to paint out the background very carefully on the negative so as to render it pure white in the print and thereby show the light grey glassware better. (See Plate 30 and Color Plate V.)

With either black or white backgrounds it will probably be necessary to remove the images of the edge-reflection cards from the negatives before printing. If the background is black, scrape the images off with a knife; if it is white, cover them while painting out the background.

Electronics

Electronic equipment is a common photographic subject. Panel faces, boxed components, and printed circuits can readily be handled by the methods described in the section on metal objects (see also the section on black objects in Chapter 12). But showing electrical circuitry clearly sometimes presents special problems, particularly in shadow control.

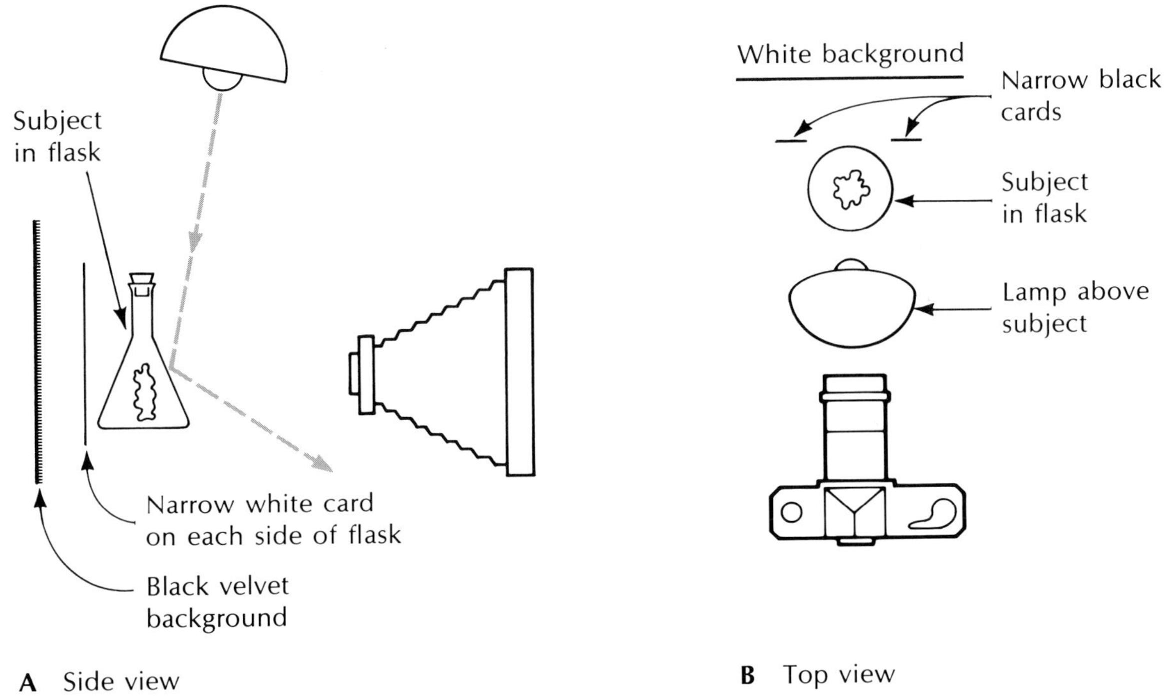

FIGURE 52
Lighting subjects in round glass containers. The lamp is placed high so that specular reflections from the container are directed away from the camera lens. Narrow cards placed on both sides of the container and a little behind it provide edge reflections that delineate it against the background. See Color Plate V.

A Side view of a setup using a black background, shown with a view camera.
B Top view of a setup using a white background, shown with a 35 mm camera. Either type of camera could be used with either setup.

The great difficulty is to show clearly all the wires, connections, and myriad electronic components that make up modern circuitry, without ambiguity and confusing shadows. This can usually best be done by placing one or another of the available types of ringlights before and surrounding the camera lens. If much of this kind of work is contemplated, there is available a specially designed cold-cathode-tube lighting device that is really excellent, though rather expensive (the Hinelight Model B). Considerably less expensive and still quite effective lighting units can be built by combining the large, medium, and small fluorescent ringlights (8-, 12-, and 16-inch Circline lamps), which are available at any good electrical shop, into one concentrically mounted unit. Electronic flash ringlights can be used with the smaller subjects, but they are less useful with larger subjects. Microelectronic circuit boards can be photographed well using a small form of beam-splitter (see Figure 20C).

Either of these two lighting setups combines several functions: (1) it penetrates cavities, (2) it lights flat plates perpendicular to the optical axis by reflection, and (3) it minimizes or eliminates shadows of the individual wires and components.

If color photography is to be done, the fluorescent fixture is less appropriate. The Hinelight illuminator mentioned above is best here, since it is designed to produce light of the correct color temperature. (See Chapter 11 for further explanation; see Kodak publications AE-3 and H-9 for suggested correction filtration for fluorescents, if they are used.)

Should suitable ringlights not be available, the best compromise is very low-contrast reflector-diffuser lighting or light tenting.

For complex types of subject matter that contain many types of components, one can light the whole works according to the needs of the single most important feature, arrange a compromise type of lighting that yields tolerable renditions of several features, or try to light each component separately; this last can become difficult, if the end result is not to be most peculiarly heterogeneous in appearance. The demands of the subject dictate what will be done. In cases of really unusual complexity, it may be best simply to diagram the setup and use photographs to provide detailed coverage of vital portions. The great variety of possible subjects makes more detailed discussion impractical.

ART OBJECTS AND ANTHROPOLOGICAL ARTIFACTS

Coins

Coins, medallions, and similar objects can be lit by a variety of means. A quick and easy means of making photographs of small groups of coins, while retaining a high degree of legibility, is to use a fluorescent ringlight around the lens, with a group of coins laid directly on an aluminum-foil background, as described earlier (see Figure

PLATE 30 ▶

Subjects: Apparatus II—Clear Plastic and Glass.

A Clear plastic apparatus (×0.8), photographed using view-camera movements to keep the vertical elements visually parallel. Transparent items of this sort are usually best photographed against a white background, curved up behind the subject so that there is no horizon line. Then the background can be opaqued on the negative to enhance visual contrast, as was done here. In removing the background it is convenient to use an opaque tape, such as the very thin Scotch #600 black tape, to delineate all straight edges. It is applied to the emulsion side of the film. Then opaque paint is applied. A brush is used to follow all the curved edges first, and then the remaining background is painted over. Where two taped straight edges meet, it is a good idea to minutely round the corner with a brush in order to avoid having the corner look artificially sharp. The lighting can be done by shining one or two direct flood lamps on the subject so that a few small highlights are present. These make the picture look "glassy." Avoid large specular reflections, which obscure information and look clumsy. Otherwise, the lighting angles are not critical. (Originally photographed for R. Poyton.)

B When the glass serves merely as a container rather than as a subject, the whole approach is different. For this picture of fruiting Oak Root fungus cultured in a flask (about ×0.8), a single high flood lamp was directed sharply downward from the upper right. The main surface reflections are directed down and away from the lens, and the subject is well revealed. The black velvet background tends to conceal the edges of the flask. There is some minor condensation that could be removed by gentle heating with a portable lamp or hair dryer. (Originally photographed for R. D. Raabe.)

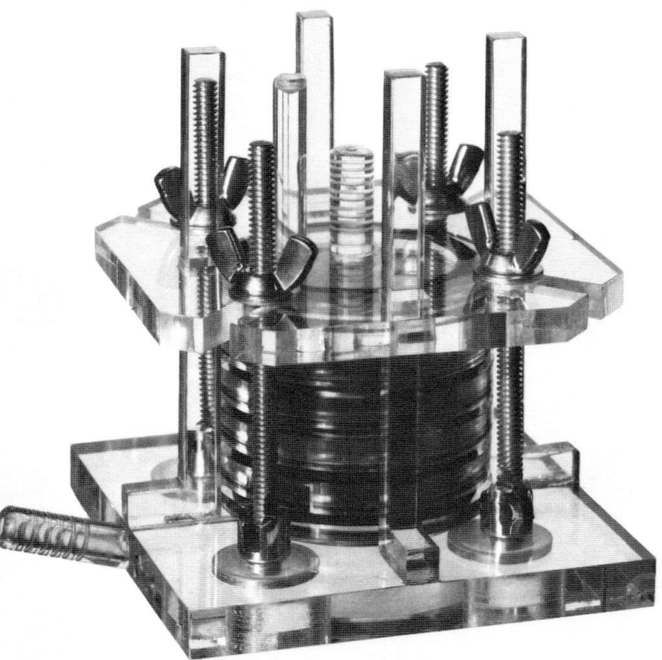

A

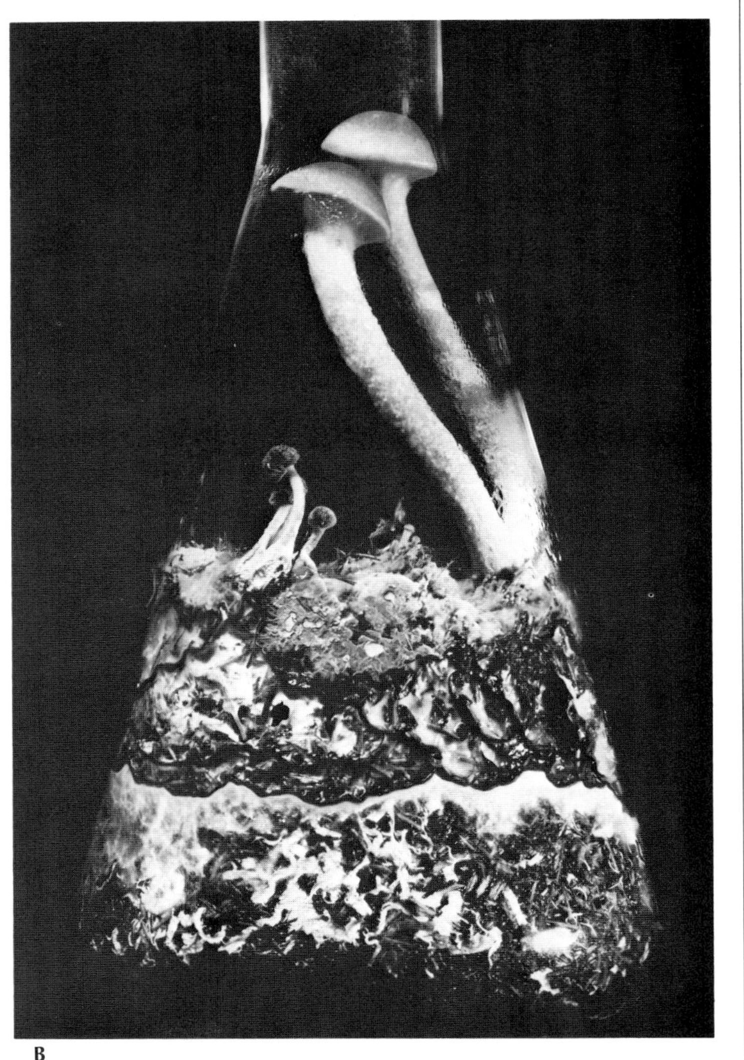

B

14). Since not all coins have the same degree of reflectivity, it may be necessary to print to several densities in order to display properly all the coins in a group. Grouping by surface appearance can be a help here. If differential printing is needed, it can be done by cutting out suitable prints from sheets printed at various levels, or it can be done all on one sheet of paper by using printing masks made of cut-out black paper to vary the exposure time given to the various coins; this can be tedious, but it is very effective.

For ultimate quality in coin and medallion photography there is a better method, which usually entails photographing one coin at a time. The coin is placed beneath a vertically mounted camera on a sheet of glass supported above the usual white-card background. Diffuse window light is used to light the coin, which is turned to the light for the best lighting of portrait heads or other details, and the background is separately lit by a beam of artificial light sufficiently strong to render it pure white in the final print. A reflector may or may not be needed at the subject level to fill the shadow areas (see Figure 53). It is important to determine the correct orientation of the coin or medallion and then light it so that the relief work appears to be lit from the top left, the top, or the top right. If the lighting comes from below, the relief will appear to be reversed. (Reflector-diffuser lighting can closely simulate the effect of this setup.)

Extremely low relief can be shown best by the use of a beam-splitter for axial lighting, as described in Chapter 4. The tone of the subject, whether light or very dark, is unimportant, since the photograph will be a record of the degree to which light is reflected by the surface texture rather than a record of the actual subject tones. Thus, the method is also useful for photographing inlaid bimetallic objects, such as certain coins and medallions. Even though such a subject might be worn quite flat, the pattern will show because different metals usually reflect light to different degrees, owing to their composition. The visual effect will be similar to that of the differentially reflective fossil shown in Plate 34B.

Paintings and Other Flat Art

Paintings and other flat artwork, including etchings, engravings, and so on, can usually be done readily with normal copy lighting (see Chapter 14). For black-and-white reproduction, paintings are photographed on panchromatic film in order to retain a scale of relative brilliances close to that of the eye, and so that a full range of color filters can be used to alter the relative brilliances as may be needed. In either color or black-and-white, shiny surface reflections and hazes can be removed completely with polarizing filters, when artificial lighting is used. Paintings that are very large but still transportable can be evenly lit most easily by photographing them in direct sunlight. Polarizing filters are of little use in direct sunlight, unless the surface of the painting is heavily convoluted; polarized reflections may then yield in part to a suitably rotated filter at the camera lens.

Engravings, etchings, and lithographs are usually best photographed on one of the continuous-tone copy films, although in some cases, particularly for woodcuts and the like, high-contrast "lith" films give either better reproduction or a chance for cheaper linecut reproduction. (See Chapter 14, on copying.)

Points and Other Tools

Items made of chipped or flaked stone will be shown best if taken as examples of controlled

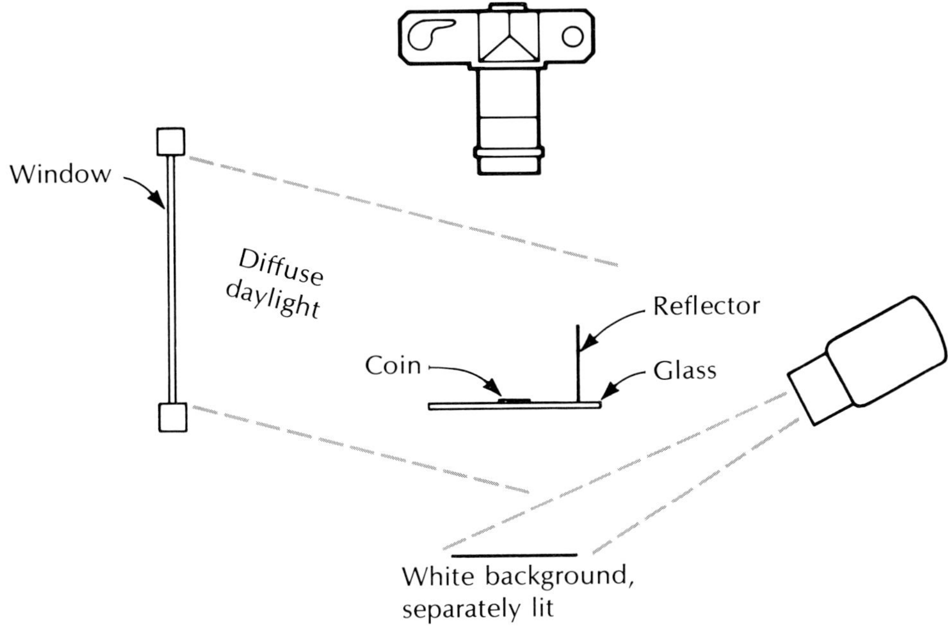

FIGURE 53
Lighting coins or medallions by window light. Diffuse daylight at a low angle is excellent for showing the relief work on coins. A card reflector provides fill-in light in shadowed areas. For a white background, separately illuminate a white card with a spotlight or other lamp so that the background is about one stop brighter than the subject. Mixed light sources are not recommended for color photography, because of color-temperature problems.

reflection, as noted in Chapter 12. I have obtained my best results photographing them singly on a black background, using two or three lights. The simplest setup is a vertically mounted camera with the subject supported a little above a black velvet cloth; the support can be a short cylinder or tube, smaller in diameter than the dimensions of the piece. This support allows the use of lighting positions lower than the supporting table. When the angle of the lens axis is related to the plane of the main flaking along an edge, the choice of lighting angle is obvious, being equal to that of the lens axis but from the opposite direction, as in any lighting by reflection. Each main flaked edge must have its own light. The visual effect is one of great clarity in revealing the flaking pattern.

More generally, and for reasons of economy, it is necessary to group a number of pieces to make up a single plate for publication. You cannot provide optimum lighting for all pieces in such an arrangement, so you must compromise. For this I suggest a relatively low-angled, grazing, direct or diffuse light to show the work marks. Fill-in reflection should be minimal—just sufficient to provide some shadow detail. The light should come from just to one side of the pointed end (or the picture top, if there is no point), as this usually best indicates relief and is a visually satisfactory orientation.

Polished tools, whether of stone or bone, are well shown by diffuse light directed along their longitudinal axis, and with rather high-contrast printing to reveal their shapes better. This is particularly true of pieces bearing incised designs, including those that have been blackened for visibility by their makers.

Backgrounds in both of these lighting setups should generally be white—though bone shows well against black—and may require separate lighting to clearly delineate light-colored objects.

Pottery and Other Dishware

Vases and the like can be approached either as sculpture (see below) or as a special form of copy. For research purposes the latter approach is more common. The aim is to show the form and the nature of exterior decorations in complete detail, rather than to produce a glamour photo.

The setup uses two undiffused lamps, at about 45° to the optical axis on either side, with polarizers to remove the nearly inevitable crescent-shaped reflections. The lens should also carry a polarizer. (See Chapter 5 for details of reflection control by polarization.) The background is usually white and is lit separately so as to print white. It should not be overly large, or it may introduce nonfilterable reflections on the sides of the vase. The background brightness should be carefully gauged, since blocking out on the negative is frowned on here. The exact outline is too important to risk an error in delineating it. The lens should be of the longest available focal length to provide the best perspective and truest picture of the outline (see Figure 34).

Dishware of pottery or stone can be well photographed from directly above. A ringlight surrounding the lens will give good penetration of deeply dished items, and will also show comparative depths of dishing in adjacent pieces. The background should be a white card placed directly under the dishes, without any intervening space. With all but the very lightest of such subjects it will print as pure white. Very light subjects can be done against black velvet.

Sculpture

Sculpture is usually approached much like portraiture. The desire of the photographer is to show as much as possible of the individual character in the piece, along with the best possible feeling of the design motif. Lighting, then, is for shape and texture. I prefer a single, moderately diffuse source such as window light or a well-diffused flood lamp, directional but not harsh, with such reflector fill as is needed or desired (sometimes none, depending upon the subject). By moving the subject, the light source,

---

PLATE 31 ▶

Subjects: Masks. (See page 210.)

A Eskimo mask, Lowie Museum of Anthropology No. 2-4597, University of California, Berkeley. (Appeared in color as Plate VI in Ray and Blaker, *Eskimo Masks: Art and Ceremony,* University of Washington Press, Seattle, 1967.) Masks that look like faces should be lit and photographed like portraits.

B Eskimo mask, Lowie Museum of Anthropology No. 2-5854, University of California, Berkeley. (Appeared in color as Plate III in *Eskimo Masks.*) This more abstract design was diffusely lit from the top for a quite effective rendering.

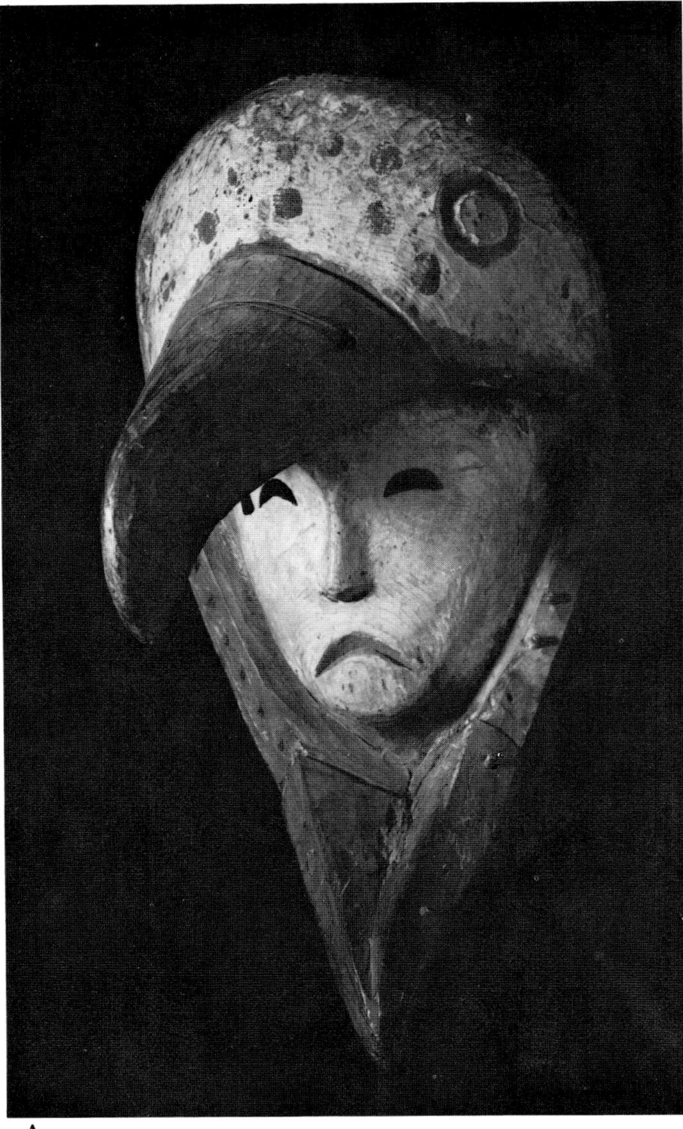

A

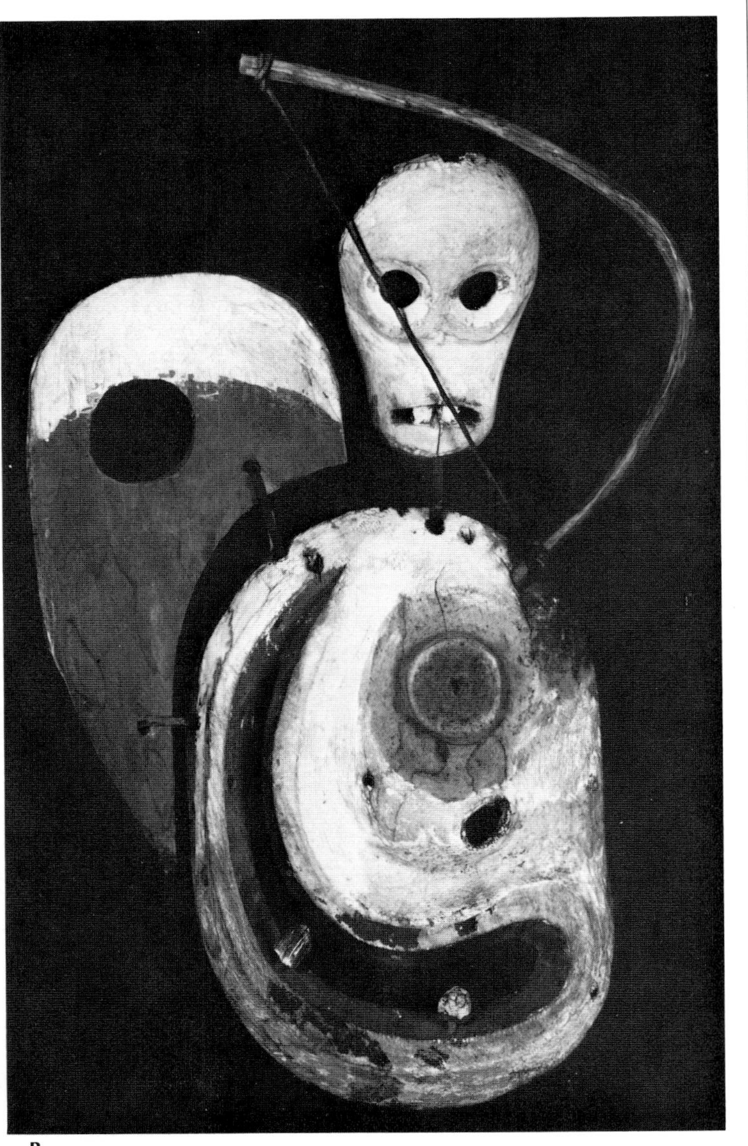

B

or the camera—together or separately—you can achieve virtually any effect desired. (With subjects too large to move, the options are, of course, reduced.) Complex lighting setups usually serve only to confuse the appearance of the photograph while draining out much of the force and import of the shapes. There are, of course, exceptions to the above, and there are those, too, who reject the whole idea of simple diffuse lighting for sculpture. Personal preference rules in this matter.

Direct frontal lighting, as with on-camera flash, is nearly always about the worst possible approach for portraying sculpture. The effect is to flatten relief, diminish surface textures, and generally bore the eye. These remarks also apply, of course, to pictures of people made this way.

Porcelains are exceptionally well portrayed by ordinary window light or by some other well-diffused, single light source. The soft diffuseness imparts excellent modeling without producing harsh highlights. Marbles and other stone works may benefit from more strongly directed sources, such as undiffused floodlights. Metal work may require either of these, or combinations of both. No pat answers can be given for any situation where the notion of art prevails. Final decisions rest on matters of esthetics and not on scientifically controlled conditions.

Masks are another type of subject matter that should be treated like human portraits. I prefer to try to find out something about how a mask was intended to be used or displayed, and to let that influence my lighting of it. In other cultures masks serve a variety of social and religious purposes, and insofar as is possible, a picture of one should tend to indicate something of the associated meanings (see Plate 31, and see Ray and Blaker, *Eskimo Masks: Art and Ceremony,* 1967).

BOTANICAL SUBJECTS

Plant materials likely to require photography are of three main types: (1) whole potted plants, (2) leaves, stems, or other portions of plants, usually essentially alive and cut immediately before photography, and (3) mounted herbarium sheets. (Dish cultures and other special cultures are described later.) The most common objectives are to show the following: comparative size; attitude of the leaves on whole plants; color differences such as those due to lesions, spotting from disease, insect damage, and so on; shape and texture abnormalities in diseased leaves; and typical characteristics of type specimens. Color differences are enhanced by suitable color filtering (if the colors to be shown are different). Water immersion of leaves or other plant portions may also be necessary if very shiny surfaces are present or if color differences exist only as different shades of the same color. These matters have all been thoroughly covered earlier.

Potted Plants

The usual points of importance in photographing potted plants are to show the general appearance and attitude of the plants, to show size and color, and to make comparisons of vigor. The simplest setup is a horizontally mounted camera with two lamps set at about 30–45° off the optical axis on each side of the camera and about 30–45° above it, pointing down at the subject. Diffusing screens are often placed before the lamps. The camera is aimed either straight in or slightly downward at the plant. In some few cases, plants are photographed at sharp downward angles or even from directly above. Here it usually suffices to place one lamp, well diffused, on each side of the plant and pointing down at it at about a 45° angle. Difficulties are rare once the requirements of the situation are clearly in mind.

Backgrounds are usually white, since most plants are too dark to show well against a black background. Where the camera points directly or nearly directly downward, the setup is as described earlier for reflector-diffuser lighting, with the plant set on a glass support and with a directly lit white card below it.

For horizontally arranged setups there is a method that results in a background that is either white or just slightly off-white, which is nearly always satisfactory. A curved white card is used as both base and background, and the pot is set, well forward, directly on it (see Figure 54). In most cases the light on both plant and background is softly diffused, so that only the slightest shadowing is visible at the base of the pot. Care must be taken to assure that the background is evenly lit and that the plant is suitably lit at the same time. If you cannot do both, give primary attention to the plant and paint out the background with opaque on the negative. (See Plate 32A.)

Leaves and Plant Parts

A very common botanical subject is one or more leaves laid flat to show color and shape differences or abnormalities. The best setup is usually normal reflector-diffuser lighting. Filters are often needed to show color effects (see Plates 3C and 9). The correct orientation is considered to be with the tip of the leaf as the top of the picture and the petiole as the bottom. Lighting is from the tip end. The relative positions of reflectors and diffusers can be varied to show any degree of surface modeling desired.

A variation of this method is to show such a leaf by transmitted light only, in order to show better the internal structures and abnormalities. Lighting is as previously described for diffuse transmitted light. Filters can still be used.

The most common difficulties with leaf pictures are (1) accidental, too strong background lighting, which results in flare around and through the leaf and loss of overall contrast (similar results come from too large white backgrounds), and (2) surface shine from waxy leaves. Reduce the background light intensity (or the background size) to eliminate the first difficulty; immerse the leaf in water or use the polarization technique to eliminate the second.

If leaves curl and refuse to lie flat, one solution is to wait until they just begin to wilt before photographing them. Most leaves will then lie quite flat. Do not let them wilt too much, or their appearance will change. Stubborn specimens can be made to lie flat by placing a sheet of glass on them, but one must then watch out for reflections, and for wrinkling of the leaf.

Stems and cut sections of stems showing lesions or other discolorations are another common type of botanical subject matter. These are lit similarly to leaves; the orientation is proper when the root end of the stem is at the bottom of the picture, with the light coming from the upper, or leaf, end. This is the correct lighting for cylindrical objects, i.e., from the end. If such subjects are crosslit, there will be considerable difficulty in controlling the contrasts, the side nearest the light source being much too light. Much more even lighting and hence clearer rendition of detail is obtained with end lighting. (See Plate 27B.)

There may be a need to dissect, lay out, and photograph the various parts of a flower. There

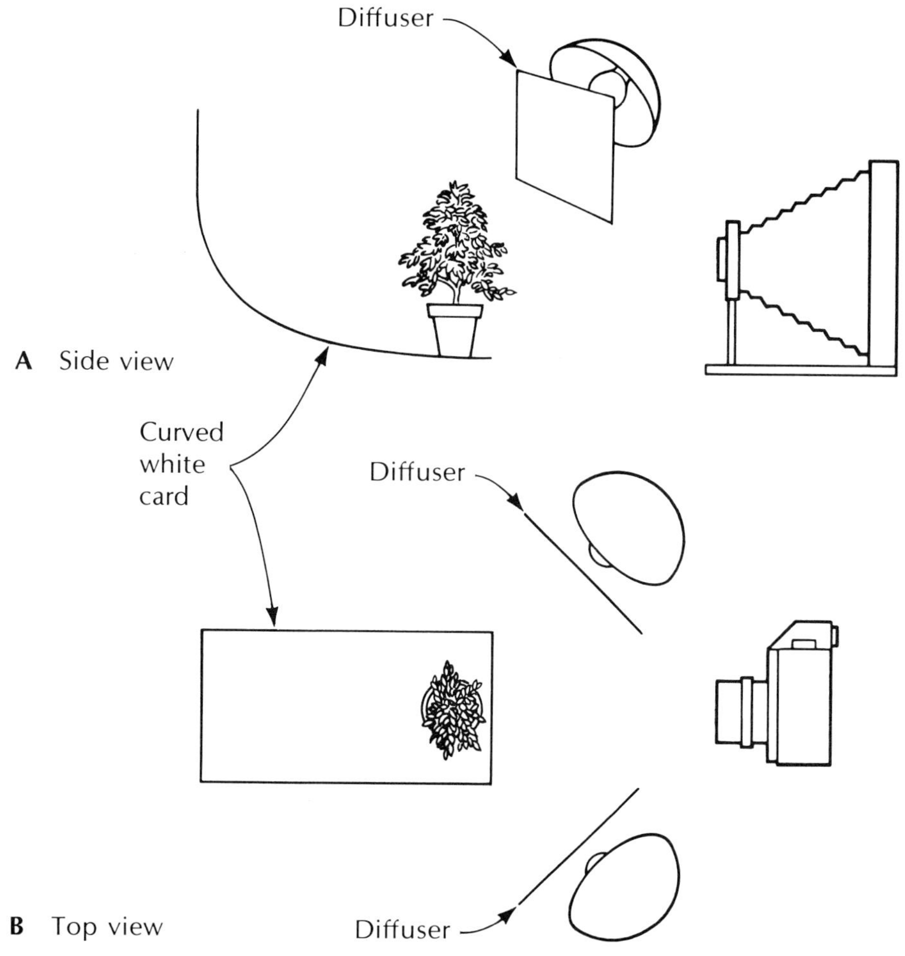

FIGURE 54
Lighting potted plants, using two diffused lamps set at about 45° on each side of the camera lens axis, and a little above it. Either type of camera shown can be used. (See Plate 32A.)

is a combination lighting method that works very well for this. The subject parts are laid out correctly on a glass support, beneath which is placed a suitably sized fluorescent ringlight. The center of this light is filled in with black velvet, which is shaded from the light of the ring by a standing circle of black paper. Then pieces of black paper are laid flat on the glass support to surround the subject and thereby cut off from the lens the direct light of the ringlight. The result so far is dark-field lighting. The next step is to use conventional direct or reflector-diffuser lighting to toplight the setup. The top and dark-field lightings are then carefully balanced for intensity. The final result will be an excellent view of all parts of the flower against a black background and with all the minute, hairlike processes shown clearly. If color film is being used, substitute for the ringlight a pair of two-mirror setups, as was advised for directional dark-field photography (see Figure 26 and Plate 8).

Herbarium Sheets

Herbarium sheets appear at first glance to be merely a variation of copy work, but there are complications. Such specimens come in all types of relief, from dead flat to completely rounded. Generally speaking, the best way to show all the features is to light to very low contrast, to minimize the shadows, and to emphasize color differences. This can be achieved by using carefully balanced reflector-diffuser lighting. If the more rounded subjects are to be shown for shape, and shadows would only confuse the issue, the best method is to use a three-ring fluorescent ringlight around the camera lens. The light is essentially shadowless, but the relief still shows well. Occasionally a more directional light may be desirable, and here the first method, with some degree of light-versus-reflector imbalance introduced, is used. In any case, a sufficiently good background, if the print will show the edges of the herbarium sheet, is simply a white card laid directly under it. See Plate 32B.

It is normal practice to include a scale, usually metric, somewhere within the picture area to indicate sizes. All herbarium sheets are delicate and require very careful handling. *Do not flex the sheet,* or the specimen on it may get cracked or broken. *Do not attempt to pin such a sheet to a wall and photograph it with a horizontally mounted camera.*

DISH CULTURES

Petri-dish cultures appear at first a simple matter for photography, yet there is sufficient variety within this classification to require quite a range of techniques. Such cultures are of three general types: (1) fungal or bacterial colony cultures on and under the surface of the medium, (2) precipitation bands formed by interactions among substances within the medium, and (3) bacterial plaques and similar phenomena, which produce a clouded effect in or on the medium, comprising discrete circles of cloudiness on a clearer background or a completely clouded background with circles of relative clarity scattered here and there.

A problem likely to be encountered in any photography of a dish culture comes from the nature of the dishes themselves. Most glass Petri dishes have concentric rings of uneven thickness in their bottoms. They may also have scratches, abrasions, or other physical deformations. This problem is countered by floating the dishes in mineral oil during photography. Several large drops of oil placed on the glass support will suffice to just float the typical Petri dish. Care must be taken to avoid bubbles of air in the oil beneath the dish, as these will be highly visible. Large bubbles mean that one or two more drops of oil are needed. A number of smaller bubbles indicate prior turbulence in the oil. Handle it carefully so as to minimize turbulence. Application with a large pipette is preferable to pouring it or using a bulb-type dropper. Glass dishes are preferred to plastic ones, even though the plastic ones have flatter bottoms. When examined carefully, many plastic dishes exhibit minute, radial, internal cracks in their bottoms; although they do not affect the use of the dish, they show up glaringly in dark-field lighting. Floating the dish in oil will not cure this defect.

Colony Cultures

Colony cultures are usually photographed by normal top lighting, either direct or diffuse (though occasionally interior detail may require transmitted light, either solely or in combination with top light). The desired emphasis in lighting may be on either color patterning or surface relief, or both. If the emphasis is on color, use evenly balanced reflector-diffuser lighting, and check the need for color filtering. If color bands are in shades of the same color, the lighting must be especially even, as high-contrast developing and printing will be needed, and this will render any uneveness of light highly visible.

Where surface texture or shape is the main point of interest, a more direct lighting is called for, with a single lamp being placed at a high angle (about 60° above the subject plane) to shorten and minimize the shadow of the forward edge of the dish. A white-card reflector is then used on the opposite side to fill shadows and provide contrasts as desired. For revealing shape alone, the contrast can be quite high, but when color is also important, the shadows should be well filled with reflected light in such a manner that, while the shapes are clearly outlined, the overall contrast is relatively low. (See Plate 33A.)

Backgrounds can be either black or white, according to needs or tastes. A white background provides a modicum of transmitted light, which is sometimes useful in showing some structures within the medium; but where it is necessary to show surface detail only, without confusion from internal features, it is best to use black.

Precipitation Bands

Precipitation bands within a culture medium in a dish can be shown by two methods. The culture can be desiccated and stained, and then photographed with diffuse transmitted light, or it can be photographed directly by dark-field lighting, using either a fluorescent ringlight below it (see Figure 25) or the mirror technique for producing a directional dark-field (as in Figure 26). The latter is particularly useful where the bands to be shown all face the same way. If the bands face in various directions, only an all-around dark-field effect, such as the ringlight produces, will be able to show them all equally well. Either of the dark-field methods will show the lesser and more inconspicuous traces more easily and clearly than will desiccating and staining.

PLATE 32 ▶

Subjects: Potted Plants; Herbarium Sheets.

A Portion of a potted plant (×1), photographed as shown in Figure 54. (Originally photographed for C. Lamoureaux.)

B Herbarium sheets are best lit by very diffuse light. The lighting can be low-contrast reflector-diffuser lighting, as it was here, or it can be done by mounting three differently sized (8-, 12-, and 16-inch) fluorescent ringlights concentrically, and placing this device so as to surround the camera lens. A scale should always be included in the picture.

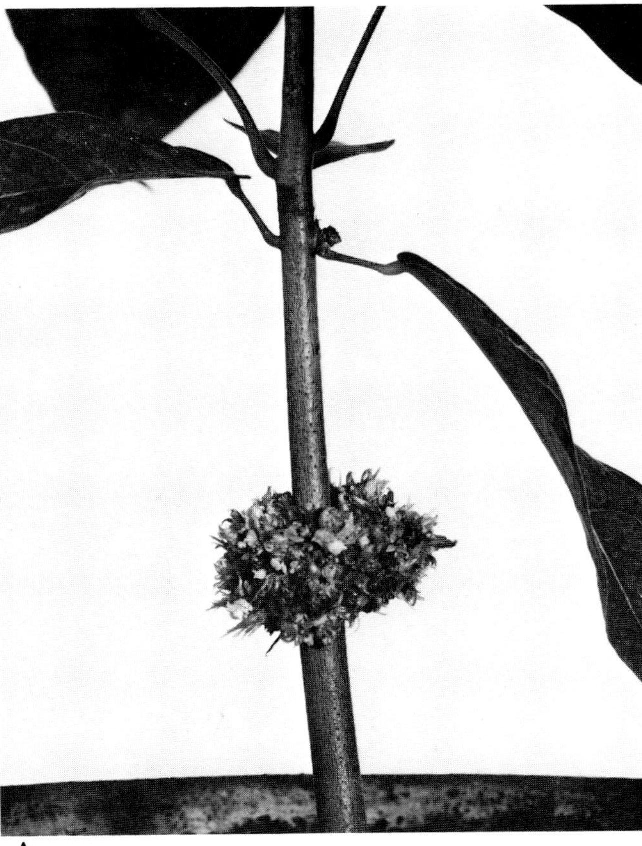

A

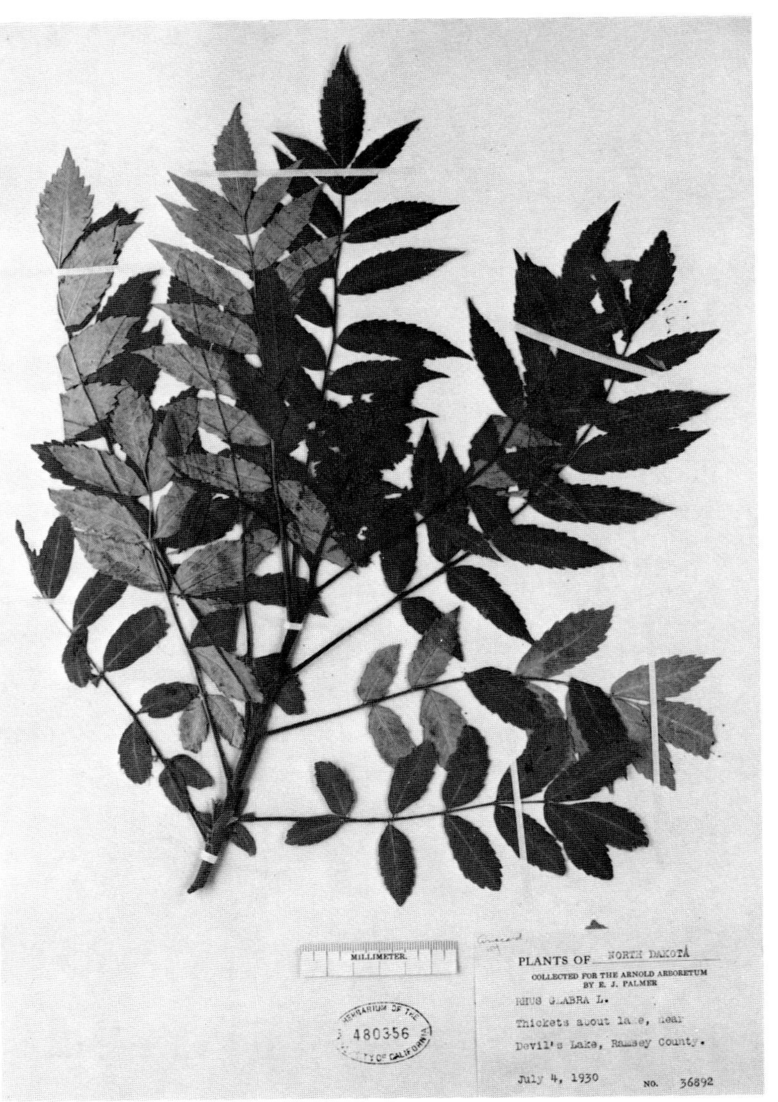
MILLIMETER.
PLANTS OF NORTH DAKOTA
COLLECTED FOR THE ARNOLD ARBORETUM
BY E. J. PALMER
RHUS GLABRA L.
Thickets about
Devil's Lake, Ramsey County.
July 4, 1930
No. 36892
480356

B

Unfortunately, the dark-field methods show dust, lint, and undissolved culture medium as well as or better than the precipitation bands. Great care, including rigorous attention to preparing and filtering the medium to be used, is necessary if one is to avoid spending long periods retouching such features off a print intended for reproduction. It is virtually certain that a little such extraneous matter will be present to show as white marks on the final prints. If the presentation is to appear competent, these must be retouched out. Even though they may be inert and sterile in the culture, their visible presence is disturbing in the print. (See the later section on precipitation bands in tubes for further information on the photography of precipitation bands.)

Plaques

Plaques show either as cloudy areas on a clearer background or as clear areas on a cloudier background. Once in a while the best solution is dark-field lighting, but usually the best result is obtained with diffuse transmitted light. Only examination of the individual plate will tell which should be used. For a dark-field example, see Plate 33B.

FOSSILS

Most fossils are either stony objects or more or less pigmented inclusions within a transparent medium (such as insects in amber). The methods of lighting fossils are various, depending upon what is visible and what is to be shown.

Stony Fossils

Stony fossils are of several general types. Some are free-standing objects, such as chunks of fossilized wood, bones, and shells, and are treated much like any other three-dimensional object. Generally, they are shown best with fairly diffuse lighting against a white background. If they are unusually light in color, however, black makes the better background.

Other fossils exist as relief impressions on a split-open stony matrix. These are best lit with a single flood lamp or spotlight, placed at a relatively low, grazing angle to the subject surface, the exact angle depending upon the depth of relief; it can be adjusted according to need or taste. If the relief is exceptionally low and flat, no reflector is used, but ordinarily reflectors can be used to throw fill light into any shadowed areas to reveal the detail within them. In some cases you may need to arrange a number of relatively small reflectors carefully around the specimen to throw small amounts of light into specific areas. Some experimentation and ingenuity will be required to photograph a difficult specimen well. A curved specimen, for

---

PLATE 33 ▸

Subjects: Dish Cultures.

A Fruiting fungus in a Petri-dish culture (×1). A single direct light, with minimal reflective fill opposite, was used to show the surface sculpturing. Lighting was from the picture top. The dish itself was ignored.

B Plaques, photographed by dark-field lighting, using a single fluorescent ringlight. The edge of the dish refracts the light strongly, so the dish shows prominently whether you want it to or not. Photographed at ×2.

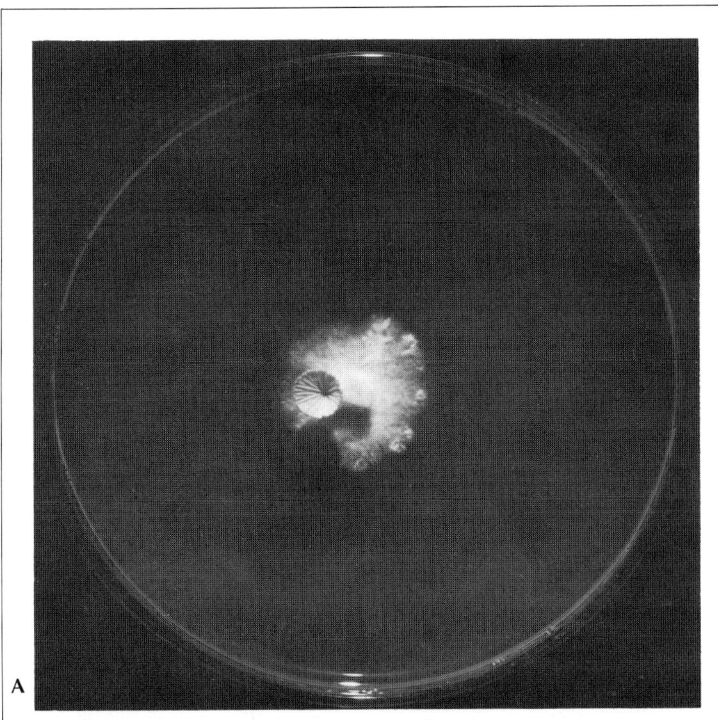
A

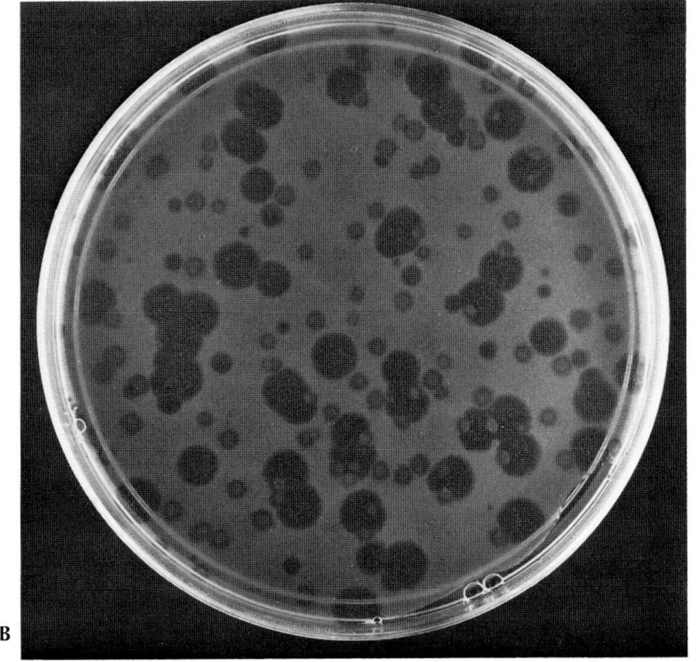
B

instance, may need to be lit as one would a cylinder. The relative orientation of lamp and subject must, of course, be one that will provide lighting generally from the direction of what will be the picture top, if the effect of reversal of relief is to be avoided.

A third type of stony fossil exists only as a stain on a rock face. Here the lighting must be low in contrast, even, and as nondirectional as possible, with little or no evidence of highlight and shadow. Lighting by a well-balanced reflector-diffuser technique works very well. Color filtering will probably help. In some cases immersion in water will improve the contrasts. Before trying this, however, check the possibility that the subject is water-soluble. If water is used, it should be distilled water, to cut down the likelihood of bubbles. Some bubbling will probably occur through the emergence of air trapped within the specimen, but this is a temporary problem. Before an exposure is made, any bubbles present from outgassing can be removed by gentle brushing with a watercolor brush. (See Plates 4 and 34A; see also the article by Blaker, "Liquid Immersion of Stain-type Stony Fossils," 1970, for additional detail on this subject.)

Carbonaceous or other highly reflective deposits on or in a stony matrix make a fourth category of fossils. They can be photographed by reflection methods with axial or near-axial lighting. The final print will then show them as highly detailed, bright objects against a darker background (even though the original may be seen by the eye as coal black against a light tan stone). See Plate 34B. If retention of color is necessary, they can be lit like the rock stain discussed above, but there may be less visible detail this way. Occasionally immersion in water may help here, although it is impractical with axial-type lighting.

In some fields of inquiry there is a convention that lighting for fossils must always come from a given single direction, either from the upper right or the upper left. Actually, the lighting direction should be that which gives the most informative view of the subject. It should never be from below center, as noted earlier, or the relief will appear to be reversed. However, it can quite logically appear to come from anywhere above center; whether from right, left, or directly above is not important in itself.

Another convention that seems to be disappearing (though not fast enough to suit me) is that of removing all coloration from three-dimensional fossils by coating or painting them with white substances. This can only reduce the visibility of fine detail. Sometimes it has been done by the sublimation of ammonium chloride. This substance must be applied with

---

PLATE 34 ▶

Subjects: Fossils; Insects in Amber.

A A stain-type stony fossil (×5), photographed by low-contrast reflector-diffuser lighting from the top. Enough directionality of lighting was preserved to just show the surface sculpturing. A Wratten 22 orange filter assisted in increasing the visual contrast.

B This fossil (×5) was of a material that reflected light better than its surrounding. A beam-splitter was used to provide axial lighting, and this showed the difference very effectively. (Parts A and B originally photographed for W. Berry.)

C Insect (Hymenoptera: Proctotrupidae) in amber (×40), photographed immersed in mineral oil, as described on page 220.

D Insect (Diptera: Drosophilidae) in amber (×25), photographed similarly. The light lower left corner is a refraction effect produced by an angular cut in the amber block. (Parts C and D originally photographed for P. Hurd.)

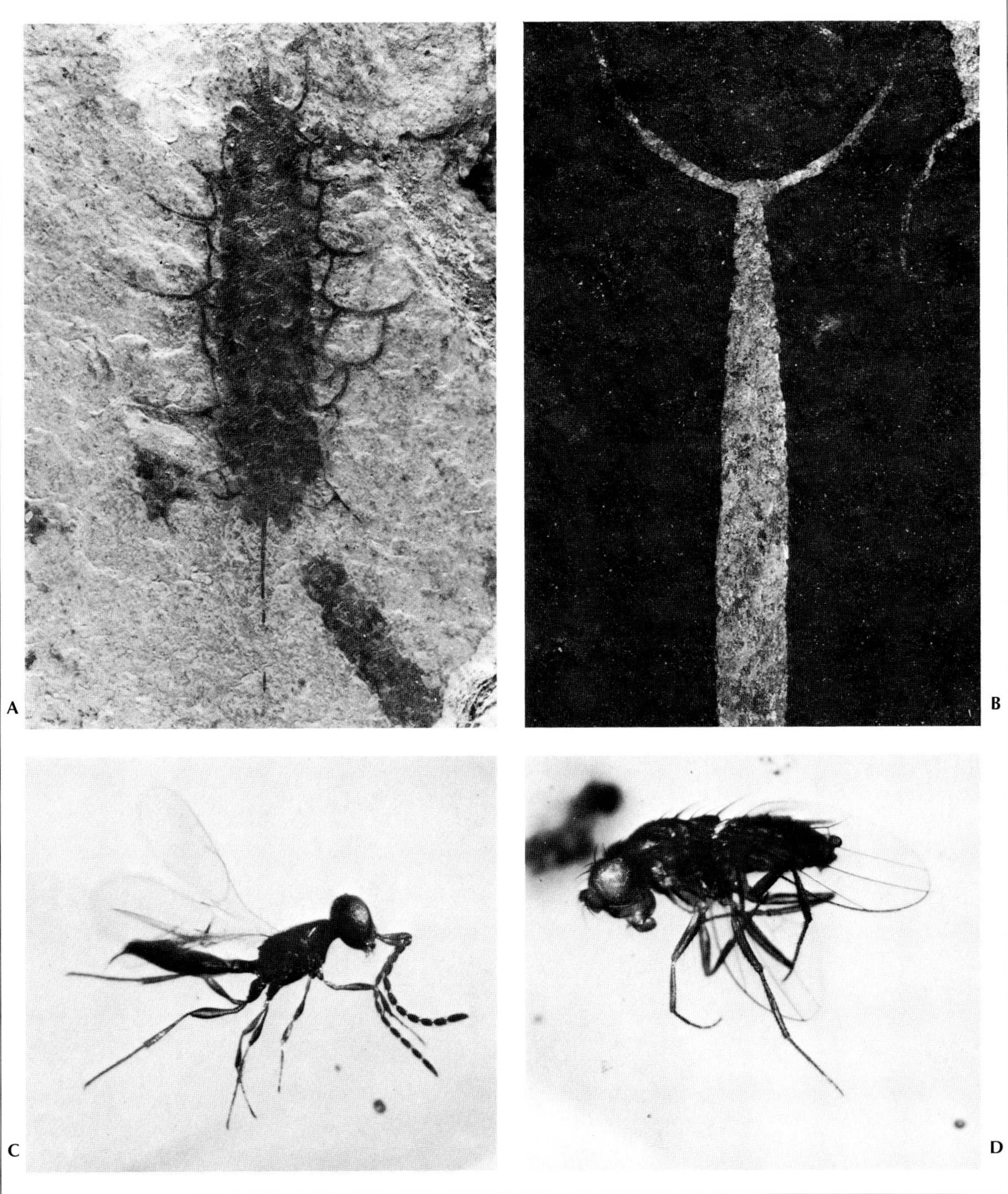
A
B
C
D

the greatest of care, or it will fill all surface sculpturing. White paint, particularly the spray enamels in pressurized cans, can be applied very thinly if care is taken, but requires quite strong solvents to remove it. I can see no reason for applying such materials in the first place. Careful lighting will reveal much more detail, and there should be no confusion between color and shape if it has been done well.

Amber Inclusions

Insects and various other types of living matter are often found trapped and fossilized in amber or other hardened natural resins (hereafter referred to collectively as amber). When the amber has been selected, cut, and polished, it is often photographed to aid in examining and recording the included matter. Most of the subjects are quite small. The methods used for photographing them are—except for the problem of dealing with the amber itself—the same as for any other small object of similar aspect (see the section on insect materials, below).

The main problems in working with amber inclusions are the existence of distortions resulting from uneven shapes and tilted surfaces, and reflections from those surfaces. Fortunately, the method for avoiding both of these problems is the same. Prior to photography the amber is immersed in mineral oil, which has an index of refraction close enough to that of the amber to eliminate both the reflections and the refractions. The oil makes for messy working conditions (it must be kept off the camera and all its accessories), but the results are worth it. The use of oil does introduce one unusual problem: paper used for reflectors and diffusers will be rendered translucent by the oil and will not act as desired in controlling the light. Such reflectors should be made out of white celluloid or other material that will not be affected by oil immersion. The diffusers can usually be placed outside the dish, so that no contact is made with the oil. (See Plate 34, parts C and D, and Color Plate VIA; see also the article by Blaker, "Photography of Insects in Amber," 1969, for expanded coverage of this subject.)

GEOLOGICAL SPECIMENS

Geological specimens in the round can be treated like the stony fossils. In terms of lighting and photography, they are similar. Exceptions to this are the thin sections normally intended for photography through the microscope, and crystals.

Thin Sections

Thin sections of geological materials are usually photographed between polarizers, in order to record and analyze aspects of birefringence. This can be done with the compound microscope for detailed study, or using the transmitted-light low-power technique, as described on pages 162–163.

Certain types of sections, usually photographed at relatively low magnifications, are approached differently. Among these are micaceous or foliated-rock thin sections, in which strong linear effects are present in the structure and are to be recorded. These are best photographed using the low-power directional form of Rheinberg lighting, as described on pages 164–165; this is a specialized photomacrographic technique that has a surprising number of applications.

For making very low-power survey photographs, thin sections can be done very simply with quite good results. Just use a photomacrographic camera setup with diffuse, transmitted light, as shown in Figure 55A. When directional dark-field effects are needed, the minor variation of that technique shown in part B will do nicely. A horizontal camera setup could be used, but the vertical setup is more common and is quite satisfactory. (See Plates 22 and 23).

Crystals

The photography of crystals differs from that of other geological specimens in that it entails the use of controlled specular reflections. It would be possible to predict where lights should be placed were it not for the number of faces to be illuminated; the lighting is best balanced for a good average effect by a process of trial and error.

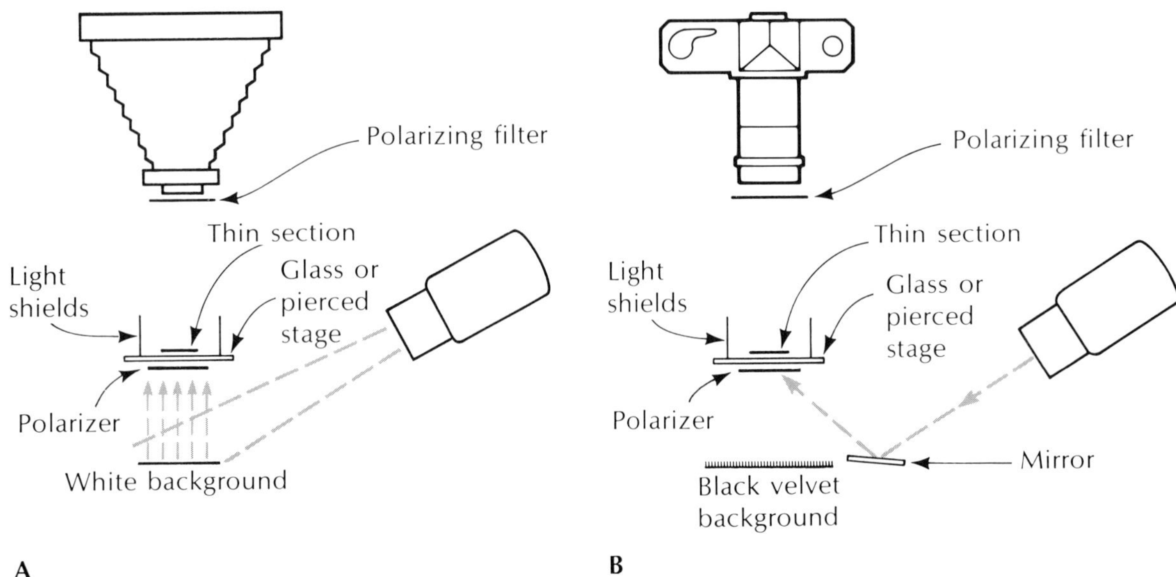

FIGURE 55
Lighting geological thin sections for low-magnification photography. Various lighting methods can be used, according to the kind of mineral and the nature of the effects to be shown.

A Polarized diffuse transmitted light, used to obtain a good general view of granular patterns as revealed by polarization. (See Plates 22 and 23.)
B Polarized directional dark-field lighting, used to show linear structural effects.

In my experience, the problem is best solved by working in a semidarkened room and using a small pen flashlight to test for the correct lamp position. To do so, you look through the viewfinder (or at the ground-glass image) while moving the penlight around. You will soon find one position that gives a good overall effect. Then it is just a matter of substituting the lamp for the penlight, in that position.

Most crystals can be photographed very satisfactorily using only one lamp, which can as well be flash as normal incandescent lighting. In the few cases where two lamps are needed, you find the first lamp position as described above, and fix that penlight in position. A second penlight is then used to determine the position of the second lamp, in the same manner. If you are doing flash photography the picture can be made by double exposure, if a second lamp is needed, as long as you know where to place the lamp each time. (See Color Plate VII.)

The purpose in moving the penlight around is *not* to find an angle that gives a maximum specular reflection from a given crystal plane, but rather to find an angle that gives a good *average* reflection from most or all of the planes. It is not difficult to do this.

CASTS AND IMPRESSIONS

Casts

Casts, being almost completely rounded, or even fully three-dimensional, are photographed much like any other fully shaped subject. Facial casts are treated like portraits. Casts of objects are lighted as though they were the original itself.

Some cast materials have special characteristics that must be recorded with unusual care. Representative of this sort of subject are dental casts, where upper and lower jaw impressions have been taken and have been placed together on a metal articulator. These are photographed as follows. Two lights are placed so their beams cross the face of the subject. This provides a grazing light along both sides, so that the shapes of the teeth are clearly shown. These lights must be carefully positioned, so that the lighting as seen from the camera position will be evenly distributed. They can be either direct or diffused, according to the circumstances.

At this point, a special problem arises. With such dental casts one of the primary objectives is to show the existence, sizes, and positions of gaps between opposing and adjoining teeth. With the lighting setup described above, these gaps will be submerged in the general shadows about the teeth. To show them clearly, special steps must be taken.

First, the background should be a piece of deep-nap black velvet. Then the space between the casts, representing the patient's mouth, must have some wisps of cotton or fiber-glass fluff placed in it. There should be just enough to scatter the light, not block it. Now a spotlight is directed into this fluff-filled space from the rear and slightly to one side. The light will be scattered and refracted by the fluff in such a manner as to fill the mouth space with a diffuse glow. As seen from the camera position, any dull-looking area is a sign of too much fluff, which should be thinned out. Finally, cards are so placed as to keep the spotlight beam from touching any part of the casts except the interior space (see Figure 56). Correctly done, the final print shows the casts in shades of light grey against a black background, and with the gaps between the teeth

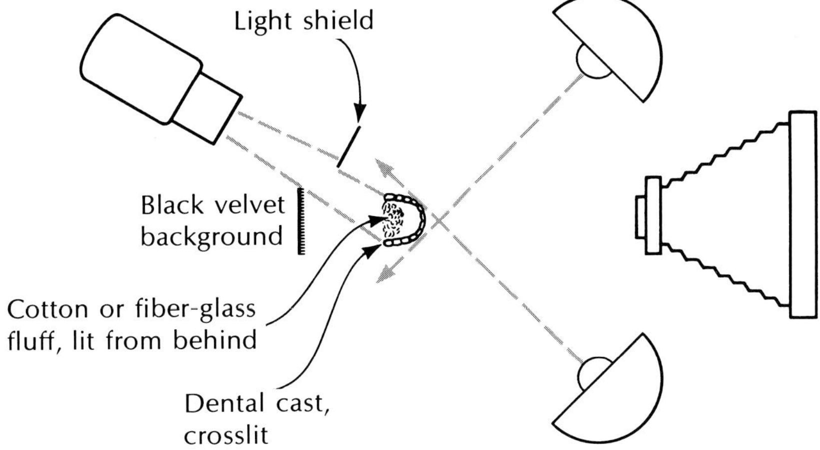

FIGURE 56
Lighting dental casts to show two features: the shapes of the tooth surfaces and the shapes and positions of gaps between the upper and lower teeth. To avoid confusion with shadows, the gaps are made to appear white. To do so, the inside of the cast is filled with cotton or fiber-glass fluff and lit from behind so as to be about one stop brighter than the front lighting. The teeth are shown well when crosslit by two flood lamps. (See Plate 35A.)

(and them only) as clearly defined pure white areas. (See Plate 35A.)

Impressions

Impressions are generally a relatively simple photographic task. The light should be grazing, to indicate relief. With small specimens the technique is the same as that used for relief fossils. Where the impressions are large, as with squeezes (papier-mâché impressions) of cut-stone inscriptions, the lamp is placed relatively far away, to minimize the falloff of light across the subject; no attempt is made to reflect light back across it, since to do so would lower the relief contrasts. Equalization of tones across the picture is accomplished in the final printing. The use of grazing direct sunlight may be convenient; if it is used, there will be no fall-off of light.

About the only question remaining is whether the final picture is to appear as one of the impression itself, or whether it is to appear to resemble the original subject matter (as with inscriptions, which must be legible). In the first instance, used particularly where the original material itself is a cast or impression and the object that made it has long since disintegrated, the impression is lit, as is customary, from somewhere generally at the picture top. If the photograph must resemble the original inscription rather than its impression, the impression is placed—as is normal with any impression—with the side bearing the sharp imprint of the original subject facing the camera. The lighting is then set up to come from the picture *bottom,* usually bottom right. If the negative is then printed reversed, the inscription will be legible and the relief will appear depressed rather than raised, as was the actual inscription, with the light appearing to come from the top left. Since the impression is itself actually a reversal of the original subject's relief, this apparent re-reversal will roughly recreate the relief of the original subject. (See Plate 35B for an example of such reversed lighting.)

Replicas

A replica is simply a very high-quality impression. These are now much easier to make than they were a few years ago, the materials employed usually being some form of quick-setting rubber or rubbery plastic. Most of the subjects are relatively small, and so require normal closeup or photomacrographic techniques, but the lighting should probably follow the suggestions presented for doing impressions.

Microreplicas are basically the same thing, but on a smaller scale. The casting material is usually a thin transparent medium applied to the original surface by means of a solvent (see the article by Smith, "Micro Replication," 1967–68, for details of manufacture). The photography of microreplicas is accomplished either with photomicrographic methods or with photomacrographic transmitted-light methods. Since the microreplicas are transparent and unstained, as a rule, you may find some advantage in using deliberately uneven lighting methods, to give a three-dimensional-looking "shadowed" effect (see page 157).

One form of microreplica picks up surface material from the original subject as a very thin colored layer. The appearance of this type of replica is as though you were looking at the subject itself, through a fairly thick plastic coating. Such replicas are best treated as though they were the original subject—that is, by using top lighting in an appropriate manner, according to the shape, color, and sculpturing of the surface. Surface reflections from the plastic coating can be eliminated by immersing the replica in distilled water, or by using properly oriented polarizing filters over both lamp and lens, as described on page 76.

INSECT MATERIALS

Most of the technical knowledge required for the successful photography of small objects in general has been presented earlier. But insects,

PLATE 35

Subjects: Casts; Impressions.

A Dental cast, photographed as shown in Figure 56. (Originally photographed for A. D'Amico.)
B Modeling-clay impressions of antique seals. The clay was worked to pliability, and the surface was lightly and evenly dusted with talcum powder to prevent sticking. Lighting was direct, and grazed at a rather low angle. It was directed at about a 45° angle across the impressions, so as to show both horizontal and vertical markings with equal effect. The lighting direction, from below and to the right of the subject, makes the relief look reversed when the print is inverted; thus the impression resembles the seal here, and the lighting appears to come from the upper left. To see it as an impression, turn the page upside down. (Originally photographed for E. Gans.)

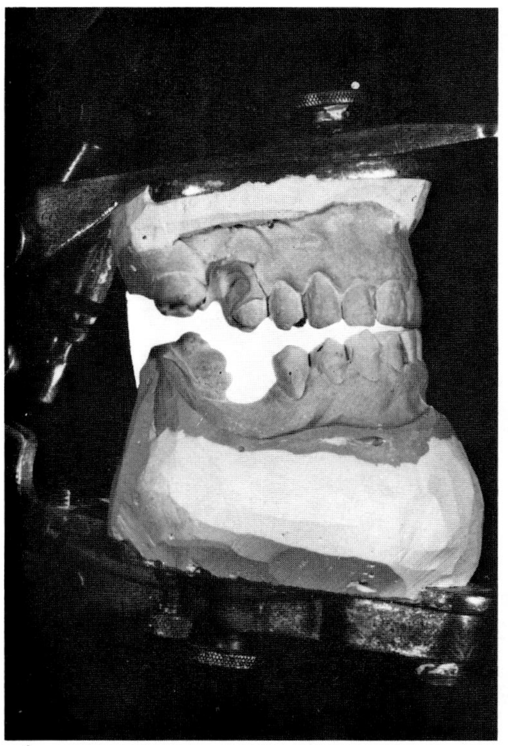
A

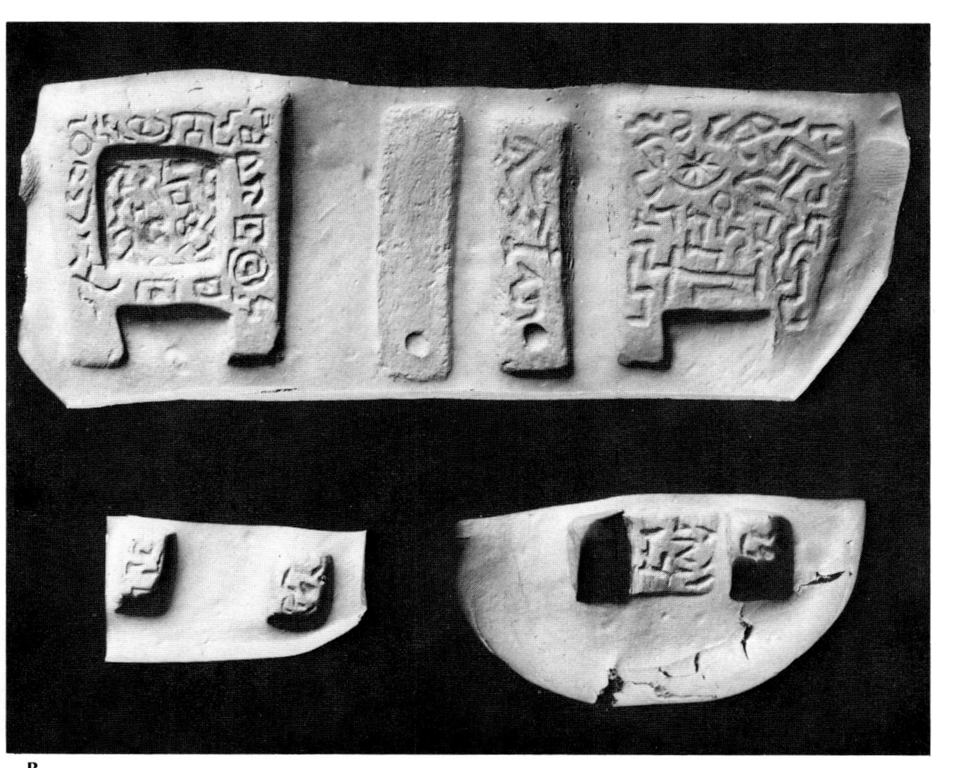
B

being extremely varied in appearance, particularly small, and unusually complex in structure, require some special comment.

Lighting presents the greatest single difficulty, once the general procedure of working at magnifications is understood. The problem is the small size of the subjects: many are too small for you to see just how the light is falling upon them. The solution, as with all really *small* objects, is to observe the specimen through a dissecting microscope while varying the lighting until the desired effect is obtained. Then the specimen is placed under the camera and the lighting setup is carefully duplicated. After checking the results at the ground glass and correcting as necessary, the exposure is calculated and the picture made.

Some photographic writers feel that the only ethical way to photograph any insect is in the wild, with no studio work or manipulation of the subject allowed. This is certainly valid when the normal living habits of the insects are the primary concern. But when the insect being studied is extremely small, or when the primary concern is not its normal habits and stance, but rather its detailed structure, then field work becomes very impractical and laboratory work is both imperative and entirely correct. The latter approach will be emphasized here, and lighting suggestions for particular types of materials follow. (See Blaker, *Field Photography,* 1976, and Ross, *Insects Close Up,* 1953, for expanded coverage of the field photography of living insects.)

Eggs

Insect eggs seem like a good subject for beginning the discussion. Many such eggs are white or very light in color. Photography in natural locations—on leaves, bark, other insects, and so on—is common (see Plate 5C), but if the eggs have been isolated, the background should be black. The eggs are placed directly on a piece of black velvet or on a piece of glass just above it. Isolated dark eggs are, of course, done better against a white background. (See Plate 36A.)

The lighting depends upon circumstances. If the egg is textured and of a matte surface, lighting is by the normal reflector-diffuser method, with the fixtures reduced in size proportionally. Reticulated surfaces, either matte or shiny, can be lit by a grazing light to emphasize relief, particularly if the egg is of the common, flattened "fried egg" configuration (see Color

---

PLATE 36 ▶

Subjects: Insect Eggs, Larvae, Pupae, and Adults.

A Grasshopper egg mass (×8), with direct floodlighting from the top right to show the surface sculpturing. (Originally photographed for W. W. Middlekauff.)

B Larva of the Ponderosa Pine-Tip Moth, *Rhyacionia zozana* (×1.8). There is a frass deposit next to the larva, and a silk deposit next to a bud at top center. Reflector-diffuser lighting was from the picture top. (Originally photographed for R. E. Stevens.)

C Translucent pupa (×3.6), photographed with diffuse light from the picture top, without reflective fill. The resulting shadows allow the mouth parts and other structural details to be clearly seen. The pupa gave troublesome surface reflections, which were removed by polarizing the light (a polarizing screen was placed *inside* the diffuser and a polarizing filter was on the camera lens). The multiple tiny bright spots are surface sculpturing. (Originally photographed for J. Chemsak.)

D Pinned specimen of *Eurygaster alternata* (×8). This is reflector-diffuser lighting, modified as described in the text for lighting beetles. (Originally photographed for S. Vojdani.)

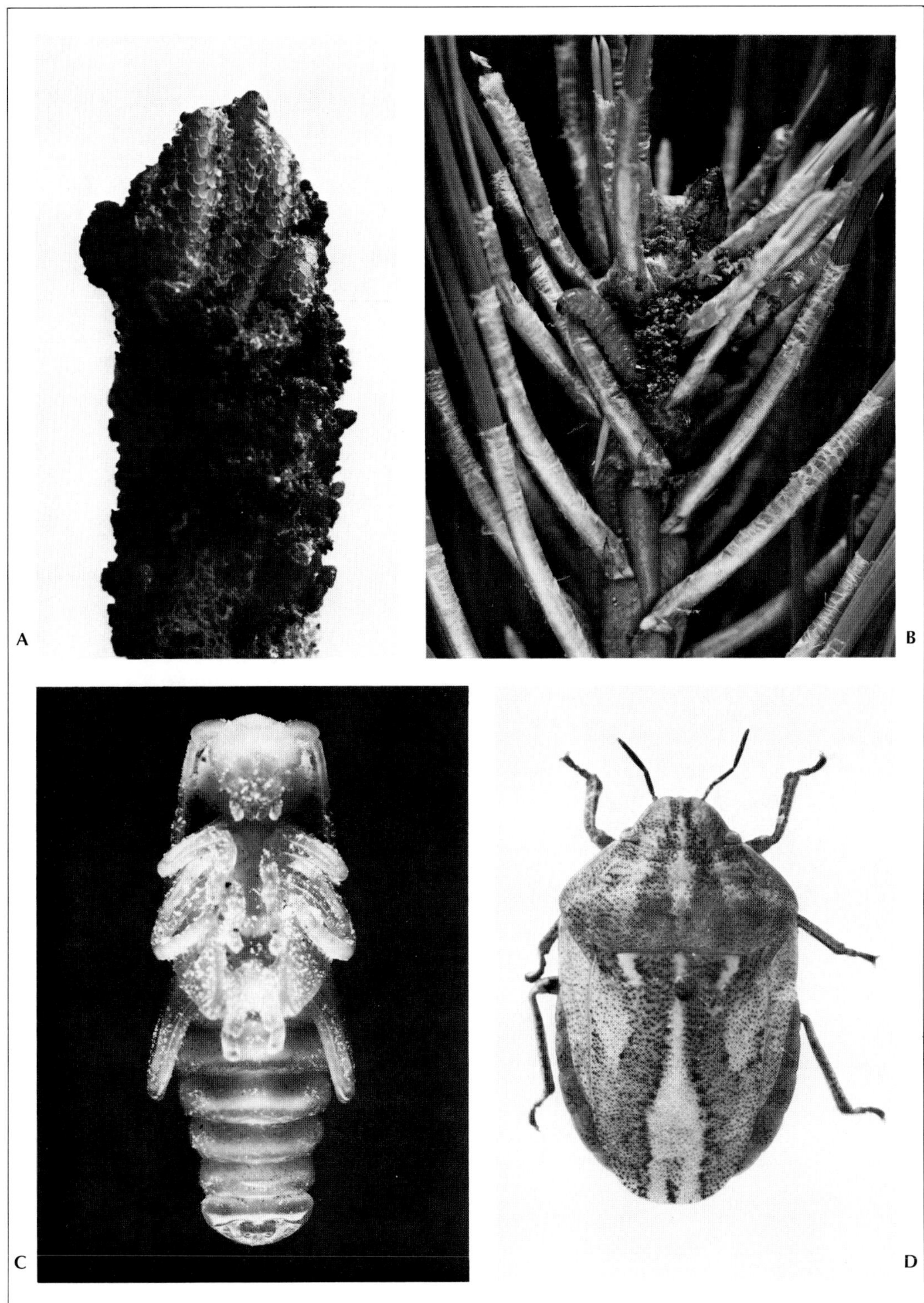
A
B
C
D

Plate IIB). Eggs on stalks, such as lacewing eggs, are best shown in profile against a black background, with lighting arranged to emphasize the edges and to show the stalk.

A special problem is found with eggs that have a highly polished surface, yet with an inconspicuous honeycomb pattern—a not unusual appearance. Diffuse light does not show the pattern well, so the egg is lit with two direct lamps, one at each end (or one direct lamp and a small mirror simulating a second one). The effect is to provide a definite highlight from each lamp, and within those highlights the pattern will show clearly. Although the pattern will not show as clearly elsewhere, the lights can be so placed that one can infer its existence all over the egg.

With all such egg materials, and indeed all insect materials, the subject must be protected from overheating by placing a water cell before the lamp, with anything but small electronic flash units.

Those who work with 35 mm cameras will find it a good idea to employ high-resolution technique here (see Chapter 7). Image magnification can be increased by the use of tele-converters (see the section on increasing the magnification, in Chapter 6). See Plates 2, 5C, 36A, and 40A, and Color Plate IIB, for examples of insect-egg photography.

Larvae

Since larvae tend to be active (in many instances being constantly engaged in feeding), by far the most satisfactory means of photographing them is by the closeup flash method. They are most easily and appropriately pictured in natural circumstances. If the work is done in the laboratory, they should still be seen on genuinely appropriate food stock, unless the photography is being done solely to provide anatomical records. (See Plate 36B.)

By using high-resolution techniques (see Chapter 7) coupled with the use of closeup flash and tele-converter image magnification, you can make high-quality photographs illustrating even the fine detail of living insect larvae.

Preserved specimens can be photographed using normal photomacrographic techniques. Treat them as described for pupae, below.

Pupae

Pupae can be roughly divided into two general classes: those that are dark and opaque, and those that are white or light and somewhat translucent.

The dark pupae are treated with normal reflector-diffuser or direct-light reflector lighting, according to the need, and are photographed against a white background if they are isolated from their natural surroundings. There are seldom any great difficulties here.

The white or translucent pupae are, if isolated, photographed against black velvet. Usually the best lighting is provided by a single direct lamp about 45° above the subject plane, at the head end. Filling of the shadows is effected by a white-card reflector opposite the lamp. The harsh highlights caused by damp or shiny surfaces are eliminated by placing a polarizing screen in front of the lamp and a polarizing filter at the camera lens. Rotate one of them while observing the ground-glass image, and fix it in position when the reflections disappear (see Plate 36C).

The pupae must be protected from the heat of the lamps. Extreme heat will damage them, and even gentle warming may initially stimulate them to movement. Also, many pupae become active if disturbed, and may flop around wildly. If left a minute or so under the lighting to be used, however, they will usually quiet down, and exposures running even to 20 or 30 seconds can be made without sacrificing sharpness.

Pupae that move frequently or that do not settle down after responding to a disturbance are best photographed by means of the closeup flash technique.

Beetles

Because of the complexity of their structures and the multiplicity of their types, beetles are a photographically important order of insects. Two features of great interest to researchers are the general structure and the color patterns. Because of frequent problems with surface shininess and because much beetle research is carried out with preserved specimens, I will first discuss their photography as static subjects in the laboratory. The showing of color patterns alone is often aided by the use of color filters. Suitable lighting for simultaneously showing color patterns and general structure consists of a slight modification of normal reflector-diffuser lighting.

A single lamp (most conveniently a spotlight or one of the more powerful microscope lamps), aimed at the head end of the beetle, is directed downward at an angle of 30–45° and lights both the insect and a white background below its support. The diffuser can be plain white tissue paper or, if more directionality of lighting is desired, a piece of translucent matte celluloid. The latter diffuses the light somewhat less than the tissue. (See Plate 36D.) This lighting takes good care of the whole frontal section of the beetle, but one problem remains.

Nearly all beetles have wing cases that round off at the tail end, roughly as a more or less flattened quarter-section of a sphere. Using a simple white-card reflector to fill in at this end will produce an unrealistically light, crescent-shaped reflection on this portion of the wing cases. The way to avoid this, at the same time providing soft, even light to reveal the sculpturing and wing-case coloration fully, is to mask the lower part of the reflector with a piece of black paper that extends up to a level just above the center line of the beetle (just as is done for spherical objects, but here on one side only).

Some beetles have another characteristic that is tough to deal with. The wing cases, instead of having the usual gently curved cross section, are strongly curved and meet at the center in a sharply depressed groove. Almost any form of lighting results in longitudinal highlights and shadows that, in black-and-white photography, look much like color striping. (In color photography the effect is also present but is less likely to be visually ambiguous.)

A method for at least lessening the problem, and sometimes eliminating it, is to reverse and modify the normal lighting scheme. Place the lamp at a rather low angle at the tail end of the beetle and the reflector at the head end. Use no diffuser, but place a neutral-density filter—the *only* effect of which is to decrease light intensity—before the lamp in such a way that the insect is shaded by it while the background and the reflector both receive the direct and undiminished light of the lamp. The strength of the neutral-density filter must be such that the diffuse light reflected from the card at the insect's head is slightly stronger than the direct light from the other direction; the reflector should be relatively low and wide.

The result, then, is that the head end is lit by diffuse reflected light, and the wing cases by a rather low-angled direct light. The appearance of normal relief is maintained by having the stronger light come from the head end. The ambiguity in the wing-case rendition is at least lessened and may be removed by the direct light up the groove. (This method is a variation of lighting for cylindrical objects, as discussed in Chapter 12.)

Shiny black beetles and similar subjects present another special problem in lighting. Since most such beetles have relatively undetailed wing cases but have considerable sculpturing about the head area, the lighting that gives the most natural appearance is a single, high, direct lamp placed at the head end. No reflector is used, as it would only cause unnatural-appearing reflections on the tail end of the wing cases. If this method is correctly used, the result will be excellent delineation of the frontal sculpturing and a natural appearance of the wing cases—that is, very dark with small bright highlights to indicate shininess.

When the insect is alive and moving about, a minor variation of this method is achieved by the use of a single flashbulb (not electronic flash, the flash head of which is quite large), without a reflector. Flash exposures with certain subjects, such as black insects, usually require abnormally short flash-to-subject distances because of the high degree of absorption of light by the subjects. Exposure straddling will help in getting the correct exposure.

A second method is sometimes used if less realism is necessary but where maximum overall surface sculpturing must be clearly shown. Here a light tent that is lit evenly from all around surrounds the insect. This provides omnidirectional, ultrasoft lighting and an effect of overall highlighting. That is, the whole insect will appear rather light in color, with sculptural details as dark lines on it. There will be relatively little impression of glossiness. Figure 57A shows a good method for achieving this effect, and Plate 37A illustrates it. Color Plate III was made using a similar setup, but without the tail-end mirror or the cutout in the light tent.

Where accurate detailing of minute surface pitting is required, rather than the showing of relatively gross sculpturing, it may be better to employ a more or less overall specular-reflection effect. This can be done by using several direct lights, but is easier to do by arranging several small mirrors so as to reflect the light from a single light source to various parts of the subject's surface. The lighting may not be totally even, but it can be made to show virtually all of the pitting that is present. This method is shown in Figure 57B and the effect is illustrated in Plate 37B. If you have the specialized equipment, a Leitz Epi-Mirror setup will give similar effects,

---

FIGURE 57 ▸

Lighting black beetles or other dark, shiny subjects is a problem because they absorb light so well. Two methods for making dorsal views are illustrated (see Plate 37).

A A variation of light tenting that gives overall diffuse highlighting; it is especially good for showing surface iridescence.
B A variation of direct lighting in which several small, bright specular reflections are scattered over a generally well-lit whole; it is good for very shiny insects, with or without surface pitting or other sculpturing.

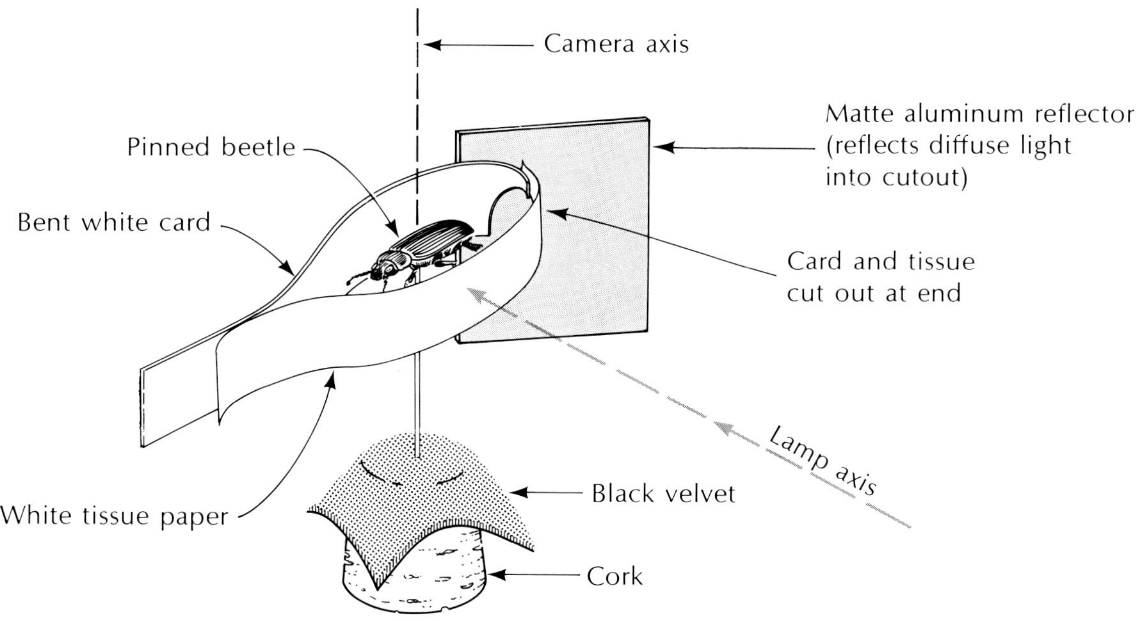

A Variation of light tenting

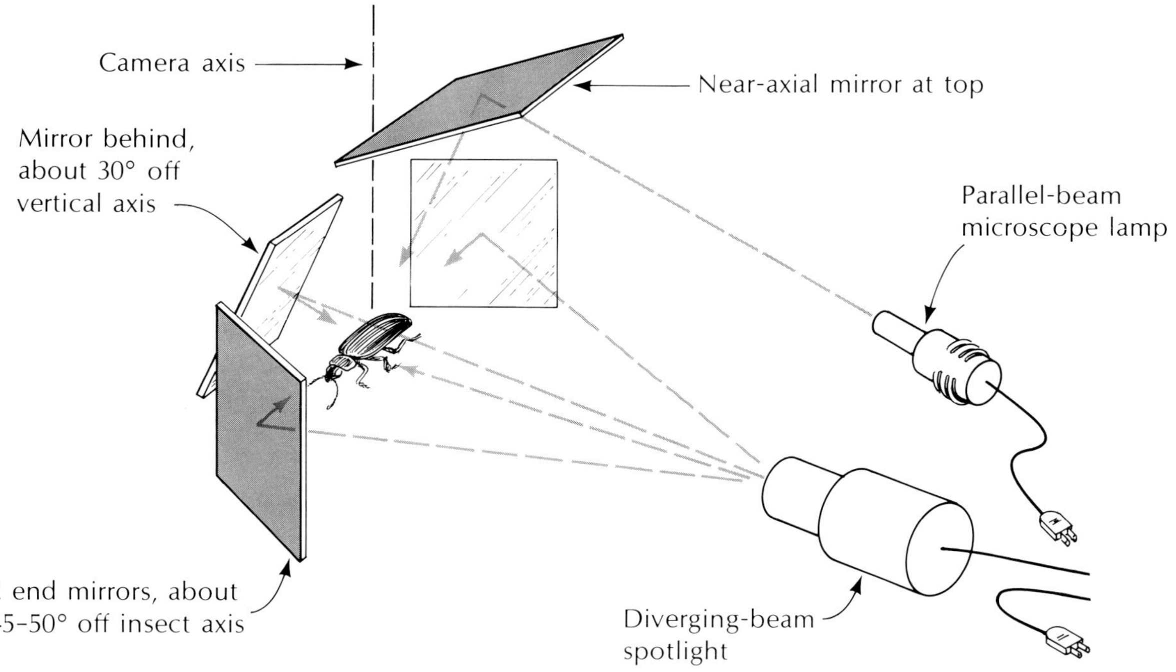

B Variation of direct lighting

but usually with a dark center spot where the mirror was pierced for the lens.

Transparent-Winged Insects

Insects with transparent wings present a special problem in photography. If the body of the insect is at all dark, it is difficult to show both it and the transparent wings adequately in the same black-and-white print (the problem is slightly less severe but still present in color photography). Where overall appearance is to be shown, a good method is to use a dark background, light the body to emphasize edge delineation, and play a light on the wings at such an angle that the reflection will cause them to show their patterning to the camera. In color photography with light-tenting, placing the insect on a medium-toned background can give good results (see Color Plate III).

To show an insect pinned with its wings spread out against a white background, you can light it with reflector-diffuser lighting. To make the wings show well, paint out the background on the negative, and print so that the wings are seen as a very light grey against a pure white background. Expose the dark body less than the wings in printing, to even out the appearance. Properly done, the final visual effect will look quite natural. See Plate 38A.

Pinned Insects

As photographic subjects, pinned insects in general present two problems, both associated with the presence of the pin. In dorsal views the pinhead may obscure important detail. The best solution for this is to place the pin correctly in the first place. But if it is too late for that, cut the pin off, carefully, just above the insect's body. Hold the pin with fingertips or forceps below the insect's body, to damp any vibrations produced when the pin is cut; this will lessen the risk of damage to the specimen. If cutting the pin does not suffice, it will be because the act of pinning has itself destroyed the wanted detail. When removing the pinned insect after the photography, hold the lower part of the pin firmly with the forceps just above the celluloid, and press down lightly on the celluloid with a fingertip to damp any vibrations that might damage the specimen.

The second problem arises when the lighting throws the shadow of the pin across the background. This can be prevented quite simply. A piece of medium-weight celluloid is used as a support for the subject instead of the usual glass plate. The pin is inserted into a hole previously made for it, and the background is placed at a little distance below the celluloid. A handy way of holding the celluloid stiffly is to cut it to fit

---

PLATE 37 ▸

Subjects: Beetles.

Shiny black beetles are photographically particularly difficult, especially if surface sculpturing is to be shown. Examples of two different approaches are shown, one more suitable for showing gross detail and the other for fine sculpturing.

A Beetle (×4.5), photographed in a modified reflector-diffuser fixture, as shown in Figure 57A. The heavily sculptured wing cases are especially well illustrated.

B The same subject, using the multiple-mirror method shown in Figure 57B. This method does better on the finer detail just behind the head. (Originally photographed for J. T. Doyen.)

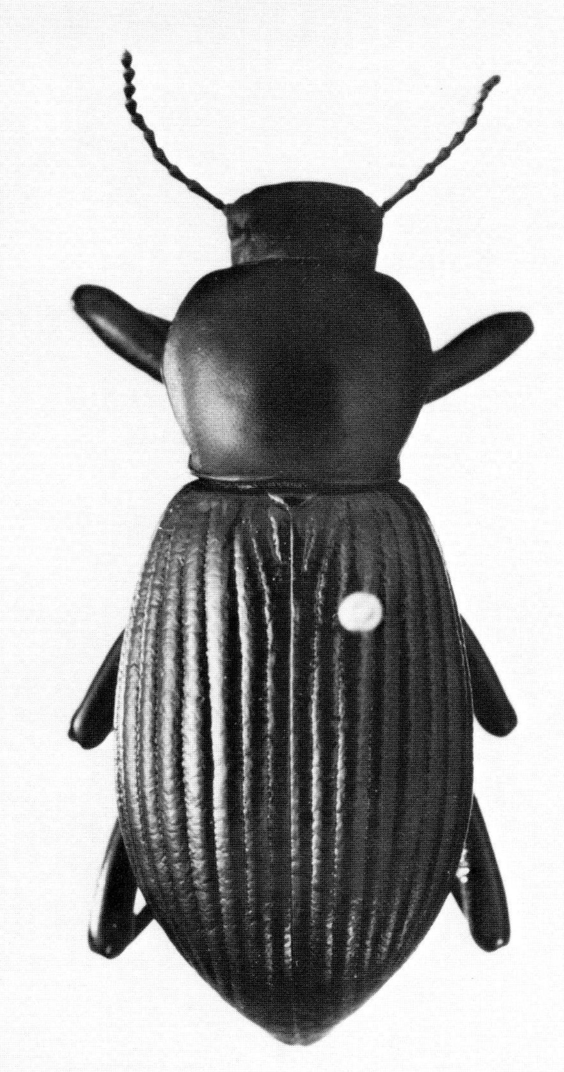

A

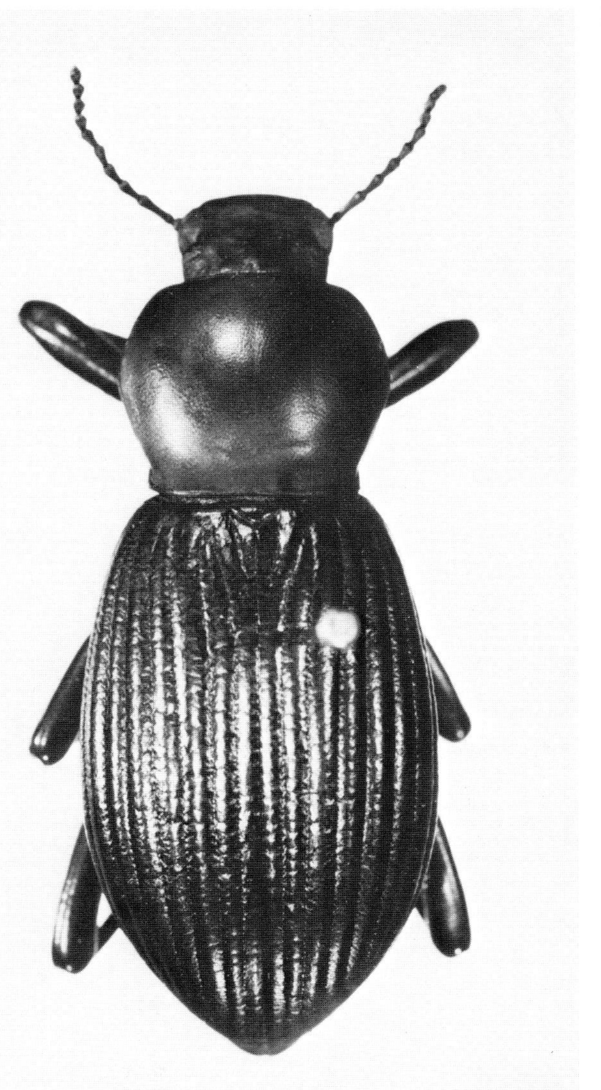

B

one of the plastic snap-together frames that are made for holding $3\frac{1}{4} \times 4$-inch film slides for projection (Polaroid #632 slide mounts do nicely). The whole assembly can then be set across two blocks of wood above the white-card background. The background should not be too large, or it will cause edge reflections on the subject. See Figure 58 for details of the setup, and Plates 36D, 37, and 38A for examples.

Actually, pinned insects should be relaxed, de-pinned, and temporarily reset so as to show legs and other appendages to the best advantage, before photography. And, of course, if a series of related specimens are being shown, all should be in the same position to facilitate comparisons. Many entomologists, it seems, are reluctant to take these steps. Too bad, because the results can be well worth the effort.

Moths and Butterflies

Moths and butterflies are generally quite simple to photograph. They are usually photographed as mounted specimens with their wings spread out; lighting is low-contrast reflector-diffuser lighting, intended to emphasize the wing coloration. With black-and-white films, selective color filtering may help. With color films, the lighting remains the same, but of course there is no color filtering except as may be needed for correcting the color balance.

Insect Galleries in Wood

Insect galleries in wood can be photographed in such a way as to show clearly the galleries themselves and the sculpturing produced by the insect's mouth parts, or they can be photographed primarily to show their contents. The desired result dictates the lighting to be used.

For the first task mentioned above, it is most useful to light with a single direct lamp, angled according to the height of the relief and aimed across the general line of the galleries at about a 45° angle. The exact adjustment depends entirely upon the individual subject and upon the final effect desired. A white-card reflector is used opposite the lamp to adjust the contrast

---

PLATE 38 ▶

Subjects: Transparent-Winged Insects; Pinned Insects.

A Transparent-winged insects, such as this formally mounted grasshopper (×1), are best photographed against a white background, which can be painted out on the negative to enhance the visual contrast, as was done here. They are treated much the same as glass or clear plastic apparatus. In dorsal views of pinned insects it is a good idea to render the head of the pin somewhat out of focus so that it will not be confused in the picture with surface detail of the specimen. Lighting here is by the reflector-diffuser method. The background is a white card given the same light as the subject (controlled overexposure, as when trying for pure white backgrounds, would make the printing of the wing excessively difficult and probably low in contrast). (Originally photographed for D. Rentz.)
B A lateral view of a pinned bee fly (×1.5), also photographed by reflector-diffuser lighting. Here, however, the usual controlled overexposure was used to give a pure white background (in the original print). In this, as in other work with white backgrounds, be sure to avoid excessive overexposure, as it will produce optical flare; this will result in attenuated edge effects, loss of overall contrast, and apparent loss of sharpness. This subject was photographed with a vertically mounted camera, the pin being thrust horizontally into the side of a cork. (Originally photographed for R. Merritt.)

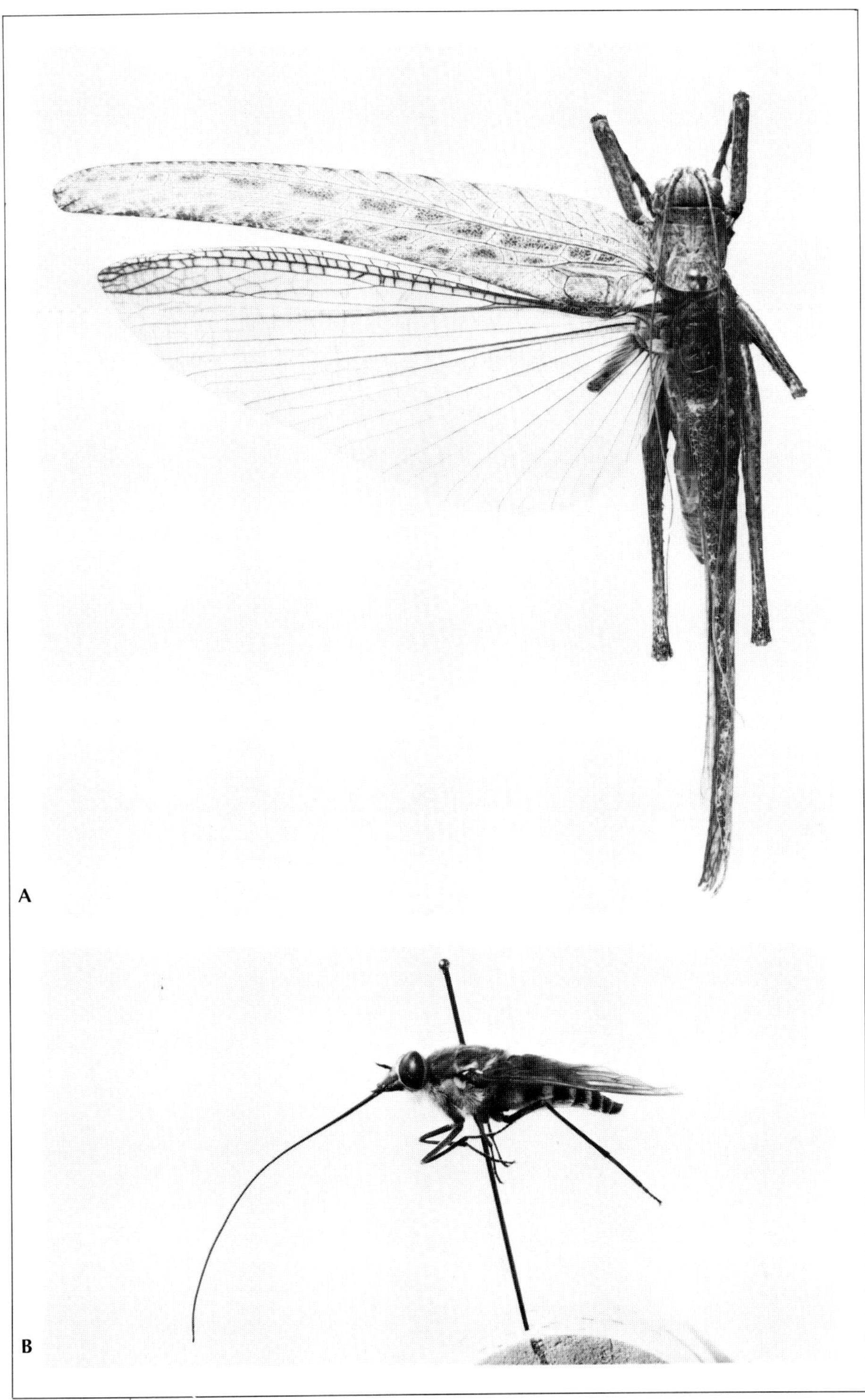
A
B

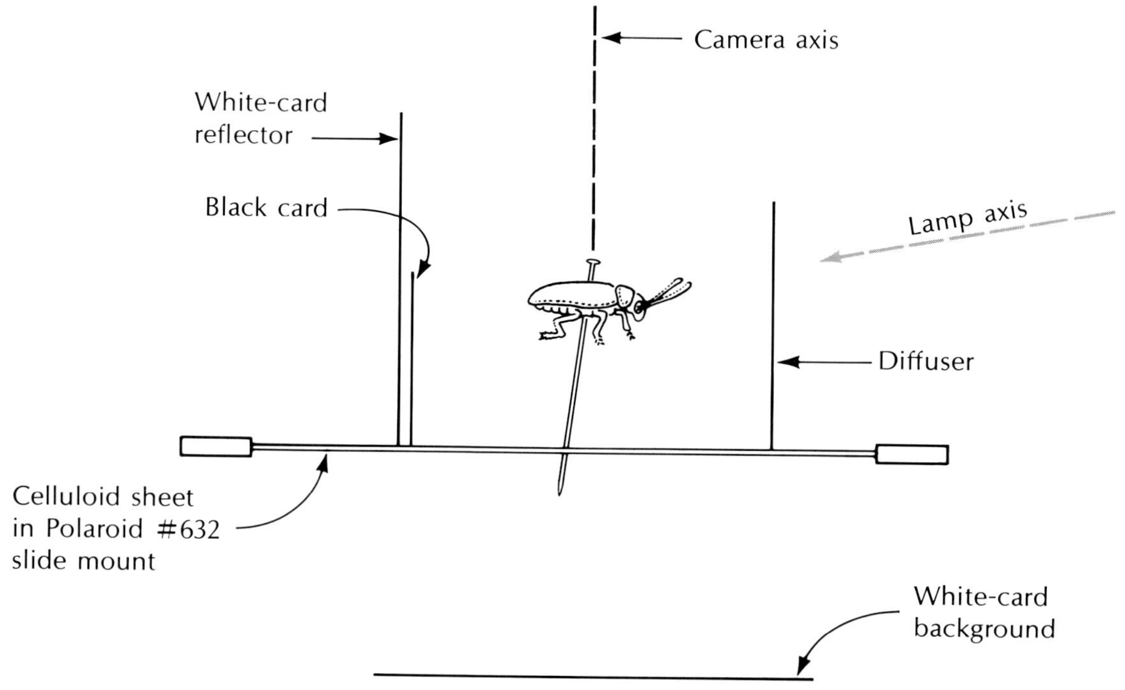

FIGURE 58
General setup for photographing pinned insects. This is a variation of reflector-diffuser lighting, with a black card introduced to block reflections from the downward-curved posterior end of the subject, as needed (this is similar in effect to the black paper ring used in lighting spheres—see Figure 50). (See Plate 36D.)

and partially fill shadows. It is most properly placed parallel to the line of the galleries rather than at 90° to the light path, as would otherwise be customary. This placement keeps the amount of shadow fill roughly constant along the length of the specimen. Properly done, the effect is to provide a good amount of detail on all flat or near-flat surfaces, a shadow next to one wall of the gallery, and a highlight illuminating the other wall. For a pictorial example, see Plate 39A.

Where the insect is the main point of interest and the gallery serves merely as its container, the lighting must be different—usually much lower in contrast. A good result is usually obtained by using reflector-diffuser lighting adjusted to give a soft, nearly directionless light; such directionality as remains should be approximately from the picture top. This affords good general detailing and usually adequate lighting of moderately deep cavities and their contents. If the cavity is unusually deep and the insect is deep within it, then axial or near-axial lighting will be needed to achieve the necessary penetration of the cavity and delineation of the subject. (See Plate 6A.) Axial lighting is also helpful in showing insect eggs that have been partially embedded in the floors and walls of galleries. Although it is not penetration of a cavity that is usually sought in this case, the eggs will be shown much more prominently because they will reflect more axial light than the rougher, less shiny wood.

Silk Deposits

Silk deposits, being made up of extremely fine strands of material, can be quite difficult to portray unless certain special steps are taken. Spider webs and other primarily radial silklike structures can be lightly sprayed with a very fine mist of water, causing tiny droplets to form all over the web. With one light placed on each side of the structure, much as for copying, each droplet is clearly edge-lit, and the aggregate effect is a clear delineation of the entire web pattern.

Most worms that spin silk, as well as spiders that spin sheet webs, produce relatively amorphous masses of fibers that lack the fine patterns of the orb webs spun by other kinds of spiders. Careful examination of these massed strands will usually show a preponderant general direction of the deposit, however. A good practice here is to use a single direct light at 90° to this line of deposit, with a reflector opposite to fill shadows in the whole area of the picture. Each strand that is thus lit will appear as a discrete fine line of light in the picture, owing to refraction (see Plate 39B; see also Plate 36B). If there is more than one prominent direction of alignment of the strands, you will have to place a lamp for each one.

Leaf and Needle Miners

Leaf and needle miners can be photographed quite normally, once the top surface of the mined leaf or needle has been peeled back to expose the occupant. And if you wish to show the external appearance of the mined leaf or needle, the best methods are those normally used for any such botanical subjects (see Plate 5B). But if you wish to show the larva actually at work within the leaf, something else is required.

A shadowgraph or silhouette effect is usually the most appropriate means of doing this. Some subjects are shown best with a strong, collimated beam of transmitted light. This will require a condenser lens below the subject, as for low-power photomicrography (see Chapter 9, and Figure 43A there, for details of the setup). Other subjects, particularly needle miners, may show best when a directional form of dark-field lighting is used. In this case, the mined needle should be placed at 90° to the light beam reflected up from the mirror. (See Figures 26 and 43B for details of useful setups.)

Tiny Active Adults

These are a real test of the photographer's patience and skill. Magnifications of ×10 or more may easily be required simply to show general form, stance, and habits. (Detailed structure may be visible only in photomicrographs made of killed and mounted specimens, or in pictures made with the scanning electron microscope of living or dead specimens.) Such high magnifications severely limit the depth of field, absorb light, restrict the field of view to an area substantially smaller than the usual area of the subject's activity, and exaggerate the insect's apparent speed of motion.

If the insect is walking and if a statically mounted camera is to be used, the most practical method is to prefocus the camera at a point very slightly above the surface of a clearly delineated area; when the insect passes across this area, make a picture using a high-speed electronic flash lamp to stop the motion—a flash duration of at most $\frac{1}{1000}$ second may be required if all parts of the insect are to be sharp. Light falloff due to the magnification and its accompanying extension of the camera bellows will often require the use of an accessory lens to concentrate the light beam. And the subject may need to be protected from the heat of the flash with a water cell. Experimentation may be needed to determine the correct exposure. See Figure 59 for examples of useful setups.

Much patience will be needed in waiting for the insect to do what is wanted of it, somewhere within the area depicted on the film. At any given image magnification, therefore, the larger the film size, the better your chances.

A much more practical approach is to use 35 mm photography. It is possible to obtain image magnifications as great as ×6 directly on the film, and to enlarge in printing at least 15 to 20 times, thus obtaining a final print magnification of 90 to 120 times actual size, all without significant loss of photographic quality. The basic setup is with a macro-type lens set for ×1, using the closeup flash technique with augmentation of the image magnification by teleconverters (Chapter 6), and high-resolution technique (Chapter 7). You may be amazed at the high quality of the images thus obtainable. And it can be done with insects that are fully alert and moving around. See Plate 40A.

A glass cage can be used to hold active or dangerous small subjects for photography with either large or small cameras (see Figure 60 for details of construction). Useful cage materials include 2 × 3-inch microscope slides or $3\frac{1}{4}$ × 4-inch projection-slide cover glasses as the cage faces, and either 1 × 3-inch microscope slides or lengths of square Plexiglas bars as the ends, tops, and bottoms. Transparent silicone adhesive, sold in tubes in hardware stores, is a good, fast-drying material for fastening them together. It sets quickly to a permanently rubbery consistency, makes a watertight joint, and holds firmly.

The same cages can also serve as small aquaria for the photography of aquatic insects, tadpoles, small fish, etc. See Figure 49 and the section on aquarium photography in Chapter 12 for information applicable to the flash photography of subjects in aquaria.

PLATE 39 ▶

Subjects: Insect Galleries; Silk Deposits.

A Insect galleries in wood (×1.5). Although the branch is basically cylindrical, the lighting is across the subject from the upper right—about 1:30 o'clock—in order to show clearly both the galleries themselves and the sculpturing, or "toolmarks," made by the insects on the floors. The lighting is direct, with minor fill from a card reflector placed parallel to the left edge. (Originally photographed for J. Chemsak.)

B Silk deposit on a cone (×5). The lighting is direct and from the upper left—about 11 o'clock—with reflector fill opposite. The direction of lighting is roughly 90° to the axis of the main silk strands, to assure maximum visibility. There is a living larva just above the silk deposit. The background is a piece of black velvet. (Originally photographed for R. W. Stark and J. N. Borden.)

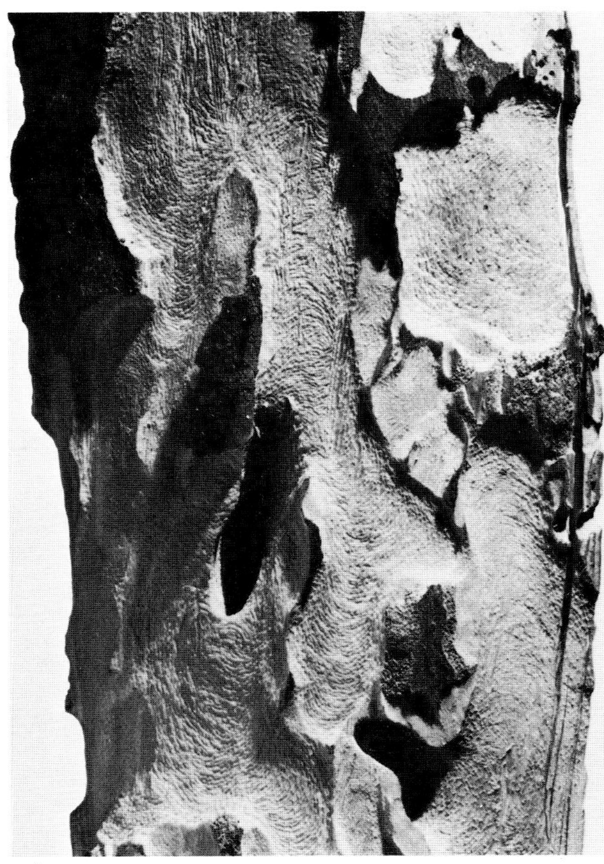

A

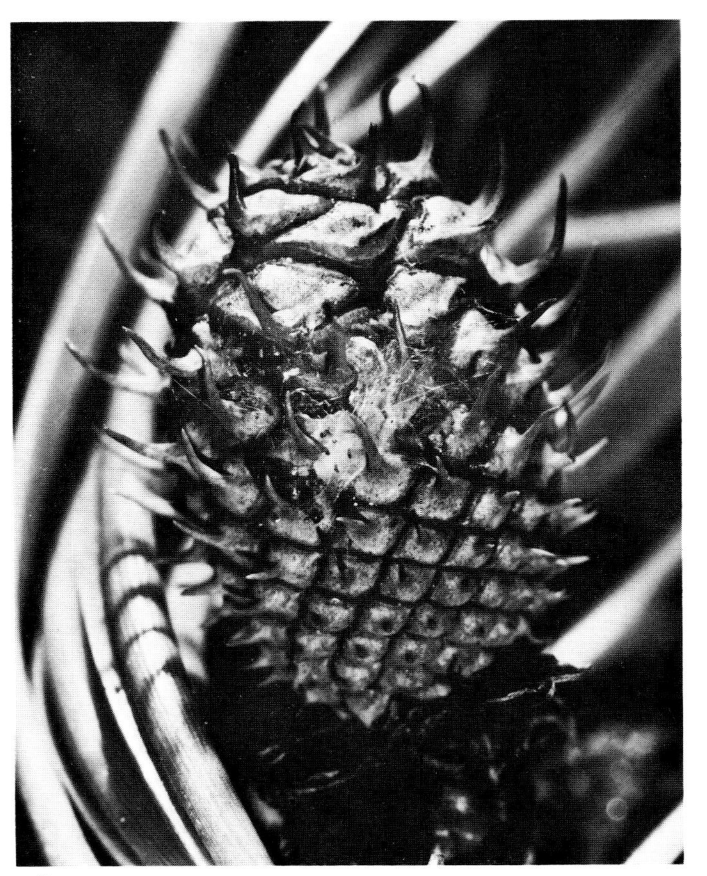

B

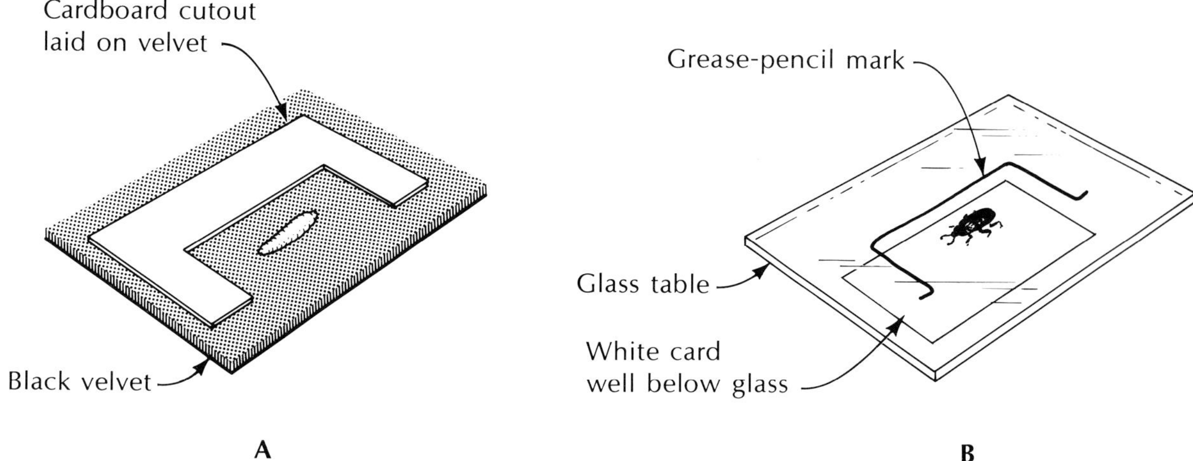

FIGURE 59
Photographing live, nonflying insects with large-format cameras requires a means for outlining the area of the subject plane that will be covered by the film frame. The subject can be placed within that area, or it can be chivied into crossing it; when it does, the shutter is released to make a flash exposure.

A Light-colored subjects, such as many larvae and pupae, can be shown well against a black background.
B Darker subjects show better against a white background. Some of the more active subjects can be slowed down by putting them on a slippery glass support table.

See Plate 40, parts B and C, for examples of subjects photographed in glass cages—the former with a statically mounted view camera using sheet film, and the latter with a 35 mm camera.

Other methods are required for the photography of flying insects. The full-scale investigation of insect flight entails a complex setup using high-speed flash with electronic triggering. Dalton's book, *Borne On The Wind,* 1975, is illustrated with superb examples of this type of work, and provides basic information on how to accomplish it. See also Edgerton, *Electronic Flash, Strobe,* 1970, for circuit diagrams of the equipment likely to be needed.

Limited photography of insects in free flight can be accomplished with ordinary 35 mm equipment, if you have the patience and perhaps a little luck. The method uses a camera equipped with an attached L-shaped wire frame mounted in front of it to outline the image area; it is located exactly in the principal plane of focus. The lens-to-frame distance varies according to the focal length of the lens and the image magnification chosen. A high-speed electronic flash unit is used to stop the subject and camera motion. You stalk the chosen insect until you can manage to place the wire frame around it as it flies; then you release the shutter, and with it the flash. It isn't easy, but it can be done (see Blaker, *Field Photography,* 1976, for details of this and other field-photography techniques).

Insects that repeatedly come to the same location (e.g., a wasp returning with prey to a nest hole, insects pollinating a particular flower, etc.) can be photographed in the act of landing or taking off, without wire frame finders, electronic triggers, or other special equipment. You determine the flight path, set the camera firmly in the correct position—with electronic flash to illuminate the target area and to stop subject motion—and wait. Knowing what the film-frame area will be, you use a cable release to actuate the shutter when the insect is correctly placed and doing what you want it to. You must use a zone-focus method here—that is, you place the camera parallel to the path of expected flight, focus in the correct plane, and then use a small diaphragm opening to maximize the depth of field.

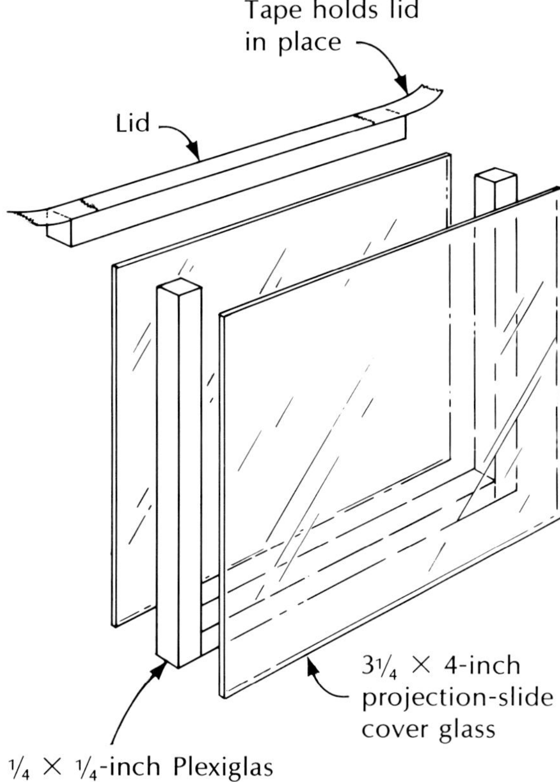

FIGURE 60
A transparent container for holding live (including flying) insects, or water for aquatic specimens. In a thicker version the top, sides, and bottom are all 1 × 3-inch microscope slides. For cages the pieces can just be taped together (Scotch "Magic" tape is suitable); for aquaria, fasten the pieces with transparent silicone adhesive (sold in tubes in hardware stores). Aquaria do not require a lid, except for flying fish. . . . (See Plate 40, parts B and C.)

INVISIBLE SUBJECTS

Sometimes photographs are needed that reveal phenomena that are virtually invisible because they occur in transparent media. There are several photographic lighting techniques that can be used to make such effects visible in pictures.

In photomicrography, dark-field and phase-contrast techniques are widely used for these purposes (see the numerous references to dark-field lighting throughout this book; since the phase-contrast technique is equipment-specific, your dealer is the best source of both equipment and information; see also the book by Bennett et al., 1951, as a source on phase contrast). Dark-field photography can be done routinely in any image-magnification range, not just in photomicrography. It is less well known that the phase-contrast technique is also adaptable to closeup photography and photomacrography. P. C. Diegenback's good how-to account in *Scientific American,* 1970, offers a method by which a variety of phase-contrast effects can be obtained at very low image magnifications.

Although he uses only an experimental subject (a streak of Canada balsam), the method is equally adaptable to any small transparent subject (e.g., the transparent capsules surrounding the spores of certain water ferns undergoing fertilization).

Another technique, though rather technical and requiring specialized equipment, is Schlieren photography. This too is a physical method for revealing invisible events. It takes advantage of the differing densities (and hence refractive indexes) of the air surrounding an object to show the effects of air speed, turbulence, heat, or other factors. The place to begin searching the available literature on this method is Kodak publication P-11; see also the book edited by Engel (1968).

Not everything requires a highly technical approach, however. You will find useful information in the section on subsidiary techniques in Chapter 9, where there are references to applications of dark-field lighting, Rheinberg lighting, deliberately uneven transmitted light, and so on—all of which can be used in a variety of contexts. (See Plates 7A, 16, and 20D for examples of essentially transparent subjects photographed by these means.)

I will provide one detailed example of an unusual subject in closeup photography to give an idea of how you can use simple but unorthodox methods to accomplish difficult photographic feats.

The problem was to photograph the "weeping" that occurs on the inside wall of a wine glass when the wine is swirled, or simply allowed to stand undisturbed. (This was to illustrate a point in Amerine and Roessler, *Wines: Their Sensory Evaluation,* W. H. Freeman and Company, San Francisco, 1976.) The "tears" of wine, as the drops seen flowing down the inside of the glass are called, consist primarily of water. The difficulty is that both the glass and the liquid are transparent. Any use of an evenly toned background rendered the drops invisible.

PLATE 40 ▶

Subjects: Active Insects.

Highly active insects and small arthropods are inherently difficult to photograph. There are several methods of photography that work well.

A Newly hatched first-instar bug (Hemiptera) on its own egg mass on a leaf (×20). Photography was by the closeup flash technique, using a basic ×1 setup augmented with a 3× tele-converter to achieve a ×3 image. It was further enlarged in printing. (This picture also appeared as Plate 35a of Blaker, *Field Photography: Beginning and Advanced Techniques,* W. H. Freeman and Company, San Francisco, 1976.)
B Female Brown Recluse, or "Violin," Spider, *Loxosceles laeta unicolor* (×2.5), the nominal reference being to the violin-shaped pattern on the top of the head. This spider is poisonous and can inflict a bite that ulcerates, so it was not handled directly. It was dumped from its container into a straight-sided pan, where it typically ran to a corner and stopped. A glass cage (see Figure 60) was pushed up until the edge touched the spider, which immediately entered it. The cage was then capped. Since spiders move fast or not at all, it was possible to make a 30-second time exposure for detail photography, using reflector-diffuser lighting. (Originally photographed for R. Doty.)
C Female sand fly, *Lutzomyia vexatrix occidentis* (×16). A male is seen in dorsal view, out of focus in the background. The insects were momentarily anesthetized with CO_2 for transfer into a glass cage. Once revived, they moved rapidly and nearly constantly, so the camera was immobilized and the cage was moved by hand to locate and focus on standing specimens. Exposure was by electronic flash. Photography was at ×2.25, with further enlargement in printing. High-resolution 35 mm technique was used. (Originally photographed for S. Iyala.)

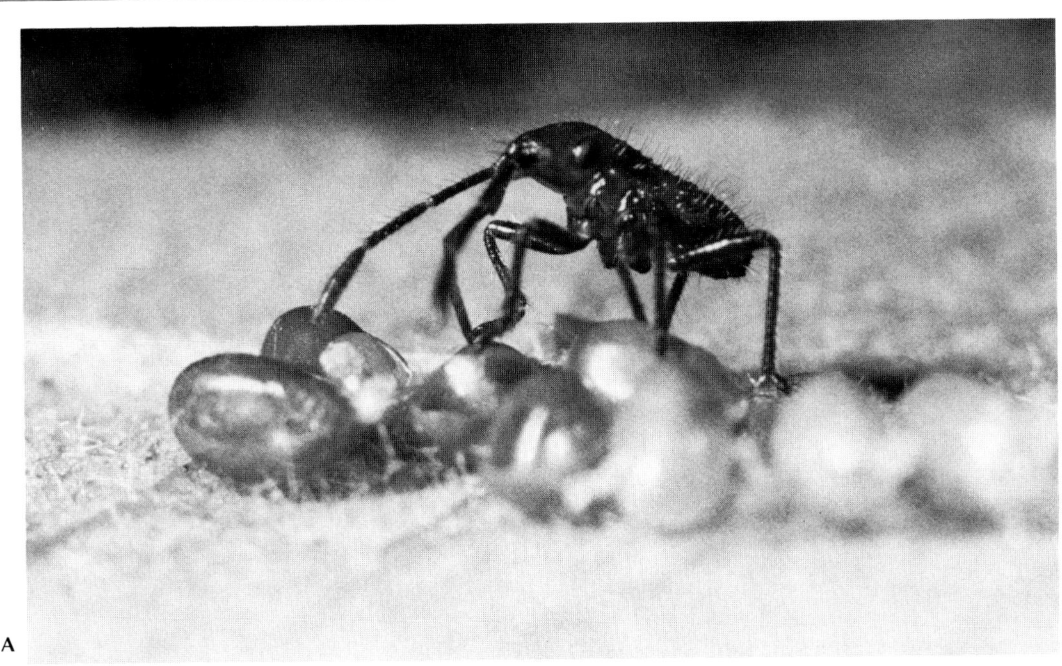

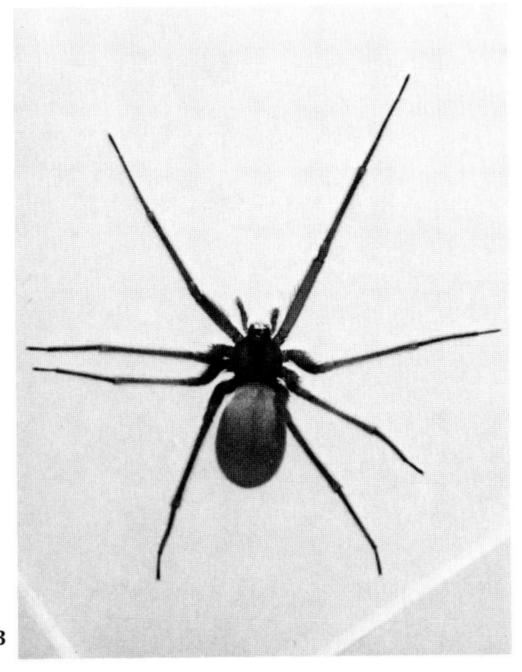

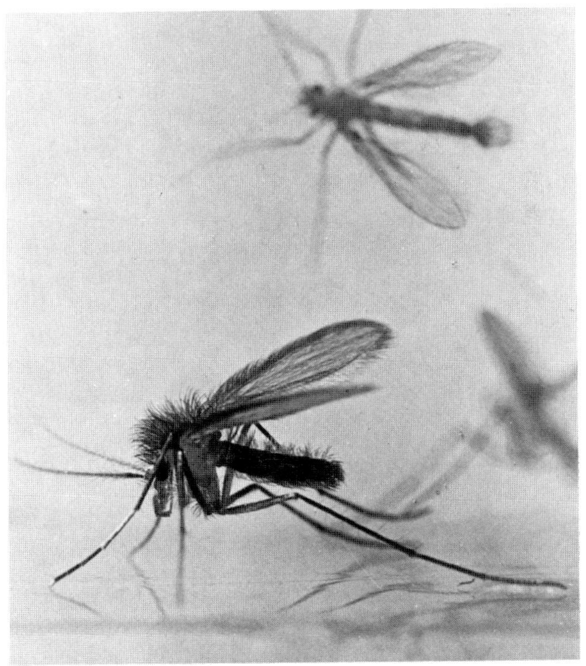

A single drop of liquid would be quite well revealed through the use of deliberately uneven transmitted light, but multiple drops are hard to make visible simultaneously. Your eye sees the effect because you move the glass against the uneven background made up of objects in the room. To photograph the effect with a still camera, you can use a patterned but out-of-focus background that will provide visual edge refractions around each drop of liquid.

Experimentation revealed that the optimum effect was achieved with a background made of a sheet of grey cardboard with a black grid on it, made by laying 1/4-inch-wide strips of black tape 1/4 inch apart. When placed at the right distance behind the subject, with the lens aperture at the optimum setting, each drop of liquid was clearly visible. Since the setup was specific for lens focal length, lens aperture, image magnification, distances, and background pattern, I will provide the details. But any change in the conditions would require different settings, and further experimentation would be needed.

I used an 8 × 10-inch view camera with a 12-inch focal length lens closed down to *f*/11. Image magnification was ×1, and the subject was placed 12 inches in front of the background. Exposure was by flash, to stop the motion of the tears as they ran down the inside of the glass. Different widths and spacings of the grid lines produced patterns that were either too large or too small for optimum visibility of the tears. At *f*/8 the grid was too far out of focus, and at *f*/16 it was too sharp. Even under optimum conditions the negative produced was very low in contrast, and required printing on a very high-contrast paper (Brovira #6, with the developer heated to about 80°F (27°C) to further increase the contrast). The result is shown in Plate 41.

The visual effect is of a regular pattern of dark and light areas, with the glass and the tears shown up by dark edge lines arising from refraction effects. The background shows in low contrast because as subjects in photographic images go out of focus, their contrast decreases.

The purpose of the foregoing description is to show that you must apply some knowledge of optical effects in order to solve unusual photographic problems. Since it is not possible to predict the nature of all future problems, you must be constantly aware of the kinds of things that can affect photographic subjects—things such as reflection, refraction, scattering, polarization, and so on.

PEOPLE

Portraits

It may seem strange to include a section on portraiture in a handbook for scientific photography, until one remembers that scientific research is done by scientists, who may need (or like) to have their pictures taken. Many scientists are at one time or another asked to provide pictures of themselves for publication with articles or reviews, on book jackets, or for publicity use in connection with meetings, lectures,

---

PLATE 41 ▶

Subjects: Invisible Subjects.

An 18% aqueous solution of ethanol "weeping" after being swirled in a wine glass. Photographed at ×1 and reproduced here at ×0.8. A full explanation begins on page 242. (Originally photographed for Amerine and Roessler, *Wines: Their Sensory Evaluation,* W. H. Freeman and Company, San Francisco, 1976, where it appears as Plate 14.)

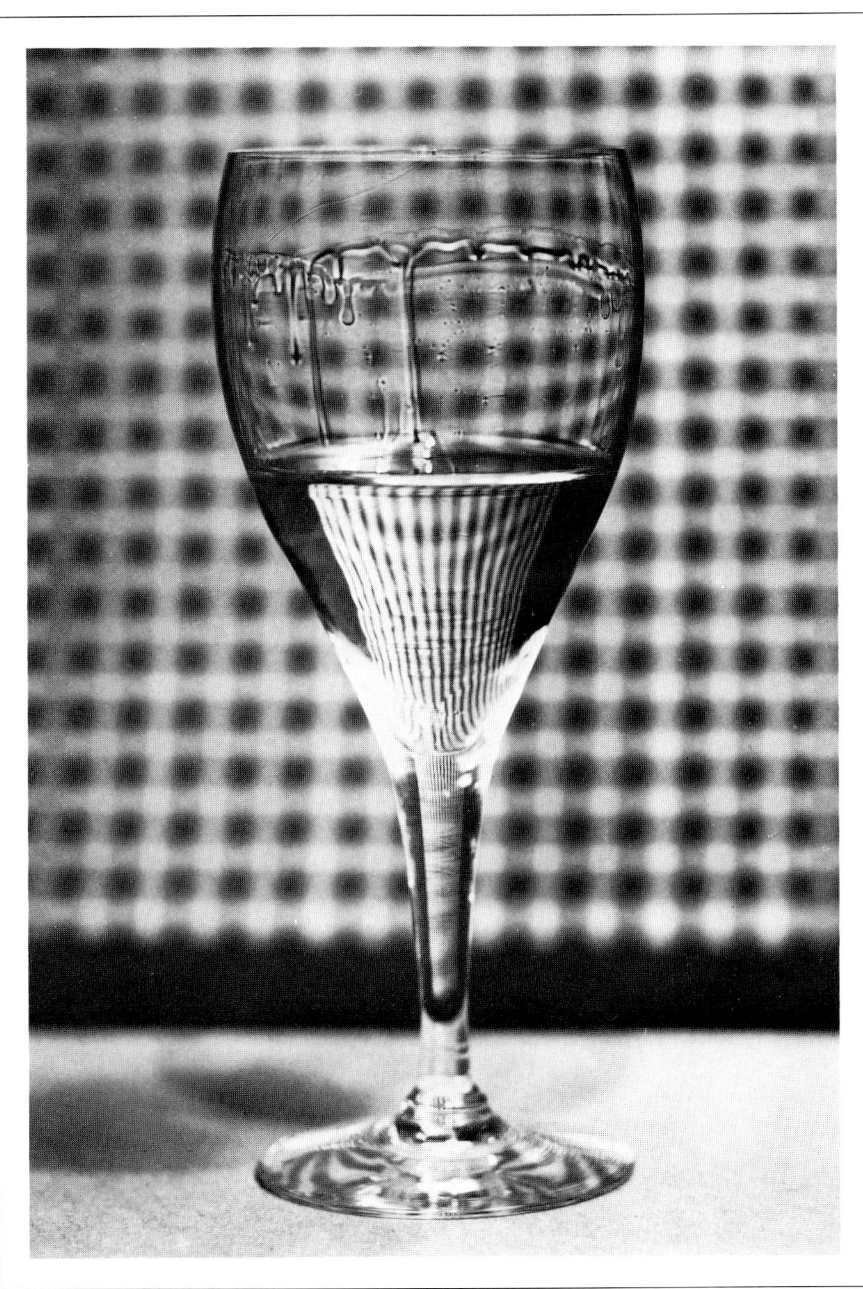

and so on. The general run of studio portraiture often seems rather unsuited to these purposes. The most common substitute is a more or less bad snapshot made by some well-meaning but photographically inept associate. Hence this section.

No attempt will be made to describe the intricacies of advanced portrait lighting, which can be quite involved, nor will any standardized lighting setups for the use of artificial light be provided. The approach will be to show how existing light can be used to good advantage to provide what is in essence a glorified snapshot—an informal and relaxed portrait of the subject as he is, without artifice. Those who wish to learn about more formal portraiture are encouraged to read Kodak publication O-4, *Professional Portrait Techniques,* which is clearly written and well illustrated. It is a good source for either amateur or professional, and offers a variety of methods.

The best source of light for achieving good results with great simplicity is diffuse window light. A pleasant appearance can be obtained by having the subject sit or stand about 4–5 feet from the window and turned at about a 30–60° angle to it. The camera is placed just inside the window, looking into the room with its optical axis roughly perpendicular to the surface of the window. The background can be simply a piece of black velvet (no shadow problems, good isolation of the subject), or it can be composed of out-of-focus elements of the subject's natural working surroundings. Filling the shadows on the side opposite the window is accomplished by hanging up a white card (or a sheet of newspaper or even a white lab coat) and adjusting its distance to provide the degree of fill desired. For best results—good sharpness, reasonable depth of field, and minimum grain—I prefer very fast films in rather large cameras. (A typical setup might include a 4 × 5 or 5 × 7-inch camera, Kodak Royal-X Pan film of ASA 1200–1600 speed, and normal development of about 5 minutes in DK-50 developer.) The result can be a really satisfactory portrait, with a sense of relaxation and intimacy often not easily obtainable in the professional studio.

Users of smaller cameras can obtain satisfactory results by similar means. The relatively larger 120-sized cameras can use such films as Kodak Tri-X or Royal-X Pan, and 35 mm cameras can be loaded with Tri-X or Royal-X Recording Film. The Tri-X film is very suitable for general portraiture, offering a speed of ASA 320–400 (depending upon how you use it) and surprisingly unobtrusive grain if enlargement in printing is not overdone. The Royal-X films offer substantially higher speeds (ASA 1200–1600) and are interesting films to use when you want to introduce grain as a structural pattern in the picture. It is a good way of producing an abstract effect. In substantial enlargement, these films offer a crisp, evenly structured grain pattern that is very satisfactory for the purpose.

The Polaroid Land films offer good possibilities for portraiture of this type. Three films in particular are worth mentioning. The P/N film produces a positive that is useful for checking the lighting, and simultaneously a black-and-white negative of good quality, with an emulsion speed of about ASA 80. There is also a print-only film in black-and-white that offers a speed of ASA 3000; it is called Polaroid 3000. This extends the possibilities for portraiture into almost any situation. Finally, the new, improved Polacolor 2 offers rapid-access color prints with very good color fidelity and a "palette" of colors that can only be described as painterly. Marie Cosindas has achieved quite lovely results using Polacolor films for portraiture and related subjects.

Other film manufacturers produce a variety of films suitable for use in portraiture. Those mentioned above simply happen to be those with which I am most familiar. The reader is encouraged to experiment widely.

Where artificial light is necessary—for example, where the subject is to be shown surrounded by his laboratory equipment—one can still use only that light that is normally present. Most laboratories these days are lighted quite brightly. The subject is moved about until good lighting is found, and then the picture is made. A firm camera support will assist in obtaining sharp pictures. See Plate 42 for an example of portraiture in the laboratory, by existing light.

The most natural and relaxed appearance will occur if the subject sits or stands in a comfortable, normal position, with his features in repose. The subject may or may not be looking at the camera, but in any case the principal plane of focus should be at the eye nearest the camera. If this eye is in focus, all else can be slightly out of focus and the effect can still be good. If the eye is out of focus, there is an irretrievable loss. Photographically speaking, the eye is the seat of the intellect and the window of the soul, the natural center of interest in almost any face. The only likely exception to this might be in a subject who is blind; here the best point of focus may be the lips or even the hands and gesturing fingertips.

People as Types, or at Work

Two additional circumstances that may require the photography of people are not strictly examples of portrait photography. In doing ethnographic research it is often desirable to photograph individual people to illustrate typical facial characteristics, makeup, or hair arrangements. This kind of photography can be done basically the same as laboratory portraiture, but care must be taken to see that those features that are most important in the record are well lighted.

A second need that often arises is to photograph people at work (colleagues in their laboratory surroundings, or other people whose work is being studied—perhaps in ethnography). Here you can use either of two methods. You can photography them by existing light when the ambient light level is high enough and when you have films and lenses that are fast enough. No special techniques are needed; just be sure that important portions of the scene are not obscured by shadows or by intruding objects or people.

Alternatively, if you need to stop subject motion you can use flash lighting. The ordinary flash-on-camera method will virtually guarantee a usable picture in most cases, although the quality of the lighting will not be especially impressive. A better method would be to use two identical small electronic flash units, with flash-synch extension cords of 1 to 2 meters for gaining flexibility in the choice of lighting angles. With a Y-connector inserted into the camera's flash-synch socket, you can plug in both units for simultaneous firing. The lighting technique need not be complex. The *main light* (the one that will determine the relative positions of highlights and shadows) is placed so that it will illuminate the subject area in the most suitable manner. Then the *fill light* is placed very close to the camera lens. It can be on either side or just above the lens, and serves to fill in the shadows. To obtain a good balance in light intensity, the main light should be about half as far from the subject as the fill light. However, with small flash units used to illuminate rather close subjects, it is better to place the main light where it will properly light the subject, and then place one or more layers of white tissue paper over the front of the fill light. The idea is to have the fill-light intensity about one-half to two-thirds that of the main light.

For example, if you were using small electronic flash units, a typical guide number for a film of ASA 400 speed would be about 110. If the main light were placed about 7 feet from the subject, the fill light would give a good effect at about 10 to 14 feet. But if the camera itself was to be closer in to the subject—say, about 5 feet away—two layers of white tissue paper over the fill lamp, with that lamp still next to the camera lens, would give a similar lighting balance. Under these conditions you would obtain a correct exposure by setting the lens diaphragm at *f*/16, with the shutter set at the correct speed for electronic flash synchronization ($1/60$ second for most 35 mm SLR cameras). If trials indicate that the lighting contrast is too high, from too little fill lighting, remove a layer of tissue paper from the fill lamp (or move the fill lamp closer to the subject). If the contrast is too low, add another layer of tissue paper.

TUBES

Test tubes and other tubular glassware are frequently the subject of photography for research purposes. Since they present several different types of problems, this section will be divided accordingly.

Tube Slants

These are cultures in which the actual subject matter is plant material growing on the face of a slanting layer of culture medium. They require special treatment for best results. The lighting should be direct and undiffused, and always from the top of the tube (plugs must be so placed and the height of the lamp so adjusted that no shadow falls on the actual subject). Light from the bottom of the tube or tubes would not only misrepresent the usually occurring surface relief, but would also make disturbing reflections on the rounded end of the tube. No reflector is used, as it too would reflect on the tube bottoms.

Backgrounds can be either black or white. If they are to be pure white in the final print, it will usually be necessary to opaque the background on the negative, but with tubes this is not usually an arduous task, as the edges are simple in shape and easy to follow. A black background can be provided by laying the tubes directly on a piece of black velvet. Where backgrounds are black, tubes laid in groups will tend to reflect one another disturbingly, so dividers of black paper cut to a width slightly less than the diameter of the tubes are placed between the pairs. This setup will give a final picture in

---

PLATE 42 ▶

Subjects: Portraiture.

Laboratory portrait of Dr. John H. Northrop, winner of the 1946 Nobel Prize in chemistry. The lighting was existing window light only. The camera was an 8 × 10-inch view camera with an $8\frac{1}{4}$-inch lens. The film was 5 × 7-inch Kodak Royal-X Pan film (ASA 1200), developed normally. Although I also use a 35 mm camera, with Kodak Tri-X film, for similar portraits, the camera-and-film combination used here is an excellent way of getting a high-quality, apparently grainless portrait with existing light.

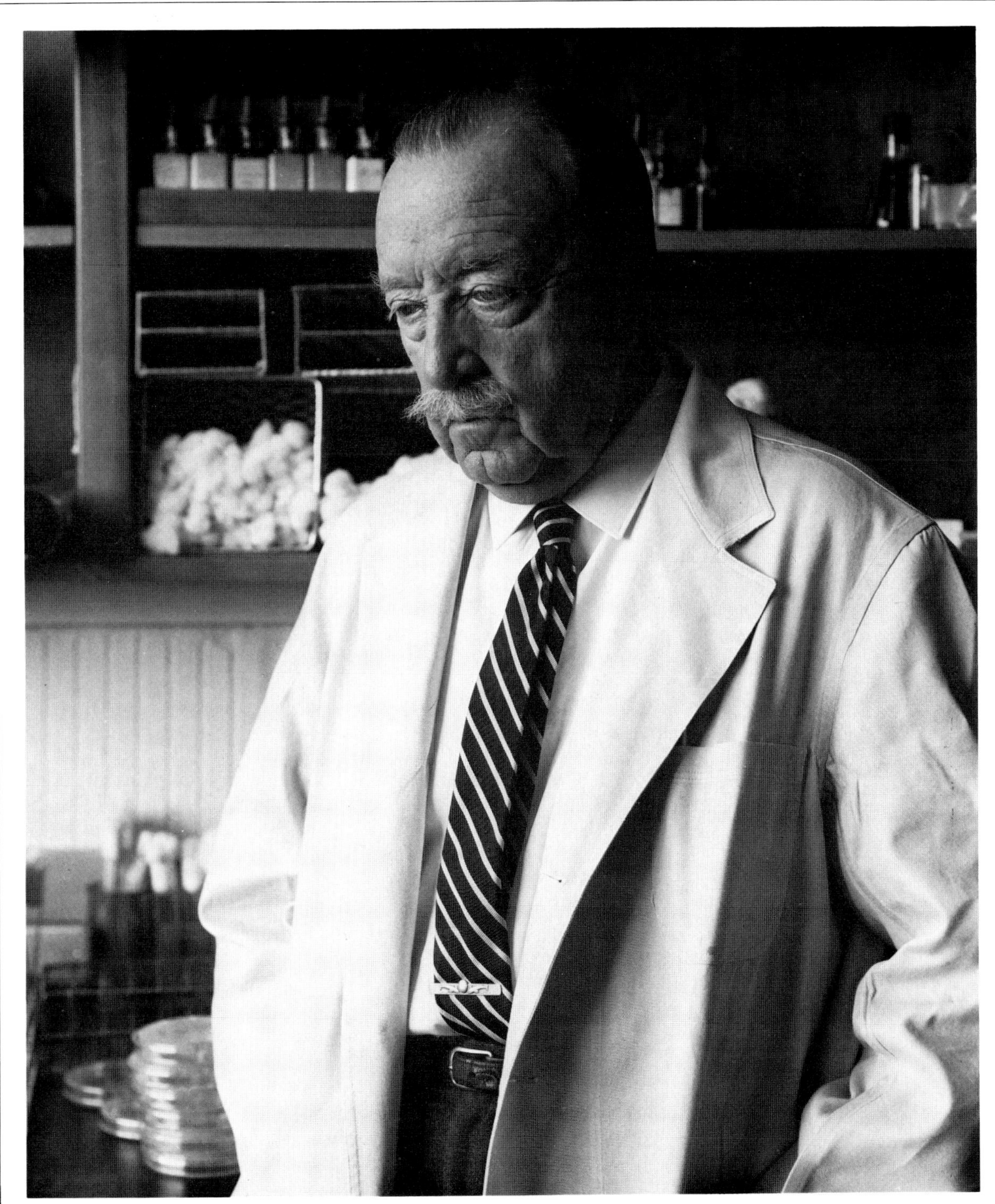

which the tubes are very inconspicuous compared to the setup with a white background, and the appearance will be much as though the cultures had been removed from the tubes entirely and just laid side by side.

All growing cultures in closed glass containers will cause moisture to condense on the inner glass surfaces. To combat this, gently warm the tubes by waving an infrared lamp or an ordinary hair dryer above the tubes until the condensation just disappears. Use care, as overheating will damage the cultures. (When in doubt, test a typical culture for heat resistance before attempting this method.) The photographic setup must be complete before the heating is done, as the picture must be made quickly before the condensation returns (see Figure 61 for details of the setup; see Chapter 10 for information on the removal of condensation and the opaquing of backgrounds).

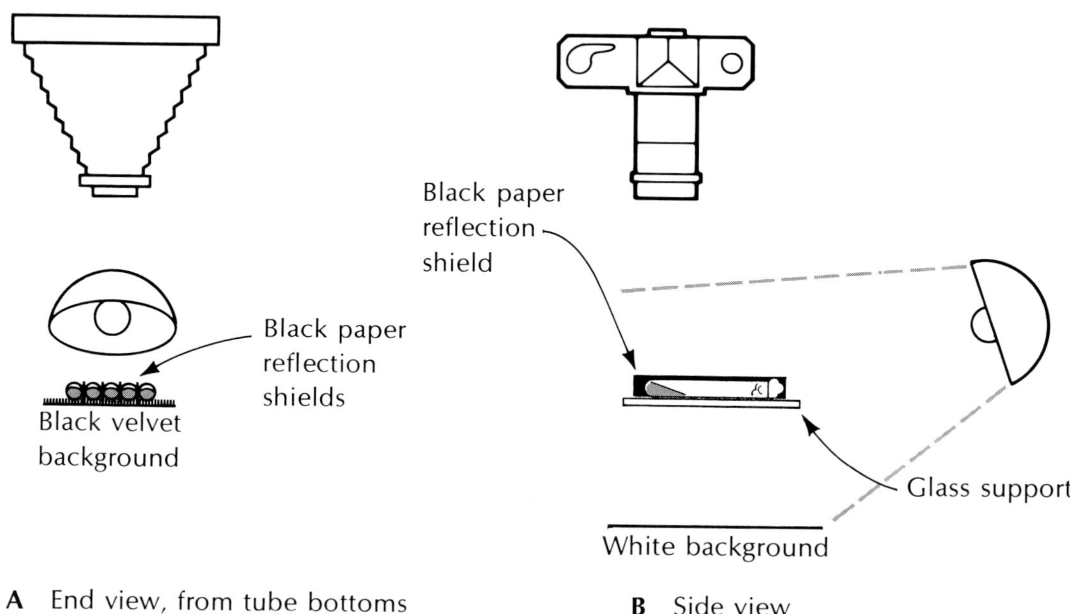

FIGURE 61
Lighting tube slants. Surface reflections between pairs of tubes are removed by inserting narrow strips of black paper as shown. Direct lighting is used, to show surface detailing on the contained growths.

A View of the setup from the tube bottoms, shown with a black background and a view camera.
B Side view, shown with a white background and a 35 mm camera. Either background or camera can be used, according to preference.

Liquids in Tubes

Liquids in tubes, and transparent gels that have colored bands and are contained in tubes, are fairly common photographic subjects. The best pictorial result will probably be achieved by using a lighted white card behind the tube as a diffuse source of transmitted light, with no frontal light on the tube at all. Either color or black-and-white films can be used with this setup. There will be no reflections on the tube itself to divert attention from its contents.

If the white background is too small or too far away, the edges of the tubes may be outlined by broad dark bands. The background should be adjusted in size and distance until there is only a thin dark border to indicate the size and shape of the tube.

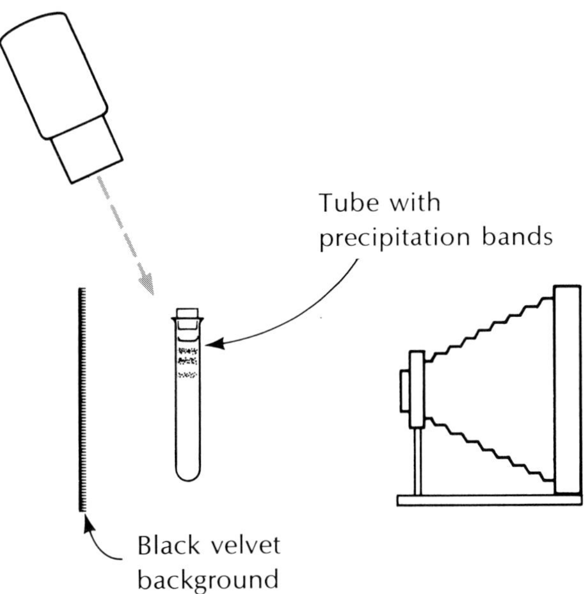

FIGURE 62
Lighting precipitation bands in tube preparations. The method shown is an application of dark-field lighting to illustrate a form of colloidal suspension, which is virtually transparent when seen by frontal or transmitted light. It requires a black background.

Precipitation Bands

Cultures containing precipitation bands within a gel column in a tube are handled much the same as similar materials in dish cultures. (See the earlier section on precipitation bands in dish cultures.) A dark-field effect, which should be directional in this case, is obtained by placing a single light above and behind the tube and shining along the tube length (see Figure 62 for details of the setup).

In this setup, as in others where the background is black, the edges of the tube can be made visible by putting a narrow piece of white card along each side of it, and adjusting their positions until a very narrow white reflection is seen all along each side of the tube. In some cases a very good effect can be obtained by using a fluorescent ringlight behind the tube or tubes, as with Petri dishes. No edge cards will be needed here, as the tubes will naturally be edged with a very narrow band of white light reflected from the ringlight.

Objects in Tubes

Photographing three-dimensional objects inside tubes can sometimes be trying, since the lighting requirements of the subject may be at odds with the need to prevent surface reflections on the tube. Usually this problem is reasonably well solved by lighting with diffuse illumination from above and in front of the tube, as was shown for use with other types of glass containers in Figure 52.

A reflector opposite the lamp usually serves only to confuse the issue by introducing unwanted reflections on the tube. Backgrounds are used as described earlier for objects in glassware: with black backgrounds, white cards at the sides produce light tube outlines; with white backgrounds, black cards produce dark outlines. With white backgrounds it may prove desirable to opaque the background on the negative so that it will print pure white and thereby be better differentiated from the glass tube.

If the subject matter within the tube requires a more complex type of lighting, it is sometimes useful to immerse part or all of the container in water, thereby killing the reflections on the glass surface. An aquarium can be used for unsealed test tubes, with the tube held at its top by a lab clamp and as much of the tube submerged as may be needed. The side of the aquarium facing the camera should be of high-quality plate glass and the camera axis should be at 90° to it, to assure the best optical conditions. (If bright parts of the camera reflect in the aquarium glass, cover them with black photo tape.) A sealed container, such as an electronic vacuum tube, in which the important subject matter is the inner components, can be placed in a tray of water below a vertical camera and kept submerged by a sheet of glass (itself under the water surface) laid over it. In either case, lighting the container's contents can then be approached in the normal fashion.

ZOOLOGICAL SUBJECTS

The great variety of zoological subjects precludes any detailed discussion here, so only general types of likely subjects will be covered. Field photography of fauna will also not be described, as it is well covered elsewhere (see Blaker, *Field Photography,* 1976, and Garrison and Gray, *Secrets of Zoo Photography,* 1972).

Anesthetized Specimens

It is seldom a good idea to anesthetize a specimen just to make it easy to handle, since the risk of injury or death is great. Anyone who uses anesthetics must be aware of their characteristics and the effect they are likely to have upon

---

PLATE 43 ▶

Subjects: Anesthetized Specimens.

As a rule it is a good idea to avoid unnecessary anesthetizing of specimens, because it is dangerous to them and is certain to affect their natural stance and behavior. However, it is sometimes the most practical route to a given end.

A Salamanders (×1.75), arranged to show comparative patterning in live hybrids. This arrangement is not due to a compulsive sense of order, but is to assure that the same area will be shown comparably on each animal. They were immersed in a chlorotone solution (which should not be touched with your bare hands because it can be absorbed through your skin) in a glass-bottomed container. Lighting was by the reflector-diffuser method, from the head end, with a white-card background below. Exposure time was about 30 seconds. (Originally photographed for A. G. Brown.)

B A similar specimen (×10.5), showing one type of structural detail in the color patterning. The details of the photography were similar. The circle at upper right is an air bubble. (Originally photographed for J. F. Lynch.)

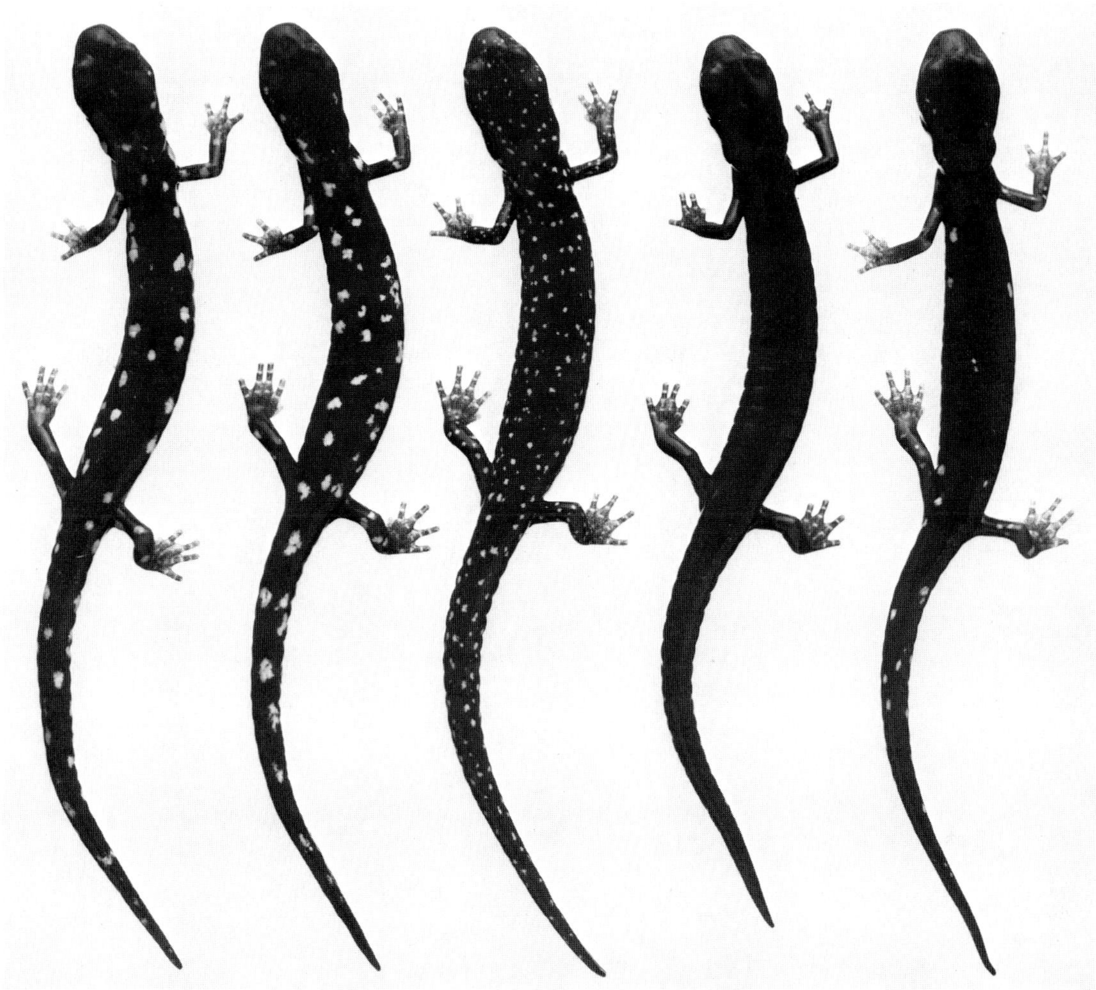

A

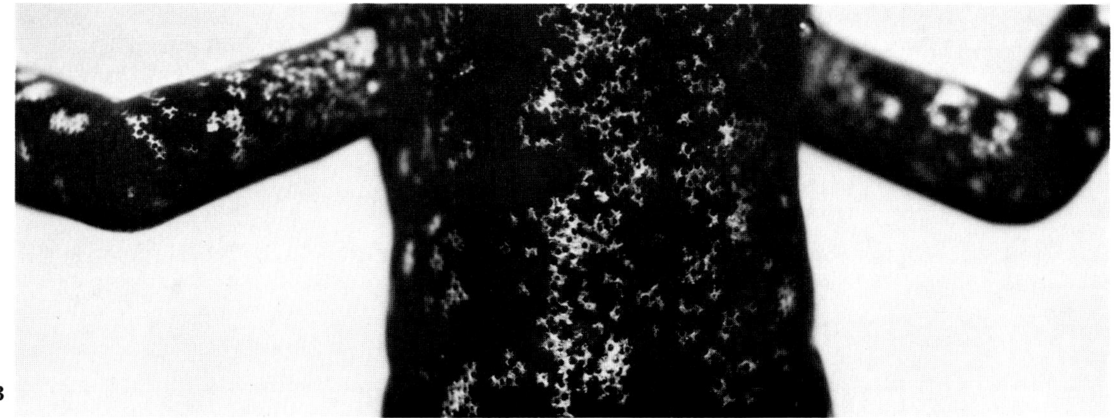

B

the subjects. Furthermore, the use of certain types of anesthetics can pose risks for the experimenter. An example is the use of chlorotone and similar materials to knock out amphibians, such as salamanders. Here the animal is placed in a tray containing a solution of the anesthetic. If the experimenter does this with bare hands, his skin may absorb some of the chlorotone, with undesirable consequences.

There are perfectly good reasons for using anesthetics of various types in the photography of living creatures, e.g., in the recording of internal pathological conditions or injuries during surgical procedures, or the recording of implantation techniques. The use of anesthetics has no bearing on the photography itself, so no special techniques will be suggested. See Plate 43 for sample illustrations of anesthetized subjects.

Bird Skins

Most commonly photographed in small groups to show comparative patterning, bird skins are usually laid out in the proper order directly on a white card. For black-and-white photographs, a fluorescent ringlight (or, more suitably, a concentric three-ring fluorescent fixture of the kind that has been described earlier) is mounted so as to surround the camera lens and thereby produce near-axial lighting of the subjects arrayed below. The soft nondirectional light obtained by this method is well suited for the job and gives exceptionally fine detailing of feather color and structures. The background will normally print either pure white or very close to it. For color photography, use a very low-contrast reflector-diffuser setup, with the light at the head end of the skins.

Bones and Teeth

Long bones are best photographed by diffuse illumination along the axis of the bone, as with other roughly cylindrical objects. Minor adjustments in the position of the lamp will serve to illustrate the shapes and textures of the jointed ends.

Skulls come in a variety of shapes, and it is difficult to give details of technique in general terms. The lighting should usually be diffuse, though sometimes a harsher form of illumination will show surface texturing better. Primate skulls, especially those of humans, may require the type of lighting prescribed for spheres (see Chapter 12, and Figure 50 there).

Jaws and teeth can be treated like dental casts, which were described earlier in this chapter. If they are joined to the rest of the skull, the

---

PLATE 44 ▶

Subjects: Bones and Teeth.

Long bones are basically cylindrical in shape, and are so treated. More complex shapes represent individual problems in lighting.

A Vertebral bones (×1.2), articulated. A medium-low lighting contrast was employed, using reflector-diffuser lighting. The direction of lighting was down the axis of the spine, to preserve the symmetrical appearance. (Originally photographed for P. Van Horn.)
B Lower left back teeth of a rodent (×10), photographed to show breakage and cavities. Medium-contrast reflector-diffuser lighting was used, with the lamp just to the right of the picture top. (Originally photographed for R. Nordstrom.)
C Teeth of a malnourished rat (×4.2). Their shape dictated lighting as for cylindrical objects, since the color pattern was the important feature. (Originally photographed for B. Reikstneice.)

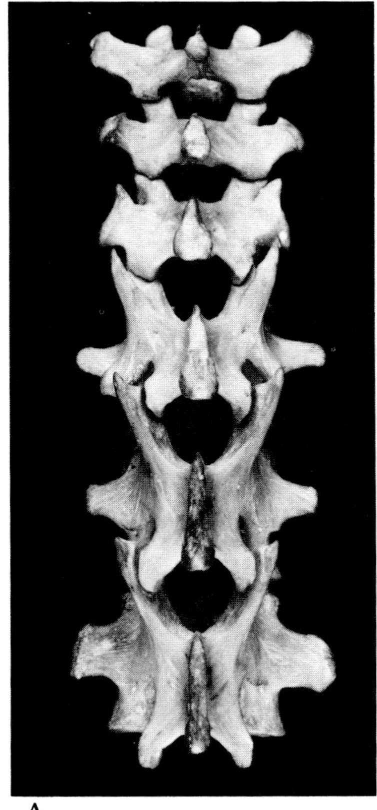

A

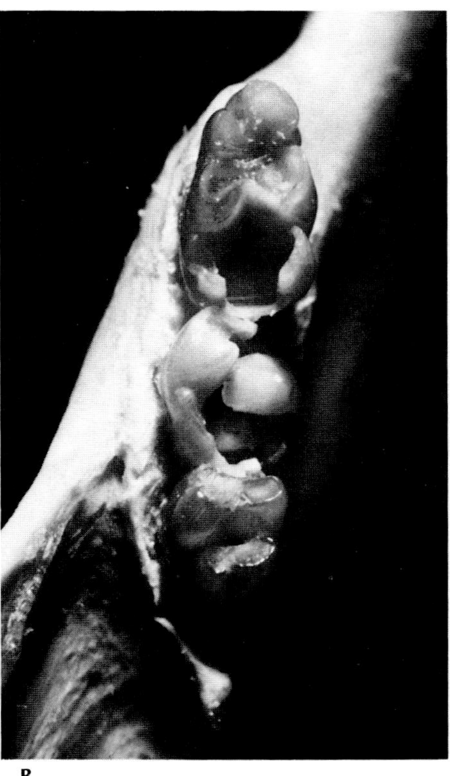

B

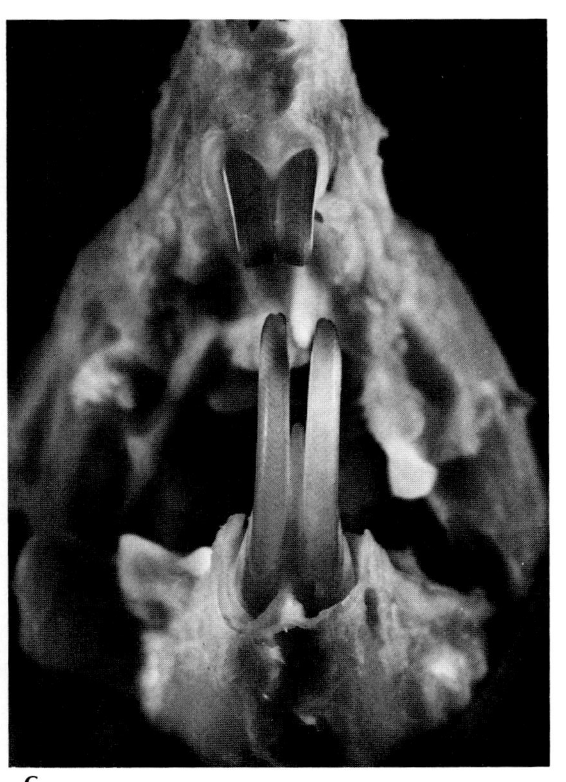

C

parallel is even more obvious (see Figure 56).

Backgrounds can be either black or white, but since most bones are quite light in color, the former seems more appropriate. The color or tone chosen for use will depend upon the intended use of the picture. See Plate 44 for examples of bone and tooth photography.

Living Animals

The photography of living animals in the laboratory can be troublesome, but is not an insuperable problem. A simple side view is the most commonly wanted pose, for the purpose of showing the form, coloration, or stance, or a deformation or other pathological condition. Elephants, camels, and other large mammals can be simply photographed outdoors, so we will limit our discussion to the smaller creatures.

The most suitable lighting arrangement will probably be that described earlier for potted plants (see Figure 54), using a curved white card (or, with very light-colored subjects, a similarly placed piece of black velvet) for a background, and well-diffused lights. Here, however, the lights may often have to be electronic flash, to stop the subject motion and obtain a picture at exactly the right moment.

To produce the most informative picture, the film frame should be fairly well filled by the subject. With animals that are likely to move around much, this is best done by measuring the subject beforehand and arranging the camera so that the field of view covered is of suitable size. A wood block or other dummy subject is then placed correctly and the camera is focused on it. The next step is to mark the background material so as to indicate the boundaries of the picture area and the principal plane of focus. When the setup is ready, the focusing block is removed, the correct exposure is determined, and the lens aperture and shutter speed are set (see Figure 63 for a typical setup).

Then the animal is placed on the background between the positioning marks, with its longitudinal axis in the principal plane of focus. It should, of course, be treated as gently as possible while doing all this. When set down, many animals will immediately set out to explore their surroundings. If the animal is set down a short distance to one side of the desired position, you can make the flash exposure while it is passing through the marked area. See Plates 45 and 46.

Amphibians and reptiles of many types can be readied for photography by a few minutes of gentle handling by a person who knows the individuals well. By this means they are calmed. With the camera and lighting ready, the animal can be set down in the right position, and will often stay put for 30 seconds or so. If it moves immediately, pick it up for more gentle handling. Needless to say, this cannot be done with

PLATE 45 ▶

Subjects: Living Animals, I.

White guinea pigs, photographed by direct lighting to show the hair structure well, with the lamp at the head end and slightly above the body axis. There is a minimal white-card fill opposite. The background is a piece of black velvet. A white background would have washed out virtually all subject contrast.

A Normal healthy animal.
B Experimental specimen, photographed identically.

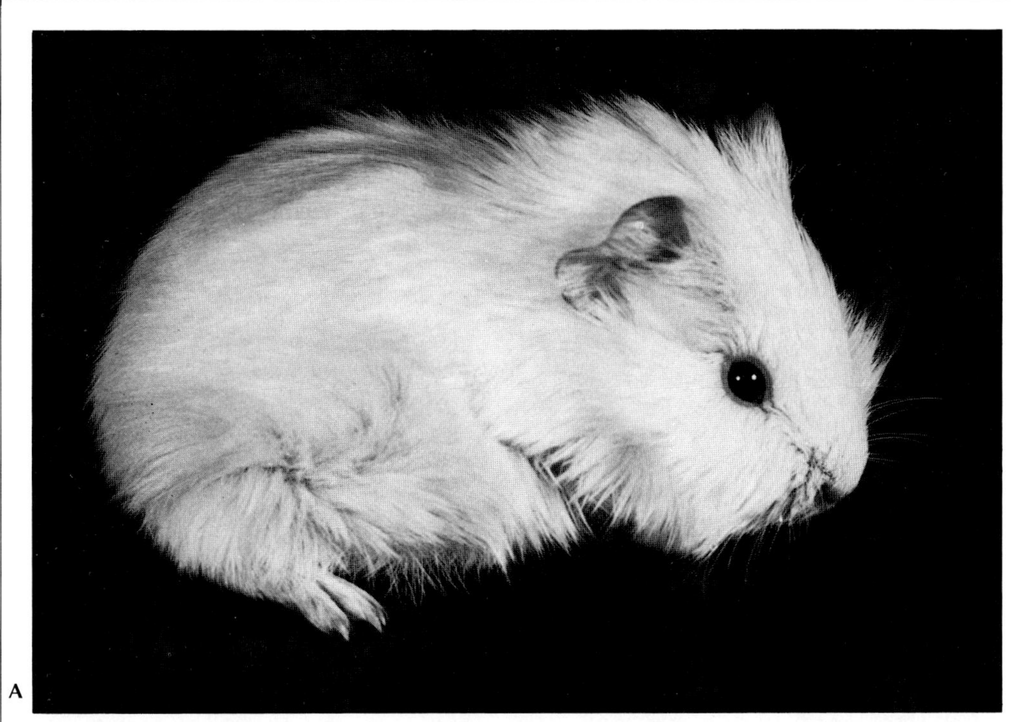
A

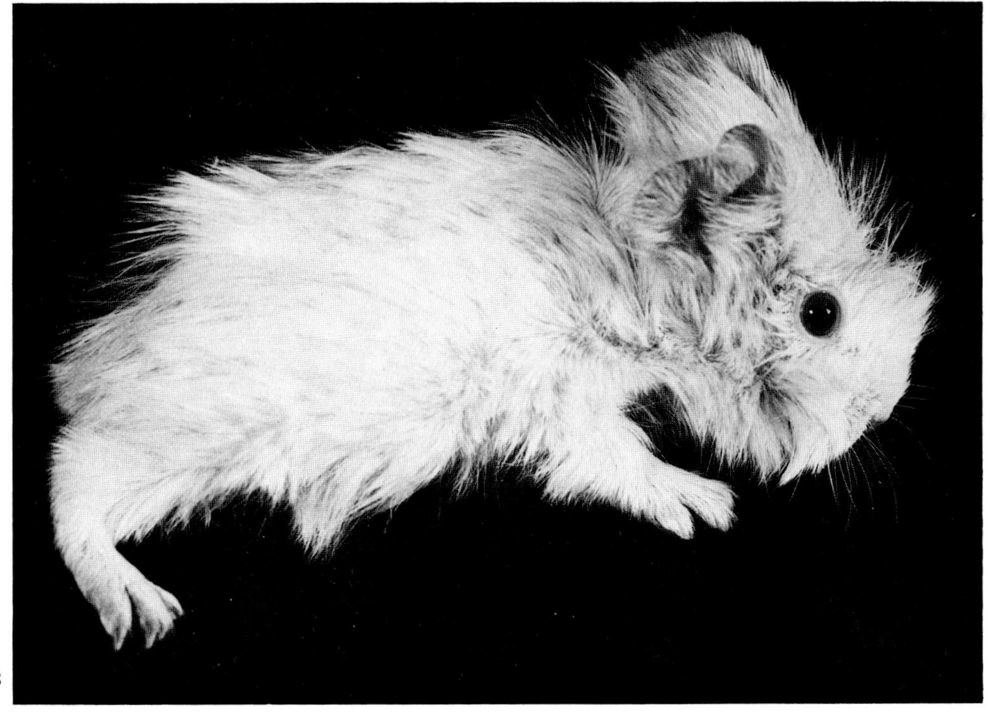
B

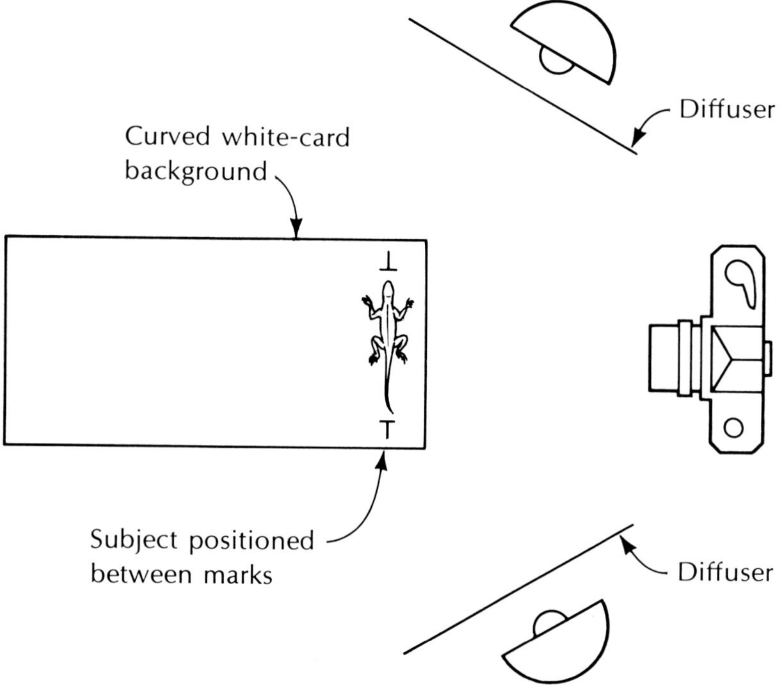

FIGURE 63
Setup and lighting for photographing live animals in the laboratory. (Note the similarity with Figure 54, for photographing potted plants.) The marks on the background card denote the picture boundaries and the location of the principal plane of focus. Two lamps are used to give equally strong lighting from each end of the animal. This setup is for a lateral view. Dorsal views can be done in a similar manner, but with the usual white background below a glass table. (See Plates 45 and 46.)

PLATE 46 ▶

Subjects: Living Animals, II.

Cat with an experimental apparatus attached to its skull, photographed on a preselected target area, as shown in Figure 63. The purpose was to demonstrate visually that the animal was alert and was minimally encumbered by the apparatus. Electronic flash lighting was used to stop its motion. A single direct light source was used, with a white-card reflector fill, opposite. (Originally photographed for O. T. Ellsworth.)

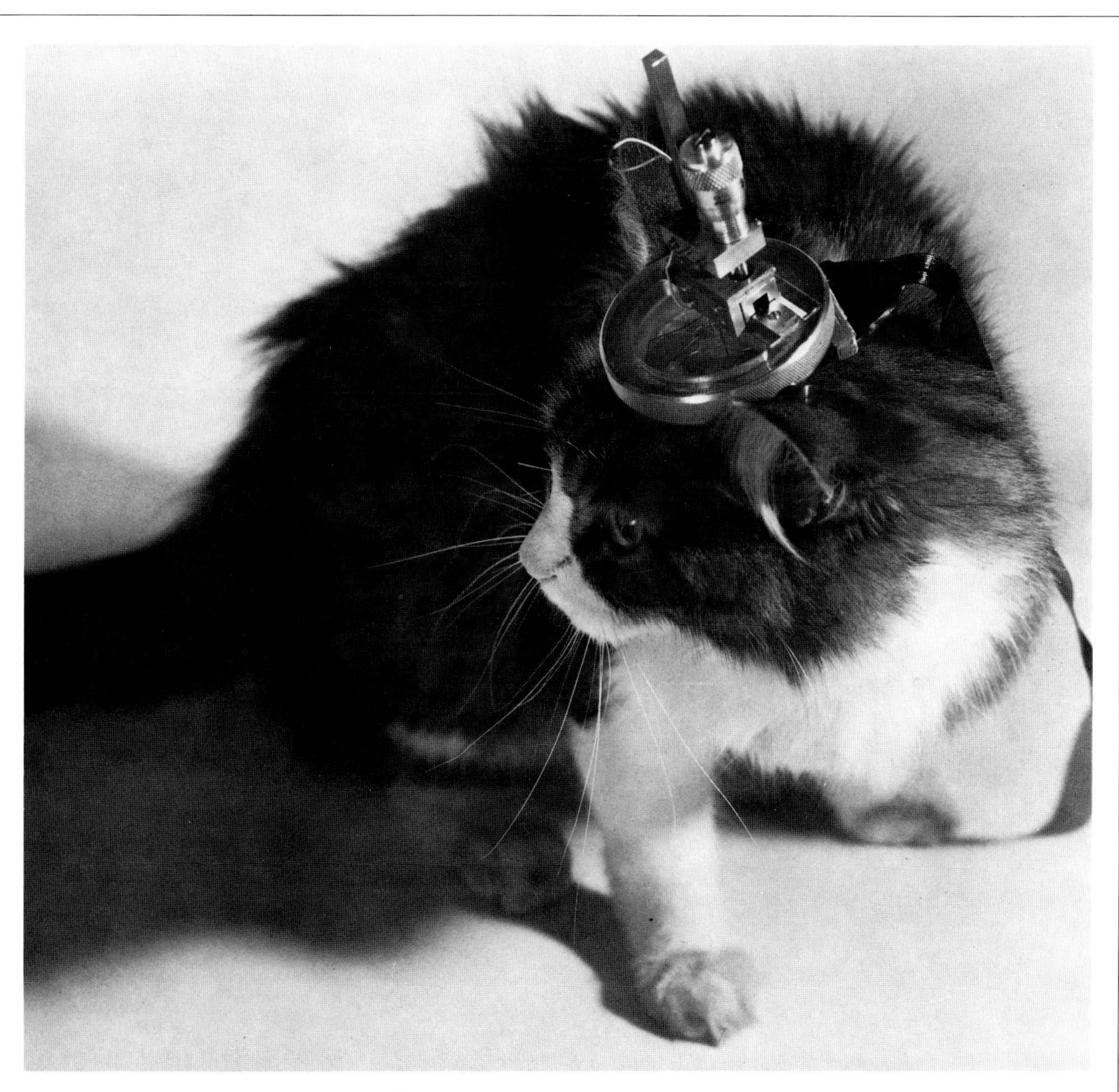

poisonous or vicious specimens, nor should it be attempted by anyone not thoroughly familiar with the particular creature. Dangerous specimens can best be photographed in a reasonably large terrarium or aquarium, depending on the species. They should then be treated like subjects in museum cases or aquaria, as described in Chapter 12.

Preserved Specimens

Animals such as fish, which are preserved in liquids, are best photographed while immersed in the liquid, using a vertically mounted camera. The most practical setup makes use of a glass-bottomed tray set above a white background. If a black background is desired, support the tray above a piece of black velvet so that the nap will not be crushed. Be careful to prevent reflections of the camera from showing on the liquid surface. The basic lighting should be reflector-diffuser lighting. See Plate 47.

Visceral Preparations

Visceral preparations and other views of animal interiors are photographed using a vertically mounted camera. There should be direct lighting from the head end or from one side, with reflector fill opposite. A polarizing screen before the light and a polarizing filter at the lens, as described previously, will make it possible to eliminate nearly all the disturbing reflections that are normally present in this type of subject matter. Eliminating these reflections by immersing the subject in liquid is usually practical only with such things as single complete organs that have been dissected out. Backgrounds, if they show at all in the picture area, should usually be white. Small animals pinned to boards for dissection will present a good appearance if a piece of white card is placed on the board prior to mounting the specimen. Any shadows thrown on this background card will be rendered very light by the reflector fill, and will not be disturbing. See Plate 48.

PLATE 47 ▶

Subjects: Preserved Specimens.

A Pouch young (47-day-old and 42-day-old) of Tasmanian Barred Bandicoot (*Perameles gunni*), preserved and photographed in liquid (×0.8); a portion of a developmental series. A white background was dictated by the subject tones. Note that when such a background is too large for an individual specimen, as it must be in a group picture, there are edge reflections on fully rounded subjects. These can be avoided by doing single-subject pictures, using a background card only just large enough. Lighting here was by the reflector-diffuser method. (Originally photographed for G. Heinsohn.)

B Rat paw with a rejected graft (×6.5). This specimen was fresh, being preserved only by refrigeration. It was treated like any fresh specimen. Lighting was direct and from the picture top, with white-card reflective fill opposite. (Originally photographed for R. Laverin.)

C Attachments and head of a parasitic worm, *Glycera americana* (×6.5). The specimen was preserved in liquid and was photographed through the liquid to prevent surface reflections. Direct lighting from the picture top was used, with reflective fill opposite. (Originally photographed for C. Reid.)

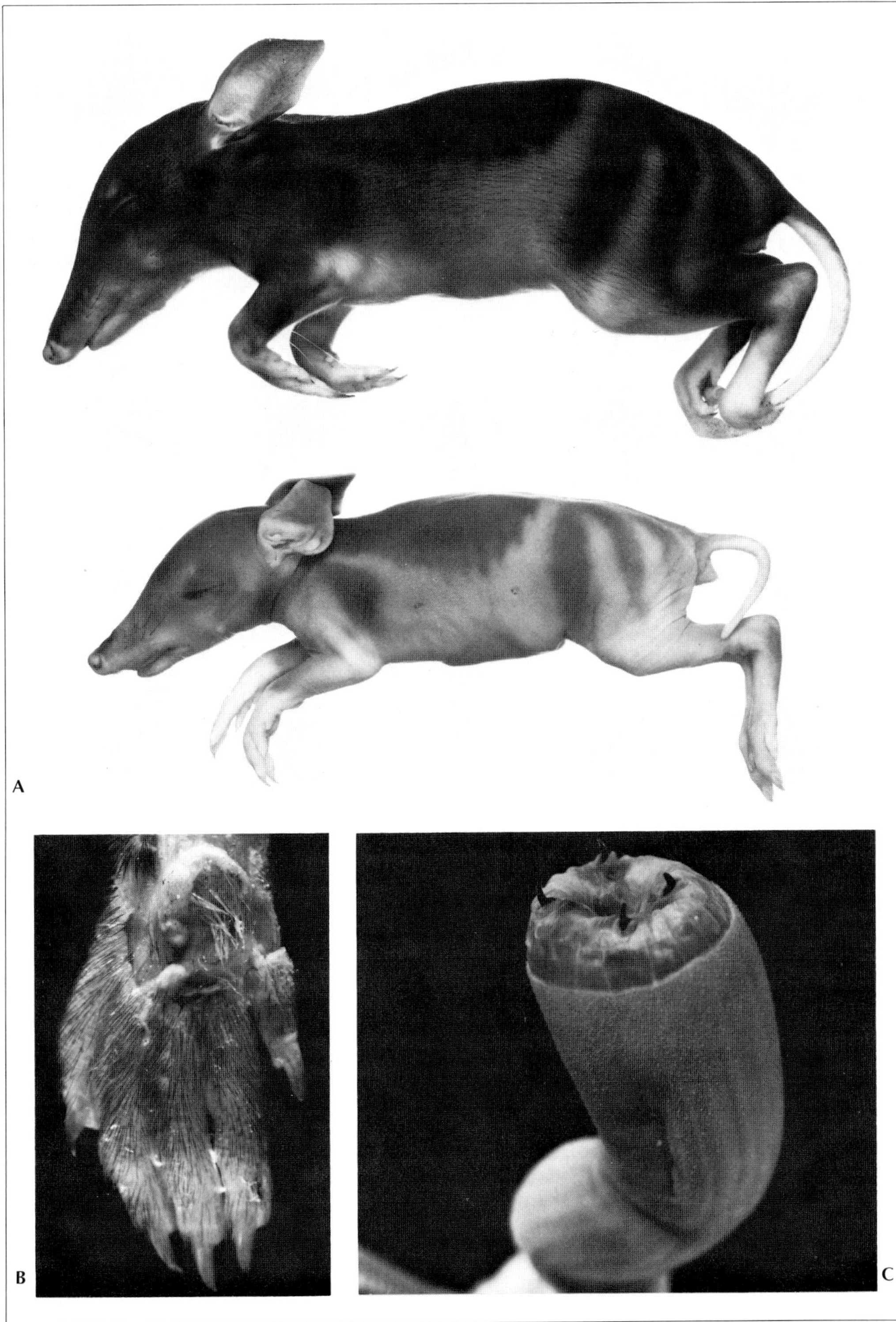
A
B
C

PLATE 48 ▶

Subjects: Visceral Preparations.

A A complete visceral spread (×1.3), with the animal pinned to a board through a white background card. Direct lighting from the upper right was strongly filled by a closely placed white card opposite. The investigator's interest was confined to the viscera, so no attempt was made to light the legs and tail well. A polarizing sheet was placed between the lamp and the subject, and a polarizing filter was on the camera lens, rotated so as to eliminate the surface reflections.

B A closeup of the central viscera of another specimen (×2.6). Here there was only a paper towel under the animal, and it shows rather unattractively at the sides. The lighting was similar to that in part A, but no polarizers were used. Instead, the specular reflections were used to indicate surface dampness, with the lamp placed so that the reflections did not obscure important information. (Parts A and B originally photographed for B. Gordon.)

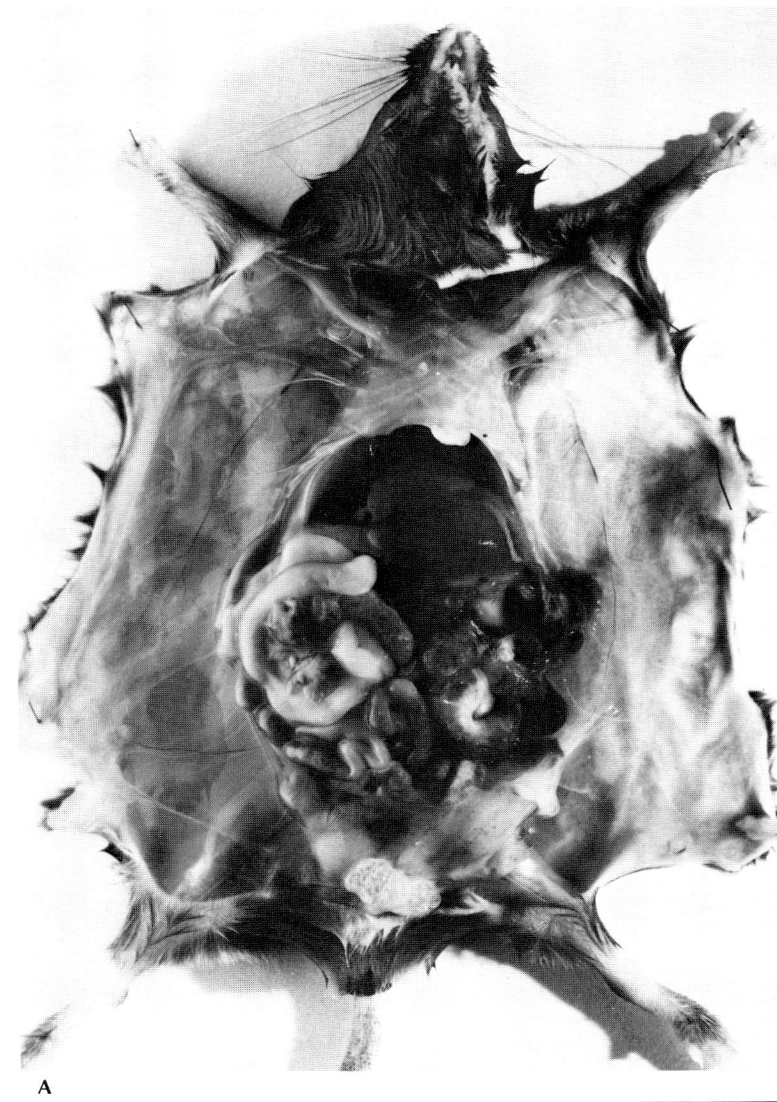

A

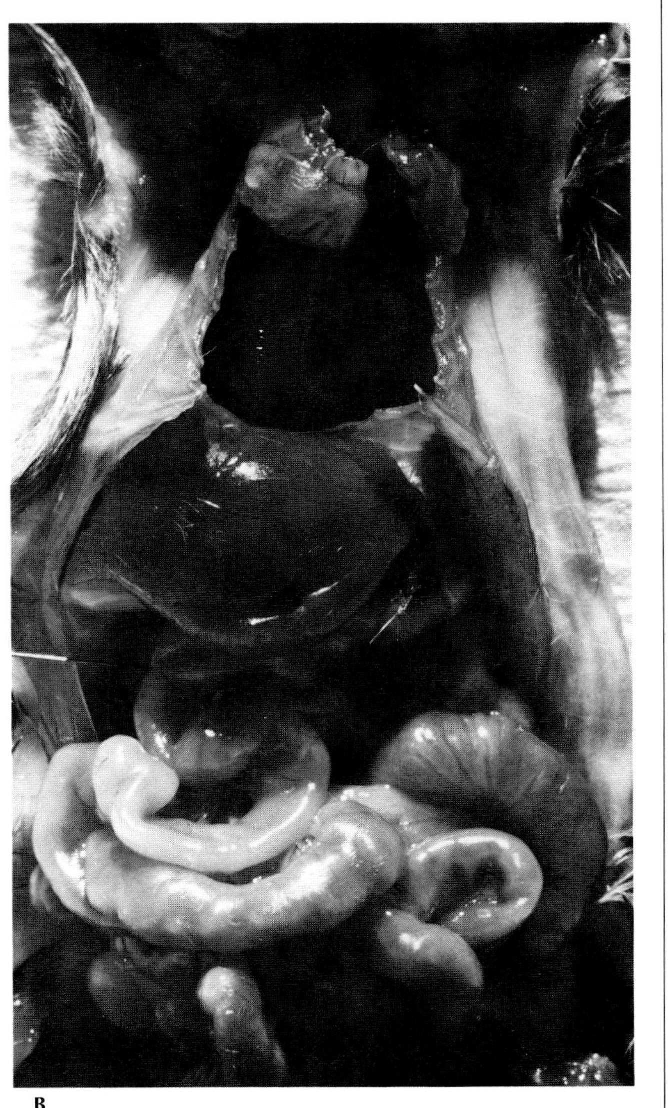

B

PART IV

Related Techniques

Although not properly considered as scientific photography themselves, there are certain photographic procedures that are related in the sense that they are much used in connection with scientific work. This portion of the book will describe those related photographic techniques that are most often needed.

CHAPTER 14
Copying

A great deal of copying is done in conjunction with scientific research and, although there are standard references in the field (see Kodak publications AM-2 and M-1), some coverage here is desirable. Ordinary documentary copy can generally be handled most economically by commercial firms or library copying services, but where more than normal care is required or it is otherwise necessary to do the work oneself, some special knowledge is required. Photostating, reflex copy, machine methods such as Xerox, diazo processes, and other such special techniques will not be covered here; the following discussion treats only straight photographic copying.

COPYRIGHT

Before engaging in copy work, you should refer to standard sources on copyright law (see the book by Hattery and Bush, 1964). Violations of copyright can be both embarrassing and expensive. Academic use of copyrighted materials in the United States has traditionally been regarded as permissible, but it has been a courtesy, not a right. At present, American copyright law is under extensive review, with substantial new legislation pending. There have been recent changes in copyright law in other countries, and more can be expected. You have an obligation to know and understand the provisions under which you will be working. When in doubt, consult a lawyer who is expert in such matters. It will help if you view the copyright laws as a justifiable protection of the substantial investments of time, energy, and money made by the authors and publishers of printed matter.

LIGHTING

The standard lighting setup for copying is two lamps, one on each side of and equidistant from the original copy material, and each set at about a 35–40° angle to the copy surface. This results in an approximately evenly lit elliptical area, which must be somewhat larger than the original copy; its size is varied by adjusting the lamp-to-subject distance (see Figure 64).

For accurate reproduction it is essential that the optical axis of the camera be perpendicular to the copy surface. This can be attained in several ways: by measuring the distances between all the components, by measuring the subject on the ground glass (this is practical only with large cameras), or by optical means (the Hasselblad company markets an optical device for this purpose). Except for engineering and similarly exacting uses, it is usually sufficient just to get close enough to a true perpendicular that measurement of the resulting photograph will reveal no irregularities.

To align a tripod-mounted camera for copying in a horizontal setup, you first choose a comfortable camera height. Then apply a strip of black tape down the wall, vertically, with a short cross strip at the camera-lens height. At the floor, run the strip out perpendicularly from the wall, beyond the expected camera position. Center the copy material on the cross on the wall; center the tripod (by its center post) over the floor line, and keep it centered each time a change of focus necessitates moving the camera. With the camera lens at the height of the wall cross, centering the subject on the ground-glass viewing screen will provide a rectilinear image.

The original copy material must, of course, be held as flat as possible. Where absolute flatness cannot be achieved, as with tightly bound books or with material that has been folded or creased, such gutters and creases should be parallel to the lighting axis. This will minimize any shadows or highlight reflections at these points. If possible, folded or creased material should be dry mounted to a stiff card, to flatten it for copying (see Chapter 17 for mounting techniques).

LINE COPY

Line drawings, such as the text figures in this book, are examples of subjects suitable for what is called *line copy.* So are sections of printed text that might be copied out of books or similar sources. Most copying of these materials is now done by means of machine processes, such as Xerox copying; but when you wish to accomplish size changes greater than such machines are capable of, when you wish to produce slides for projection, or when you want exceptionally high-quality reproduction for subsequent publication, then photographic copying with a camera is appropriate.

To be worth the trouble, the originals for photographic line copying must be of good quality. Sketches made with fountain pen, ball-point pen, or pencil are rarely suitable. Ordinary typescript is very poor, and electric typing is good only if the machine used was in good adjustment and if the typing itself was done flawlessly, preferably with a carbon ribbon, not cloth. Electric typescript may not come out pure black, but the shade of grey produced should be even throughout, with no faded portions of letters. In drawings, all lines should be a uniform solid black, without unintentional breaks or grey areas. There should be no excessive variation in line thickness. Some variation may be needed for purposes of discrimination or emphasis, but you may have photographic problems with broad and heavy lines combined with fine, spidery lines.

The object of line copy is usually to produce prints or transparencies in which there is no highlight or shadow detail—that is, copy in which all lines are pure black and the background is pure white everywhere. This is most easily done with medium-to-large-sized cameras through the use of "lith"-type films. These are extremely high-contrast, thin-base films of great dimensional stability, usually orthochromatic in sensitivity (though panchromatic films of this type can be obtained), very slow in speed, and designed primarily for use in the printing industry. (The extremely high contrast, which makes the very black lines and pure white backgrounds possible, is also what makes the evenness of the lines in the original copy important.) These films offer very high resolution and provide excellent fine-detail rendering and very sharp line edges. Ordinary films have

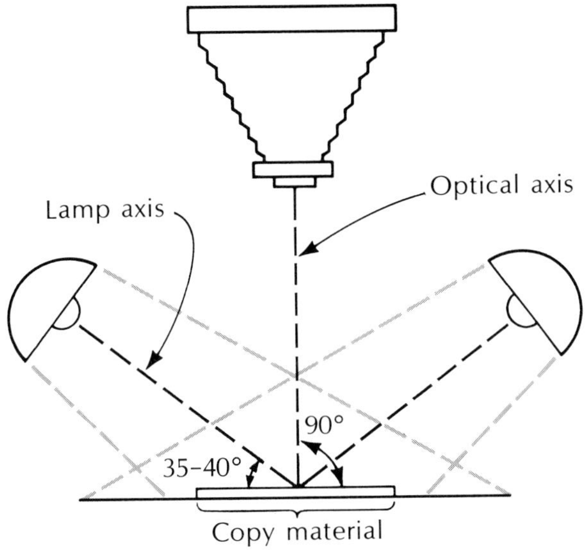

FIGURE 64
Setup and lighting for copying with a vertically mounted camera. The best contrast between black type or lines and white paper occurs when the lighting angle is about 35–40°. With unusually large copy, the lighting can be made more even by aiming each lamp at the *far* edge of the subject rather than at the middle.

A Side view of the setup, shown as used for relatively small copy.
B Top view, from the camera position. If a crease or binding gutter is aligned with the lamp axes, it will be less conspicuous in the copy. Lighting across a crease will exaggerate its appearance.

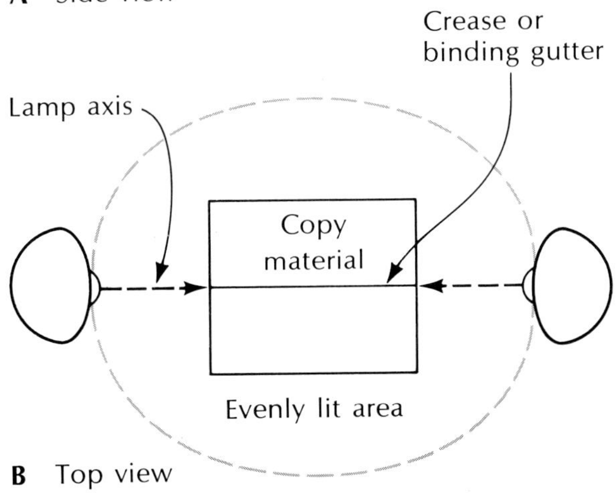

neither the contrast nor the resolution capabilities to give good results with line copy.

For 35 mm use there are available special, high-resolution films, now usually panchromatic, that can deliver either high or normal contrasts, depending upon the processing used. These films are also very low in speed—but copy doesn't move much. (Certain of these films can yield excellent high-resolution results in general photography if correctly used—see Chapter 7.)

In photographing inked line copy, particularly of large sizes, a peculiar problem may arise. When examining the ground-glass image or the finished print, parts of lines near the edges may appear light or even white, instead of the expected black. This is due to specular reflection on the ink surface itself, and occurs where the paper surface is slightly rough and has produced a reflective inked surface at an angle sufficient to throw light into the lens. Slight bending of smooth papers may also produce this effect. Shifting the lights a little will usually eliminate the problem.

A surprising number of photographers seem to think that it doesn't much matter what exposure you give to line copy in making a photographic print. *This is not so.* The correct printing exposure for a line negative should be as carefully determined as for any continuous-tone negative. Underexposure will yield a grey line that will reproduce poorly. The much more common overexposure markedly reduces line sharpness, rounds off line intersections, and increases line widths. Sharp, crisp, black lines are achieved only with correct printing exposure. The great majority of line-copy prints that I have seen showed significant evidence of overexposure in printing. To see the effect for yourself, make a test strip (see pages 17–18) the next time you print line negatives.

CONTINUOUS-TONE COPY

Anything that is not strictly line copy must be considered to be continuous-tone copy. In this category are original photographs, halftone reproductions, such as the plates in this book, most etchings and engravings, pencil and casual pen sketches, and so on. If the original material has any appreciable variations in tone within it, it falls into this category. Material that superficially resembles line copy may, upon close examination, prove to contain continuous tones.

Other types of material that must be regarded as continuous-tone copy are chromatograms, electrophoresis materials, sonograms, paintings, and color slides (the latter are treated in a separate section, below).

Black-and-white continuous-tone copying is best done with large cameras using one of the specially designed continuous-tone copy films. Exactly correct exposure and development are necessary for accurate reproduction.

If the original material is colored, a panchromatic film of normal capabilities should be used to render the relative brightnesses roughly as the eye sees them. Selective filtering can also be used here to emphasize some colors over others.

COPYING IN COLOR

The copying of color materials in color is most commonly done to provide a projection slide, either because the original material is not readily projectable with an opaque projector or because easy portability is important. Copying for color reproduction in printed matter is a highly complex process and is best left to experts in the printing trades.

The main requirements for a film to be used in making color projection slides are reasonable accuracy in the color reproduction, good contrast, and high resolution. At present, Kodachrome-II, Type A (for tungsten lighting), and Kodachrome 25 daylight film seem to be the two best choices for 35 mm work. For the less commonly seen $3\frac{1}{4} \times 4$-inch slides, the 120-size color transparency films can all be used, though I prefer not to use films that are faster than ASA 64. The very fast color films tend to be somewhat lacking in color fidelity, are grainy, and are lower in contrast than the slower films.

Color copying can be done with either tungsten lighting or direct sunlight, as long as the film and the light source are correctly balanced. Do not use fluorescent lighting—it cannot be balanced for dependable color fidelity because it is not an incandescent source. Furthermore, certain pigments will change unpredictably and drastically in color (e.g., from red to green) when copied onto color films by fluorescent light.

Large original paintings and other large colored flatwork can be most readily copied by sunlight, which will ensure evenness of lighting (you may find it very hard to light large areas evenly with tungsten sources). A good setup for making a sunlight copy is given in Figure 65, which shows a horizontally mounted camera as seen from above. Working between 10 A.M. and 3 P.M. will avoid difficulties in color balance that arise from the sky coloring in early morning and late afternoon.

Surface reflections on paintings, either as an overall haze or as a series of small glints, can be eliminated by using artificial lights, arranged for copying and polarized as described on page 76. Bright lights and wide diaphragm openings will shorten exposure times and preclude reciprocity failure, with its annoying color shifts. Polarizing filters are of little use when copying by sunlight, having no effect on overall haze reflections but sometimes affording partial relief where a convoluted surface produces small reflections, some of which may be polarized to a degree.

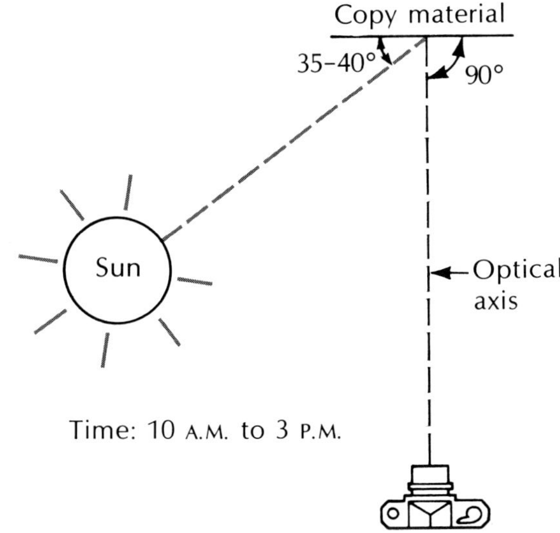

FIGURE 65
Copying by sunlight. Direct sunlight is excellent for copying large originals; because of the great distance of the source, there is no falloff of light across the subject, no matter what its size. For very large originals it may be the only practical method.

COPYING COLOR TRANSPARENCIES TO BLACK-AND-WHITE

The copying of color transparencies, or slides, is often done to provide a black-and-white print for publication, when the original photography was done only in color and reshooting is not practical. It is often not a good practice to leave this to the printer, since you are the best judge of how the print should appear. For example, selective color filtering may be needed to differentiate important tones. There is a rather wide variety of methods that can be used for copying slides, but only a few will be described here.

Owners of 35 mm cameras may find that one of the several commercially available slide-copying devices can be used with their equipment. Your dealer will be able to tell you, and instructions will be provided with the equipment. Properly used, these devices can yield quite satisfactory copies.

For those with other equipment there are two simple methods that can produce excellent results. The first is to place the color slide in the negative carrier of a photo-enlarger and project it on a piece of panchromatic film placed on the baseboard, as in normal enlarging. The work must be done in total darkness to avoid fogging the film. Perhaps the most convenient variation of this method is that in which a Polaroid Land film holder is inverted under the enlarger, and Polaroid P/N film is used to produce a good black-and-white negative of $3\frac{1}{4} \times 4\frac{1}{4}$-inch dimensions. (This was described on page 165, as a method of transmitted-light photomacrography, and the setup for it is shown in Figure 45; Color Plate IIA was copied by this means from transparency form to Polacolor 2 prints, prior to reproduction here.)

Another good method is to set up your equipment for diffuse transmitted light, as described for the low-power photography of geological thin sections on page 220, and illustrated in Figure 55A. For best results, use a black card, with a suitably sized hole, as a support. With the transparency placed over the hole and protected from top lighting, no light gets through to the camera except through the slide being copied. A variation of this method uses a cold-light illuminator, such as the cold-cathode head from certain types of diffusion enlargers, inverted under the camera, with the slide and the black-card mask set on it.

In making black-and-white copy negatives of color transparencies, the makeup of most color transparency films and the color sensitivity of panchromatic films coincide in such a way that significant improvement in appearance of the final print is gained by using a Wratten 8 medium yellow filter; I have done this in about 75% of the slides that I have copied. You should always consider the use of such a filter in any slide copying. In addition, as noted earlier, other color filtering may be needed for tone differentiation.

Many, perhaps most, black-and-white copy negatives made from color transparencies exhibit one notable trait: they are extremely high in contrast. To combat this, it should be standard practice to develop in very low-contrast developers. Printing can be simplified and improved through the use of divided development, which both lowers the overall contrast and slightly redistributes the contrasts. (See the article by Farber, 1962, or the book by Dignan, 1972, for methods of low-contrast negative development and divided print development.) Polaroid P/N film produces a negative of low contrast, and so needs no special treatment.

It is well to remember that the quality of the final result is limited by the quality of the original slide. Try to use only slides that are sharp and clear and in which the lighting is suitable for print reproduction.

SLIDE DUPLICATION

The duplication of color slides is a highly technical process, if both colors and contrasts are to be closely matched. It is therefore usually best left to qualified professionals. If you feel the need to do it yourself on a less demanding level, however, there are certain things to take note of.

Color transparency films are less than perfect in their reproduction of the colors of subjects, being made, as they are, of three or more layers of filtered emulsions. Therefore, if you copy a slide on the same variety of film, very noticeable color shifts will be introduced. The best practice, if you want to try slide duplication casually, is to copy onto a dissimilar film, e.g., Kodachrome to Ektachrome or to GAF color film. (Special slide-duplication films are made that are of relatively low contrast and that match well to films of the same manufacturer. However, they are available only in long rolls and are not very suitable for small operations.)

It is possible to do limited color correction in casual transparency copying. You should start, of course, by balancing the light source to the film being used. Then, after a trial in which you discover troublesome color shifts, you can use color-correction (CC) filters to true up the colors in a second trial. A reasonably practical method for the nontechnical worker is to place the offending duplicate slide next to the original, on an ASA standard viewing box (see your dealer for recommendations). You can then lay various color-correction filters over the incorrect slide until you come to a good guess as to the needed corrective filtering. Another trial is then made, and the process repeated as needed. Keep in mind that with this method you can achieve fairly close matches to two of the three color layers of the film, but not the third. Therefore, you have to decide what is to be sacrificed. For example, I have let a sky go green in order to retain reasonable accuracy in the colors of vegetation. You must make your own choices.

You can also expect that the contrast of a slide will be substantially increased in copying, unless you go through a very technical and extensive procedure of film masking, which is best left to an expert. You may find it at least helpful to copy onto one of the faster color slide materials, such as high-speed Ektachrome, since these are of lower basic contrast than the slower films.

COPYING TIGHTLY BOUND BOOK PAGES

Many books are bound very tightly and cannot be opened wide enough for good copying of the pages without the danger of breaking the binding, if the traditional flat-open method is to be used. There are two methods that can be used to copy partly opened books, however.

In the first, and simpler, method you open the book to a 90° angle, using an adjunct to the copy board consisting only of a base block to hold the uncopied pages out of the way. A rubber band will suffice to hold them against the book's cover board, out of view of the lens. If the facing page is covered with a piece of black paper there will be no reflection of light from it onto the copied page, which would otherwise show uneven lighting halfway across the page.

A second method, somewhat more complex, can be used with old or rare books that can scarcely stand opening at all. Here the book need only be opened to 45°. A high-quality first-surface mirror of adequate size in a 45° mounting is then inserted into the partly opened book. The camera is placed so that it looks into the book with the lens axis parallel to the page to be copied, at 90° across the page and, of course, at 45° to the surface of the mirror. The page to be copied will be seen clearly, and as far into the gutter as the leading edge of the mirror can safely be placed. The lighting is set up so as to enter the book at a grazing angle across the page, from both ends of the book.

A first-surface mirror must be used because an ordinary second-surface mirror—with its silvering on the *back* of the glass—would give a double image: one from the silvered side, as expected, and the other, somewhat less distinct but sufficient to confuse the issue, from the front surface of the mirror glass.

It should be remembered that the printing will appear reversed, because it is being seen in a mirror. Therefore the negative must be reversed when it is printed.

CHAPTER 15
Slide Making

People in the sciences often need projection slides for presentation at meetings, for classroom use, or for illustration of appeals for research funds. There are numerous ways in which slides can be made, but I will describe only a few methods, each of which offers certain significant advantages. As in the discussion of copying, I will consider only those methods that make use of conventional photographic equipment and materials.

STANDARDS FOR SLIDE ORIGINALS

In making up or gathering materials to serve as originals for reproduction as projection slides, the most common errors are the inclusion of too much information on a single slide, the use of excessively complex presentations (such as multiple rows of figures, rather than a graph), and the assumption that material printed in articles or books is automatically well suited for projection purposes. The amount of information on any one slide should be strictly limited, because the viewer cannot be expected to remember much detail when there is but the single brief chance to scan it. All diagrams, graphs, etc., should be examined critically to see if the same information could be carried by a simpler form of presentation. A good professional illustrator can be of great assistance in the planning stage, as well as when it comes time to draw the material. Conventional maps are very poor as slide originals because they combine large size with very small lettering and symbols. Maps should be redrawn, with all relevant details shown in a scale suitable for slide use.

There are two printed sources that are of significant value in assisting one to design materials for slide presentations. These are Kodak publications S-22, *Effective Lecture Slides,* and S-24, *Legibility—Artwork to Screen,* a pair of brief, inexpensive, and very much to-the-point pamphlets. Every scientist or producer of slides for science should have these available for ready reference.

COPYING ON POLAROID LAND SLIDE FILMS

For sheer rapidity of access, no other photographic process presently on the market equals the Polaroid Land system of making slides by direct positive copying (that is, without the need for an intermediate negative). Polaroid makes two black-and-white slide films: one of high contrast, for line originals, and one of medium contrast, for continuous-tone originals. If all of the manufacturer's directions are carefully followed, the quality of such slides will be very satisfactory. And you can be ready to project within a few minutes after the exposure, if you use the very practical snap-together plastic slide mounts provided by Polaroid, or their equivalent.

Some people consider the Polaroid Land films to be anachronistic in this age of 35 mm photography, since the slides produced are for $3\frac{1}{4} \times 4$-inch projectors. There are two points to consider in this regard.

One is that if you do prefer to use the large slide size—and it offers very attractive screen quality—the Polaroid Land slides are by far the lightest and most portable large slides there are. In fact, I have used Polaroid's plastic slide mounts to contain large film slides made with conventional films, in both color and black-and-white, for clients who wanted to combine large-size quality with easy portability. Aside from having a slight propensity to "pop" during projection, which simply requires refocusing, they serve as well as any other large slides.

The second point is that Polaroid Land slide emulsions are on a thin plastic base that can be cut with ordinary scissors. Therefore you can, if you wish, copy in image sizes suitable for 35 mm framing, perhaps copying as many as four originals per film, and then cut them to fit the snap-together slide mounts that are commercially available for 35 mm films.

At this writing there is no Polaroid Land color transparency film on the market, but there seems reason to believe that one may be forthcoming soon.

COPYING ON 35 MM COLOR FILMS

The simplest method of 35 mm slide making using conventional films is to copy the original material on color transparency film. Either color or black-and-white material, including line copy, can be reproduced quite satisfactorily. Original photographic prints, printed reproductions in either color or black-and-white, line drawings, or such research materials as chromatograms or sonograms can all be made directly into satisfactory slides by standard copying methods.

The technique is not without its limitations, but they are not severe. Line materials may have a slight color cast to the background because the film's contrast is a little low for line work.

Using the fairly new Ektachrome film designed for photomicrography may help here, since it has enhanced contrast.

Black-and-white continuous-tone materials may have a very subtle color toning because neither photographic papers nor the inks used in printing are always totally neutral in color. However, if the film and lighting are properly balanced in the copying process, this is the single best method of making high-quality slides of photographic prints. The most suitable film is Kodachrome-II, Type A, with photoflood lighting, or Kodachrome 25, with sunlight.

COPYING FOR SLIDES WITH BLACK-AND-WHITE NEGATIVE MATERIALS

Although it is a somewhat cumbersome and time-consuming two-step process best suited to relatively large-scale operations, the negative/positive slide-making technique is hard to match for consistently high quality.

You can make slides by contact printing an appropriately sized negative onto another piece of film, but I do not recommend it, because of the potentially serious dust problems (which show up much more severely in slides than in paper prints, and are almost impossible to retouch) and because of the possibility of getting Newton's rings when the two films are pressed together (Newton's rings are alternating light and dark bands caused by optical interference when two translucent surfaces are in uneven contact). Instead, I suggest a projection process.

My preference is to transilluminate the negative and then photograph it with a camera. (A bank of fluorescent tubes, mounted close together and faced with two layers of tracing tissue, or the cold-cathode lamphouse taken from a diffuser enlarger, makes a good light source for this purpose.) One can also place the negative in a photo-enlarger and project the image onto the second film, as in printing.

Line Copy

Excellent line slides can be made in any size desired, from 35 mm up to 8 × 10 inches (the larger sizes would be used in overhead projectors). The best film to use is a good lith-type sheet film, such as Kodak's Kodalith or the equivalent. You can also obtain glass projector-slide plates, in both high and medium contrasts and in 2 × 2-inch and 3¼ × 4-inch sizes, but I prefer to use films because of their greater versatility.

In this procedure the first step is to make a good line negative, exposing long enough to produce a black background when processed, but being careful not to overexpose, as this will tend to fill in fine lines. After processing the negative, transilluminate it and copy it, again using a lith film in the camera.

The smallest size of sheet lith film commonly available is 4 × 5 inches, but this method produces good results even in 35 mm image sizes. Those who have only 35 mm equipment should use Kodak High Contrast Copy film, or an equivalent such as Fuji Microfilm, H & W Control VTE Ultra Pan, or Agfa-Gevaert Microfilm. Exposure determination requires a little experimentation at first. Kodak lists their films as having a speed of ASA 64 for line-copy purposes, but I feel that this produces a negative unduly lacking in density; I therefore recommend using a speed of ASA 32 or perhaps a little less. Otherwise, the method of use is the same as that described for sheet films.

Continuous-Tone Copy

Good slides can be made from any adequate continuous-tone negative, including photomicrographs and general scenes; but if you are making a copy from printed matter or a photoprint, I suggest the use of such professional graphic arts films as Kodak Gravure Copy film or a close equivalent. Sepia-toned originals, such as some old photographs, will require the use of a medium yellow filter on the camera lens for best results—otherwise the contrast will be too low.

The second exposure can be made on a medium- or high-contrast projector-slide plate or on a non-color-sensitive film of the type that Kodak calls Fine Grain Positive (available in sheet form and in 100-foot rolls on 35 mm stock). The contrast can be changed over quite wide ranges by minor changes in processing. For best control, I prefer to use sheet films so that I can vary the developer and development time to match the contrasts for each slide.

DIRECT POSITIVE BLACK-AND-WHITE SLIDES

Another black-and-white slide making method suitable for relatively large-scale operations uses direct positive materials, in which the film in the camera is processed to become the slide, as with color transparency films.

As noted at the beginning of this chapter, there are Polaroid Land direct positive slide films, in both medium and high contrasts, that provide for good-quality, rapid-access slide making.

Among 35 mm camera owners in the United States at this writing, the film most commonly used for making direct positive black-and-white slides is Kodak #2551 Super Speed Copy film. It is not a general-use film, and must be specially ordered through large dealers serving major educational and government institutions. It is available only in 100-foot rolls, in 35 mm size.

Super Speed Copy is a very slow film despite its name, being rated at about ASA 1.2; the correct exposure is best determined by trial, as there is some variation in the speed from batch to batch. My informant, Donald G. Harvey, recommends the use of four 100-watt household bulbs in small desk-lamp-type reflectors, grouped in pairs at about a 3-foot distance on either side of the copy, at the usual 35–40° angle to the surface. For line copy, try an exposure time of 25–30 seconds at *f*/5.6. For continuous-tone copy, a double exposure is required: about 15 seconds at *f*/5.6 for the copy, followed by 5–7 seconds with the copy replaced by a white card. This brief second exposure is a "flash" that lowers the contrast of the film. Varying its length varies the film contrast.

Normal processing, subject to minor variations from batch to batch of film, is about 4 minutes in D-11 developer at 68°F (20°C), in a standard roll-film tank, agitated gently for 3 seconds every 30 seconds. Fixing and washing are done as for other 35 mm films. The reversal of tones is a result of the normal processing.

This method of slide making is especially appropriate in quantity work, as the contrast can be varied at will from frame to frame on the same roll of film. The line slides produced are of very fine quality. The continuous-tone slides are of generally good quality, tending only to lack real blackness in the dark areas, owing to the "flash" method of contrast control. But this is not critically important with most original materials.

Similar slides can be produced on high-resolution films such as H & W Control VTE Pan or

VTE Ultra Pan through the use of H & W Control Reversal developer. The film and developer, and full instructions for their use, are available from the manufacturer (The H & W Company, Box 332, St. Johnsbury, Vt. 05819). Made properly, slides can be obtained that can be projected to unusually large image magnifications without loss of sharpness. The results are otherwise quite similar to those achieved with the materials discussed above, except that the film speeds are substantially faster than that of Kodak Super Speed Copy film; the recommended exposure indexes for VTE Pan and VTE Ultra Pan are 50 and 16, respectively. A disadvantage is the necessity to give a second film exposure partway through the film processing. (See the manufacturer's data sheets for full information on the techniques.)

Direct positive slides can be made on almost any black-and-white film, if you use suitable reversal processing (reversal-processing kits are available from several manufacturers); but I recommend using one of the three systems described above, for their special qualities of rapid access, easy control of contrast, or high resolution.

PRODUCING LINE SLIDES IN COLOR

There are various reasons for wanting your line slides to appear in color. Color slides are, of course, inherently more attractive to the eye than are black-and-whites. More important is that color can be used to differentiate or emphasize certain data, and it thus enables you to make your point more quickly and effectively. It also seems appropriate for use when you are giving a presentation that is illustrated primarily with color transparencies of subject matter, but with occasional line slides to explain and amplify facts. Using the traditional black-on-white line slides would give unexpected visual jolts of glare, as each one came up. It is quite easy to make very readable slides containing color, designed so that there is no impression of glare.

Use of Color Originals

The simplest method is to copy colored originals onto ordinary color transparency films. Colored pencils, pens, or crayons can be used on a colored or black construction-paper background to make any form of original copy desired. Ordinary copying methods will then produce satisfactory color line slides for most purposes. Such slides are most appropriate for relatively informal presentations, but if the artist is skilled they can stand up in any company.

Negative Slides

Another easy method of slide making that spares the audience the glare of traditional black-on-white slides produces negative slides with colored backings. You simply use a high-contrast black-and-white film to make a good, dense negative, and then you mount it with a backing composed of colored transparent plastic or gel. Theatrical lighting gels are both cheap and very satisfactory. Used without the colored backing, the white lines tend to glare unpleasantly, but the colors mute the glare and increase readability. If lines of type or blocks of information are to be differentiated, two or more gels of different colors can be used, each backing the appropriate area of the slide, and held in place with bits of tape or drops of glue. The visual effect is pleasant, and the lines remain very sharp.

A somewhat more direct process uses Ektachrome transparency film which is processed in Kodak C-22 chemicals (used for processing color negative films), as a negative. The technique is described more fully in Kodak publication P-100-17, *Reverse-Text Slides in Color.* If, for instance, you photograph a conventional black-on-white line original through certain color filters, the line material will appear white on a background of the approximate complement of the filter color (for example, a Wratten 4 yellow filter will produce a deep blue background when the color slide film is developed as a negative). The catch is in the nonstandard processing. It cannot be done with the Kodachrome films, but requires the Ektachromes. Some commercial processors will do C-22 processing of these films upon request. Otherwise, you must do it yourself (ordinary color negative films cannot be used because of the overall orange color of their built-in filtering).

A variation of the method uses colored inks or colored tapes on a white backing to make the original copy material. When copied and processed, and without the use of filters, the result is that of complementary-colored lines on a dark—not black, but rather neutral-toned—background.

Negative Prints, Copied

Elaborate graph presentations, such as line graphs with lines in several colors, can be done by making a negative print from a black-and-white line original. This requires that you first make an intermediate positive transparency (a conventional black-on-white line transparency, that is), and then make the print from that. Once the print is dry, it is mounted on a card for convenience in handling, and the white graph lines are overlaid with thin strips of colored, pressure-sensitive tape (these are obtainable in a wide variety of colors and widths in art-supply stores). When finished, the artwork is copied conventionally on Kodachrome or other color transparency film. The effect is of white and colored line materials on a black background. The lettering is usually best left white.

Double-Exposed Color/Black-and-White

There is a simple way to make colored slides from conventional black-on-white line material that project as white lines on deeply colored backgrounds. The effect is pleasant to look at and easy on the eyes. It is best done so as to produce cool-colored slides, as the warmer colors are more likely to produce unpleasant impressions. In my opinion the all-around best color to use is a deep blue.

The first step is to produce a conventional black-and-white line negative on lith film. This is then placed on a light box and photographed on color transparency film. The negative is then removed, and an appropriately colored filter is placed on the camera lens (or a theatrical gel is placed over the light box—either method works just as well). A Wratten 47 deep blue filter produces a nice color effect, as do similarly colored theatrical gels. A second exposure is made, on the same film frame, of the light from the light box as colored by the filter.

The color temperature of the light produced by the box is virtually immaterial, as long as the light is basically white, since the filters used are so deeply colored as to override the normal differences. Thus, fluorescent lamps are, for once, no barrier to color photography.

To gain initial exposure information, read your light meter through the filter and then make a progressive series of trial exposures, each having one stop less exposure than its predecessor. Both exposures of the pair (i.e., of the negative backed with white light, and of the colored light separately) should be of the same length. Record the exposure information for each film frame. After the film is processed, examine the results and make a choice. All subsequent work can then be done with the same camera settings. The processing required is that normally specified for the film, and no special instructions need be given to the processor.

CHAPTER 16

Printing Old Negatives

As the history of modern science lengthens, and with it the history of photography, the reprinting of old negatives has come to be seen as a way of making useful and interesting time-related comparisons, of assisting in the analysis of the scientific methods of long ago, and of giving the present day a previously neglected record of history itself. Thus, the negative has become a document, a research source, a valuable record of the past.

BACKGROUND

Although the Talbotype and its fellow negative/positive processes date back to the very earliest years of photography, the making of photographic negatives became widespread only with the appearance, in the middle of the nineteenth century, of the wet-plate process, in which glass plates were coated with light-sensitive emulsion at the scene of the photograph. Various processes, soon using dry emulsions, were in common use up to the 1920s, and many glass-plate negatives are still used in special applications. Flexible-based films were introduced in the latter portion of the nineteenth century, and came into nearly universal use by the second decade of the twentieth.

Many museums and academic departments associated with colleges and universities have files of both glass and film negatives dating well back over the past hundred years, or more. Unfortunately, too many such collections are improperly stored and incompletely catalogued. There are often found in old filing cabinets or tumbled into cardboard cartons, and carelessly stored in some of the more remote recesses of the institution. If these often valuable records are not to be irretrievably lost, time and money must be spent to resurrect and catalogue them, and see to their proper storage.

FILM NEGATIVES

Although historically they came later, film negatives require first attention because they have special characteristics. It is both dangerous and usually illegal to store old film negatives without proper care, especially the early nitrate-based films. With age, these tend to become very brittle, and may crumble at a touch. Alternatively, they may stick together in inseparable clumps. Worse yet, old negatives made prior to the introduction of modern "safety" films are subject to unpredictable spontaneous combustion, and once ignited they burn fiercely, producing noxious fumes. They are therefore a danger to the personnel and facilities of the storing institution, as well as to themselves and to other items stored nearby. ("Safety" films are so labeled in a notice stamped along the film edge.)

The first step in salvaging such materials must be the immediate segregation and removal of all suspect film negatives to safe, fireproof storage facilities *specifically designed for this purpose.* Then a well-trained professional should be given the job of copying all unsafe negatives onto new duplicating-film stock as soon as possible. The Smithsonian Institution, in Washington, D.C., has done much of the recent research into techniques of restoration and duplication of old photographic materials, and should be queried for all relevant data. I will not attempt here to discuss advanced techniques for the handling, restoration, and storing of old films.

GLASS NEGATIVES

Negatives made on glass-based emulsions do not present the fire danger of the nitrate-based films, nor do they otherwise deteriorate in the same manner. Other than outright breakage of the glass, there are several types of damage that can occur over long time periods.

Aging of the emulsion may cause it to separate from the glass backing along the edges, with ensuing brittleness and physical breakup. Fortunately, this is an edge effect only, and usually does little or no damage to the main image. When plates that received incomplete initial fixation are stored stacked and unprotected, light coming in from the edges can result in slow chemical changes that produce staining or fading of the image, beginning at the exposed edges and working its way inward.

Fungus and mildew can attack any photographic emulsion (new or old, color or black-and-white, glass or film) if the humidity is not carefully controlled. The effect can appear as localized circles of image degradation or as an overall pattern of fine lines. There is very little that can be done to repair this damage once it has occurred, but there are processes that can arrest its further progress (as a starting point, see Kodak publications AE-22 and C-24). See Plate 49 for a recent print made from an old, damaged glass-plate negative.

A third problem, and the only one whose solution can safely be undertaken by a nonprofessional, is the formation of a scum on the base side of glass negatives. Some of this is residue from antihalation coatings (usually reddish in color), the rest being unidentified deposits, possibly from pollutants in the air. I never try to clean or repair old emulsions, but I do carefully clean the *base side only* of old glass-plate negatives, to remove this scum and thereby improve the print quality. As a cleaning solvent I use distilled water, condensed from my breath onto the plate, followed by immediate careful polishing with a soft cloth. With stubborn deposits I sometimes lightly dampen a spot on the cloth with saliva, which is a remarkably good organic solvent. I use no liquid solvent as such, to avoid the possibility of its finding its way to the emulsion side of the plate.

Glass-plate negatives must be handled with great care to prevent breakage. Also, I have learned (the hard way) never to print them in an enlarger using any form of incandescent illumination, whether condensered or diffused, because of the heat that can be generated; instead, I use only enlargers with cold-cathode light heads for this work. Glass-plate negatives cannot be guaranteed to withstand even the mild heating that comes from incandescent lamps in photo-enlargers, without cracking. They are not *likely* to crack, but the risk is not worth taking with unique and irreplaceable materials.

CONDITIONS AFFECTING THE PRINTABILITY OF OLD NEGATIVES

There is what seems to me to be an erroneous impression abroad that old negatives are, as a class, different from other photographic negatives, and in some way more difficult to print. Aside from the fact that age provides the opportunity for all sorts of damage to occur, there is no greater difficulty in printing old negatives than new ones. And new ones can have faults, too. I believe that this impression of a difference in kind is due to a failure to fully understand the nature of the films and the operating conditions that prevailed in earlier photography.

Neither films nor plates in earlier times had panchromatic emulsions; they were either non-color-sensitive or they were orthochromatic in sensitivity. A surprising number of younger photographers have apparently never used a black-and-white emulsion that was not panchromatic, and hence they are not prepared for the appearance of prints made from other types of negatives. Among the visual effects to be expected are a relative lack of contrast in the sky areas of outdoor pictures and a failure to record reds and oranges.

Early photographers generally lacked the means to measure light accurately, so the exposure of films was not well controlled. Overexposure tended to "block up" the highlight areas of a picture, and they consequently print to very low contrast. Since the emulsions were very slow, and photographers had to strain constantly to counter the effects of camera and subject motion, there was a great likelihood of marginal underexposure. This results in poor rendition of dark-area detail.

Although you can do nothing about the failure of emulsions to record light of certain

PLATE 49 ▶

Printing Old Negatives, I.

Breaker Bay, Farallon Islands, 1885, photographed by W. Otto Emerson on a $6\frac{1}{2} \times 8\frac{1}{2}$-inch glass plate (printed in 1973 by the author). This plate is an unnumbered possession of the Museum of Vertebrate Zoology, University of California, Berkeley. Although the basic image is intact, most of the common problems of old negatives are present. There are mildew spots, edge degradation of the image, and, at the right edge, minor emulsion frilling.

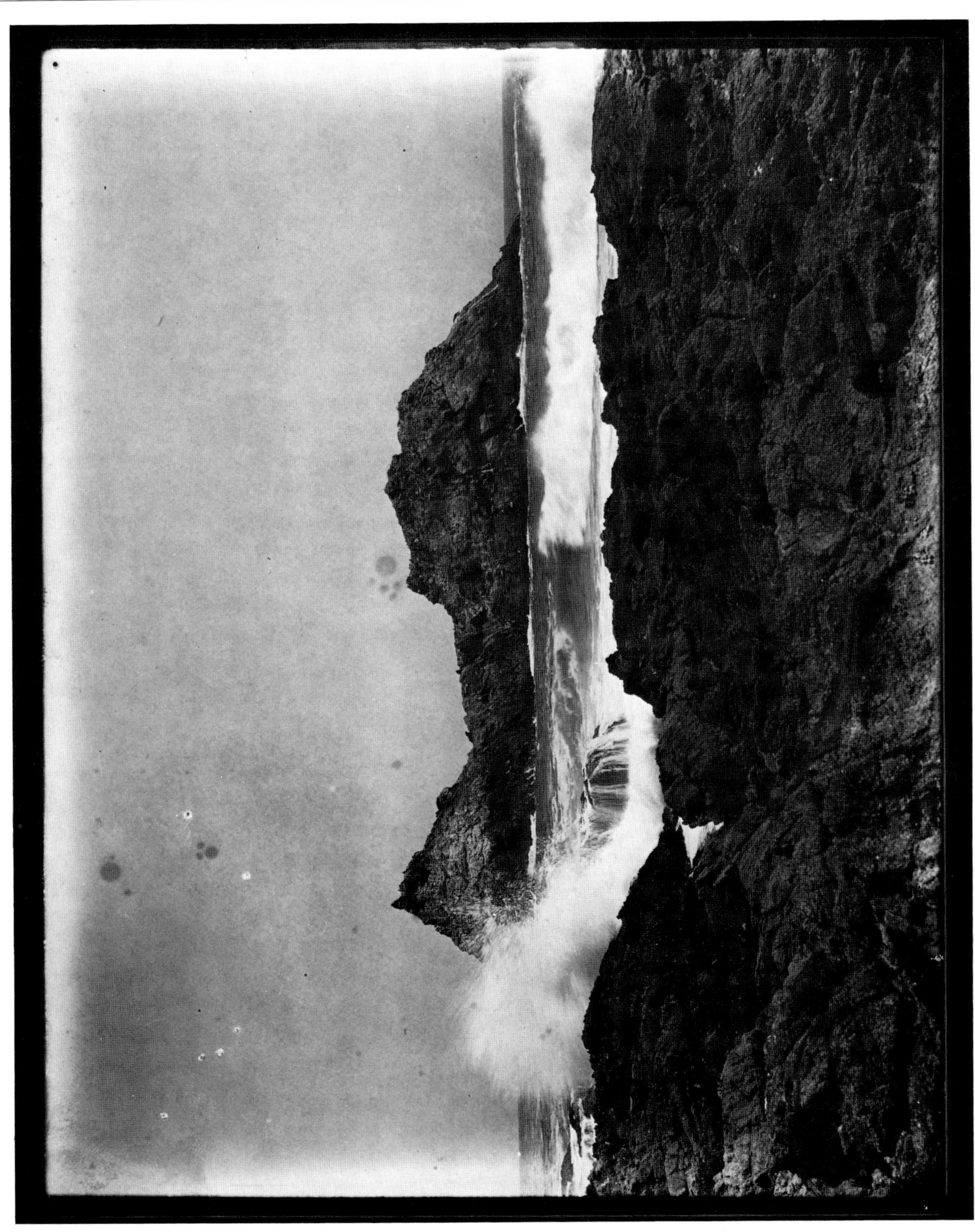

wavelengths, you can take steps that will improve the printed appearance of the images that were recorded.

The fading or staining that appears in some incompletely fixed or improperly stored negatives is not readily countered. I suggest that restoration of these materials be left to a specialist in the field. In the meantime, since the main subject matter of most pictures tends to be concentrated in the center of the negative, it may be possible to crop off such damaged portions in printing some pictures, without undue loss of information.

PRINTING METHODS

Printing old negatives is very much like printing any other negatives, unless you run into one or more of the problems mentioned in the previous section.

If your only aim is to increase the visibility and contrast of sky tones, you can increase the overall contrast by using appropriate grades of printing paper. Where doing so would adversely affect other elements of the picture, you can increase the contrast locally. Sky areas are often overexposed naturally because of the inherently greater brightness there in most weather conditions. Thus, you must give extra printing exposure to those areas of the negative in any event, using the technique of differential printing (see Chapter 1). If this additional exposure is done with a high-contrast printing filter on the enlarger lens, using variable-contrast paper, your objective of a local increase in contrast will be achieved. Variations of this technique can be used to solve any localized contrast problem, allowing you to reduce or increase the contrast as needed, if you have analyzed the problem correctly and if you are careful.

A marginal but generalized underexposure can be countered most readily through the use, singly or collectively, of the following expedients:

PLATE 50 ▶

Printing Old Negatives, II.

A General View of Camp, Jenning's Lodge, Oregon, 1906, photographed by W. L. Finley on a 5 × 7-inch glass plate (printed in 1973 by the author). Although there is no significant negative degradation, there are two notable problems. There is considerable light flare through the trees at the top left, owing to the lesser ability of earlier films to minimize halation, and this requires skill in printing if the effect is to be reduced to a tolerable level. In addition, there was much off-axis lens aberration, so only the center of the picture is really sharp. This cannot be corrected.

B Young Condor on Post, Steamboat in Background, Jenning's Lodge, Oregon, 1906, photographed by W. L. Finley and H. Bohlman on a 5 × 7-inch glass plate (printed in 1973 by the author). This is an excellent example of high-quality photography. Both of the glass plates reproduced on this page are the property of the Museum of Vertebrate Zoology, University of California, Berkeley.

Finley and Bohlman did extensive field research on California Condors in the area of Altadena, California, in 1906, traversing extremely precipitous terrain and doing excellent view-camera photography under very tough field conditions. When they returned to their home territory in Oregon they took with them the young bird shown in these two pictures. A number of their pictures from this period—but not these two—were published in C. B. Koford, *The California Condor*, Dover Publications, New York, 1953.

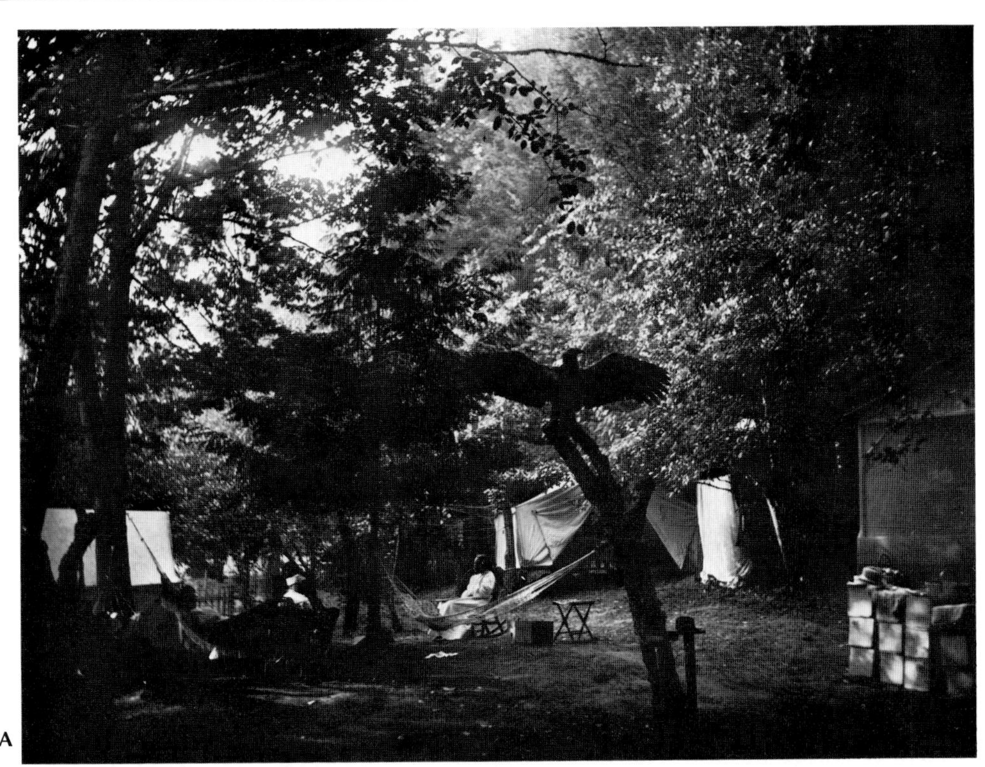

A

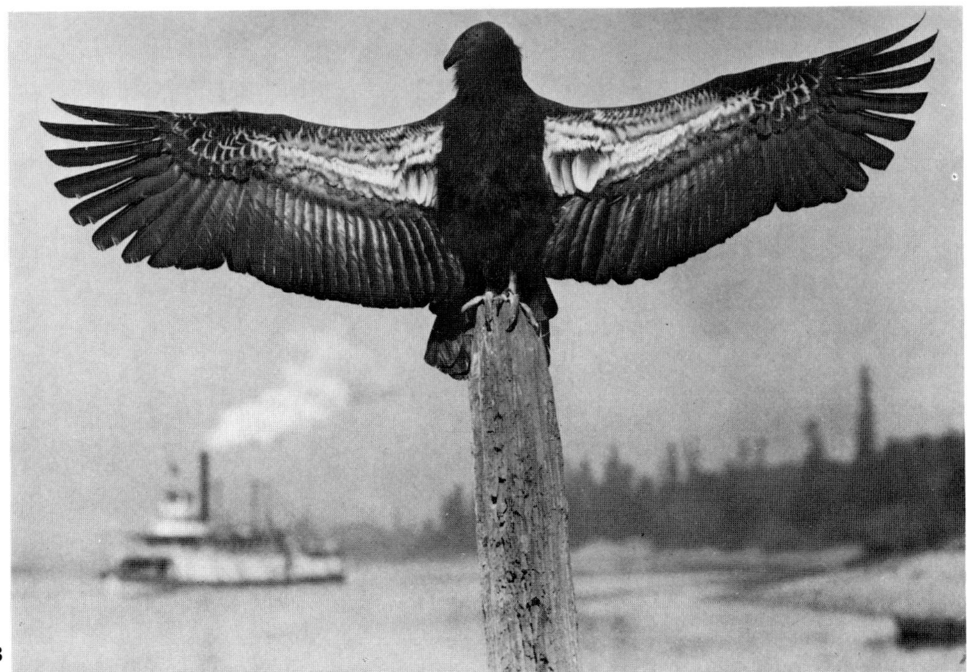

B

1. Printing to overall higher contrast.
2. Increasing the contrast selectively in the dark areas.
3. Making use of divided development in printing.

The technique of divided development is described in detail on page 21. Development is limited locally by the amount of developing agent that has penetrated the emulsion in the first immersion; when that is exhausted in the second solution, no further development takes place, no matter how long the second immersion. The more heavily exposed dark areas exhaust the developing agent first, and action stops there while the middle tones and light areas catch up somewhat. The overall contrast is lessened, but more importantly, the dark areas do not get as fully developed as usual. The effect is to equalize the contrast range throughout the entire image area, so that there is printed contrast in all tonal categories.

Do not be misled into thinking that divided development is best for *all* negatives. It is not especially good for those with normal exposure or slight overexposure. But for negatives that are a little underexposed, it can be the saving grace.

Because the overall contrast is reduced in divided development, you must counteract this effect to get the best quality possible in the final print. The usual procedure is to make the best possible print using normal development. Then, using the next higher grade of paper (in terms of contrast), you make a new print with about 10% less exposure time (or you make a new test strip). The exposure must be exact, because you can play no games with the development time—but that is as it should be anyway. Then, when the new print is processed in divided developer, the result should be a print in which the middle and light tones look about as they did in the normally processed print, but in which the dark-area contrasts are substantially increased and improved. The effect will be to substantially improve the appearance of the print as a whole. (See Plates 49 and 50 for examples of recent prints made from old negatives.)

PART V

Final Preparation for Publication and Viewing

CHAPTER 17

Preparing Photographs for Publication

In this chapter the publishers referred to are those who publish textbooks and monographs for the world of science, and the editorial staffs of scientific journals. (The practices followed in presenting materials to trade-book publishers or to the editors of consumer magazines are generally similar, but may differ in some significant details. The latter is particularly true when the author or photographer is new to publication and is submitting material on speculation to a large-circulation magazine.)

PUBLISHERS' STANDARDS

Many scientific journals and some limited-circulation magazines, as well as most publishers of nonfiction books, provide printed instructions concerning the preparation of manuscripts and their illustrations. The journals usually include these in one or more issues per year; they are seldom more than about one page in length. If you plan to submit material to such a journal, it is important to read these instructions early, and follow them to the letter. I have seen a photograph rejected for publication because it was $\frac{1}{64}$ inch larger than the specified maximum size.

Book publishers provide much longer and more detailed instructions to authors, often running to many pages and occasionally approaching book length themselves. The difference is due to the much greater complexity and flexibility in the structure of books. Failure to follow these instructions in preparing material for publication can lead to lengthy delays in the editing and production processes, and the extra expense may be cause for rejection of an otherwise worthy manuscript.

The directions regarding illustrations are usually quite short and easy to understand. They also tend to be fragmentary, because the nature of the illustration program can vary widely according to the subject in question. There are two primary factors to consider in regard to photographs, in particular.

Paper Surface and Type

Most publishers require a glossy surface on prints submitted for publication. The reason for this is that prints having textured surfaces *must* be avoided. The texture is difficult to deal with in the photocopying processes used in the making of printing plates. The usual requirement for photoprints made for publication is that the paper be of the glossy type. It is not usually important whether the surface was actually glossed. Thus, a print made on glossy-surfaced conventional paper could simply be air-dried to a semi-gloss. This is easier to accomplish than a good glossing job.

One of the newer introductions to the photographic market is the resin-coated (RC) paper, a plastic-based material that comes to a high gloss in simple air drying, lies reasonably flat without being mounted, and has much less need for washing in processing than do conventional printing papers. Glossy-type RC papers are, in my opinion, the best materials to use for printing photographs for publication.

To Mount, or Not

Many publishers specifically tell you not to mount your photographs. The reasons for this are to allow the designer some flexibility in laying out the pages and to avoid complications introduced by improper mounting. When you are submitting material to such publishers, follow their instructions, but be sure to give full instructions of your own if a plate is to have more than one picture in it, if it is to have labeling applied by the publisher, if it is to be reduced by a certain amount, etc.

If you are submitting to a publishing house that asks for mounted prints, or to one that allows it (and you wish to do it), the following detailed information will be useful.

ADHESIVES FOR PRINT MOUNTING

Prints can be applied to stiff backings with almost any adhesive, but some are more suitable than others. Rubber cement should be avoided completely in mounting photographs, because it contains substances that will probably stain the photographic image fairly quickly. White glue can be used, but it is very difficult to mount a print with it without causing the print to wrinkle. It can be used to tack a print down by its corners to a piece of typing paper when you are submitting a simple report, but it is a poor choice for preparing material for publication.

The two best mounting methods for professional-looking presentations are heat mounting and pressure-sensitive mounting. The former, usually called dry mounting (as opposed to wet mounting with glues or pastes), is by far the best established method and produces a very nice, flat piece. Pressure-sensitive mountings are of three types: (1) commercial mount boards having a pressure-sensitive coating, which is usually covered with a protective facing that is peeled off when you use the board; (2) spray-can adhesives, with which you apply a sticky film to a mount board of your choice; and (3) so-called double-stick tapes, which can be applied in strips or all over the back of a print, to stick it to a mount board of your choice. Double-stick tapes also have a protective facing that is peeled off to prepare the tape for use. I use them for applying labels to prints, as well as for mounting certain types of prints.

MOUNTING OF PRINTS FOR PLATES

Any prints that are to be sent to the publisher mounted should be placed on boards, using the techniques described below.

The mount board should not be overly large. I have found it best for journal-article and book illustrations to use an $8\frac{1}{2} \times 11$-inch board so that it can conveniently be packaged along with typescript. The actual picture size should never be less than the intended final plate size. Query your editor for dimensions, if they are not supplied in the publisher's general instructions. Many publishers prefer to have oversized photographs that can be reduced in the printing process. A typical allowance is for a 50% reduction. I prefer to find out the plate size to be used, and print to those dimensions; but there are exceptions to all rules. If you know the final dimensions, you may wish to write them on the mount border or on the back side.

Each mounted plate should be marked for orientation; the usual way is to write "top," with an upward-pointing arrow, in the mount border on the appropriate side. Unmounted prints should be similarly marked on their back side. Use pencil only, and *use a very light touch,* so as not to cause visible impressions on the print surface. Also write in full identifying information, including your name and the plate number, still in pencil. At least as important as anything else is the image magnification factor, where applicable. Ideally, this should be written on the back of a print as soon as it's dry. If the print is to be reduced for publication, the reduction factor must be taken into account in the magnification figure given in the plate caption.

Conventional Black-and-White Prints

The preferred method of mounting conventional black-and-white prints is dry mounting. In this technique you use commercial dry-mount tissue, which is available in photo supply stores. It looks rather like a sheet of waxed paper, and the individual sheets are separated in packaging by sheets of pinkish tissue. Convenient use requires two tools: a dry-mount press, which comes in several forms but is essentially a heated pressure platen (many camera stores have a dry-mount press available, either free or for rent, for the use of customers), and a tacking iron, which is used to stick the print loosely to the mount board before inserting it into the press.

You can dry mount with a household pressing iron, as long as it produces *no steam*—otherwise the print will be spoiled. Only the very lowest temperature setting can be used, and even that may be too hot for some types of prints—particularly color prints and Polaroid prints. The procedure for dry mounting is as follows:

1. Place the print face down on a smooth, clean surface, such as a clean blotter or a piece of smooth mount board.
2. Apply a sheet of dry-mount tissue to the back, using a size that slightly overlaps all

four sides of the image area of the print. Then use the tacking iron to attach it at the center of the back of the print, being careful not to mark the print through too much pressure. If the print sticks to the tissue when you pick up the tissue and shake it, it is adequately attached.

3. Trim the print and the dry-mount tissue together to assure that both are exactly the same size and shape. All corners should be square and all edges smooth and straight. Either guillotine or rotary-type print trimmers can be used, if kept adequately sharp. It is almost impossible to trim a print adequately with scissors.

4. Lay the trimmed print, with its attached tissue, face up on the mount board (suitable boards in a variety of surfaces, thicknesses, and colors are available in photo supply stores, but a smooth white board—either single or double thickness—is best for publication use). Center and align the print on the board. Then, carefully lifting each corner of the print in turn, without lifting the dry-mount tissue, use the tacking iron to fasten the tissue to the board, thus definitely locating the print and preventing it from moving in the press.

5. Place the mount with its loosely attached print face up in the dry-mount press. A protective sheet should be placed on top before pressing (you can use clean, heavy-duty brown wrapping paper, but you may prefer to use the commercially produced sheets made for this purpose). Then put the press down on the sandwich, and keep it there for 20–30 seconds. At the end of that time the print should be smoothly and permanently bonded to the mount board.

The temperature of most dry-mount presses can be varied at will over a variety of settings. Consult the instruction sheet for the temperature to be used for a given print paper and mounting tissue. A temperature that is too high or too low will prevent proper sticking, and too much heat could damage delicate papers.

Conventional Color Prints

The conventional color prints can be dry mounted, as described above, but will require a lower temperature setting on the dry-mount press. See the instruction sheet for details.

Resin-Coated Papers

Both black-and-white and color printing papers are now being supplied in resin-coated (RC) stock, which offers many advantages in use. Conventional dry-mount tissues will not stick to RC papers, so a special tissue must be used. It may require a lower than normal press temperature, but used as directed, it will work very well. Too high a temperature will melt the resin surface.

Polaroid Land Prints

The print surface of conventional Polaroid Land prints is very delicate, and cannot stand heating. You should therefore use some form of pressure-sensitive mounting for these. I have used Scotch Double-Coated Tape No. 666 very successfully. This is an exceptionally sticky tape with a protective facing that is peeled off just prior to use. It can be laid along the four back edges of a print, or you can cover the whole back of the print. Be sure that there are no overlaps of tape, or they will show through as bumps when the print is mounted. Once in place, the protective facing is peeled off and the print is applied *carefully* to its mount board. It cannot be moved afterward, so be very sure of your placement. Apply the print first along one edge, and then smooth it down toward the opposite edge so as to avoid leaving air bubbles under any part of it. This method is good for any relatively small prints, mounted singly or in groups.

With spray adhesives, place the print face down on a piece of scrap paper, and apply the adhesive according to the directions. Then mount the print as described above.

Pressure-sensitive boards are not too satisfactory for publication purposes, since these are best for "bleed" mounts, where the print goes right to the edge of the mount board.

LAYOUT OF MULTIPLE PLATES

Combining two or more photographs in one plate is justified when the pictures relate to one another in some specific, comparative manner. The mounting of the individual pictures must be done impeccably, with all edges perfectly straight, all corners perfectly square, and all joints carefully butted. If the prints are not mounted carefully the overall appearance will be sloppy. The printer may have to cut off parts of one or more pictures to even things up, and in so doing may remove something of importance. Protect your interests through careful work.

I prefer to leave thin white lines between the pictures of a set, to make all the edges distinct and without unintentional tonal blending; but if this is done, it must be done very well. You may prefer to butt-mount the prints so that they touch all around, and then direct the printer to strip white lines in between. If so, check your proofs for errors. And, of course, leave room in your composition for the lines.

LABELING OF PRINTS

Although most pictures can be adequately explained in their captions, it is often necessary to apply certain types of informational labeling directly to the photographs. Examples of photographs labeled as for journal publication are shown in Plates 4, 12, 15, and 16.

Indicators of Scale

The most common type of label is a line or bar to indicate image magnification, especially in photomicrographs. The simplest method of applying it is to take a knife point and score a line of the correct length on the emulsion side of the negative, before printing. Such a mark cannot fall off, because it is part of the print. It is also very narrow, and so will not obscure information in the picture. If this method is undesirable, if the mark must leave a white line when printed, or if it must be applied to the print itself, you can use the narrow pressure-sensitive tapes employed by artists for making graph lines and the like. If opaque tape is applied to a light area of the negative, it will print as a white line or bar. Applied to the print, it can be either white or black, according to its background. If that background varies in tone, you can apply parallel stripes of both black and white, butted along the common edge.

The numerical value of the line or bar should appear directly on the print. The neatest method is to use rub-on numbers and letters, applied *after* the print is mounted (if they are applied *before* it is mounted, they will melt in the press).

If tape lines or other labels are used on the surfaces of prints, attach a protective tissue over the mounted print (see the section on protection of plates after makeup, below) and draw on it the position and length of the line, and any included lettering, so that the printer can replace it if it is lost.

Lettering on Prints with Ink

It is quite practical to letter directly on the surface of a mounted print, perhaps using a lettering machine to assure a neat appearance. Resin-coated papers of some types, particularly the Ilford make, will accept ink (or even penciled notes, on working prints) very readily. Do not just scrawl on the print, as this will ruin its good looks and probably make it unpublishable—even if the offending item is just a scale indicator. Keep in mind that most publishers are "neat freaks," and quite rightly so. To most people, a well-ordered presentation is a sign of a well-ordered mind, and so the appearance of your work will affect its acceptance by your peers.

Application of Printed Labels

Another way of adding information to photographic prints is to print it neatly on a piece of stiff white paper (e.g., a piece of 3 × 5 card), and then apply that to the surface of the print. White glue will stick permanently to *some* photo papers, but will eventually fail on others. Double-stick tape is a better adhesive for applied labels.

Rub-on Lettering

Commercial brands of rub-on letters, numbers, arrows, and signs are very useful, and are exceptionally neat when well applied as labels to photographic prints. However, not all brands are equally compatible with given brands of printing paper. You must test to be sure of the applicability and durability. When rub-on letters are applied, they must be carefully burnished down, and they must be protected afterward, to prevent damage or loss. If a print is to be heat mounted, any rub-on letters must be applied only *afterward;* otherwise they will melt in the mounting press.

Use of Overlays in Labeling Photographs

Lettering and symbols of a complex nature are sometimes applied to a transparent plastic overlay, to be combined with the photograph in reproduction. This is generally done by the publisher, using information provided by the author. You must check the proof copies of any such plates with special care, to be sure that the correct overlay was combined with each picture when the composite plates were photographed by the typesetter's cameraman, and that the relative sizes and positions of the labels were not inadvertently changed in reproduction. (No one, after all, is perfect.)

Even when other labels are to be put on such an overlay, it is best to place the scale indicator, if any—*including its numerical value*—directly on the print. In no case should the numerical value be left off the print and placed in the caption; to do so is to invite the possibility of error or omission in the publishing process, particularly if the print, with the scale indicator on it, is to be photographically reduced.

PROTECTION OF PLATES AFTER MAKE-UP

Once you have added anything to the surface of a print, or have gone to the trouble of putting together a complex multiple plate, you owe it to yourself to protect it from damage in handling. The standard method is to cut a sheet of tracing tissue that is the same width as your mount board, but about an inch taller. The extra inch should be folded over the top of the board, and taped to the back along its full width. The fold-over should always be at the picture top, no matter whether the print and its board are arranged horizontally or vertically.

PRESENTATION OF COLOR TRANSPARENCIES TO PUBLISHERS

Color reproduction can be done from photographic color prints as well as from transparencies, but the majority of color illustrations in articles and books are made directly from color transparencies. Since it is not practical to present color slides as made-up plates, an alternative method of presentation must be used.

Packaging for Presentation

Probably the most practical way to present transparencies to a publisher is to insert them into the clear plastic, $8\frac{1}{2} \times 11$-inch, loose-leaf transparency holders that are available in most camera stores. 35 mm slides should be left in the cardboard mounts, as they come from the processor. Each slide should be labeled with your name (and perhaps your address), and the top should be indicated. Any identifying numbers should also be written on the cardboard slide mount, e.g., the plate number and the image magnification (if applicable).

Larger transparencies can be placed in similar plastic holders, which are available for all sizes up to and including 8×10 inches. Again, each transparency should carry full identification, preferably fastened to the film itself. Large transparencies need not be mounted in frames—just keep them fully protected in slip-on plastic sleeves.

Use of Drawings or Photo Copies in Layout and Labeling

Multiple plates that are to be made from color transparencies are best laid out as drawings that show the relative placing of the component pictures. If detailed labeling must be added in printing, you may find it convenient to make up black-and-white copy photographs. These can be mounted as a plate in the correct configuration, and with the labeling added just as you wish to see it in the final form. An elaborate presentation is not necessary, but whatever *is* done should be sufficient to indicate all the relationships and identifications clearly.

PACKING OF PRINTS AND SLIDES FOR SHIPPING

Damage in the mails is an ever present possibility. Valuable material for reproduction absolutely must be given adequate protection. Single unmounted photographs can be sandwiched between sheets of sturdy, uncreased, corrugated cardboard. The strength is improved if the corrugations in the two pieces run at right angles. The sandwich should be placed in a heavy-duty envelope, perhaps of the padded sort made especially for mailing delicate materials. Groups of plates should be boxed, with a sheet of corrugated cardboard on the top and the bottom. Similar packing will protect single or multiple packs of plastic transparency holders. Full name and address information should be placed on the inside and the outside of the package.

CHAPTER 18

Mounting Prints for Wall Display

When the goal is to make a photograph look good in a public display, there is an unavoidable factor of personal taste involved in any discussion of its preparation. This chapter must therefore be regarded as a statement of my opinion rather than of fact. It is based upon a number of years of experience in the public showing of photographs, as well as many years of viewing other people's shows. Nevertheless, you should feel free to disagree with my remarks, as you see fit.

MOUNTING MODERATE-SIZED PRINTS ON BOARDS

The least expensive and most commonly used method of presentation of photographs for wall display is to dry mount them on some sort of board. The techniques for doing this have been quite fully covered in Chapter 17.

The best boards for mounting are those that have been especially made for photographic use, incorporating materials that are free of any sort of chemical contamination that would tend to damage photographic papers and emulsions over long periods of time. Really contamination-free boards are not common, and at present it is hard to make recommendations. However, there is a growing interest in the use of such materials. By the time this book is printed it should be possible to obtain dependable information concerning archivally safe mounting boards from photo suppliers. For present purposes I will assume that there is less concern with archival permanence than with the displayed appearance of the picture. It does take quite a long time for even the contaminants normally found in the cheaper cardboards to have any effect.

The purpose of using a wide-bordered card mounting is to isolate the photograph from the possibly disturbing effects of the wall against which it is to be seen. The walls of picture galleries usually have a plain, neutral-toned finish to avoid problems of visual conflict with displayed works of art. However, photographs made for scientific purposes may end up in any of a very wide variety of display situations. Thus, the question of visual isolation assumes greater importance.

Color of Mounting Board

There are as many ideas about the proper color of mounting boards as there are photographers; however, I feel that it is possible to apply at least a modicum of reason to this matter.

Photographers have used everything from white to black, including all conceivable shades of grey and a wide variety of colors, in boards for backing prints. In my opinion, the very commonly used white or off-white boards introduce glare in print viewing, and thus tend to reduce the visual impact of the photograph itself. A large black surround has a different effect, in that it tends to give a feeling of heaviness and generalized darkness to the picture, making it look as though it had been overprinted. Colored boards seem inappropriate with black-and-white prints, and with color prints they must be kept from either clashing with or competing with the colors of the print. On the whole, therefore, it seems most appropriate to use a grey board of some tone.

After much experimentation I have come to the conclusion that the best tone to use for the great majority of photographs, either color or black-and-white, is a medium-dark neutral grey. It does a very nice job of providing a glare-free and noncompetitive background for virtually all prints. To be specific, I prefer to use a Strathmore 924-A mounting board. For prints of any size likely to be mounted in this manner, the width of board extending beyond the picture should be in proportion to the size of the print. I suggest a width equal to about 30–40% of the short dimension of the print at the top and on both sides, and about 40–45% at the bottom. A picture that is mounted exactly in the middle of the board, measured from top to bottom, looks a little low to the eye.

Some photographers, probably influenced by the practices of magazine layout artists, like to use off-center mounts. On the whole I find this practice disturbing to the eye and irrelevant to the needs of a photographic display. I see no virtue in having the photograph set in one corner of its mount.

Edging of Prints

Because most photographs are made up of a wide range of tones, some of the greys in a picture may tend to blend with that of the mounting board. Furthermore, it is essential to the very concept of composition that a picture be clearly framed in its own boundaries.

For those reasons I consider it very nearly essential to have a strip of white around the edge of the picture, to set it off from the mount board. You thus achieve a clear delineation of the edge of the picture. But it should not be too wide, or it will introduce glare. Again, it should be in proportion to the size of the photograph. As examples, I would suggest a width of about ¼ inch (about 6 mm) for a 5 × 7-inch print, about $3/8$ inch (9–10 mm) for an 8 × 10-inch print, and about $1/2$ inch (12–14 mm) for an 11 × 14-inch print.

This white edging is, of course, provided for in the printing. You simply use the enlarger easel to provide adequately wide borders. My own practice is to allow a somewhat wide border in printing, and cut it to a satisfactory width when mounting the print.

An exception to the foregoing recommendations occurs when the print has a pure white background around an isolated subject, especially when it is to be displayed with white-bordered prints. Here, for purely visual reasons, it is sometimes useful to rule a narrow black line around the print, in from the edge a distance corresponding to the width of the previously recommended border strip. This can look a little precious if overdone, so try it out on a spare print first.

FRAMING MODERATE-SIZED PRINTS

If you need or prefer a more permanent, more protective method of display, the thing to do is to frame the picture.

Frames

The ornate frames often used with paintings tend to look ludicrous with photographs. There seems to be something about the photographic medium that demands a simple frame. Delicate print surfaces are far better protected if you use glassed frames.

Good frames are available that provide narrow borders in either a dull black or brushed aluminum finish around the outside of the mounted print. These provide an attractive setting for most photographs.

Some people feel that the glass in the frame should be of the so-called non-glare type, but I strongly disagree. Such glasses actually have a microscopically dimpled surface, with a moderate grain effect, that breaks up hard reflections. Unfortunately, in doing so it spreads a visual haze over the picture. This might not matter with some types of presentation, but by its very nature a photograph invites close inspection. Anything that introduces an artificial visual effect between the photograph and its viewer is unsuitable. If reflections are a problem because of the type of lighting or other aspects of the surrounding, try tilting the framed picture slightly forward at the top. Any reflections from eye level or above will thus be directed downward, away from the viewer's eyes. If the floor is somewhat dark in tone, there will be little likelihood of bothersome reflections from the lower levels.

Matting Prints for Framing

When pictures are framed behind glass it is traditional to mat them, i.e., to place them behind a cut-out frame of cardboard or some other material. This serves the same purpose as mounting on an oversized card: it isolates the picture from its background on a wall.

My own feeling is that matting is a needlessly fussy practice for photographs, and that simply mounting them on cardboard, as described earlier, is sufficient preparation for framing. If you feel that you want your photographs matted, however, by all means do it. Mat knives are available quite cheaply from both art and photo supply stores, and are easier to use than ordinary pocket knives. However, I have matted quite a few prints with my trusty Swiss Army Knife (use the shorter of the two blades—it works better for this purpose).

Bleed Mounting

Mounting a photograph so that it runs right to the edge of its mount board is called *bleed mounting*. It is most appropriate for large prints. There are a variety of framing supplies available for covering bleed-mounted prints with glass. Your picture-frame supplier or your photo dealer can show you the alternatives.

GROUP MOUNTS

There are times when it is necessary to mount a group of related photographs on a single backing, with or without added labeling, to make a coherent presentation of information. If the spaces between the photographs are not too wide, you can use a piece of plain white mounting board quite attractively. If the spaces are to be wider, I suggest using the grey card, as for mounting single prints.

For any such formal display I also suggest that you consult a professional scientific or medical artist who has experience in designing public displays. A sloppy display could charitably be called counterproductive.

MOUNTING VERY LARGE PRINTS

It is not very practical to try to dry mount extremely large photographic prints, because of the size limitations of most dry-mount presses. You will find it considerably easier to do a good-looking job of mounting if you bleed-mount the print with paste or glue on a suitably sized sheet of smooth hardboard.

Probably the simplest and best adhesive to use is plain old wheat-flour paste, which can be obtained in art supply stores. White glue can be used, but it is not as easy to handle. The usual method is to dampen the print thoroughly, apply the paste as a watery mix to the back of the print, pull the excess print edges (which you must plan for) over the edges of the board, and fasten them to the back of the board with brown paper tape. As the paste and the photo paper dry, the paper shrinks a little and the result is a very nice, flat job of mounting, of excellent permanence.

A very good, detailed description of this method is given in the article by Denstman, "Print Mounting: The Finishing Touch," 1968–69.

Bibliography

No attempt will be made here to list all the technical sources that would be of use to a person doing scientific photography, as the literature is far too vast. Those sources listed are among the better ones available, and should be sufficient to satisfy most immediate needs for additional information. They will also serve as a starting point for deeper research. I have added brief remarks to some of the listings, to give you a better idea of their particular merits.

The relatively large, separate listing of Kodak publications is not meant as an endorsement of that firm or its products, but does reflect the fact that Kodak publications are a highly regarded, readily accessible source of very reliable information on an extremely wide variety of photographic subjects. Note the entry L-5, which is a catalog of all the current Kodak publications. Those not stocked by your photographic supplier can be ordered by mail.

Books

Adams, Ansel, *Artificial-Light Photography* (Morgan & Morgan, New York, 1962).
Volume 5 of the Adams basic photo series. An excellent source of information on the handling of artificial light, including flash.

———, *Camera and Lens* (Morgan & Morgan, Hastings-on-Hudson, N.Y., 1970).
The revised edition of Volume 1 of the Adams series. It is a first-rate general text on the craft of photography.

———, *The Negative* (Morgan & Morgan, Hastings-on-Hudson, N.Y., 1964).
Volume 2 of the Adams series, introducing the Zone System of photographic exposure.

———, *The Print* (Morgan & Morgan, Hastings-on-Hudson, N.Y., 1964).
Volume 3 of the series, and a fine work on the process of printing.

Bennett, Alva H., Helen Jupnik, Harold Osterberg, and Oscar W. Richards, *Phase Microscopy: Principles and Applications* (John Wiley & Sons, New York, 1951).

A good general description of phase microscopy.

Blaker, Alfred A., *Field Photography: Beginning and Advanced Techniques* (W. H. Freeman and Company, San Francisco, 1976).

A broad-ranging coverage of photographic techniques applicable to outdoor photography, listing multiple alternatives wherever practical. Comes with a separate, technical booklet, *Field-Use Data,* for easy carrying.

Bomback, Edward S., *Manual of Photographic Lighting* (Fountain Press, London, 1971).

A good general description of professional photographic lighting techniques.

Cavallo, Robert, and Stuart Kahan, *Photography: What's The Law?* (Crown Publishers, New York, 1976).

A new and concise source detailing the rights and responsibilities of photographers.

Chernoff, George, and H. B. Sarbin, *Photography and the Law* (American Photographic Book Publishing, New York, n.d.).

A standard reference on the legal rights and responsibilities of photographers.

Clauss, Hans, and Heinz Meusel, *Filter Practice* (The Focal Press Ltd., London and New York, 1964).

A clear, well-organized text on the use of filters in photography. Translated from the German original.

Dalton, Stephen, *Borne on the Wind* (Reader's Digest Press, New York, 1975).

A superbly illustrated work on insect flight, with useful photographic notes.

Dignan, Patrick D., *Dignan's Simplified Chemical Formulas for Black & White and Color* (Dignan Photographic, Inc., North Hollywood, Cal., 1972).

A very useful collection of offbeat photographic formulations.

Dunn, J. F., *Exposure Manual* (John Wiley & Sons, New York, 1958).

There is no equal to this book on the theory and practice of photographic exposure.

Eaton, George T., *Photographic Chemistry—in Black-and-white and Color Photography* (Morgan & Morgan, Hastings-on-Hudson, N.Y., 1957).

A standard reference.

Edgerton, Harold E., *Electronic Flash, Strobe* (McGraw-Hill Book Co., New York, 1970).

An important reference by the inventor and major developer of the equipment for these techniques.

Engel, Charles E., ed., *Photography for the Scientist* (Academic Press, London and New York, 1968).

A first-rate technical reference featuring chapters by 16 authors of note from England, Germany, and the United States.

Evans, Ralph M., *Eye, Film and Camera in Color Photography* (John Wiley & Sons, New York, 1959).

The finest work on theoretical and psychological effects in photography that I have yet seen.

Garrison, Ronald, and Robert Gray, *Secrets of Zoo Photography* (Doubleday & Co., Garden City, N.Y., 1972).

Anyone seeking to do photography in a zoo should consult this book first.

Hattery, Lowell H., and George P. Bush, eds., *Reprography and Copyright Law* (American Institute of Biological Sciences, Washington, D.C., 1964).

A good general reference on American copyright law. There are few newer sources, because of the current state of flux in this subject. Though outdated in certain respects, it still serves as a useful source of basic information.

Loveland, Roger P., *Photomicrography: A Comprehensive Treatise,* 2 vols. (John Wiley & Sons, New York, 1970).
Without question the best work on photomicrography currently in print, and probably the best to date. It should be on the shelf of anyone interested in the subject.

McKay, Herbert C., *Three Dimensional Photography: Principles of Stereoscopy* (American Photography Book Department, New York, 1953).
Out of print, but available in many libraries. One of the best books on this subject intended for general readers.

Phillips, Wm. Revell, *Mineral Optics: Principles and Techniques* (W. H. Freeman and Company, San Francisco, 1971).
A background reference for anyone attempting examination and analysis of geological specimens.

Ray, Dorothy Jean, and Alfred A. Blaker, *Eskimo Masks: Art and Ceremony* (University of Washington Press, Seattle, 1967).
Examples in color and black-and-white of the way in which I have photographed masks. Reprinted in paperback in 1975.

Ross, Edward S., *Insects Close Up* (University of California Press, Berkeley, 1953).
An excellent source on field photography of living insects. Dr. Ross is a pioneer in closeup flash photography, and was the source of my initial interest in, and information on, the subject.

Sherwin, Robert V., *Legal Aspects of Photography* (Greenberg Publishers, New York, n.d.).
Another standard reference on law as it applies to photography, it supplements but does not fully overlap Chernoff and Sarbin.

Shurcliff, William, and Stanley S. Ballard, *Polarized Light* (D. Van Nostrand Co., Princeton, N.J., 1964).
For those of us who need a general reference.

Stroebel, Leslie, *View Camera Technique,* 3rd ed. (Hastings House, New York, 1976).
In my opinion, the best work on the theory and practice of view-camera operation.

Strong, John, *Concepts of Classical Optics* (W. H. Freeman and Company, San Francisco, 1958).
For those times when you need to go back to first principles.

Swedlund, Charles, *Photography: A Handbook of History, Materials and Processes* (Holt, Rinehart & Winston, New York, 1974).
A very well-organized and well-presented general text, for the beginning photographer or anyone who wants to fill holes in an incomplete background. In my opinion, the very best current beginning photography text.

Todd, Hollis N., and Richard D. Zakia, *Photographic Sensitometry: The Study of Tone Reproduction* (Morgan & Morgan, Hastings-on-Hudson, N.Y., 1969).
A basic text for all serious photographers.

Valyus, Nikolai Admovich, *Stereoscopy* (The Focal Press Ltd., London and New York, 1966).
A translation of the Russian original, this is the most comprehensive text on the principles and practice of stereoscopy now in print.

Zweifel, Frances W., *A Handbook of Biological Illustration* (University of Chicago Press, Chicago, 1961).
An unassuming little paperback, this book describes graphic arts techniques that are broadly applicable in scientific photography.

Kodak Publications

Number	Title	Date
AA-26	*Optical Formulas and Their Application*	1976
AB-1	*Filters for Black-and-white and Color Pictures*	1975
AC-10	*Photographing Television Images*	1973
AE-3	*Color Photography Under Fluorescent Lighting*	1976
AE-22	*Prevention and Removal of Fungus on Prints and Films*	1974
AE-81, 83, 84, 85, 87, 88, 90, 94, and 95	Known as the *Here's How* series, these booklets describe a wide variety of interesting techniques, in article form—several per booklet. (AE-90 is dated 1975, the rest 1974.)	1974
AM-2	*Basic Copying*	1975
AM-6	*Basic Infrared and Ultra-violet Fluorescence Photography*	1976
AN-6	*Photomicrography with Simple Cameras*	1976
B-3	*Kodak Filters for Scientific and Technical Uses*	1976
C-24	*Notes on Tropical Photography*	1970
F-20	*Understanding Graininess and Granularity*	1973
G-12	*Making and Mounting Big Black-and-white Enlarge-ments and Photomurals*	1974
H-9	*Color News and Documen-tary Photography with Fluorescent Lighting*	1976
L-5	*1977 Index to Kodak Information* This is the master list from which to order. It is updated each year or so.	1977
M-1	*Copying* A more comprehensive coverage than AM-2.	1974
M-23	*Photographing Chro-matograms*	1972
M-27	*Ultraviolet and Fluorescence Photography*	1974
M-28	*Applied Infrared Photography*	1975
N-1	*Medical Infrared Photography*	1973
N-2	*Cinephotomicrography*	1970
N-3	*Clinical Photography*	1972
N-12A	*Close-Up Photography*	1974
N-12B	*Photomacrography*	1974
N-18	*Medical Photography: Clinical, Ultraviolet, and Infrared*	1973
N-19	*Biomedical Photography*	1976
O-4	*Professional Portrait Techniques*	1973
P-2	*Photography Through The Microscope* The standard beginning text for virtually all photomicrographers.	1974
P-3-590	*Now Make Duplicate Negatives As Readily As You Make Prints*	1972
P-11	*Schlieren Photography*	1974
P-39	*Photomicrography of Metals*	1971
P-100-17	*Reverse-Text Slides in Color*	1970
P-114	*Kodak Neutral Density Attenuators*	1975

Number	Title	Date
P-236	*Electron Microscopy and Photography*	1973
S-22	*Effective Lecture Slides*	1975
S-24	*Legibility—Artwork to Screen*	1974
S-26	*Reverse-Text Slides from Black-on-white Line Artwork*	1975

NOTE: Most of these selections were made from the 1977 L-5 catalog; a few were published after the catalog, and a few others last appeared in the 1975 catalog. The dates given are those of the original publication or of the latest revision listed in the catalog. The catalog lists a great many other publications, but I regard the ones shown here as the most relevant to this book.

Articles

Allen, R. D., G. B. David, and G. Nomarski, "The Zeiss-Nomarski Differential Interference Equipment for Transmitted-Light Microscopy," *Zeitschrift für wissenschaftliche Mikroskopie und mikroskopische Technik* **69,** No. 4 (1969): 193–221.
The article is in English.

Blaker, Alfred A., "Basic Lighting for Shell Photography," *The Veliger* **3** (Jan., 1961): 69–72.

———, "Color Photography of Living Marine Mollusks," *The Veliger* **4** (July 1, 1961): 47–50.

———, "Detective Story," *Petersen's PhotoGraphic,* June, 1973, p. 23.
An article on insect damage to color slides.

———, "High-Magnification 35 mm Photography," *Petersen's PhotoGraphic,* July, 1973, pp. 73–76.

———, "Liquid Immersion of Stain-type Stony Fossils," *J. Biological Photographic Assoc.* **38** (Jan., 1970): 32–34.

———, "Photography of Insects in Amber," *J. Biological Photographic Assoc.* **37** (July, 1969): 168–172.

———, "Sharp Masking In Whole-Mount Photomicrography," *J. Biological Photographic Assoc.* **38** (April, 1970): 83–86.

———, "2×-3×: Extending Your Prime Lens," *Petersen's PhotoGraphic,* Sep., 1973, pp. 61–62.

Delly, John Gustav, "How To Buy A Compound Microscope," *American Laboratory,* April, 1969, pp. 8–22.

———, "Rheinberg Differential Color Illumination in Biomedical Photography," in *Biomedical Photography,* Kodak Publication N-19, Eastman Kodak Company, Rochester, N.Y., 1976, pp. 3–16. This is an important new source.

Denstman, Hal, "Print Mounting: The Finishing Touch," *Industrial Photography,* Nov., 1968, pp. 32–37, 93–95; Feb., 1969, pp. 18–20, 56–58, 62–63.

Diegenback, P. C., "Phase-contrast Microscopy is Simulated (in large scale)," letter to the column "The Amateur Scientist" in *Scientific American* **223** (Nov., 1970): 123–125.

Eisendrath, David B., Jr., "Eisendrath on Filters: Everything About Filters Except When to Use Them," *Photo Methods for Industry,* Sep., 1965, pp. 37–40.

———, "Polaroid Land 4," *Photo Methods for Industry,* June, 1972, pp. 50–52.

Farber, Paul R., "Divided Development," *U.S. Camera,* June, 1962, pp. 46, 86.
Also printed in Dignan's book—see book listing, above.

Franks, E. Harvey, "Stereopsis and Stereoscopy"

(a four-part series), *The British Journal of Photography* **119** (15 Dec., 1972): 1086–1088; **119** (22 Dec., 1972): 1110–1113; **119** (29 Dec., 1972): 1136–1139; **120** (5 Jan., 1973): 20–21.

Gumpertz, Walter E., "Critical Light Centering for Darkfield Microscopy," *Image Dynamics in Science and Medicine,* March/April, 1969, pp. 20–21.

Jackson, Ross, "Stereo Macrophotography of Biological Material," *J. Biological Photographic Assoc.* **26** (Aug., 1958): 125–128.

Keeling, Derek, "Optical Design and Aberrations 15" (a portion of a serialized test), *The British Journal of Photography,* 12 May, 1972, pp. 411–413.

Klosevych, Stanley, "On Microscopy: Effect of Dirt," *Visual/Sonic Medicine,* Aug./Sep., 1967, pp. 42–45.

———, "On Microscopy: The Microscope Objective," *Visual/Sonic Medicine,* Aug./Sep., 1968, pp. 6–13.

Koster, Lewis W., "The Didymium Glass Filter in Photomicrography," *J. Biological Photographic Assoc.* **32** (May, 1964): 59–64.

Laurence, Mike, "The Kelvin Scale," *Petersen's PhotoGraphic,* June, 1973, pp. 35–39.

McComb, Stanley J., "The Problem of Depth of Field in Photomicrography," *J. Biological Photographic Assoc.* **29** (May, 1961): 45–51.

Rothschild, Norman, "Offbeat: Fungus? Scratches? Dirt? Here's A Way To Preserve And Protect Your Slides," *Popular Photography,* March, 1975, pp. 16, 18.

Roudabush, Robert L., "Insect Damage to Color Film," *Photographic Applications In Science, Technology And Medicine,* March, 1975, pp. 28–33.

Scardino, Mike, "Stabilization Processing: A Review," *Petersen's PhotoGraphic,* July, 1973, pp. 26–31.

See also the column "On The Scene," p. 80 of the same issue, for an update of this article.

Silberglied, Robert E., "Visualization and Recording of Longwave Ultraviolet Reflection from Natural Objects—Part 1," *Functional Photography,* March, 1976, pp. 20, 24–28; Part 2, May, 1976, pp. 30–33.

Smith, Robert F., "Color Contrast Methods in Microscopy and Photomicrography" (a four-part series), *Photographic Applications In Science, Technology And Medicine,* May, 1970, pp. 24–28, 48; Sep., 1970, pp. 19–24, 36; May, 1971, pp. 19–23; May, 1972, pp. 21–24.

———, "Micro Replication," *Photographic Applications In Science And Technology,* Winter, 1967–68, pp. 24–27.

See addition in the letters column in the Spring, 1968, issue, p. 6.

Vetter, John P., "Fluorescent Photomicrography With Interference Filters," *Photographic Applications In Science, Technology And Medicine,* March, 1973, pp. 20–24, 30.

———, "The Production and Use of Rheinberg Color Differential Filters," *J. Biological Photographic Assoc.* **31** (Feb., 1963): 15–18.

Index

F

G

H

I

K

L

S

T

V

W

Z